DRIFTING DRAGONS

Taku Kuwabara

7

DRIFTING DRAGONS

Flight
37

Engine Room
& Dragon
Meat Cake

39

Flight
36

Target Practice
& Dragon
Cubano

5

Table
of
Contents

Flight
40

The Red
Lantern's
Chilong
& Dragon
Crystals
147

Flight
39

Majuro &
Dragon
Pepper Buns
111

Flight
38

Do or Dice
79

SHIP NAME		SHIP MARK	
Quin Zaza		**O Z**	
CHARACTER LIST			
Crew	TOTAL **19**		

MIKA
DRAGON MEAT FANATIC

TAKITA
NEWBIE

VANABELLE (VANNIE)
COOL BEAUTY

JIRO
MR. SERIOUS

GIBBS
VETERAN DECK BOSS

NIKO
NEVER REMOVES HAT

GAGA
FOREHEAD OF STEEL

OKEN
NEAT FREAK

ENGINE ROOM

DOUG
CHIEF ENGINEER

MAYNE
MS. MECHANIC

HIRO
APPRENTICE MECHANIC

BRIDGE

CROCCO
ACTING CAPTAIN & PILOT

CAPELLA
HELMSWOMAN

KITCHEN

YOSHI
HEAD STEWARD

VADAKIN
SETS HAIR DAILY

SORAYA
SILVER-TONGUED

FAYE
BOOKWORM

BERKO
USUALLY DRUNK

LEE
MANAGER & TREASURER

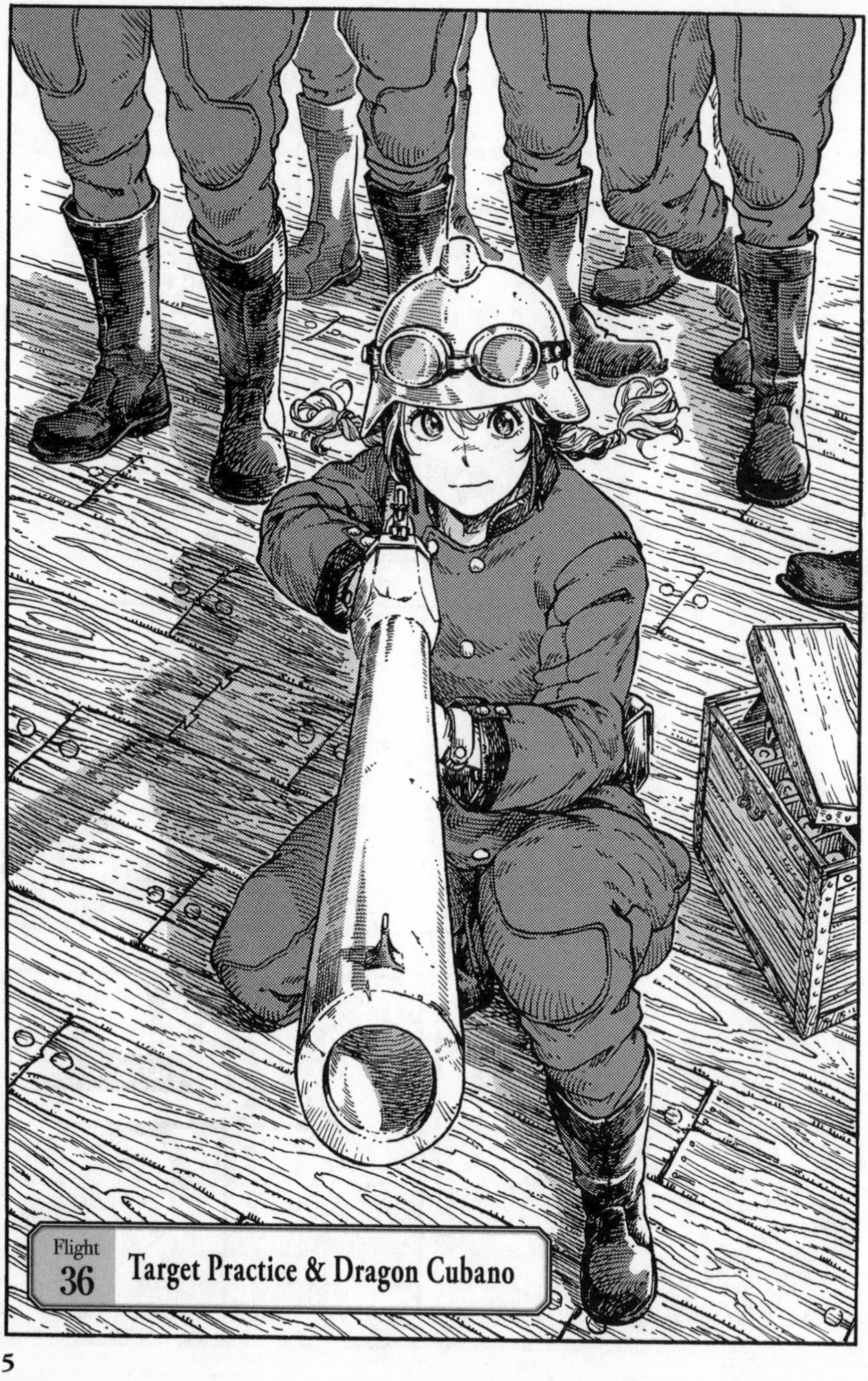
Flight
36
Target Practice & Dragon Cubano

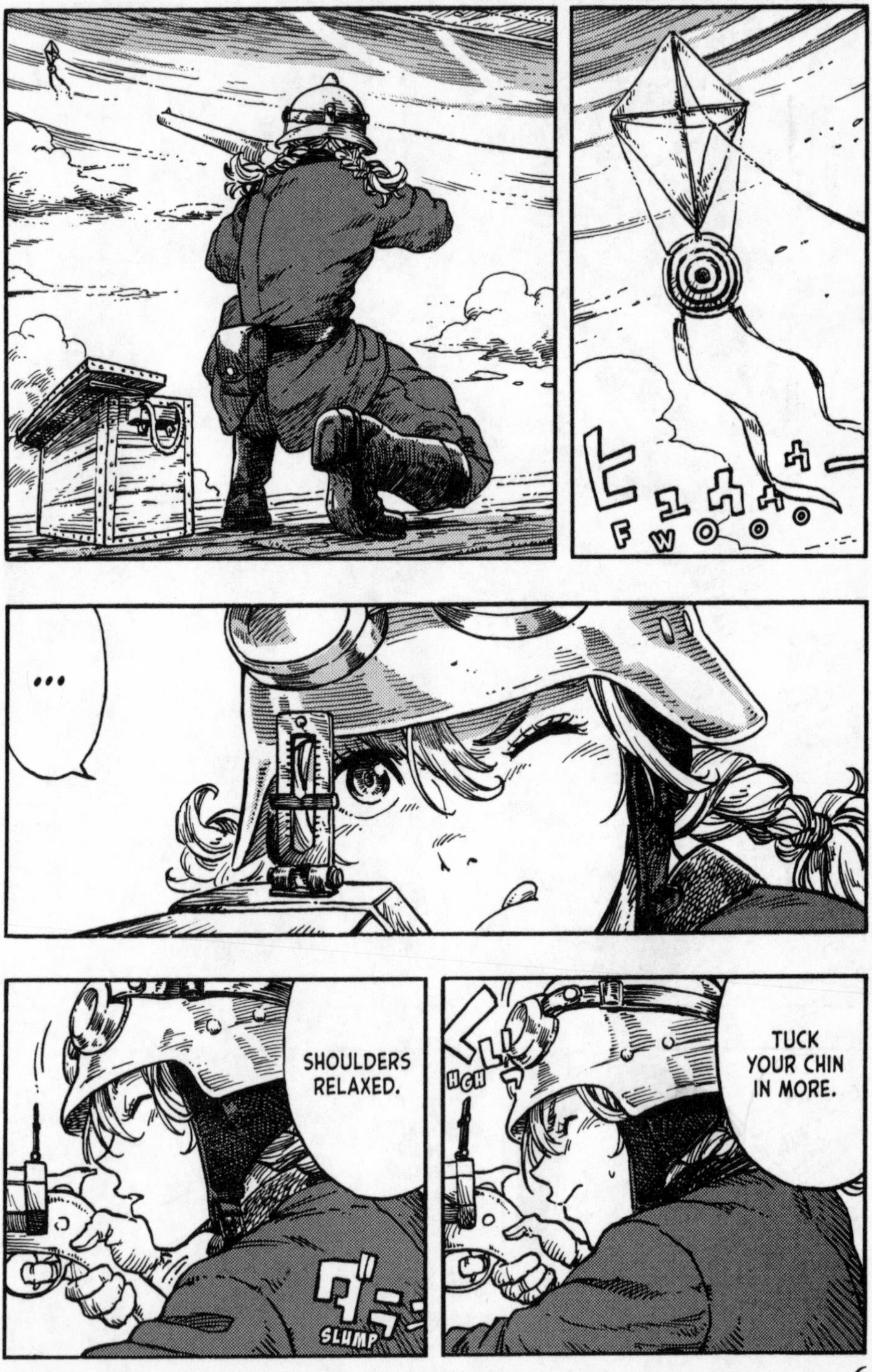
FWOOO
...
HGH
TUCK YOUR CHIN IN MORE.
SHOULDERS RELAXED.
SLUMP

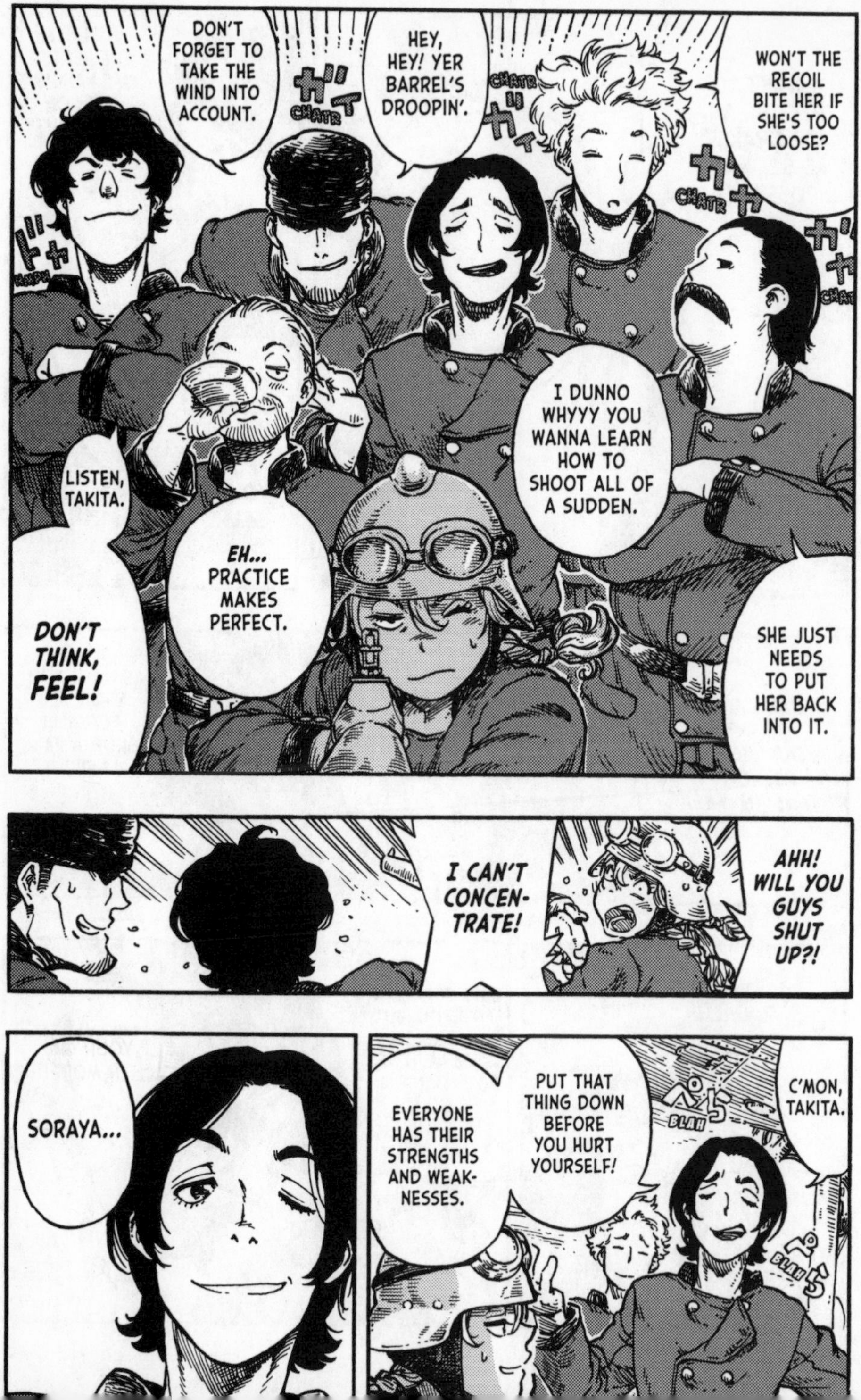
WON'T THE RECOIL BITE HER IF SHE'S TOO LOOSE?
CHATR
HEY, HEY! YER BARREL'S DROOPIN'.
CHATR
DON'T FORGET TO TAKE THE WIND INTO ACCOUNT.
I DUNNO WHYYY YOU WANNA LEARN HOW TO SHOOT ALL OF A SUDDEN.
SHE JUST NEEDS TO PUT HER BACK INTO IT.
EH... PRACTICE MAKES PERFECT.
LISTEN, TAKITA.
DON'T THINK, FEEL!
AHH! WILL YOU GUYS SHUT UP?!
I CAN'T CONCENTRATE!
C'MON, TAKITA.
BLAH
PUT THAT THING DOWN BEFORE YOU HURT YOURSELF!
EVERYONE HAS THEIR STRENGTHS AND WEAKNESSES.
BLAH
SORAYA...

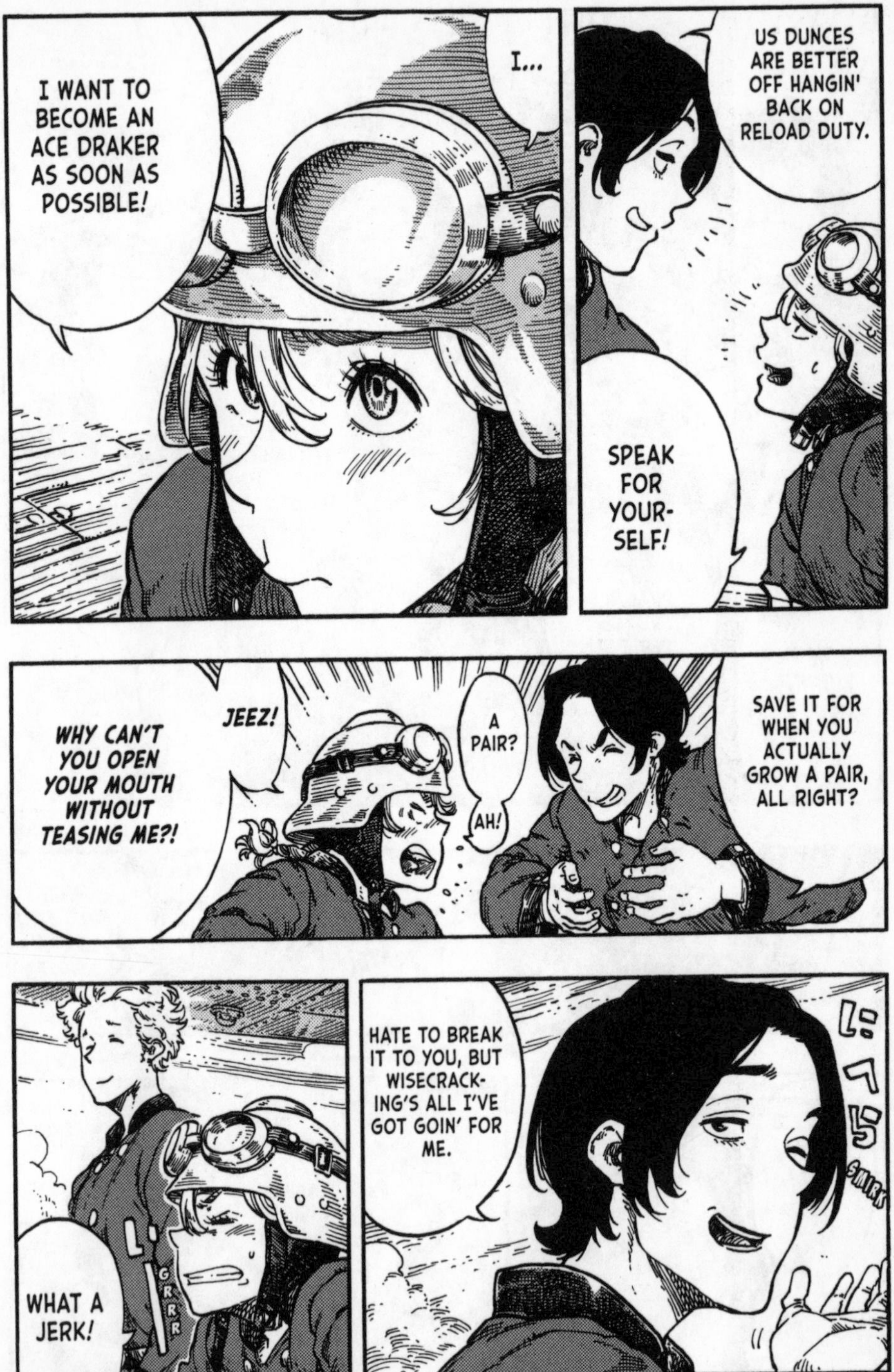

US DUNCES ARE BETTER OFF HANGIN' BACK ON RELOAD DUTY.
SPEAK FOR YOURSELF!
I...
I WANT TO BECOME AN ACE DRAKER AS SOON AS POSSIBLE!
SAVE IT FOR WHEN YOU ACTUALLY GROW A PAIR, ALL RIGHT?
A PAIR?
AH!
JEEZ!
WHY CAN'T YOU OPEN YOUR MOUTH WITHOUT TEASING ME?!
SMIRK
HATE TO BREAK IT TO YOU, BUT WISECRACKING'S ALL I'VE GOT GOIN' FOR ME.
GRRR
WHAT A JERK!

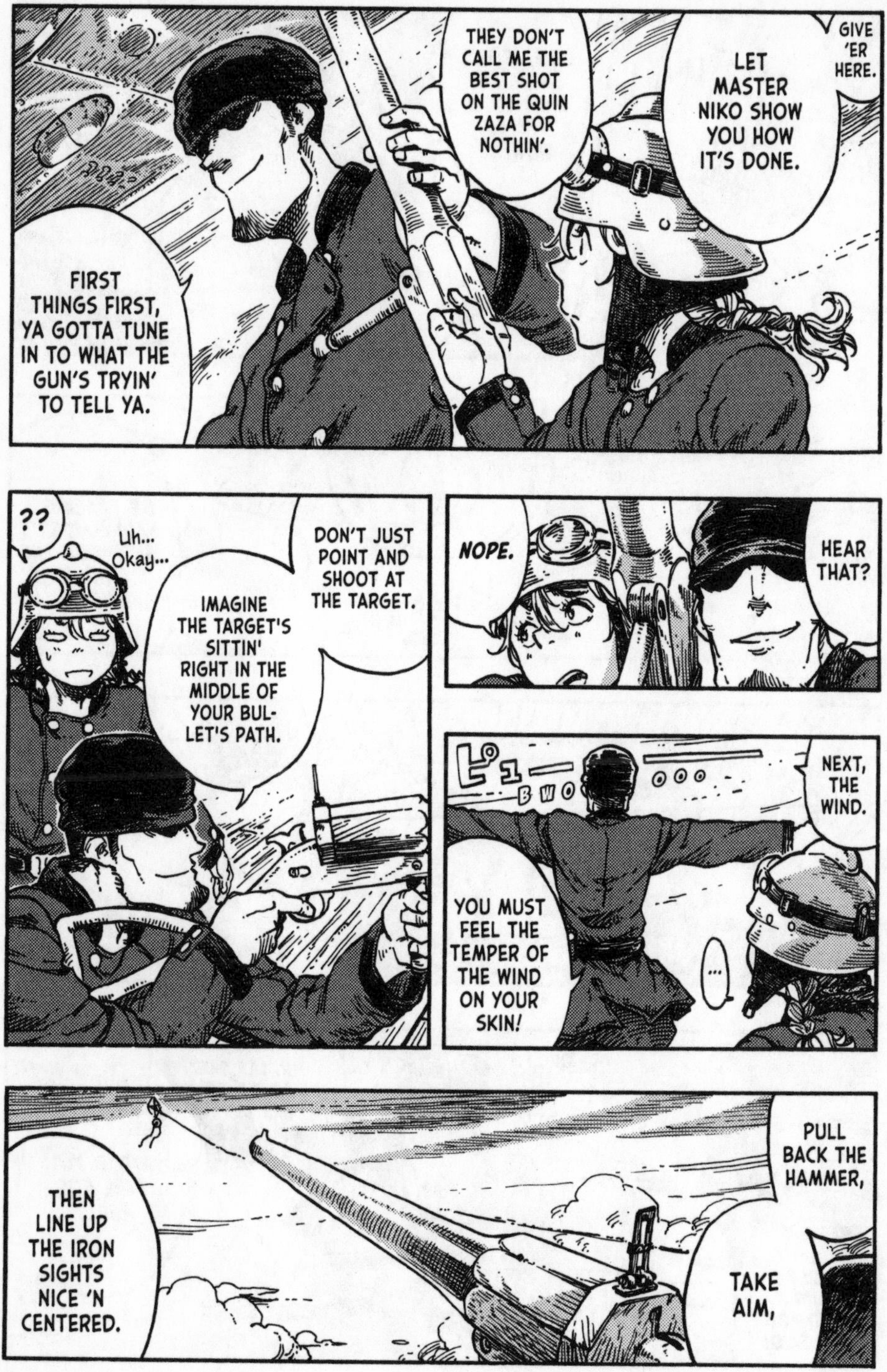
GIVE 'ER HERE.
LET MASTER NIKO SHOW YOU HOW IT'S DONE.
THEY DON'T CALL ME THE BEST SHOT ON THE QUIN ZAZA FOR NOTHIN'.
FIRST THINGS FIRST, YA GOTTA TUNE IN TO WHAT THE GUN'S TRYIN' TO TELL YA.
HEAR THAT?
NOPE.
NEXT, THE WIND.
BWO
YOU MUST FEEL THE TEMPER OF THE WIND ON YOUR SKIN!
...
DON'T JUST POINT AND SHOOT AT THE TARGET.
IMAGINE THE TARGET'S SITTIN' RIGHT IN THE MIDDLE OF YOUR BUL-LET'S PATH.
Uh... Okay...
??
PULL BACK THE HAMMER,
TAKE AIM,
THEN LINE UP THE IRON SIGHTS NICE 'N CENTERED.

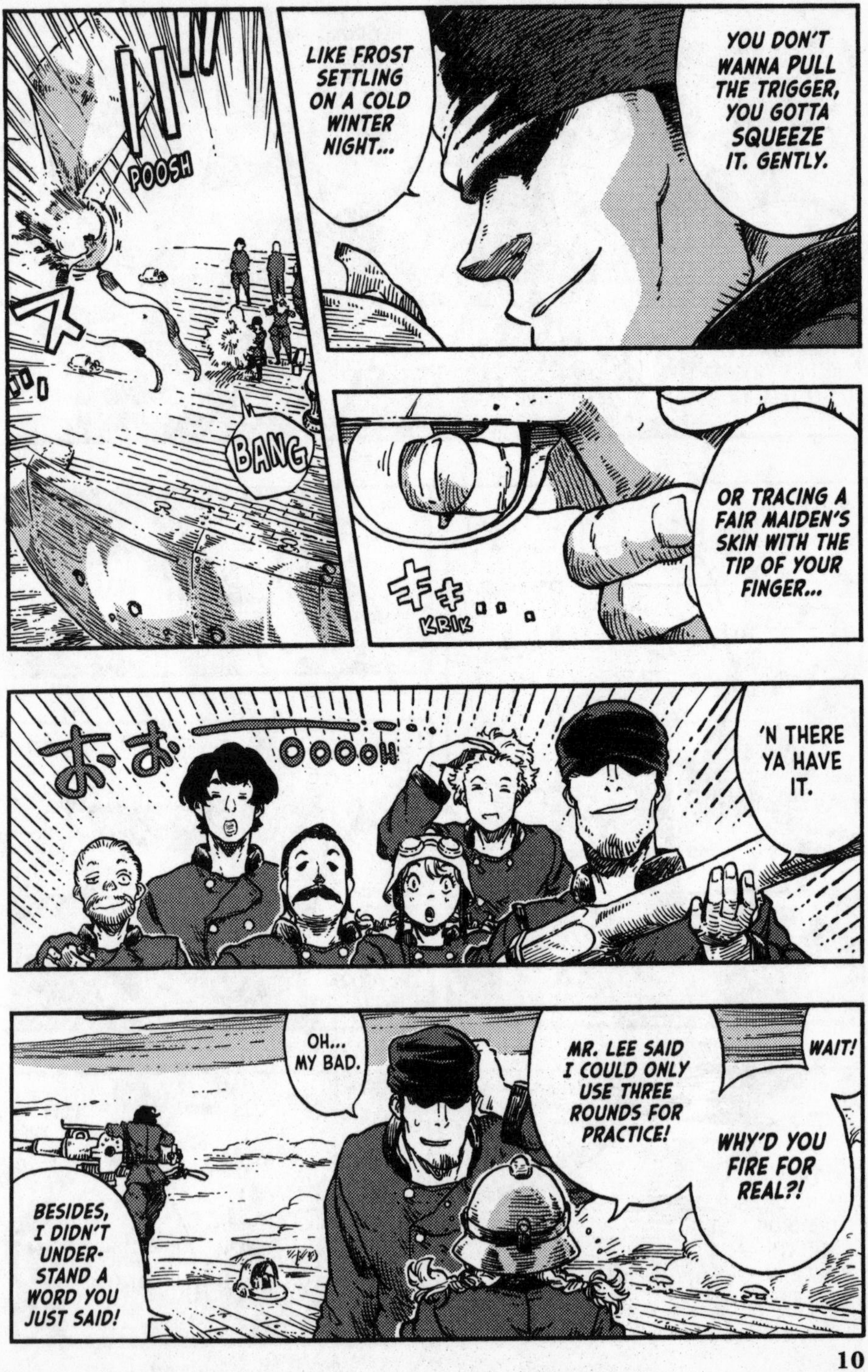
YOU DON'T WANNA PULL THE TRIGGER, YOU GOTTA SQUEEZE IT. GENTLY.
LIKE FROST SETTLING ON A COLD WINTER NIGHT...
OR TRACING A FAIR MAIDEN'S SKIN WITH THE TIP OF YOUR FINGER...
KRIK
BANG
POOSH
'N THERE YA HAVE IT.
OOOOOH
WAIT!
WHY'D YOU FIRE FOR REAL?!
MR. LEE SAID I COULD ONLY USE THREE ROUNDS FOR PRACTICE!
OH... MY BAD.
BESIDES, I DIDN'T UNDER-STAND A WORD YOU JUST SAID!

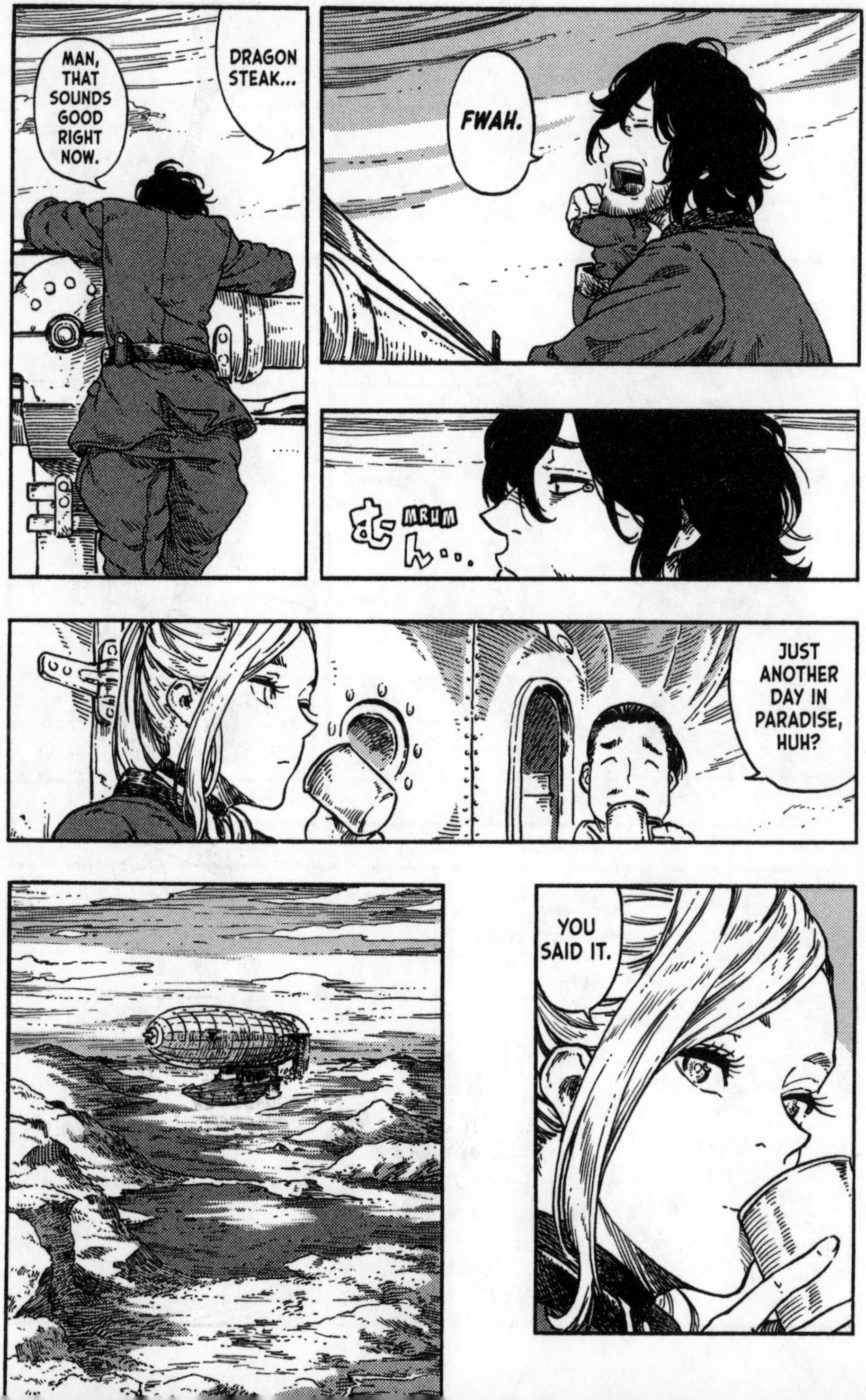
FWAH.
むーん...
MRUM
DRAGON STEAK...
MAN, THAT SOUNDS GOOD RIGHT NOW.
JUST ANOTHER DAY IN PARADISE, HUH?
YOU SAID IT.

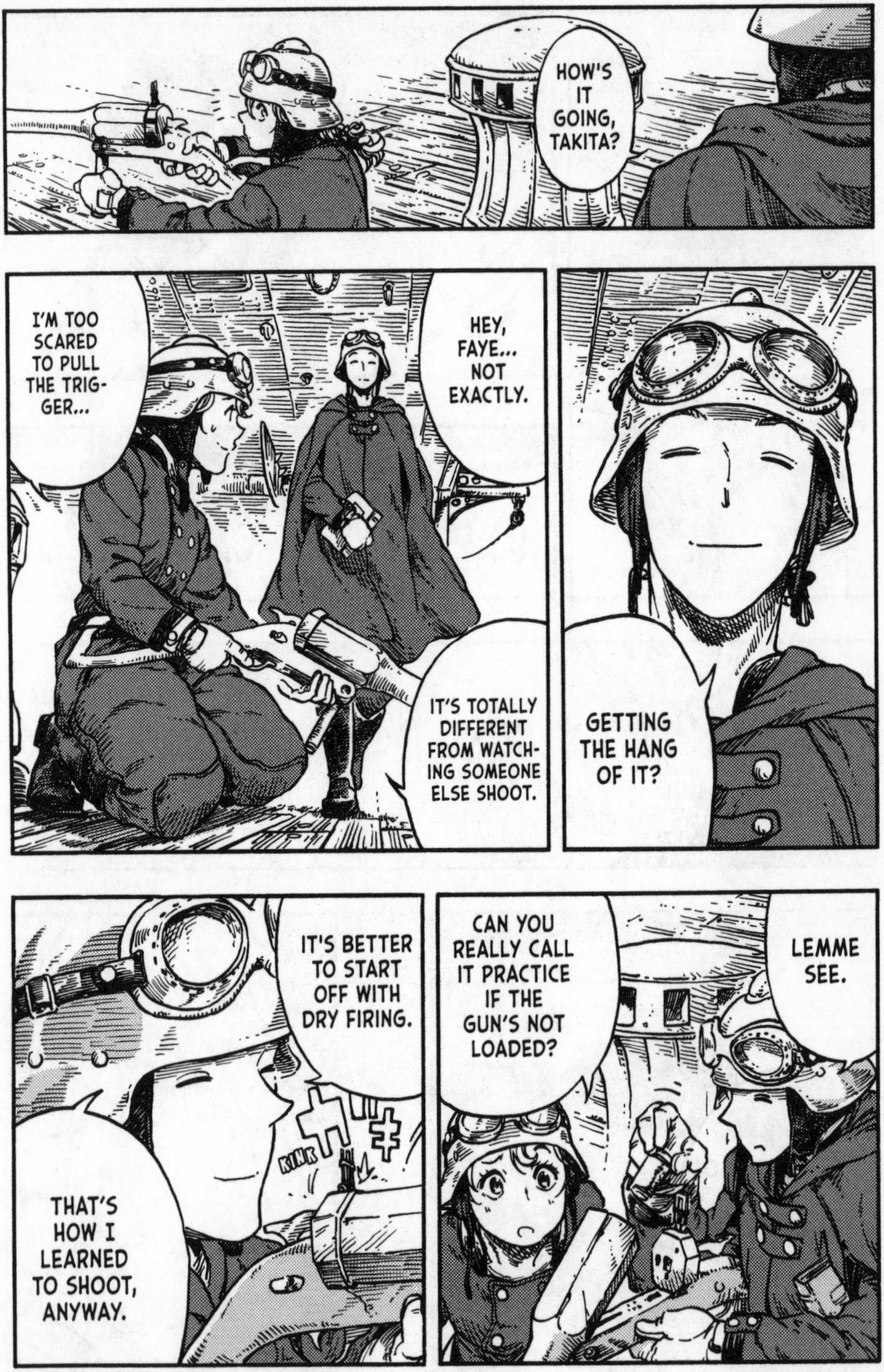
HOW'S IT GOING, TAKITA?
GETTING THE HANG OF IT?
HEY, FAYE... NOT EXACTLY.
I'M TOO SCARED TO PULL THE TRIGGER...
IT'S TOTALLY DIFFERENT FROM WATCHING SOMEONE ELSE SHOOT.
LEMME SEE.
CAN YOU REALLY CALL IT PRACTICE IF THE GUN'S NOT LOADED?
IT'S BETTER TO START OFF WITH DRY FIRING.
KINK
THAT'S HOW I LEARNED TO SHOOT, ANYWAY.

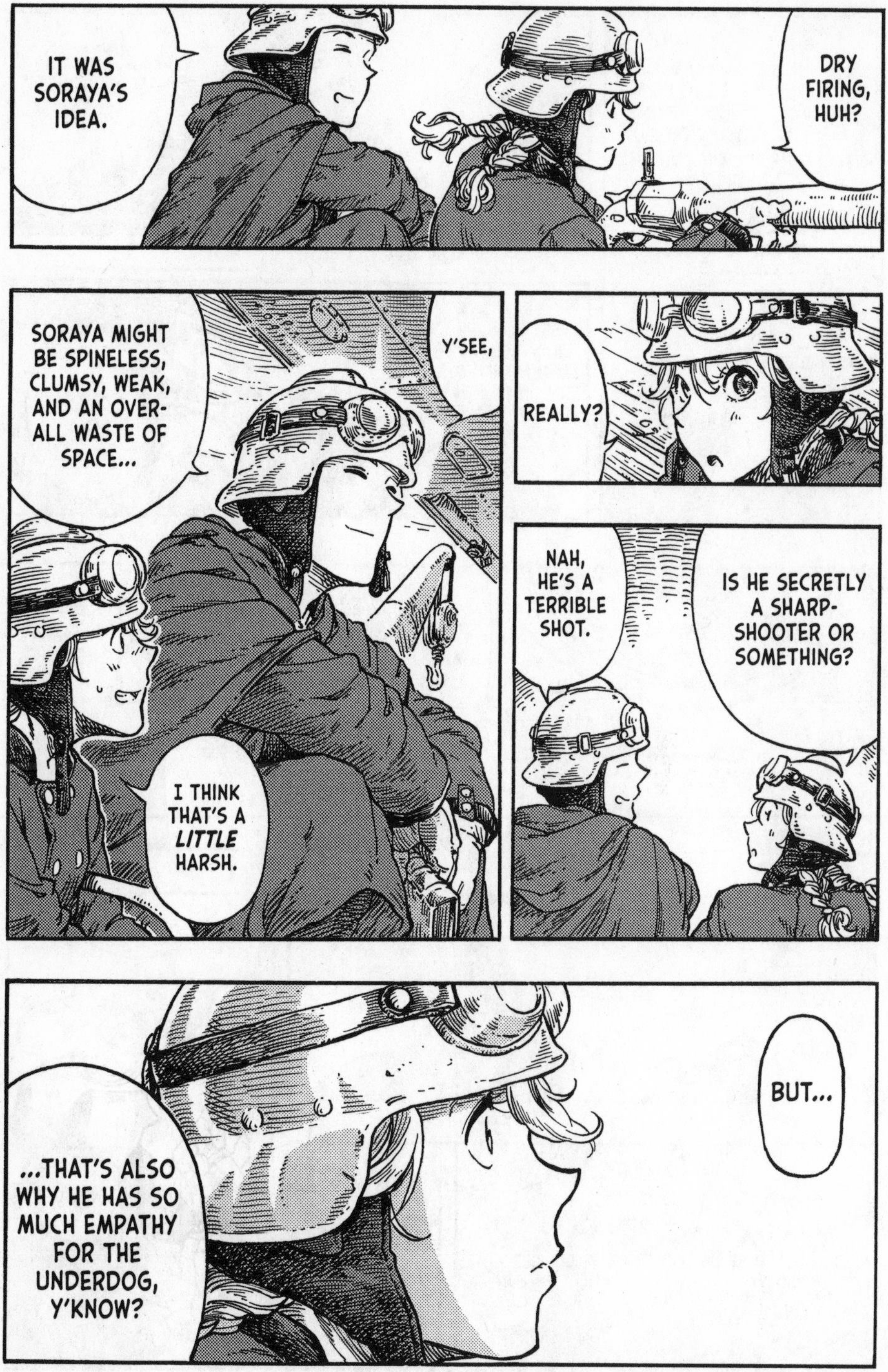
DRY FIRING, HUH?
IT WAS SORAYA'S IDEA.
REALLY?
IS HE SECRETLY A SHARP-SHOOTER OR SOMETHING?
NAH, HE'S A TERRIBLE SHOT.
Y'SEE,
SORAYA MIGHT BE SPINELESS, CLUMSY, WEAK, AND AN OVER-ALL WASTE OF SPACE...
I THINK THAT'S A *LITTLE* HARSH.
BUT...
...THAT'S ALSO WHY HE HAS SO MUCH EMPATHY FOR THE UNDERDOG, Y'KNOW?

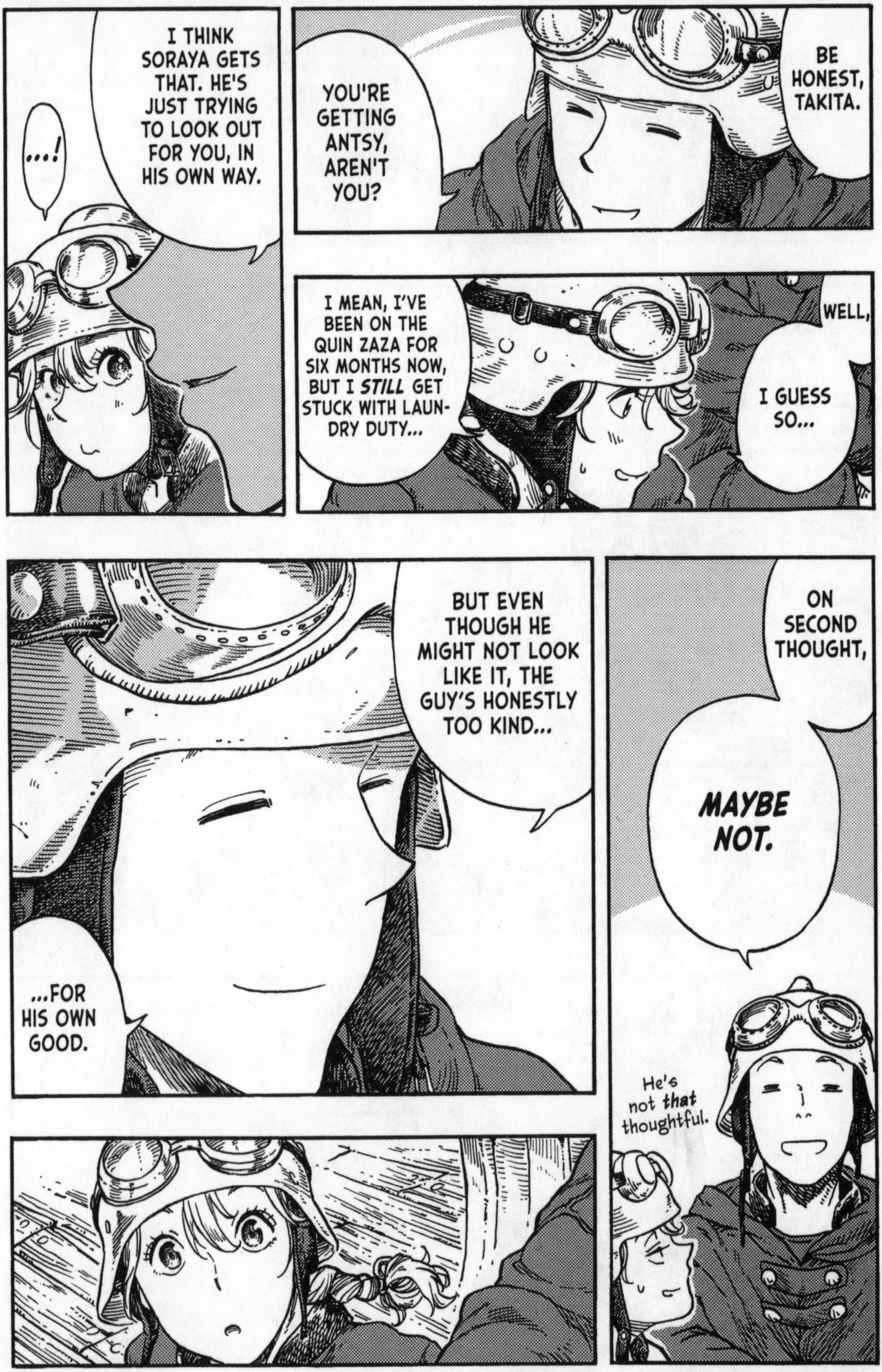
BE HONEST, TAKITA.
YOU'RE GETTING ANTSY, AREN'T YOU?
WELL,
I GUESS SO...
I MEAN, I'VE BEEN ON THE QUIN ZAZA FOR SIX MONTHS NOW, BUT I *STILL* GET STUCK WITH LAUN-DRY DUTY...
I THINK SORAYA GETS THAT. HE'S JUST TRYING TO LOOK OUT FOR YOU, IN HIS OWN WAY.
...!
ON SECOND THOUGHT,
MAYBE NOT.
He's not *that* thoughtful.
BUT EVEN THOUGH HE MIGHT NOT LOOK LIKE IT, THE GUY'S HONESTLY TOO KIND...
...FOR HIS OWN GOOD.

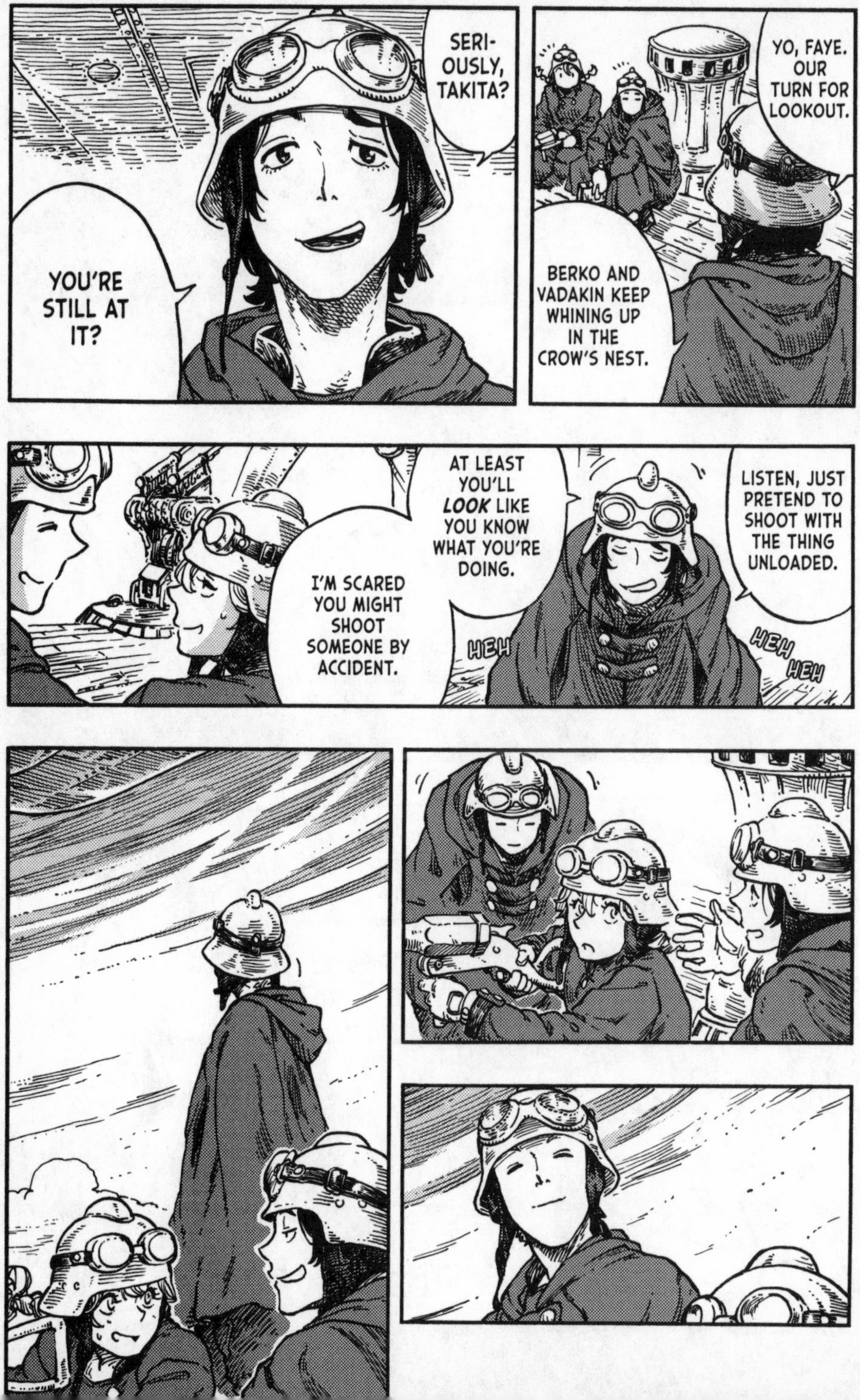
YO, FAYE. OUR TURN FOR LOOKOUT.
BERKO AND VADAKIN KEEP WHINING UP IN THE CROW'S NEST.
SERI-OUSLY, TAKITA?
YOU'RE STILL AT IT?
LISTEN, JUST PRETEND TO SHOOT WITH THE THING UNLOADED.
HEH HEH
AT LEAST YOU'LL *LOOK* LIKE YOU KNOW WHAT YOU'RE DOING.
HEH
I'M SCARED YOU MIGHT SHOOT SOMEONE BY ACCIDENT.

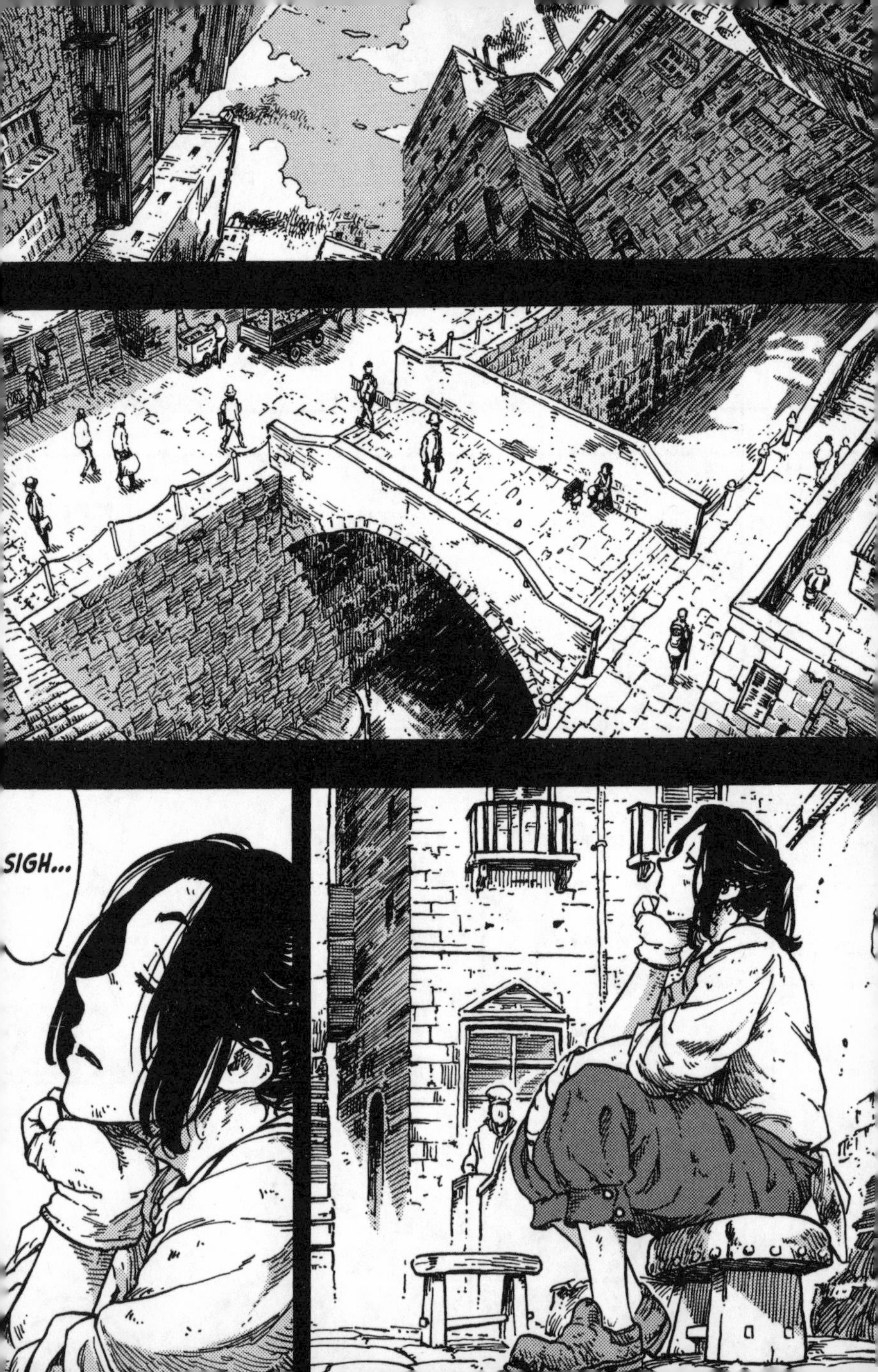
SIGH...

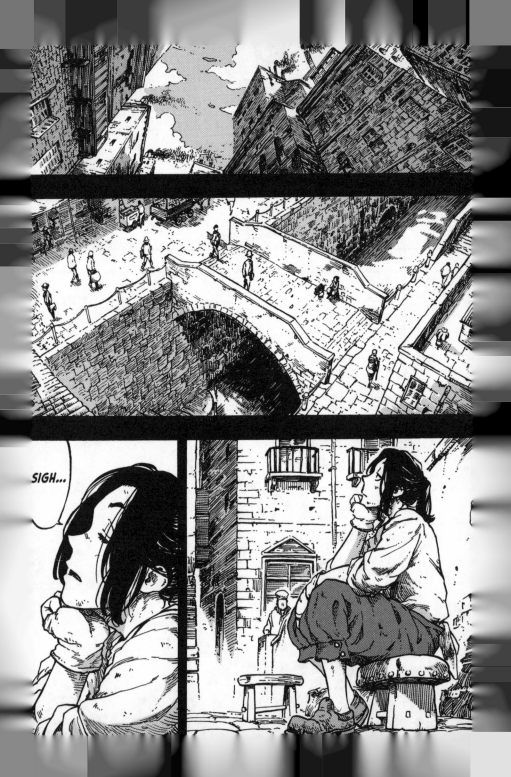

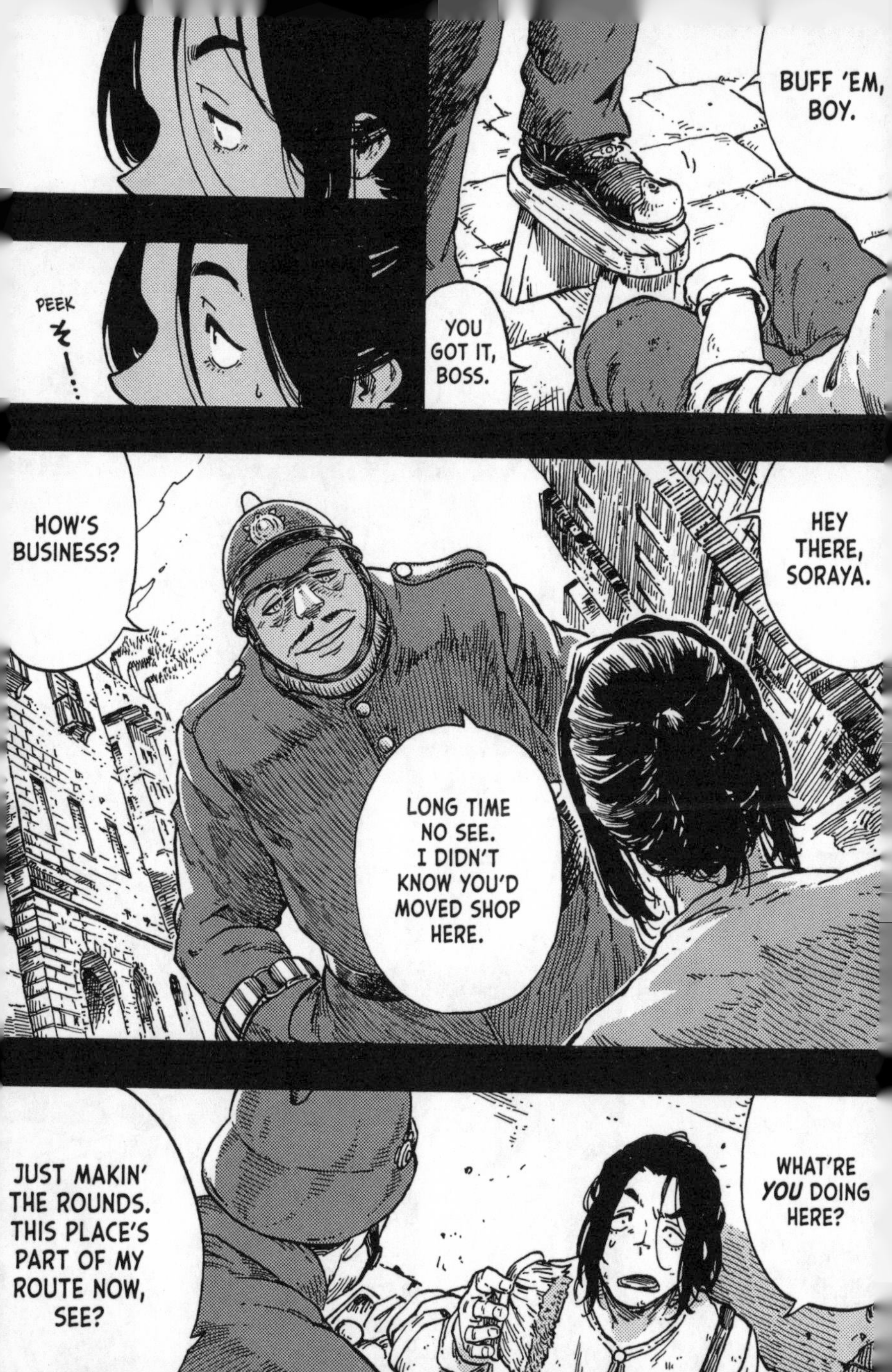
BUFF 'EM, BOY.
YOU GOT IT, BOSS.
PEEK
HEY THERE, SORAYA.
HOW'S BUSINESS?
LONG TIME NO SEE. I DIDN'T KNOW YOU'D MOVED SHOP HERE.
WHAT'RE *YOU* DOING HERE?
JUST MAKIN' THE ROUNDS. THIS PLACE'S PART OF MY ROUTE NOW, SEE?

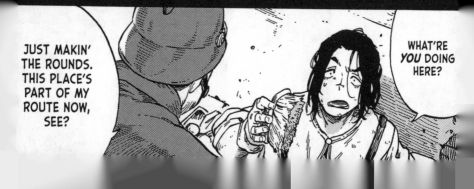

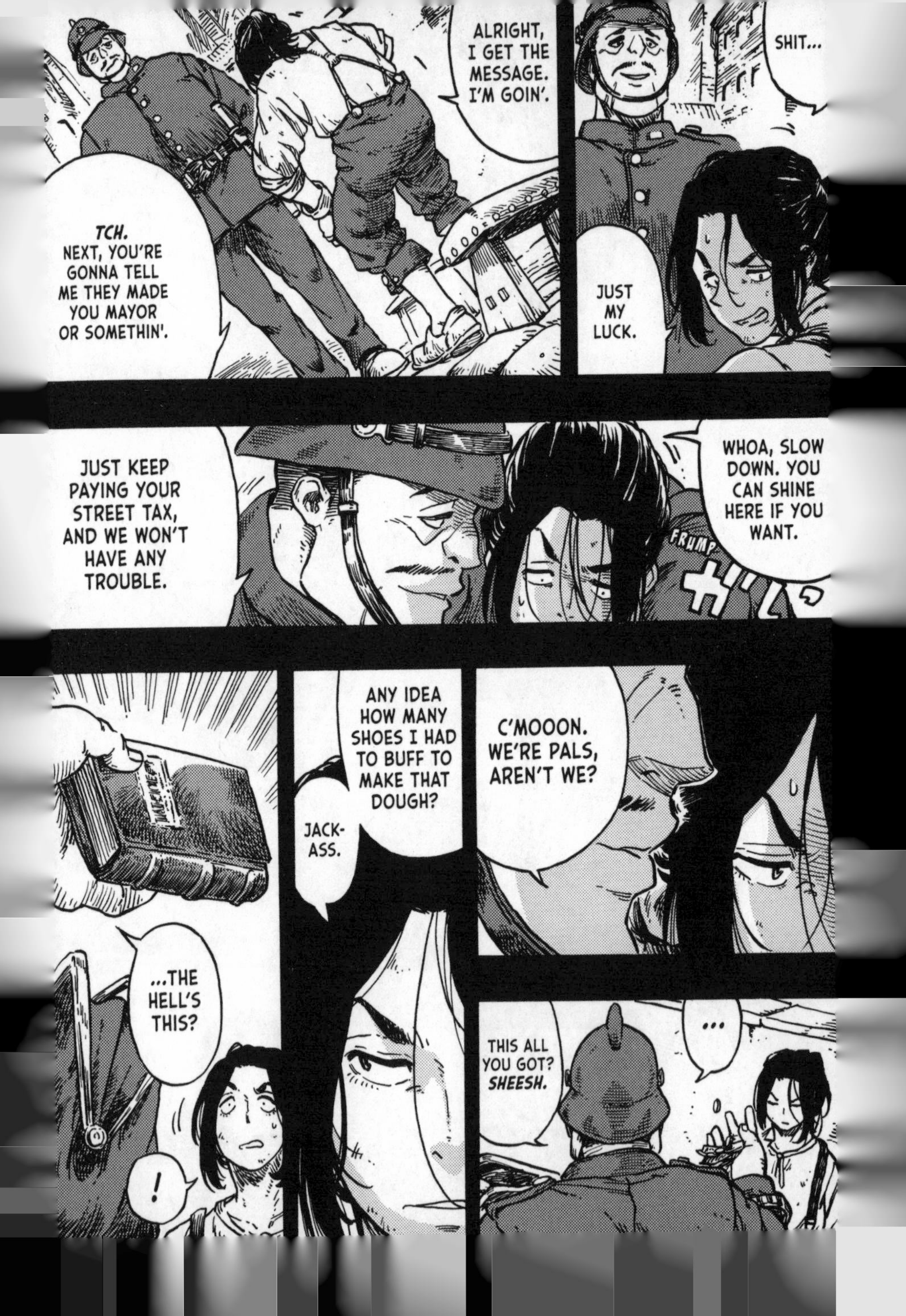
SHIT...
JUST MY LUCK.
ALRIGHT, I GET THE MESSAGE. I'M GOIN'.
TCH. NEXT, YOU'RE GONNA TELL ME THEY MADE YOU MAYOR OR SOMETHIN'.
WHOA, SLOW DOWN. YOU CAN SHINE HERE IF YOU WANT.
FRUMP
JUST KEEP PAYING YOUR STREET TAX, AND WE WON'T HAVE ANY TROUBLE.
C'MOOON. WE'RE PALS, AREN'T WE?
...
THIS ALL YOU GOT? SHEESH.
ANY IDEA HOW MANY SHOES I HAD TO BUFF TO MAKE THAT DOUGH?
JACK-ASS.
...THE HELL'S THIS?
!

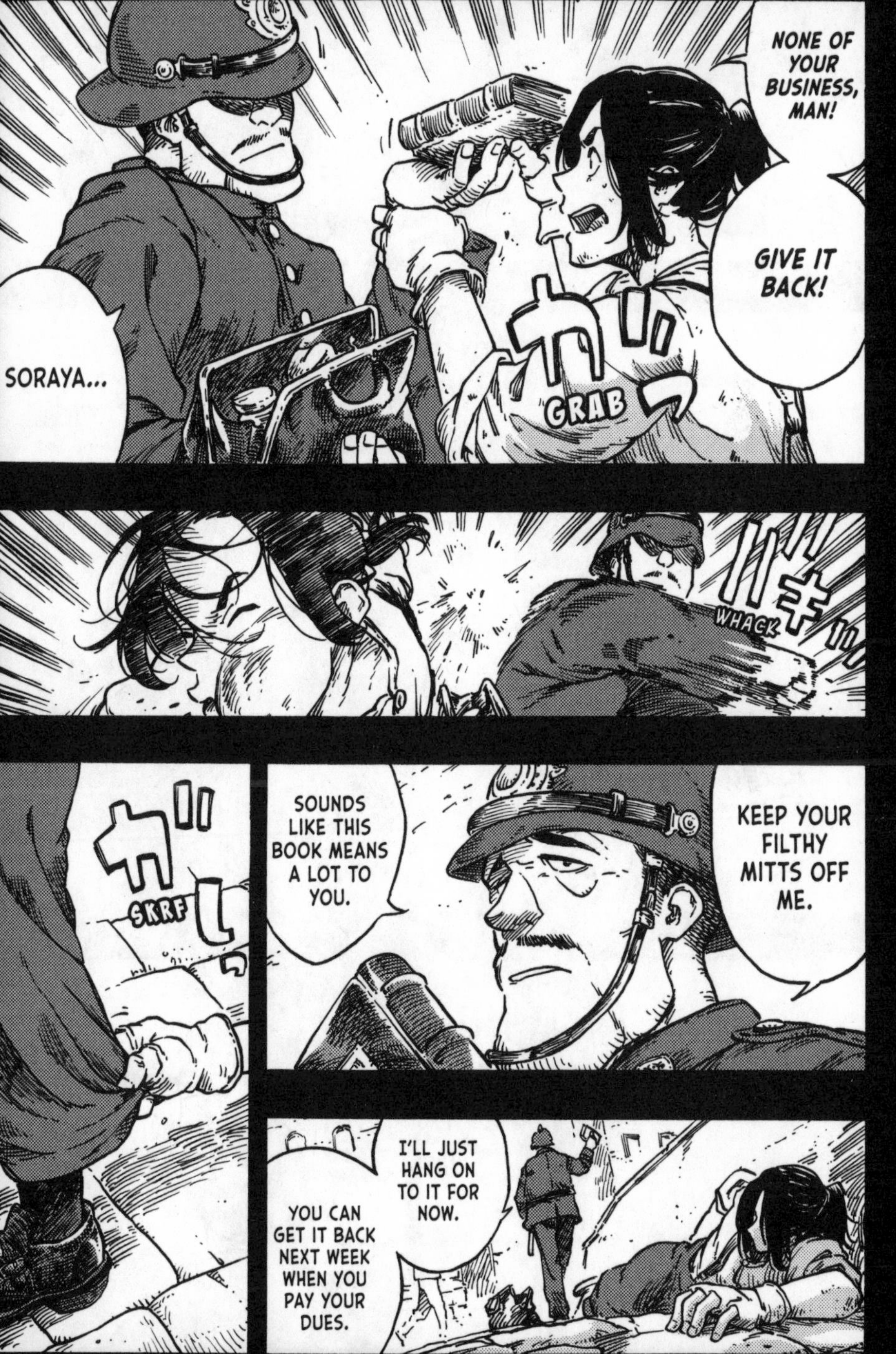
NONE OF YOUR BUSINESS, MAN!
GIVE IT BACK!
GRAB
SORAYA...
WHACK
KEEP YOUR FILTHY MITTS OFF ME.
SOUNDS LIKE THIS BOOK MEANS A LOT TO YOU.
I'LL JUST HANG ON TO IT FOR NOW.
YOU CAN GET IT BACK NEXT WEEK WHEN YOU PAY YOUR DUES.
SKRF

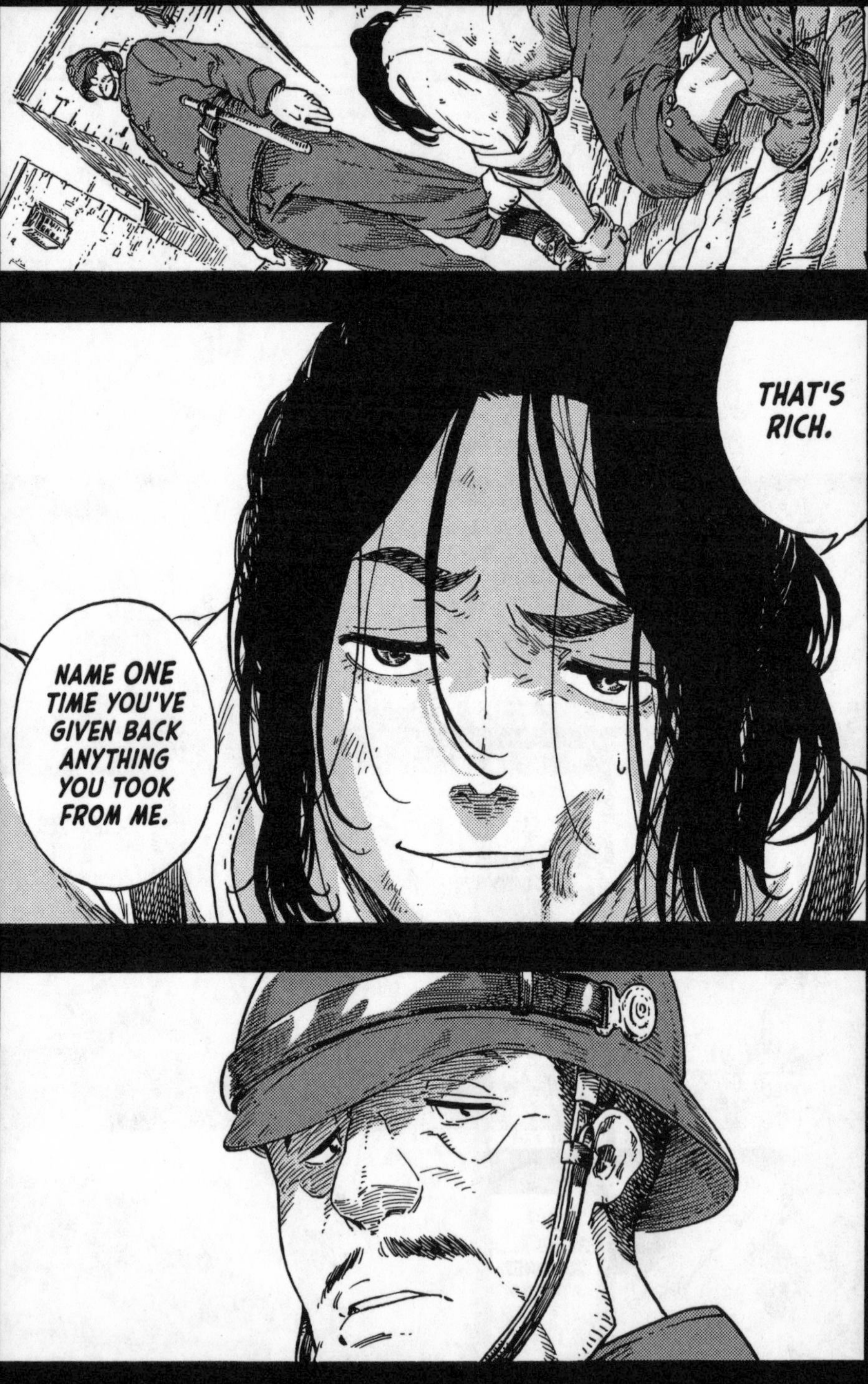
THAT'S RICH.
NAME ONE TIME YOU'VE GIVEN BACK ANYTHING YOU TOOK FROM ME.

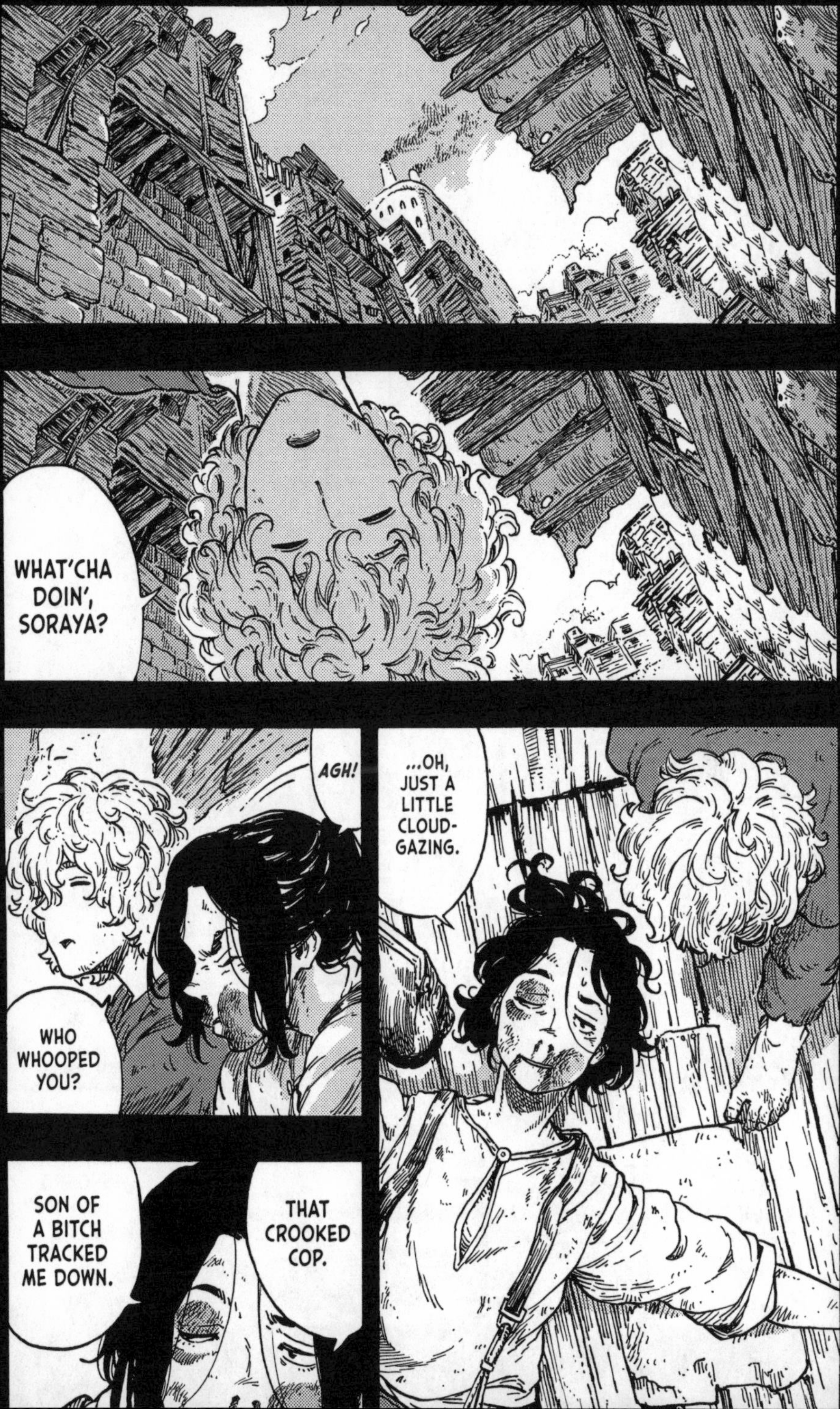
WHAT'CHA DOIN', SORAYA?
...OH, JUST A LITTLE CLOUD-GAZING.
AGH!
WHO WHOOPED YOU?
THAT CROOKED COP.
SON OF A BITCH TRACKED ME DOWN.

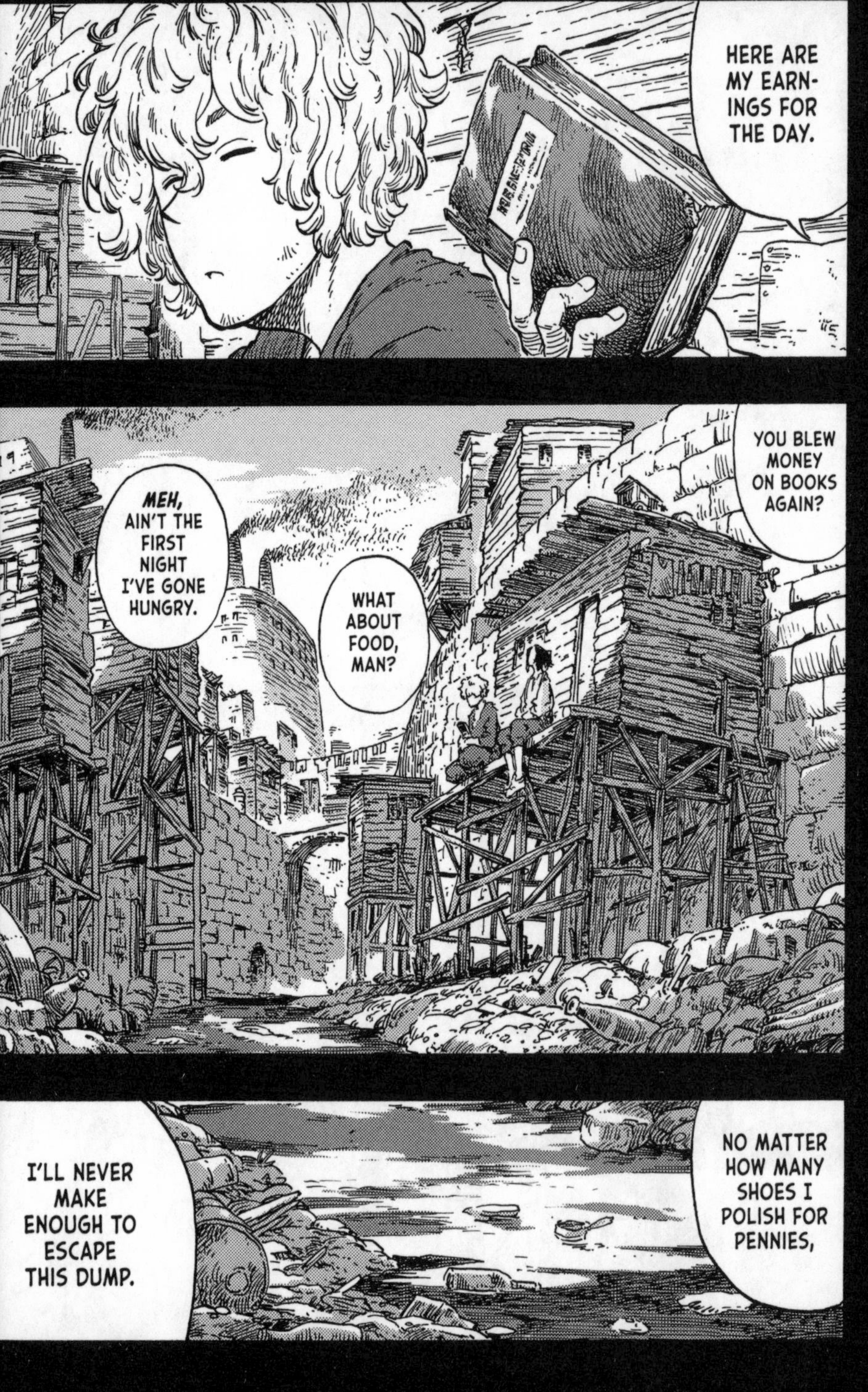
HERE ARE MY EARN- INGS FOR THE DAY.
YOU BLEW MONEY ON BOOKS AGAIN?
WHAT ABOUT FOOD, MAN?
MEH, AIN'T THE FIRST NIGHT I'VE GONE HUNGRY.
NO MATTER HOW MANY SHOES I POLISH FOR PENNIES,
I'LL NEVER MAKE ENOUGH TO ESCAPE THIS DUMP.

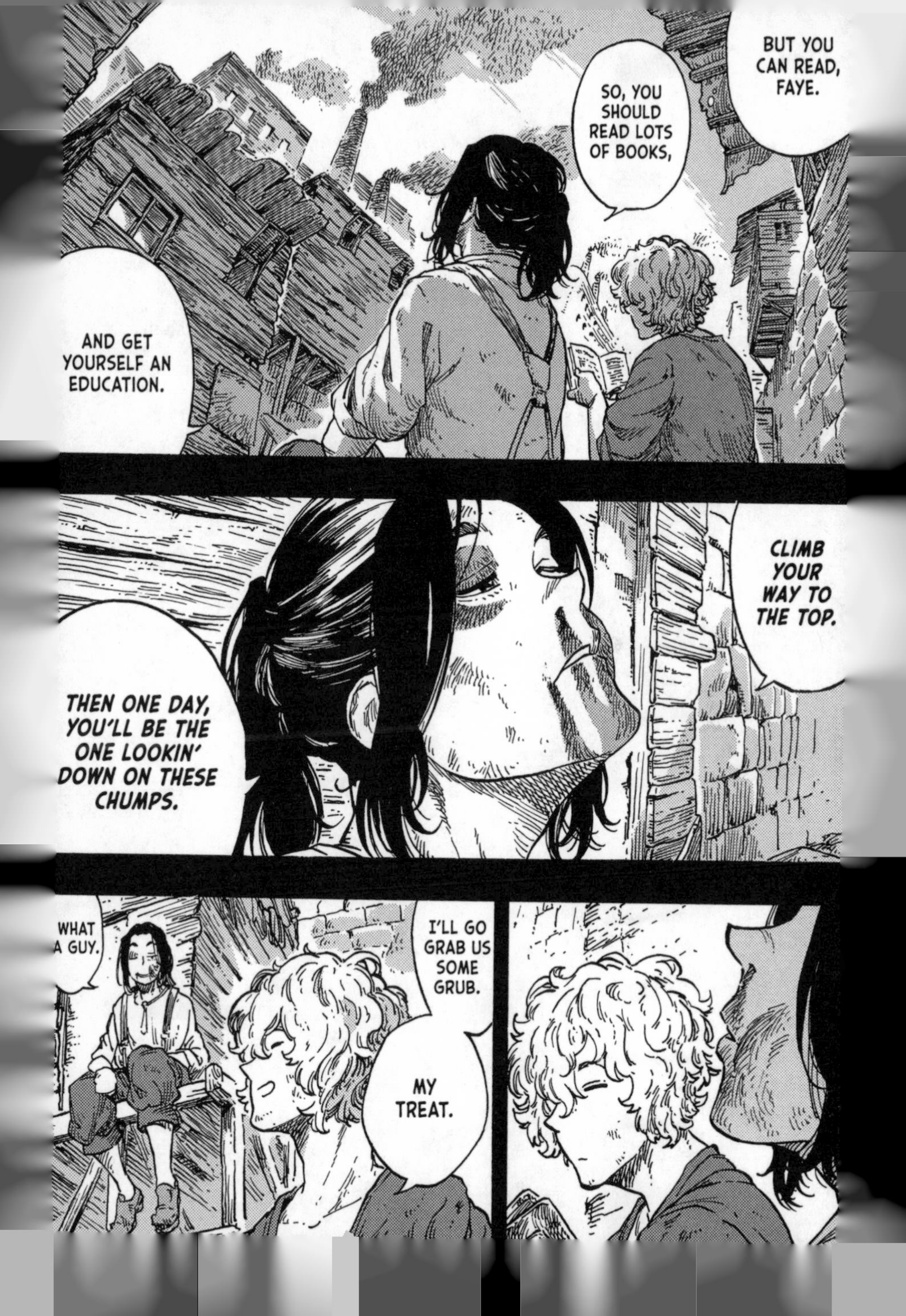
BUT YOU CAN READ, FAYE.
SO, YOU SHOULD READ LOTS OF BOOKS,
AND GET YOURSELF AN EDUCATION.
CLIMB YOUR WAY TO THE TOP.
THEN ONE DAY, YOU'LL BE THE ONE LOOKIN' DOWN ON THESE CHUMPS.
I'LL GO GRAB US SOME GRUB.
MY TREAT.
WHAT A GUY.

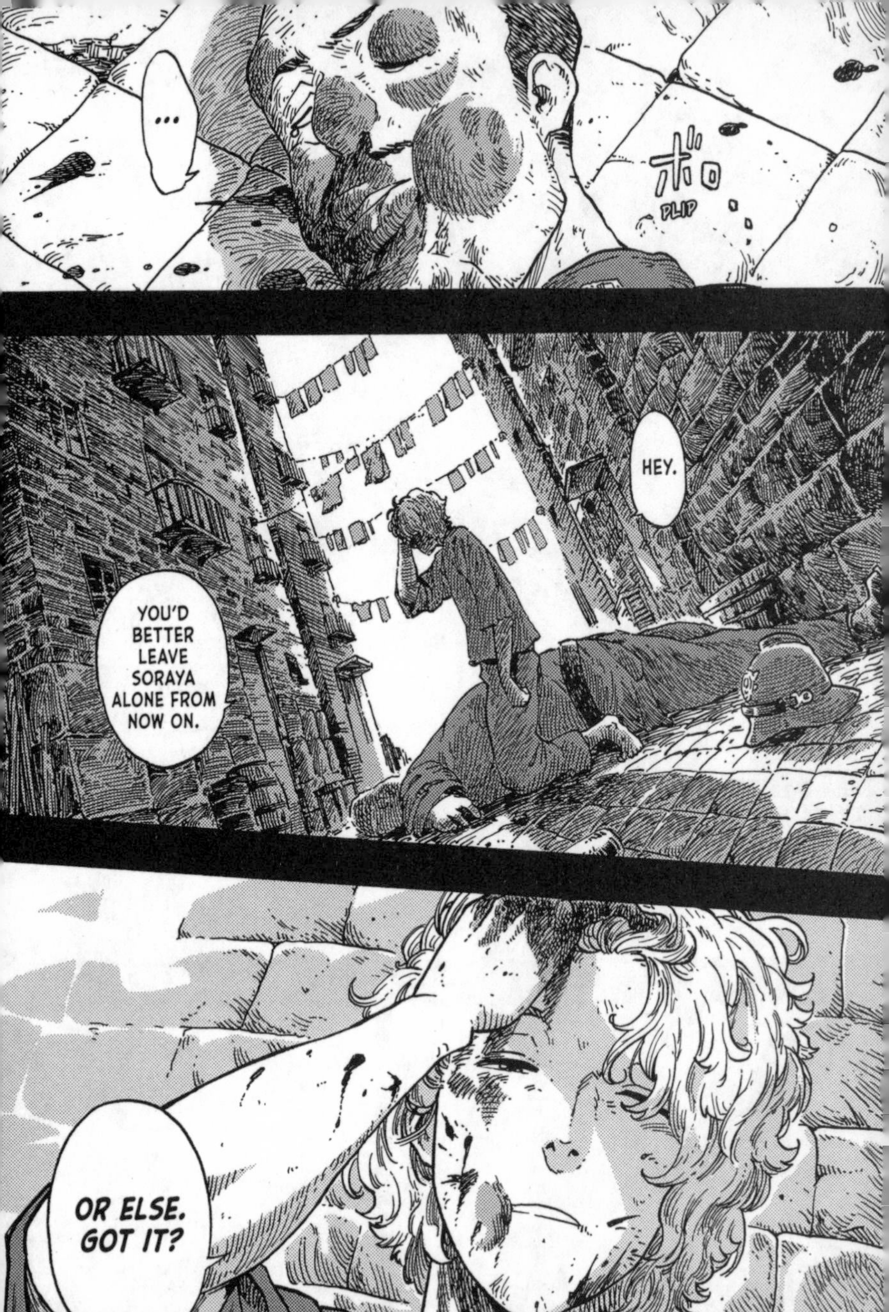
...
ボロ
PLIP
HEY.
YOU'D BETTER LEAVE SORAYA ALONE FROM NOW ON.
OR ELSE. GOT IT?

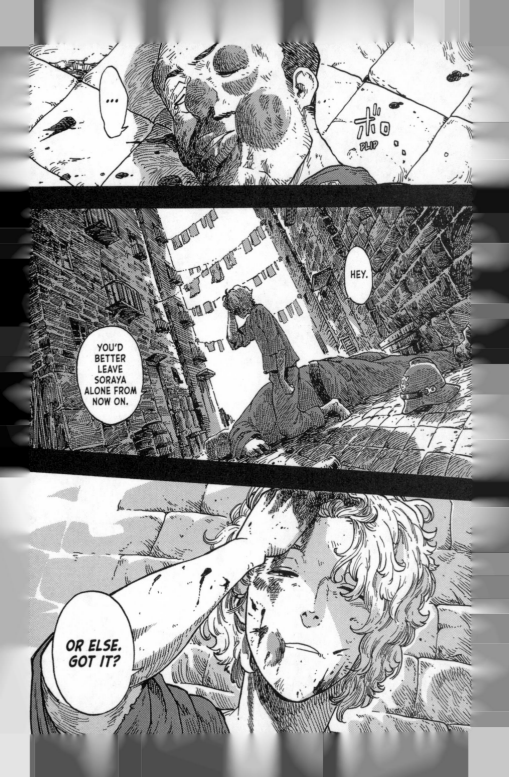

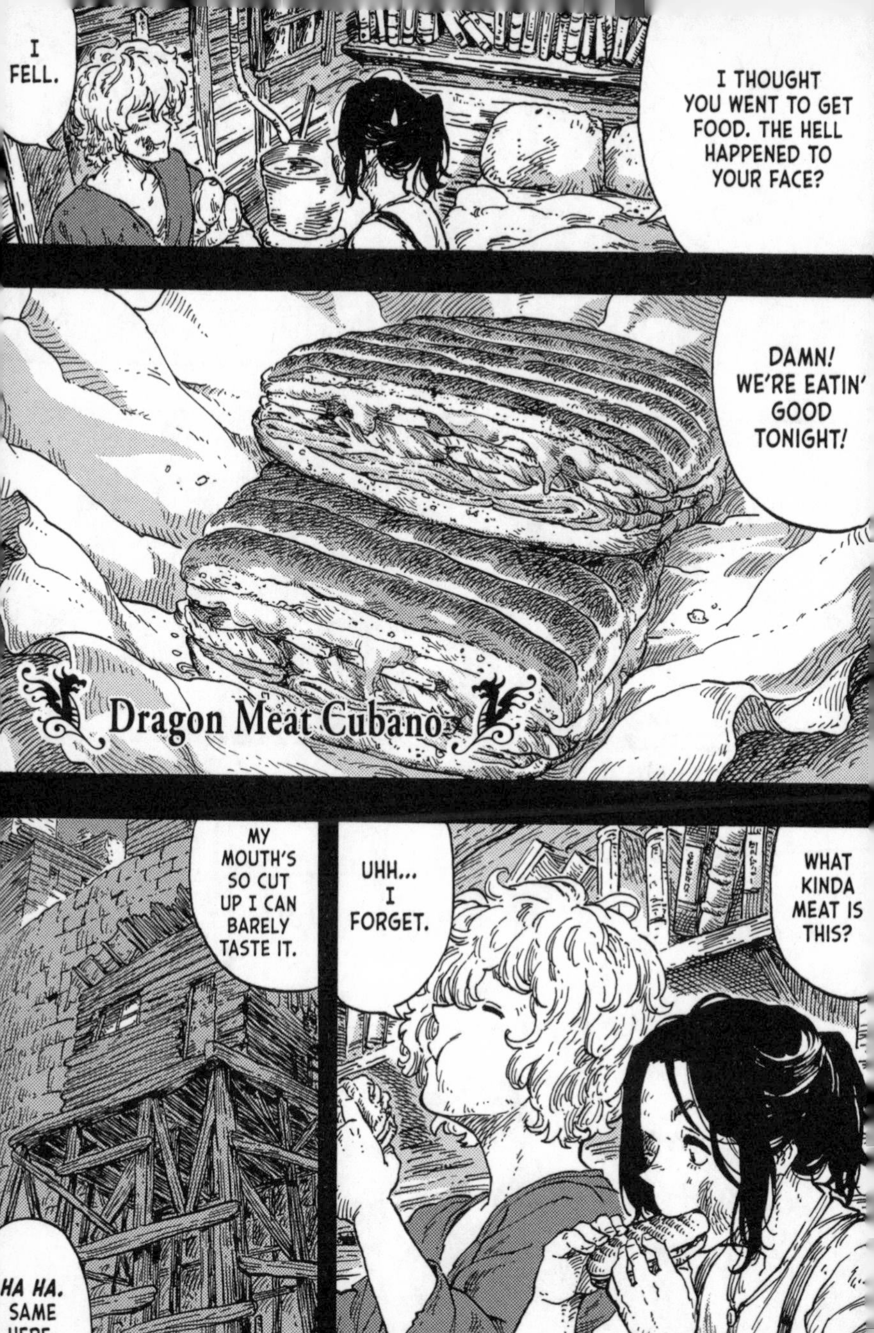
I THOUGHT YOU WENT TO GET FOOD. THE HELL HAPPENED TO YOUR FACE?
I FELL.
DAMN! WE'RE EATIN' GOOD TONIGHT!
Dragon Meat Cubano
WHAT KINDA MEAT IS THIS?
UHH... I FORGET.
MY MOUTH'S SO CUT UP I CAN BARELY TASTE IT.
HA HA. SAME HERE.

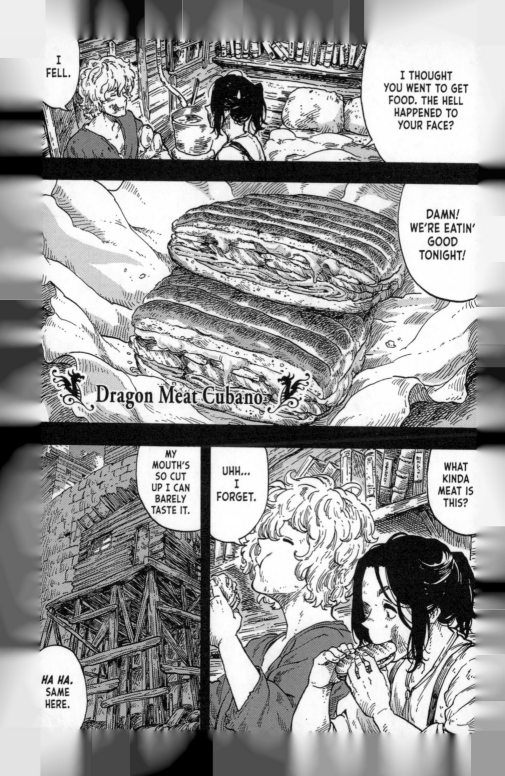

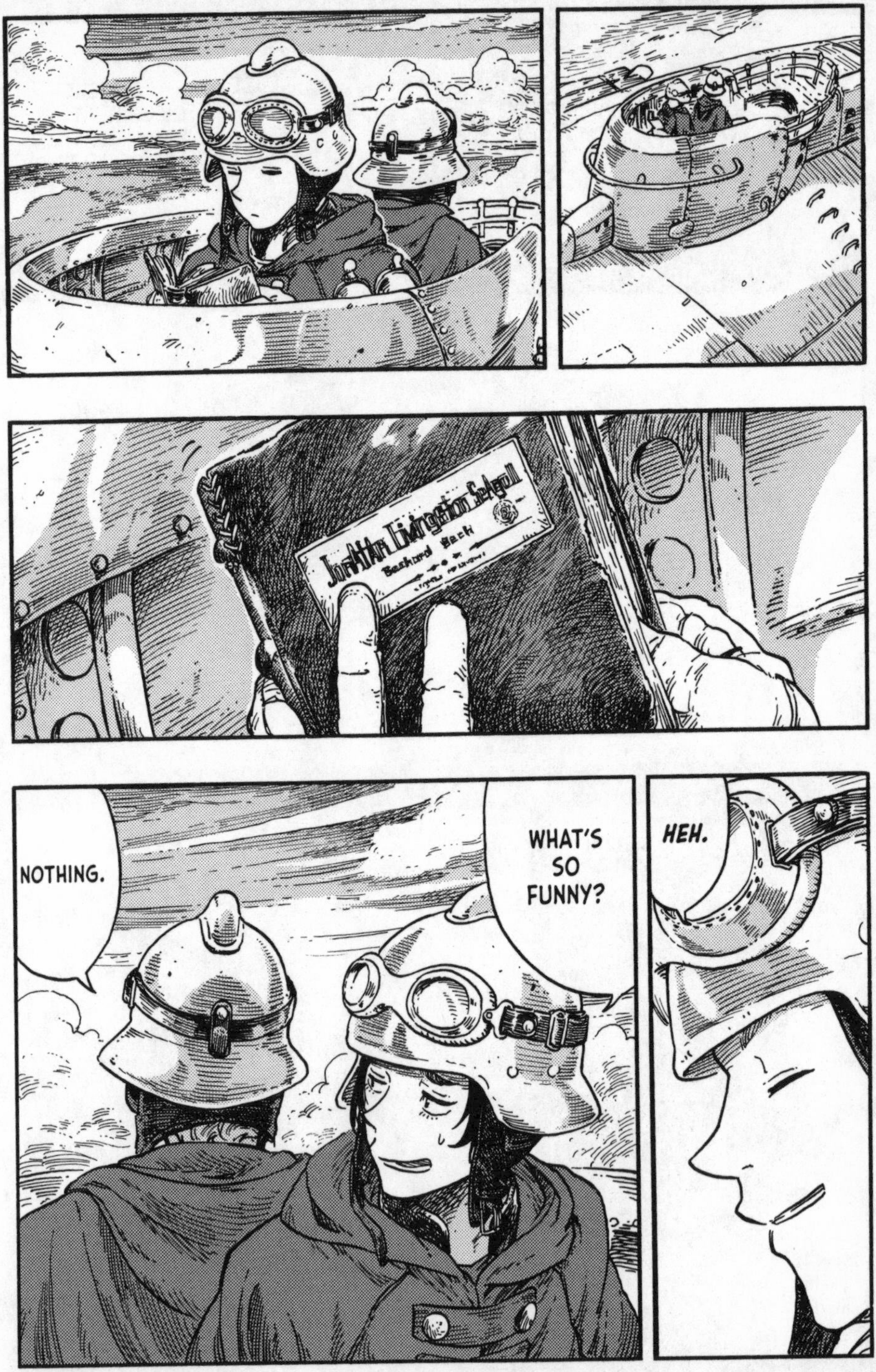
HEH.
WHAT'S SO FUNNY?
NOTHING.

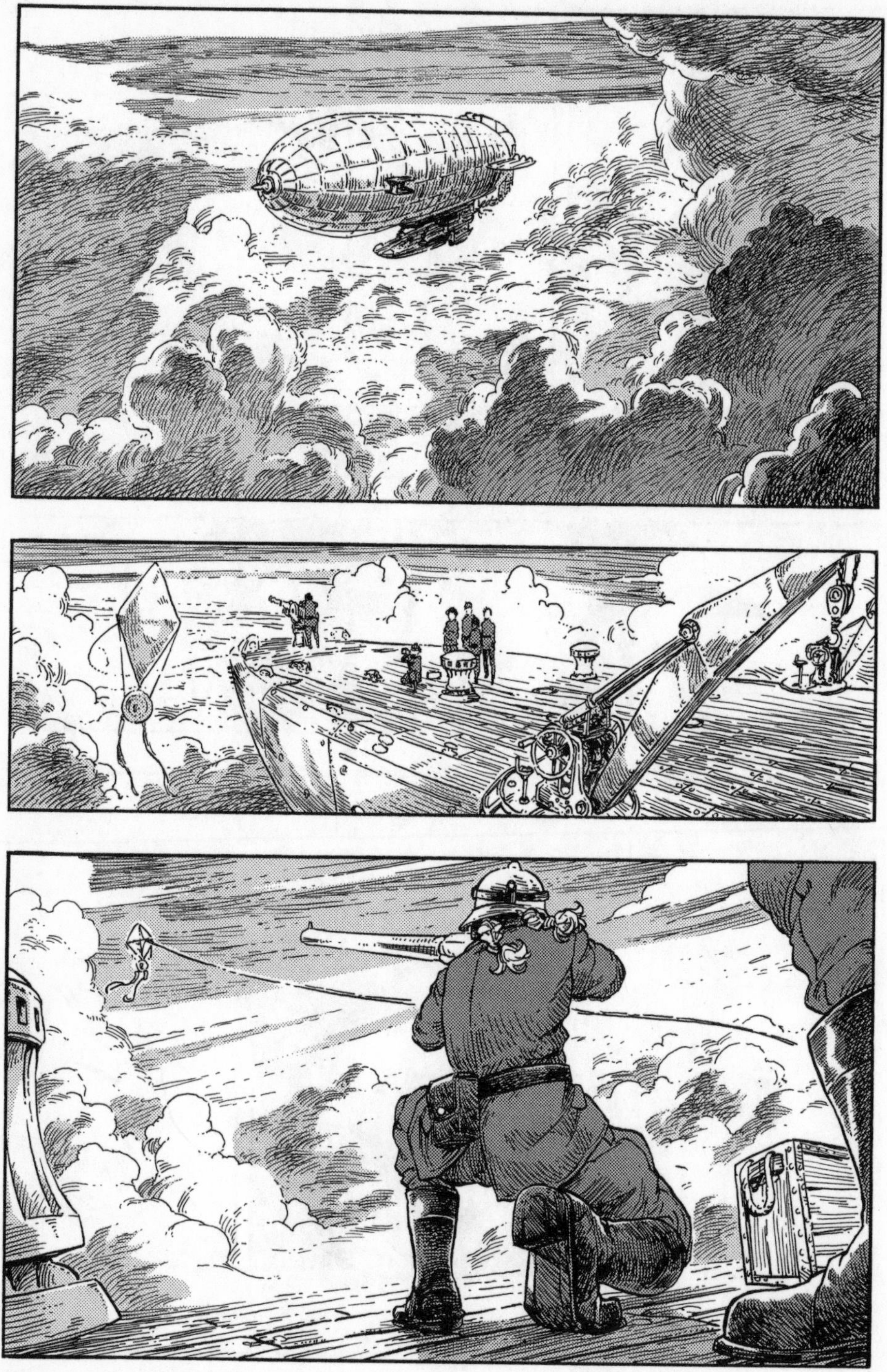

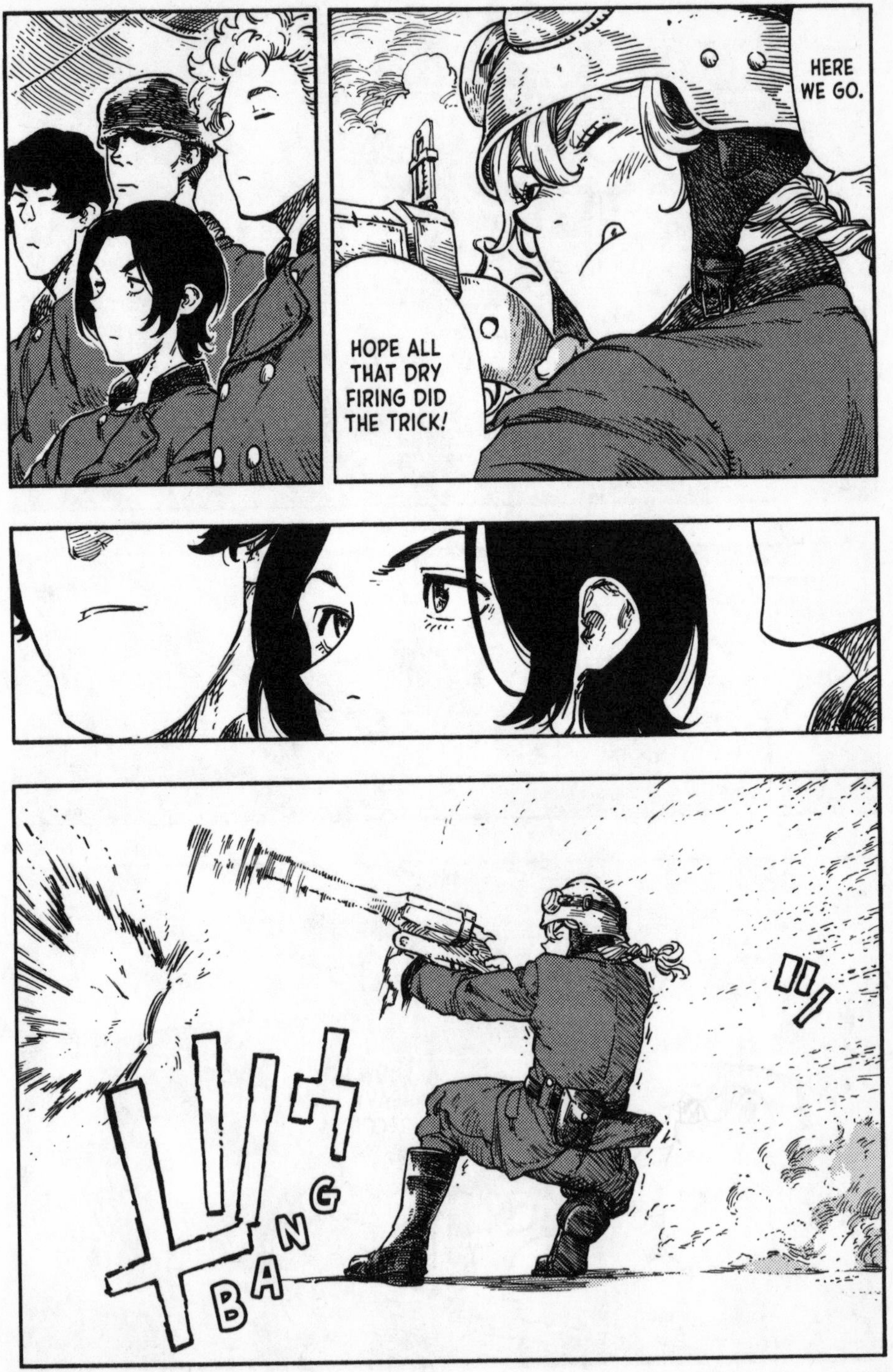
HERE WE GO.
HOPE ALL THAT DRY FIRING DID THE TRICK!
BANG

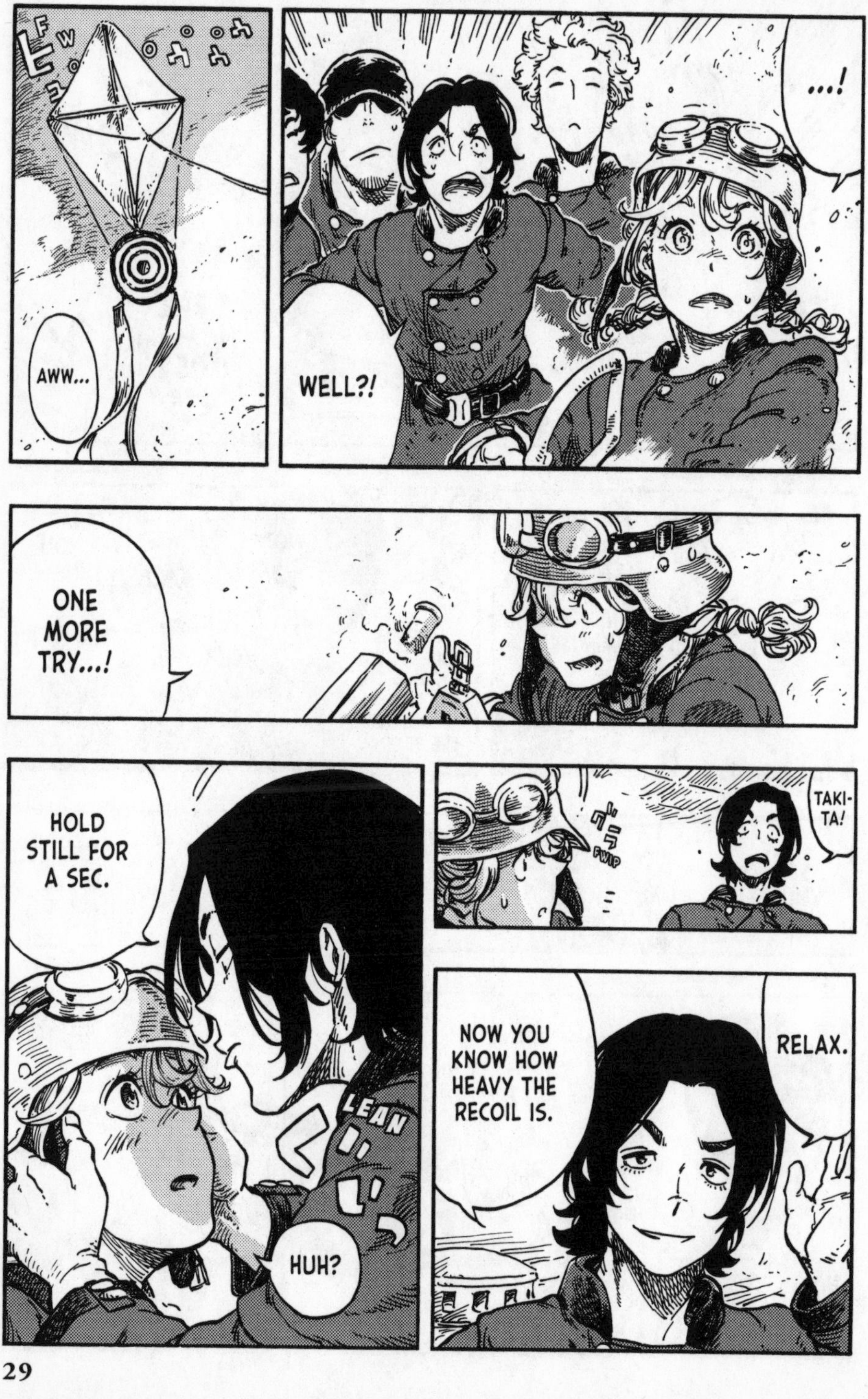
...!
WELL?!
FW
AWW...
ONE MORE TRY...!
TAKI-TA!
FWIP
RELAX.
NOW YOU KNOW HOW HEAVY THE RECOIL IS.
HOLD STILL FOR A SEC.
LEAN
HUH?

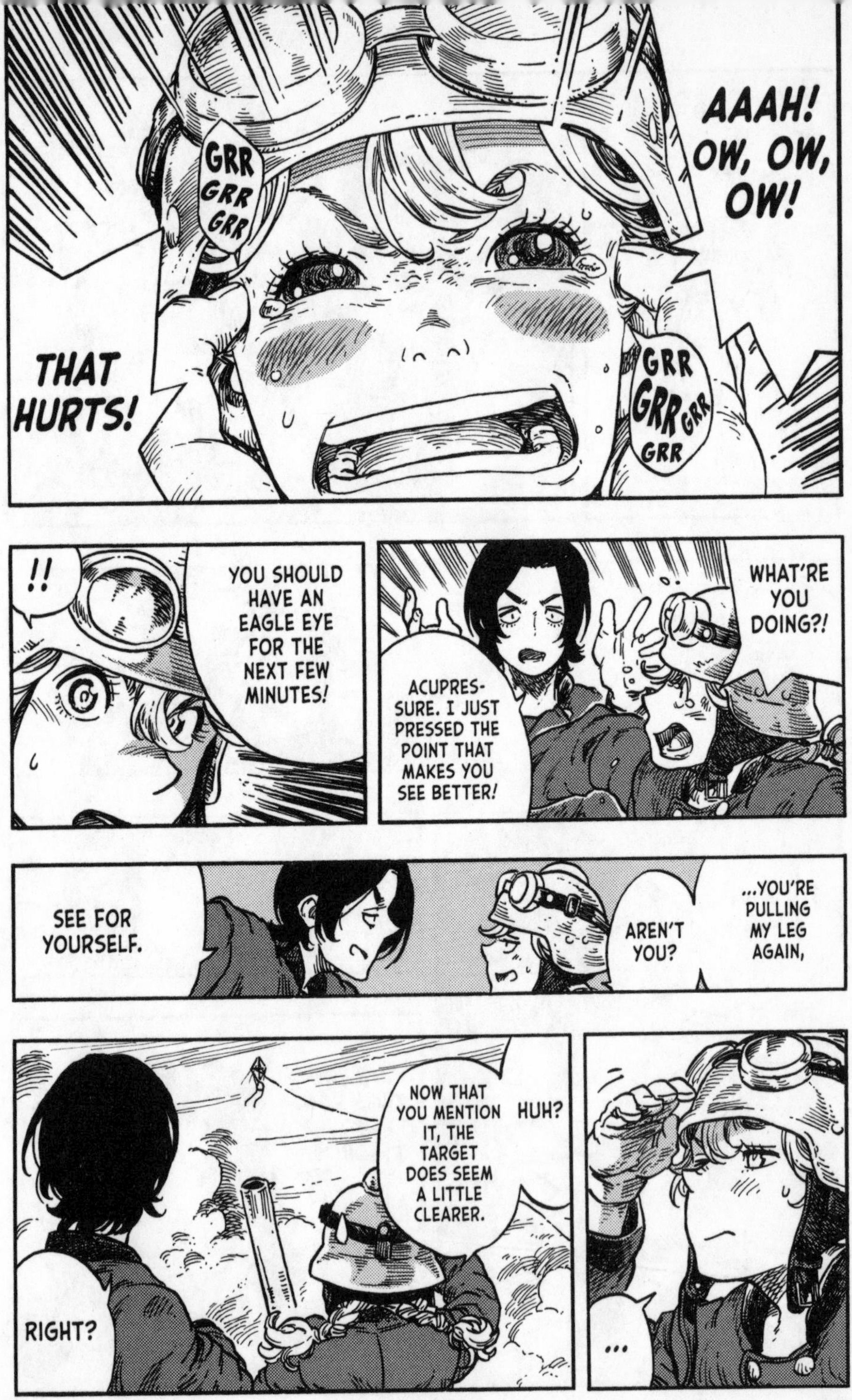
AAAH! OW, OW, OW!
GRR GRR GRR
GRR GRR GRR GRR GRR
THAT HURTS!
WHAT'RE YOU DOING?!
ACUPRES-SURE. I JUST PRESSED THE POINT THAT MAKES YOU SEE BETTER!
YOU SHOULD HAVE AN EAGLE EYE FOR THE NEXT FEW MINUTES!
!!
...YOU'RE PULLING MY LEG AGAIN,
AREN'T YOU?
SEE FOR YOURSELF.
...
HUH?
NOW THAT YOU MENTION IT, THE TARGET DOES SEEM A LITTLE CLEARER.
RIGHT?

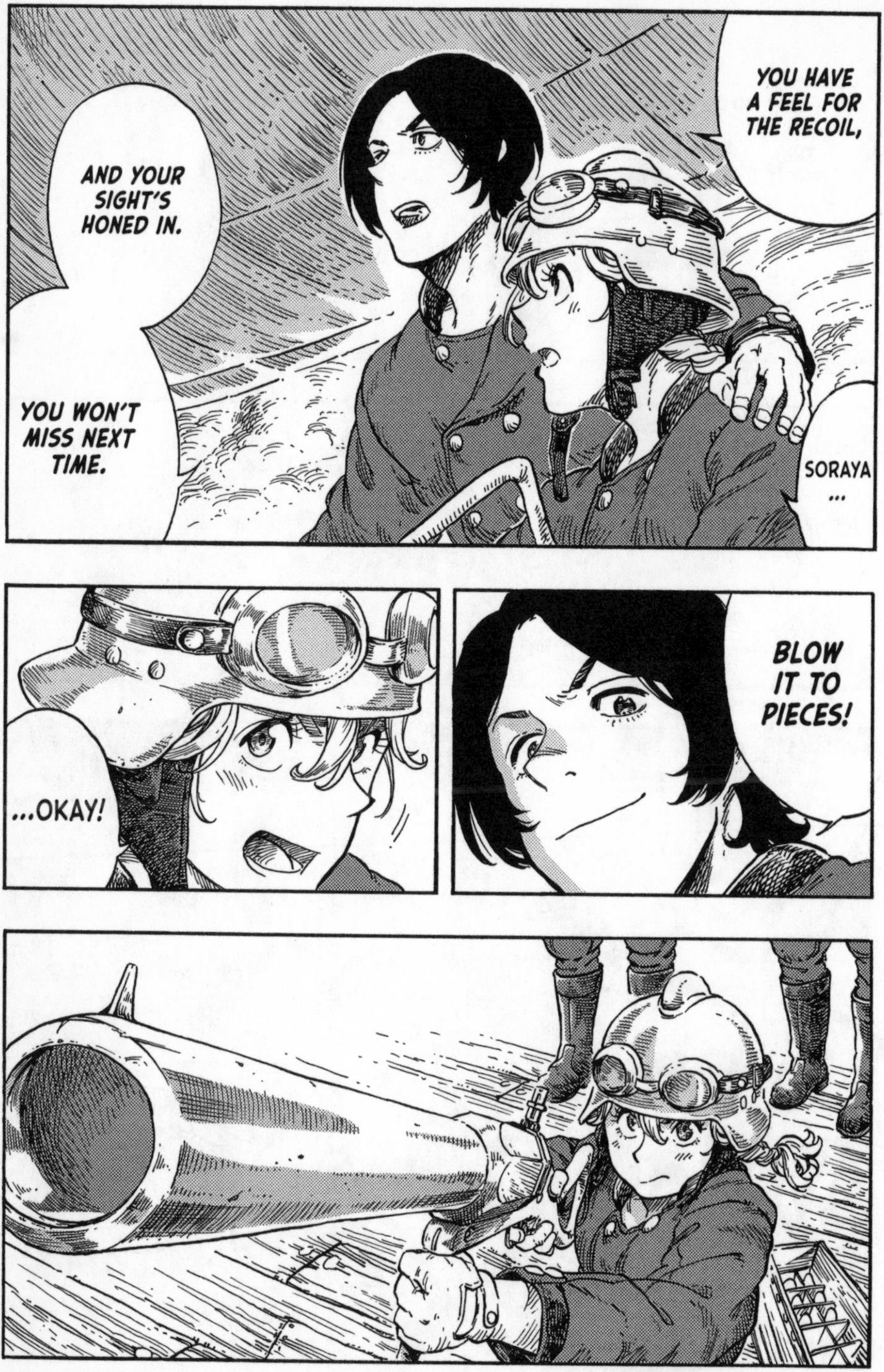
YOU HAVE A FEEL FOR THE RECOIL,
AND YOUR SIGHT'S HONED IN.
YOU WON'T MISS NEXT TIME.
SORAYA ...
BLOW IT TO PIECES!
...OKAY!

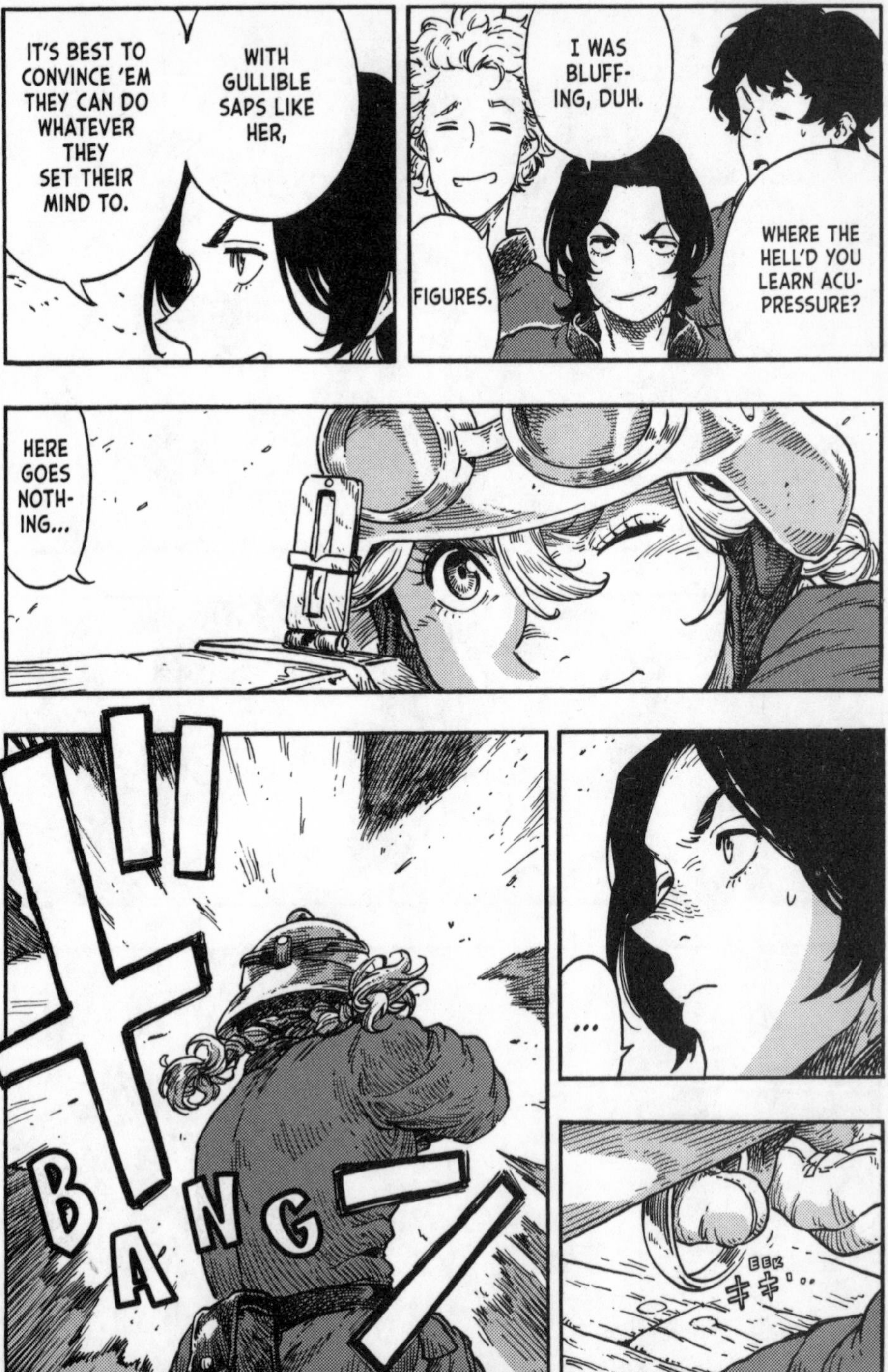
WHERE THE HELL'D YOU LEARN ACU-PRESSURE?
I WAS BLUFF-ING, DUH.
FIGURES.
WITH GULLIBLE SAPS LIKE HER,
IT'S BEST TO CONVINCE 'EM THEY CAN DO WHATEVER THEY SET THEIR MIND TO.
HERE GOES NOTH-ING...
...
EEK
キキ
BANG

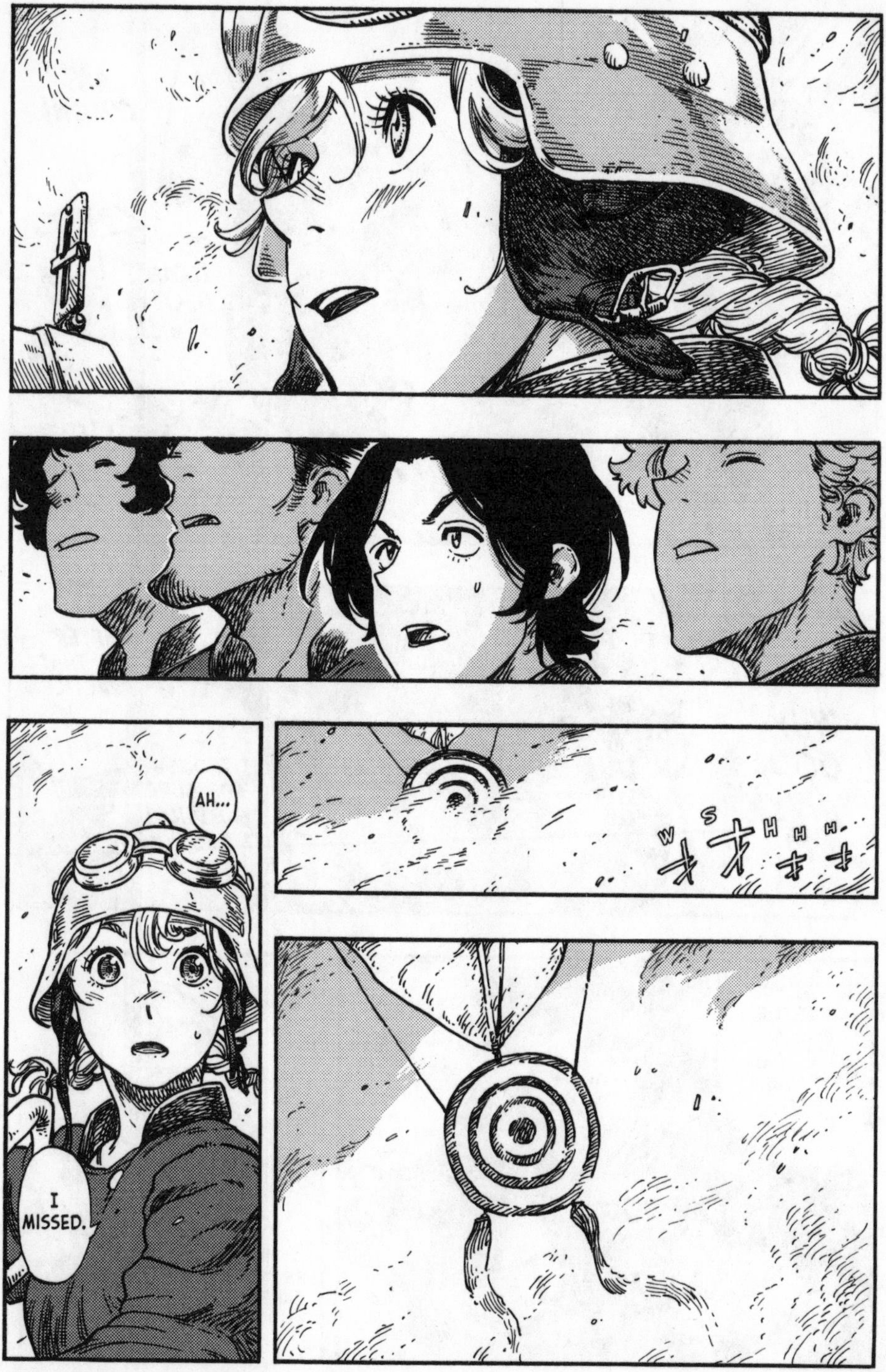
WSHHH
AH...
I MISSED.

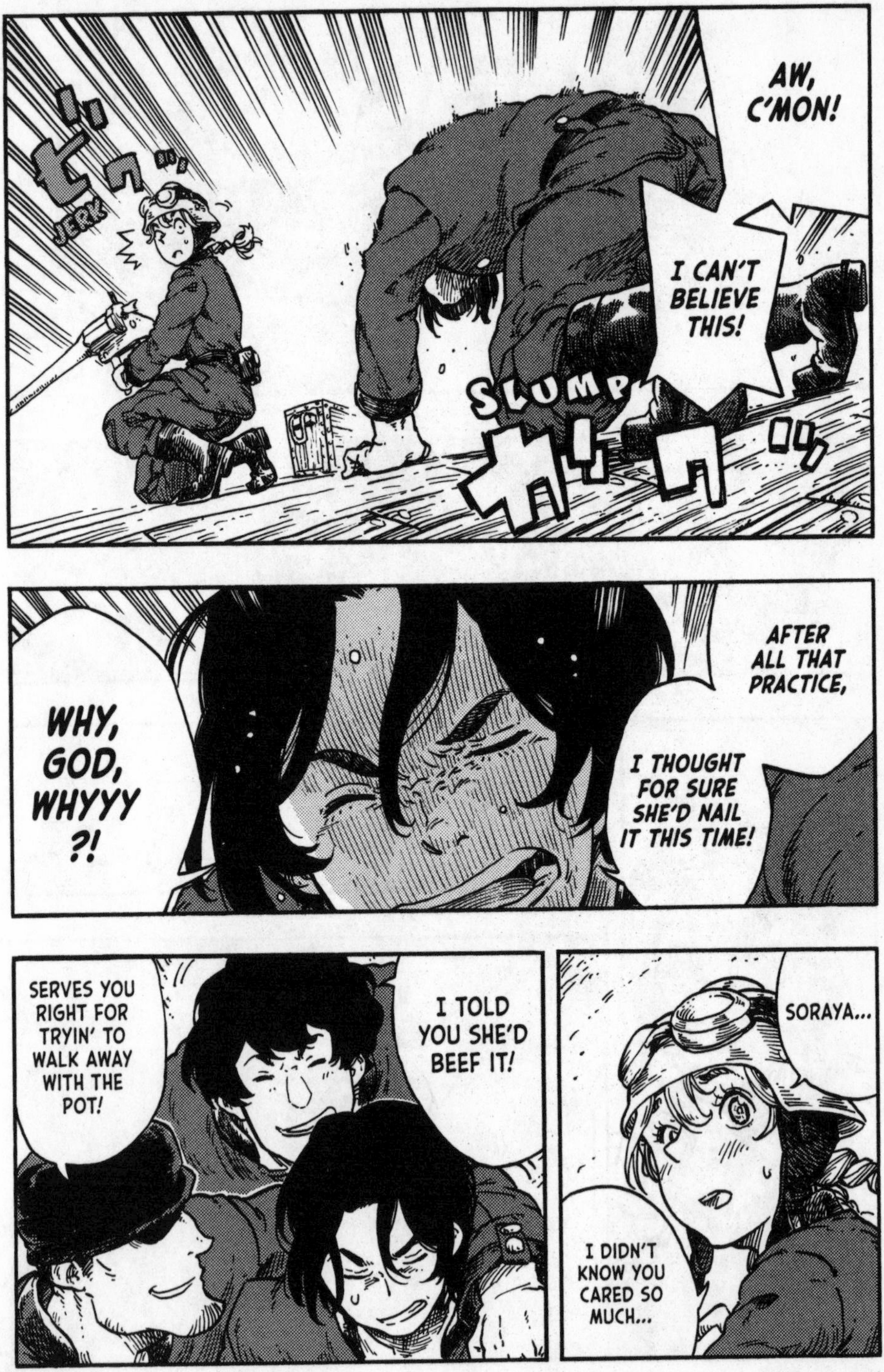
AW, C'MON!
I CAN'T BELIEVE THIS!
SLUMP
JERK
AFTER ALL THAT PRACTICE,
I THOUGHT FOR SURE SHE'D NAIL IT THIS TIME!
WHY, GOD, WHYYY?!
SORAYA...
I DIDN'T KNOW YOU CARED SO MUCH...
I TOLD YOU SHE'D BEEF IT!
SERVES YOU RIGHT FOR TRYIN' TO WALK AWAY WITH THE POT!

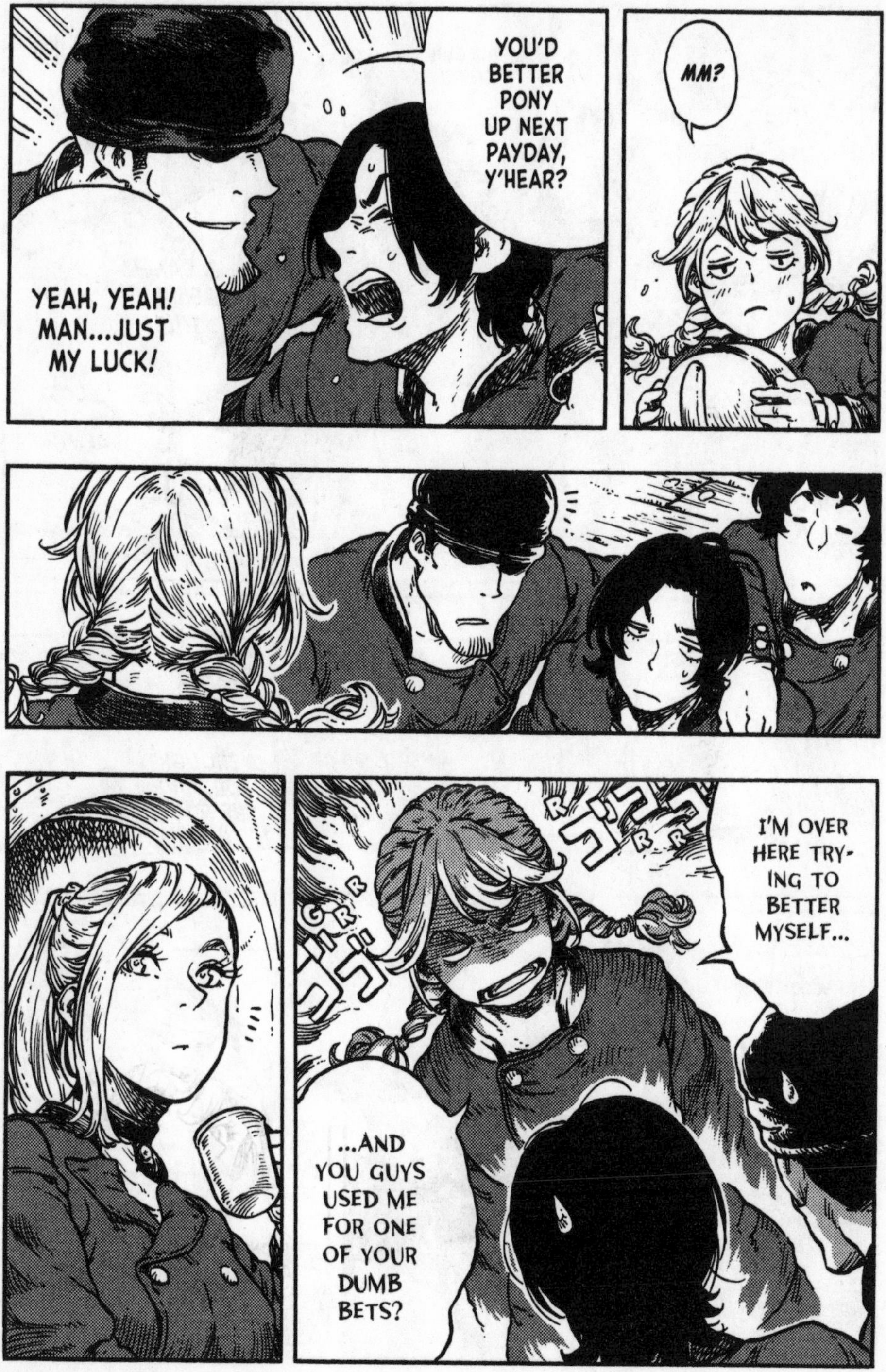
MM?
YOU'D BETTER PONY UP NEXT PAYDAY, Y'HEAR?
YEAH, YEAH! MAN...JUST MY LUCK!
I'M OVER HERE TRYING TO BETTER MYSELF...
GRR
...AND YOU GUYS USED ME FOR ONE OF YOUR DUMB BETS?

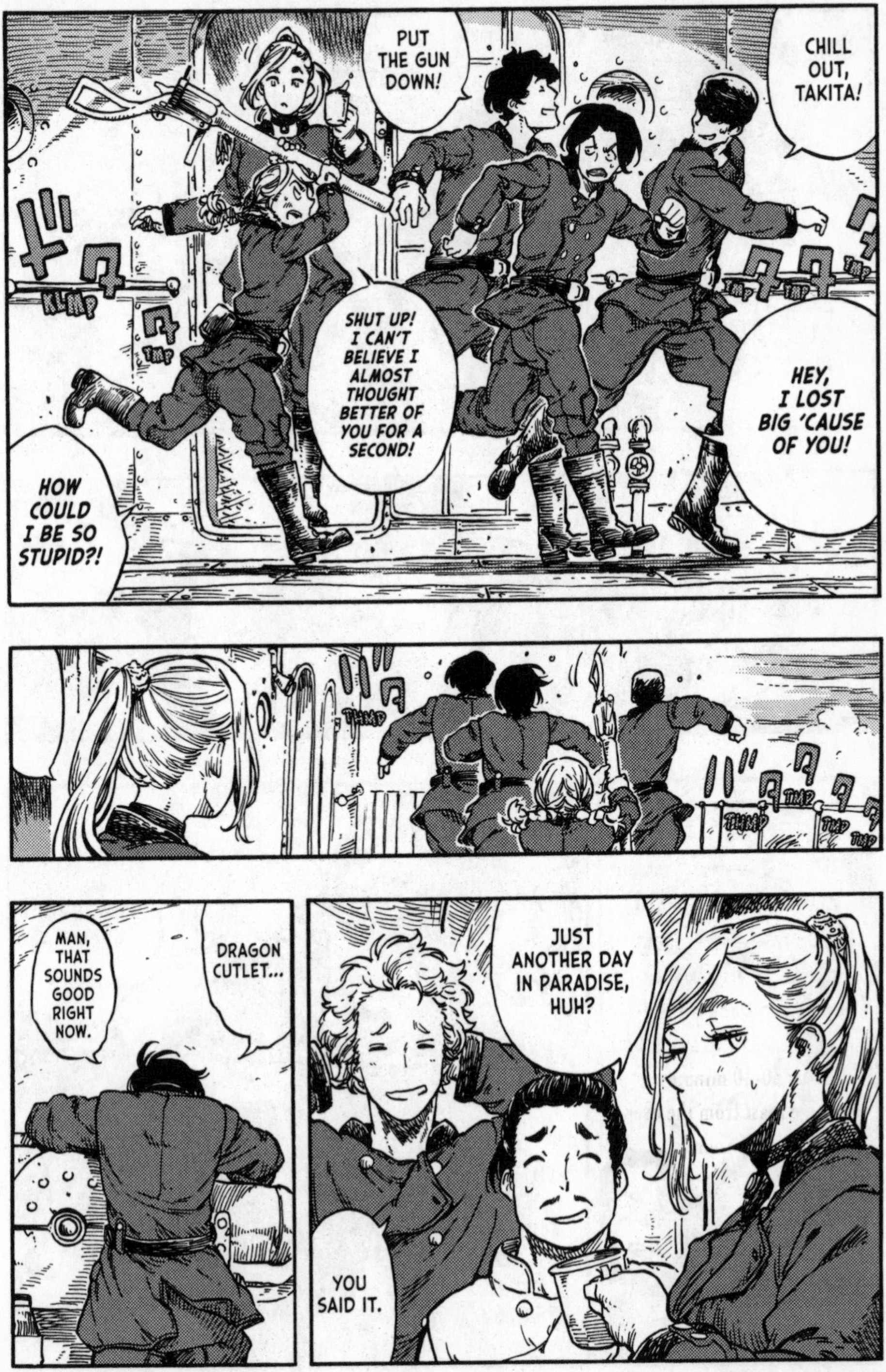
CHILL OUT, TAKITA!
PUT THE GUN DOWN!
HEY, I LOST BIG 'CAUSE OF YOU!
SHUT UP! I CAN'T BELIEVE I ALMOST THOUGHT BETTER OF YOU FOR A SECOND!
KLMP
TMP
HOW COULD I BE SO STUPID?!
JUST ANOTHER DAY IN PARADISE, HUH?
YOU SAID IT.
DRAGON CUTLET...
MAN, THAT SOUNDS GOOD RIGHT NOW.

Dragon Cubano

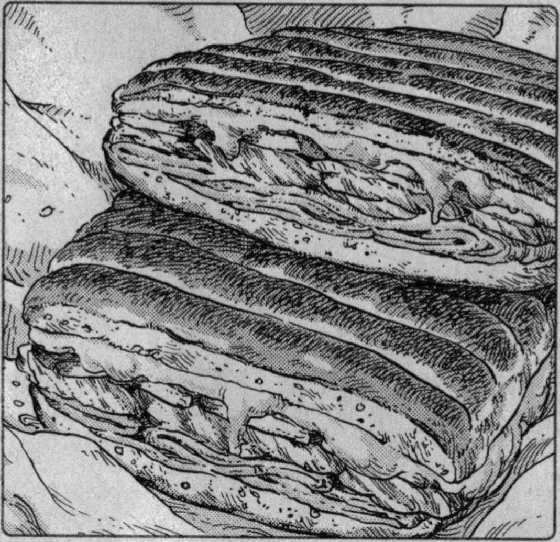

Ingredients (Serves 2)

- ✦ Dragon tail meat: 500 g
- ★Marinade:
  - Extra virgin olive oil: 3 tbsp
  - Orange zest: 1 tbsp
  - Orange juice: 5-6 tbsp
  - Lime juice: 1 tbsp Mint: to taste
  - Sliced garlic: 2 cloves
  - Powdered oregano: 1 tsp
  - Cumin: 1 tsp Paprika: 1 tsp
  - Salt & Pepper: to taste
- ✦ 15-cm baguette ✦ Ham: 3 slices
- ✦ Cheddar cheese: 2 slices
- ✦ Thinly-sliced dill pickles: 3-6 slices
- ✦ Mayonnaise: to taste
- ✦ Mustard: to taste ✦ Butter: to taste

01

First, we'll make the mojo dragon roast. Place all of the marinade ingredients in a large container and mix thoroughly to incorporate.

02

Prick holes into the dragon meat with a fork to aid in absorption and place the meat in the marinade.

03

After 2-3 hours, turn the meat over and leave to marinate overnight.

04

Heat olive oil in a pan and sear the meat on all sides. Once seared, remove the pan from the heat and transfer to 180° C / 350° F oven and bake for 30-40 minutes. Remove roast from the oven and let cool to room temp.

05

Layer sliced mojo dragon roast, ham, cheese, and pickles on a baguette halved lengthwise.

06

Grease a sandwich press with butter and toast the sandwich until the surface is golden brown. If using a frypan, toast one side at a time, pressing the top side down with a large pot or lid. Add more butter as necessary.

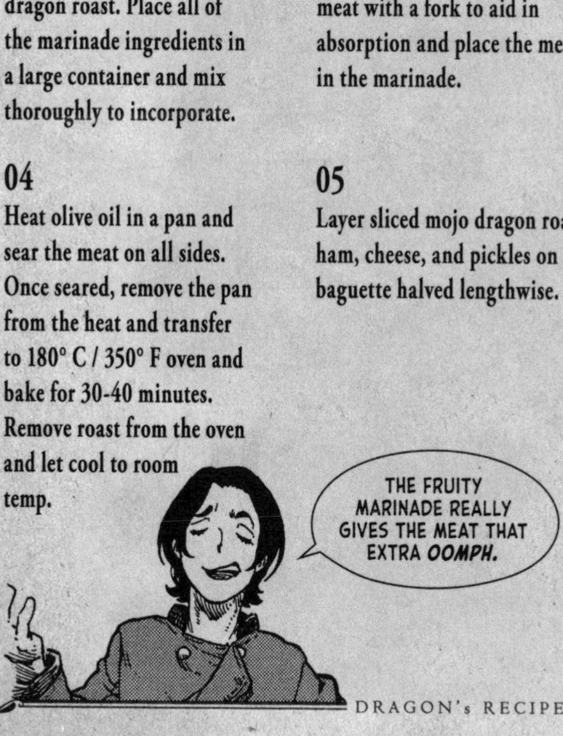
THE FRUITY MARINADE REALLY GIVES THE MEAT THAT EXTRA *OOMPH.*

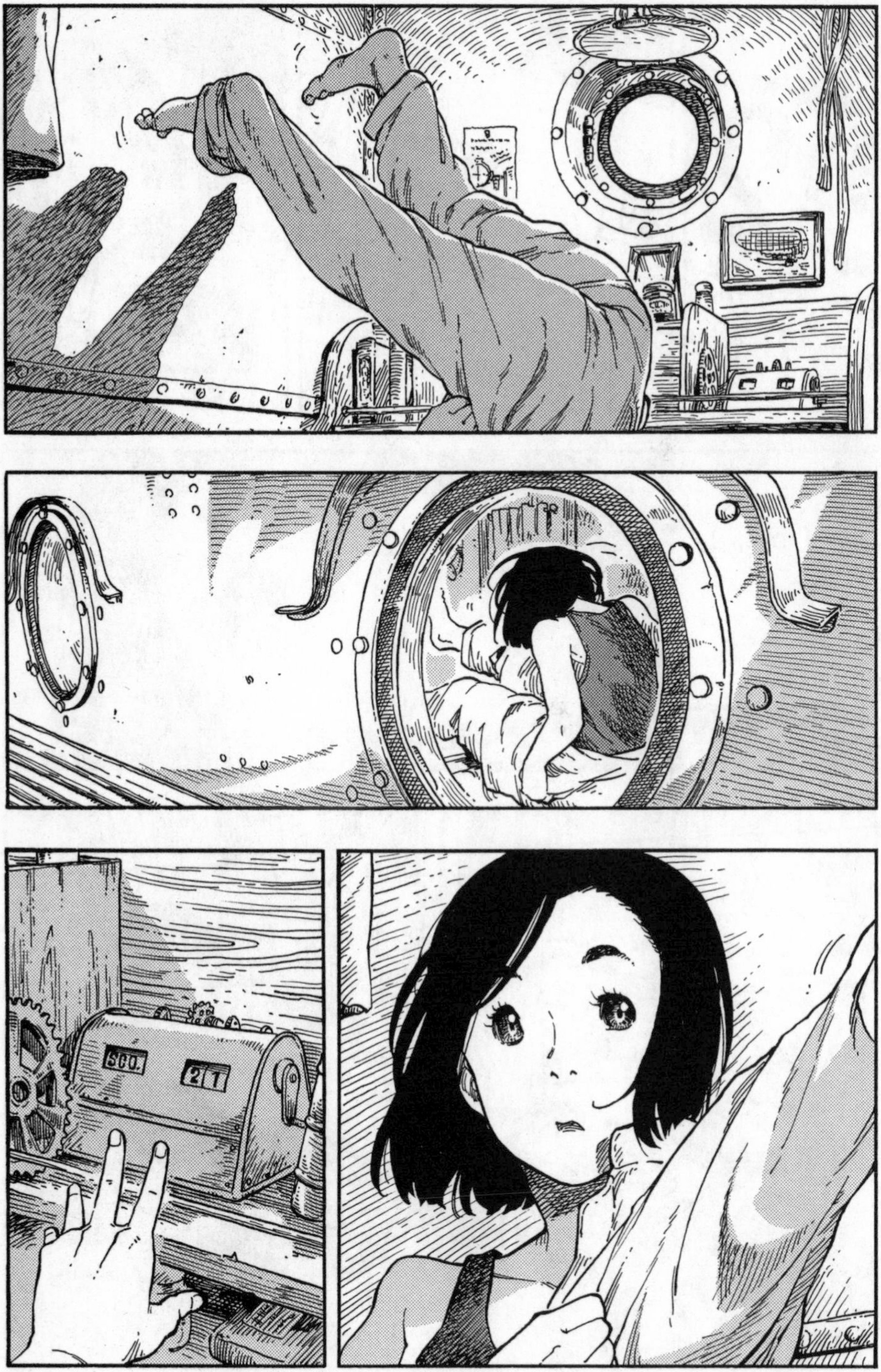
21

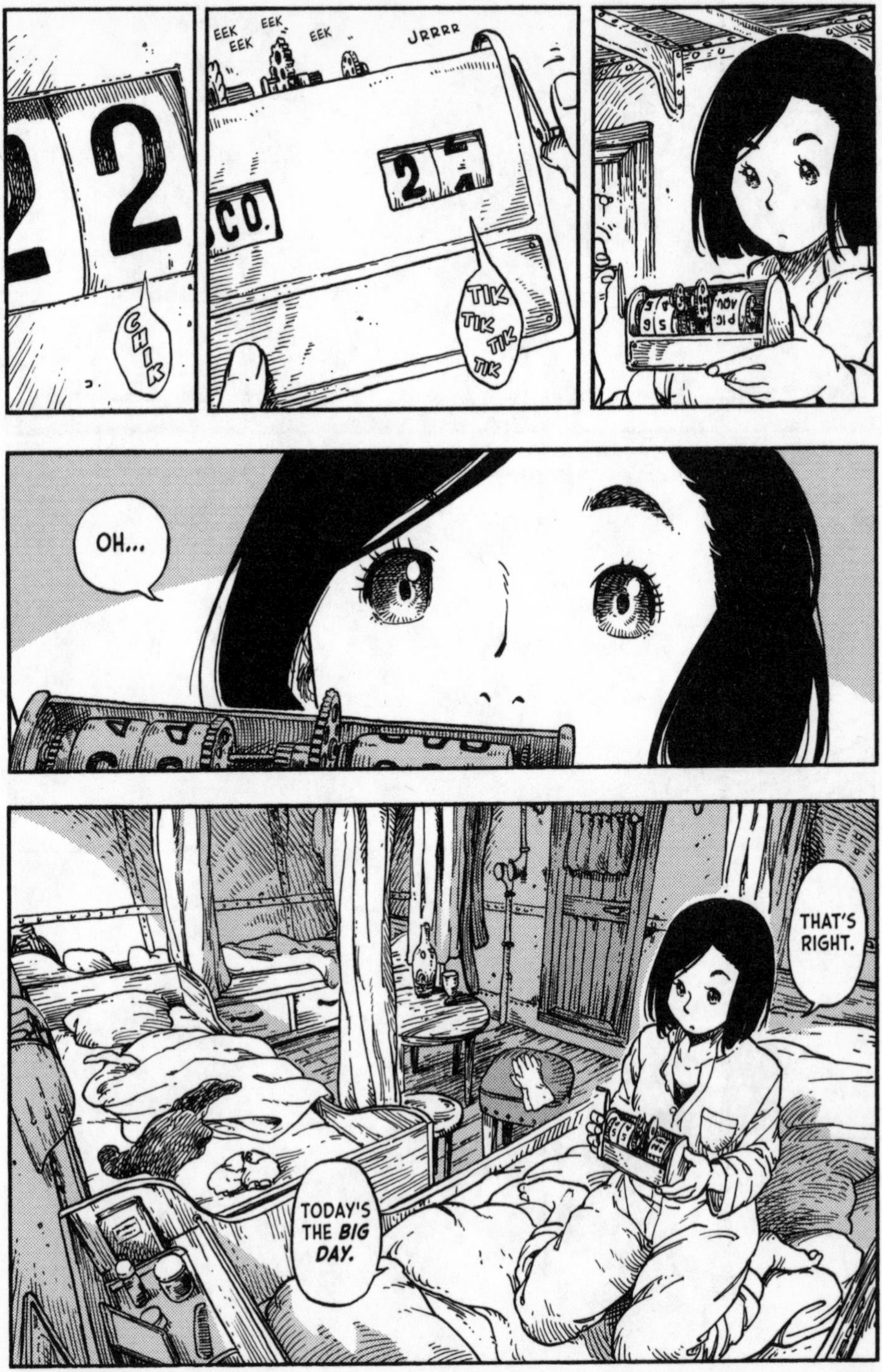

EEK EEK EEK EEK
JRRRR
CO.
TIK TIK TIK TIK
CHIK
OH...
THAT'S RIGHT.
TODAY'S THE *BIG* DAY.

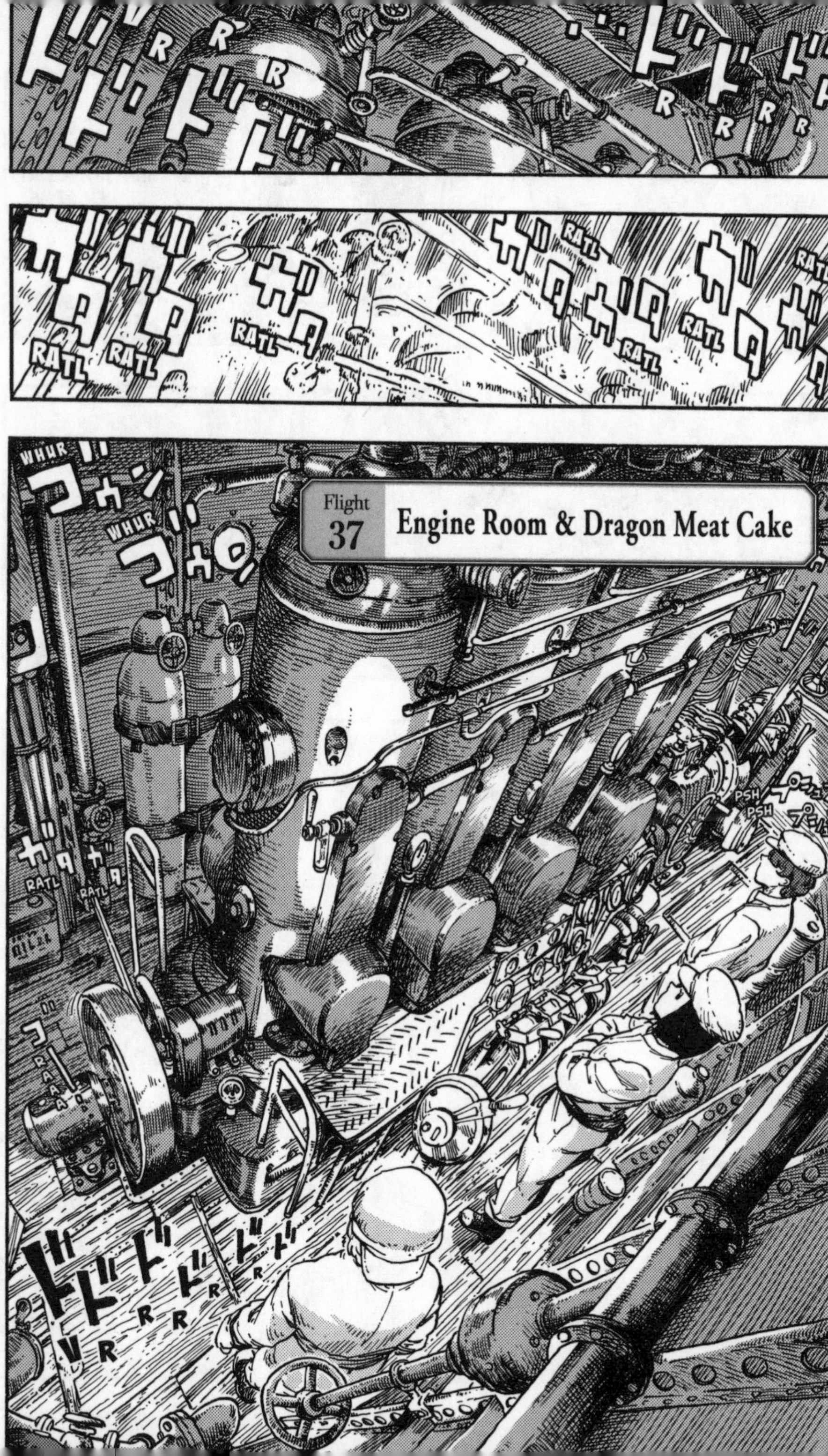

VR
R
R
R
R
R
R
RATL
RATL
RATL
RATL
RATL
RATL
RATL
Flight 37
Engine Room & Dragon Meat Cake
WHUR
WHUR
PSH
PSH
RATL
RATL
RAAA
VR
R
R
R
R
R

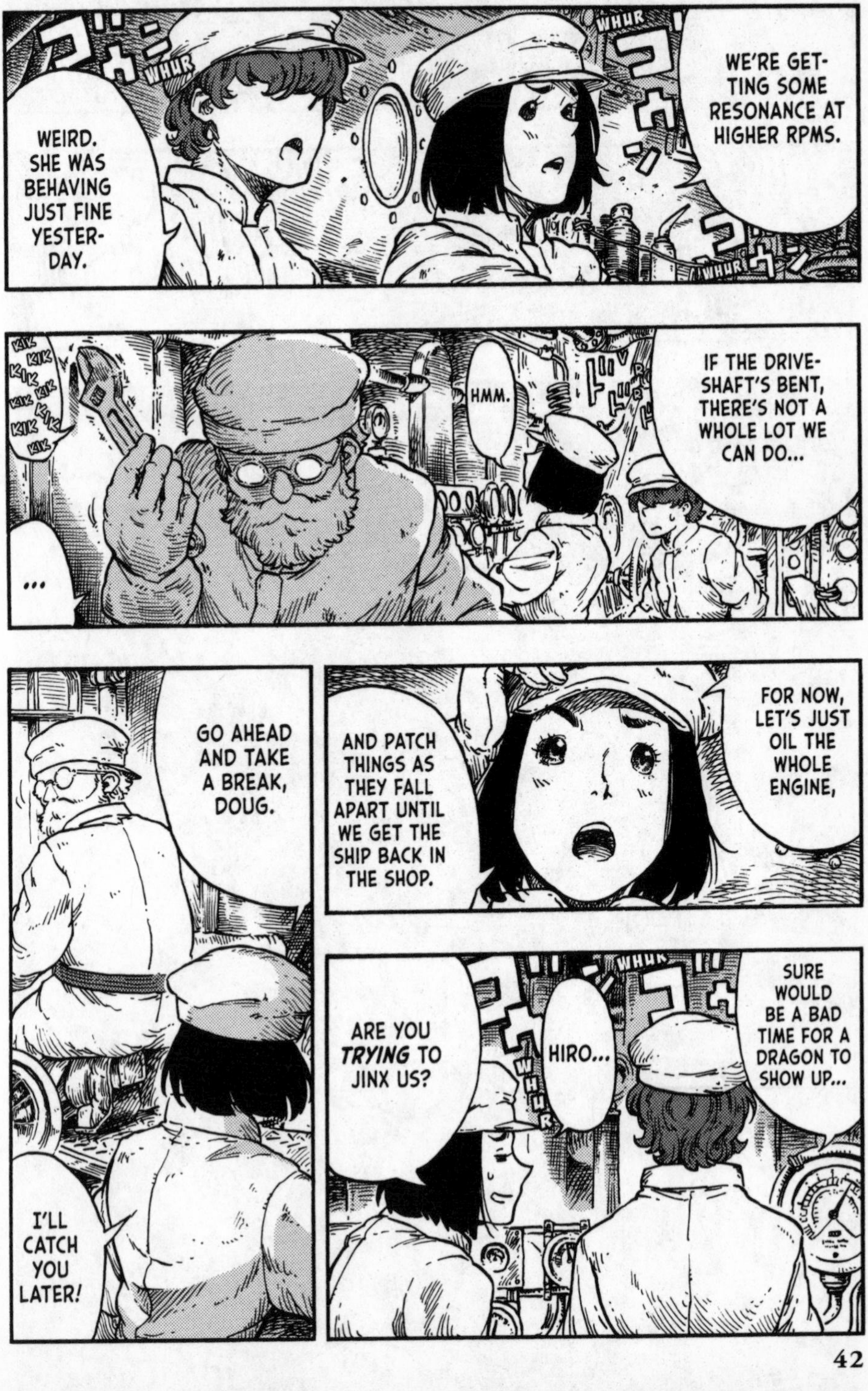
WHUR
WE'RE GETTING SOME RESONANCE AT HIGHER RPMS.
WHUR
WHUR
WEIRD. SHE WAS BEHAVING JUST FINE YESTERDAY.
IF THE DRIVESHAFT'S BENT, THERE'S NOT A WHOLE LOT WE CAN DO...
HMM.
KIK KIK KIK KIK KIK KIK KIK KIK
...
FOR NOW, LET'S JUST OIL THE WHOLE ENGINE,
AND PATCH THINGS AS THEY FALL APART UNTIL WE GET THE SHIP BACK IN THE SHOP.
WHUR
SURE WOULD BE A BAD TIME FOR A DRAGON TO SHOW UP...
HIRO...
WHUR
ARE YOU *TRYING* TO JINX US?
GO AHEAD AND TAKE A BREAK, DOUG.
I'LL CATCH YOU LATER!

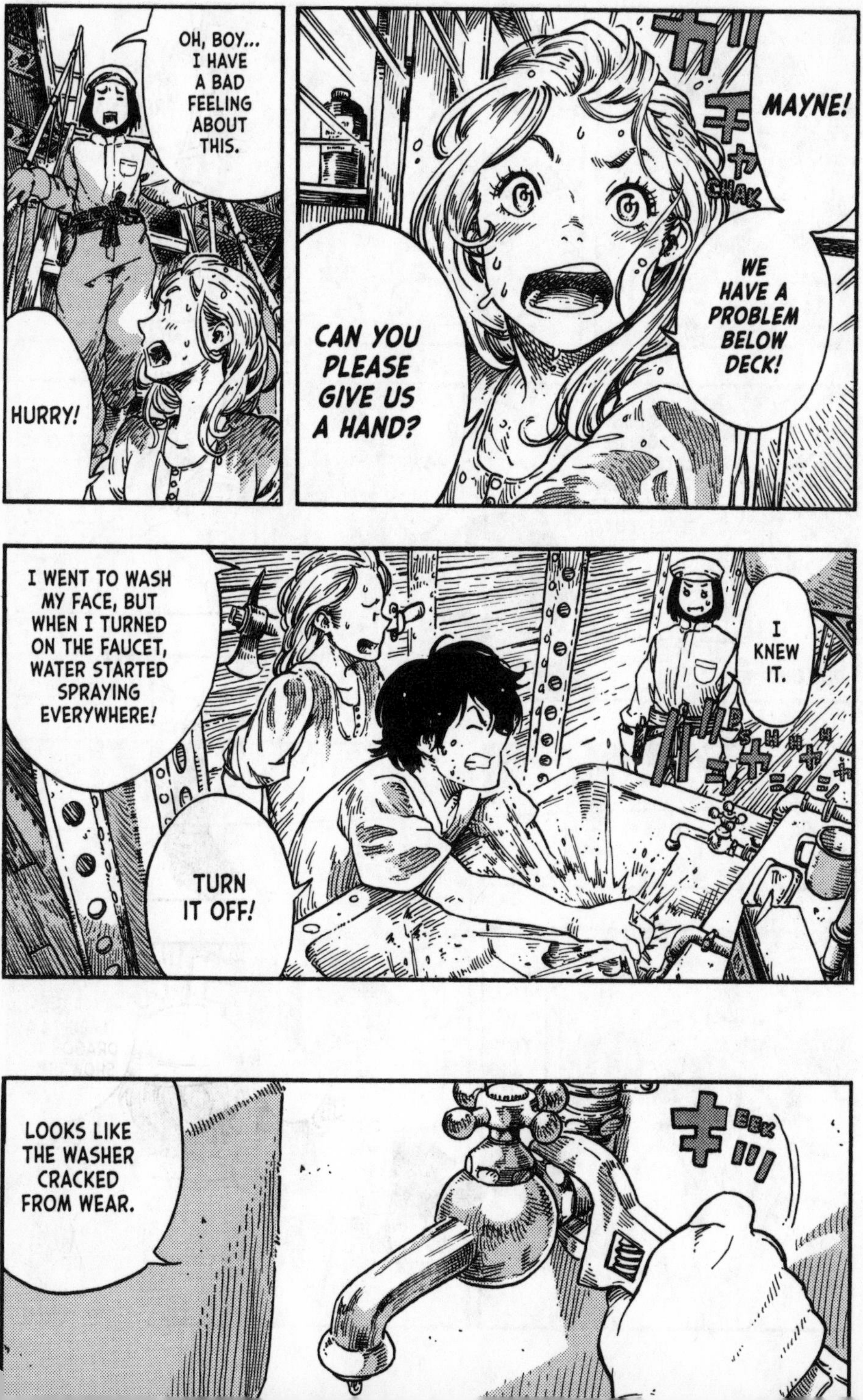
MAYNE!
CHAK
WE HAVE A PROBLEM BELOW DECK!
CAN YOU PLEASE GIVE US A HAND?
OH, BOY... I HAVE A BAD FEELING ABOUT THIS.
HURRY!
I KNEW IT.
I WENT TO WASH MY FACE, BUT WHEN I TURNED ON THE FAUCET, WATER STARTED SPRAYING EVERYWHERE!
TURN IT OFF!
LOOKS LIKE THE WASHER CRACKED FROM WEAR.

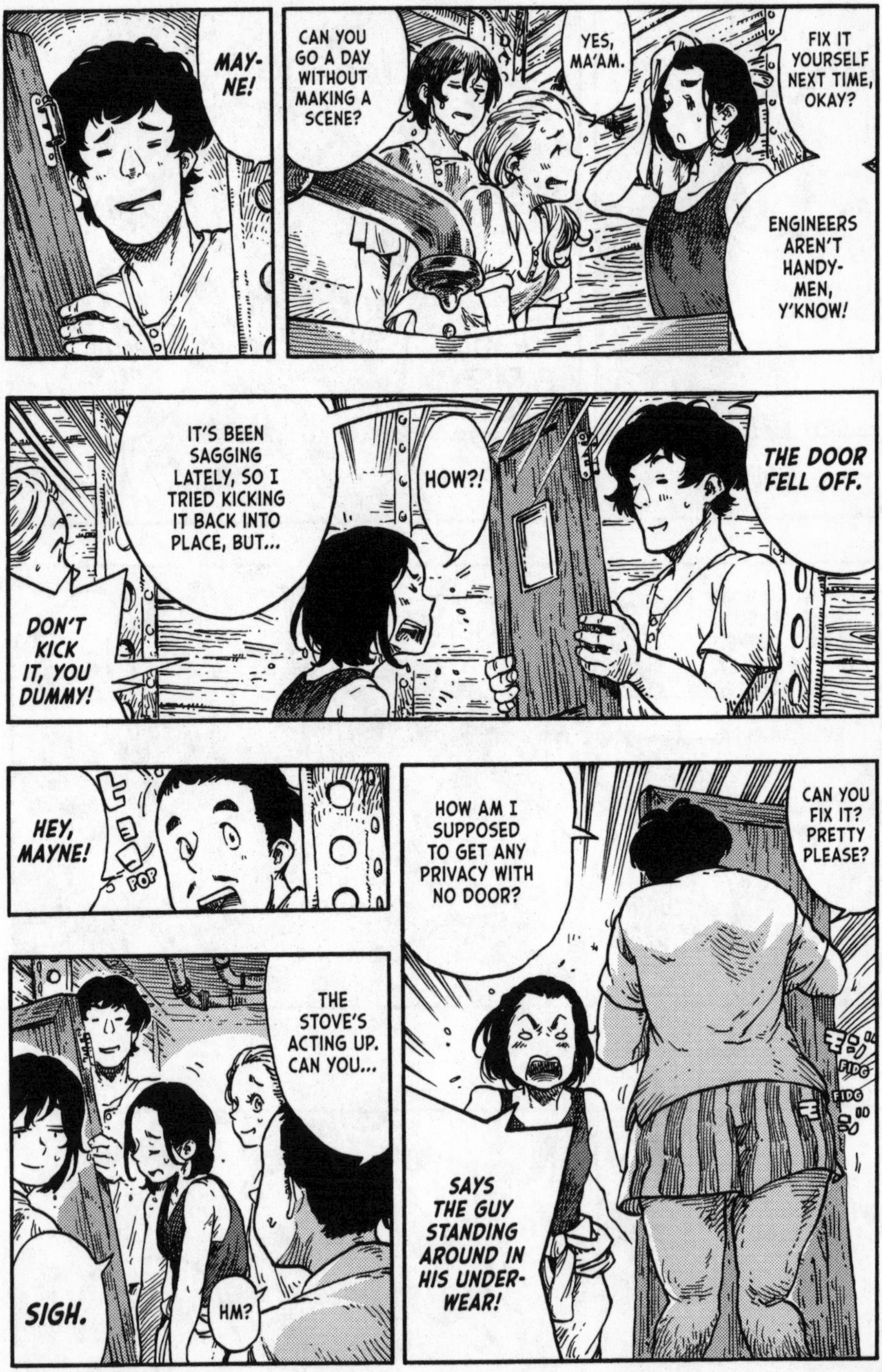
FIX IT YOURSELF NEXT TIME, OKAY?
ENGINEERS AREN'T HANDY-MEN, Y'KNOW!
YES, MA'AM.
CAN YOU GO A DAY WITHOUT MAKING A SCENE?
MAY-NE!
THE DOOR FELL OFF.
HOW?!
IT'S BEEN SAGGING LATELY, SO I TRIED KICKING IT BACK INTO PLACE, BUT...
DON'T KICK IT, YOU DUMMY!
CAN YOU FIX IT? PRETTY PLEASE?
HOW AM I SUPPOSED TO GET ANY PRIVACY WITH NO DOOR?
FIDG
FIDG
SAYS THE GUY STANDING AROUND IN HIS UNDER-WEAR!
HEY, MAYNE!
POP
THE STOVE'S ACTING UP. CAN YOU...
HM?
SIGH.

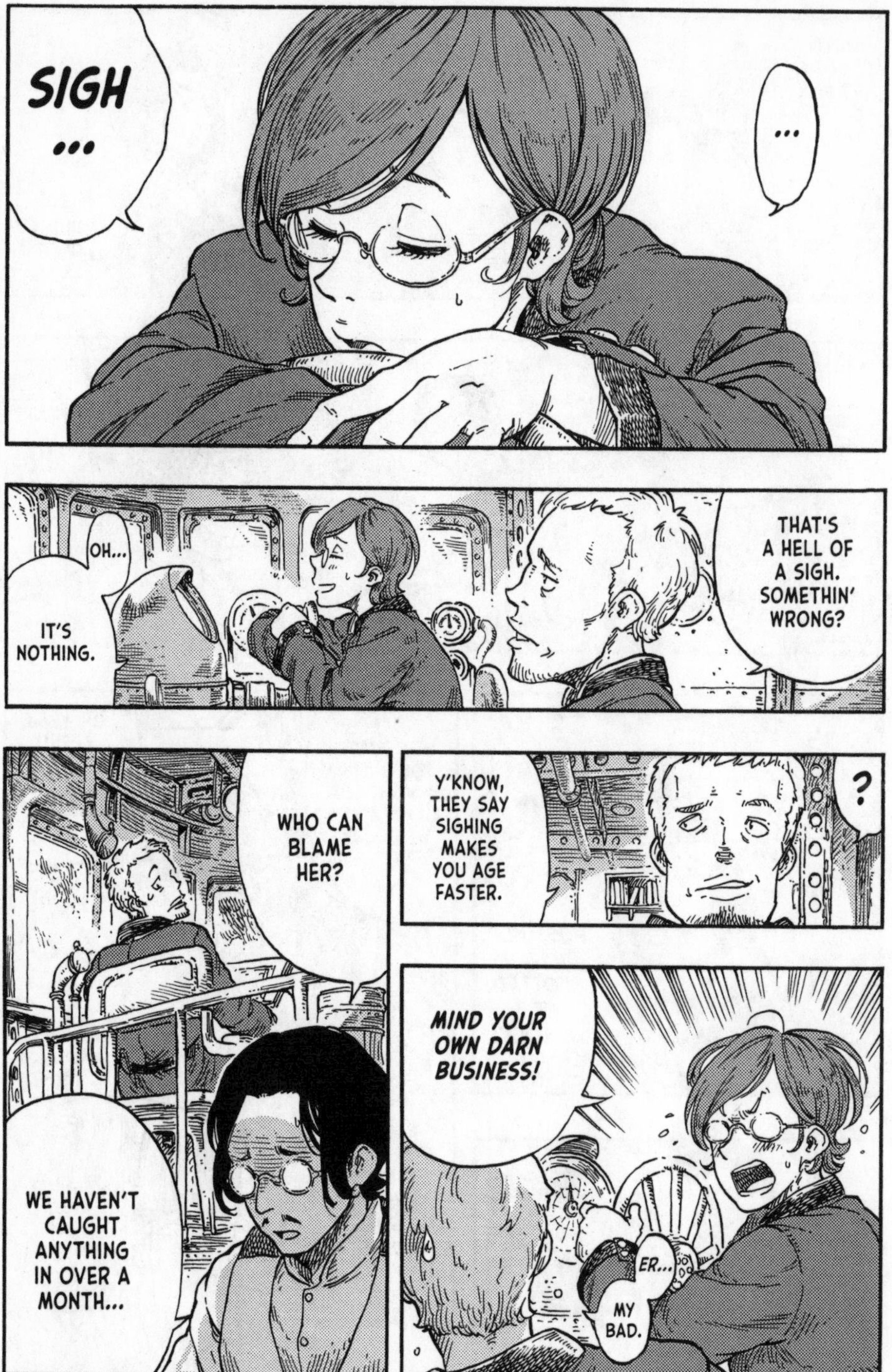
...
SIGH ...
THAT'S A HELL OF A SIGH. SOMETHIN' WRONG?
OH...
IT'S NOTHING.
?
Y'KNOW, THEY SAY SIGHING MAKES YOU AGE FASTER.
MIND YOUR OWN DARN BUSINESS!
ER...
MY BAD.
WHO CAN BLAME HER?
WE HAVEN'T CAUGHT ANYTHING IN OVER A MONTH...

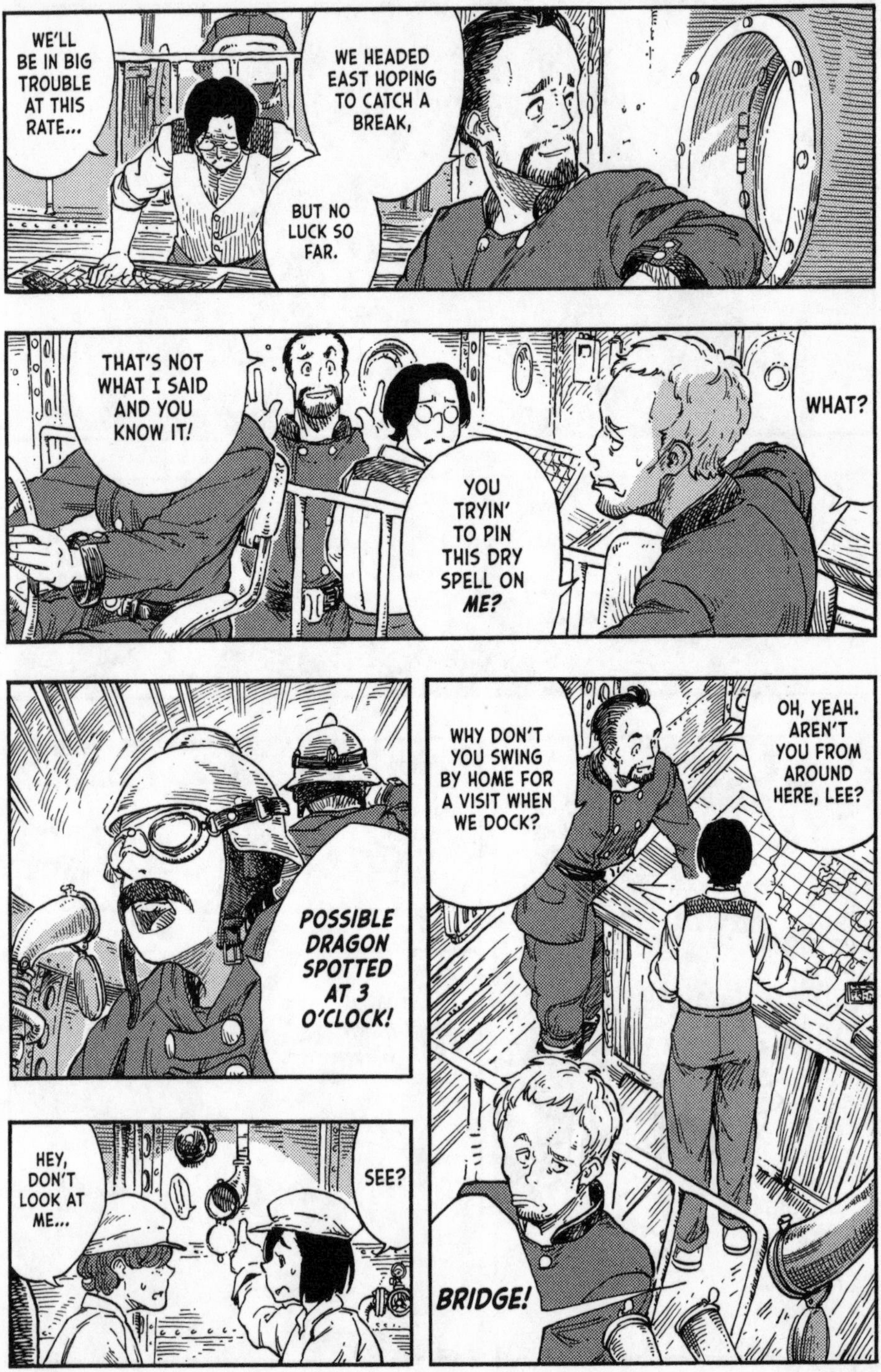
WE HEADED EAST HOPING TO CATCH A BREAK,
BUT NO LUCK SO FAR.
WE'LL BE IN BIG TROUBLE AT THIS RATE...
WHAT?
YOU TRYIN' TO PIN THIS DRY SPELL ON *ME?*
THAT'S NOT WHAT I SAID AND YOU KNOW IT!
OH, YEAH. AREN'T YOU FROM AROUND HERE, LEE?
WHY DON'T YOU SWING BY HOME FOR A VISIT WHEN WE DOCK?
BRIDGE!
POSSIBLE DRAGON SPOTTED AT 3 O'CLOCK!
SEE?
HEY, DON'T LOOK AT ME...

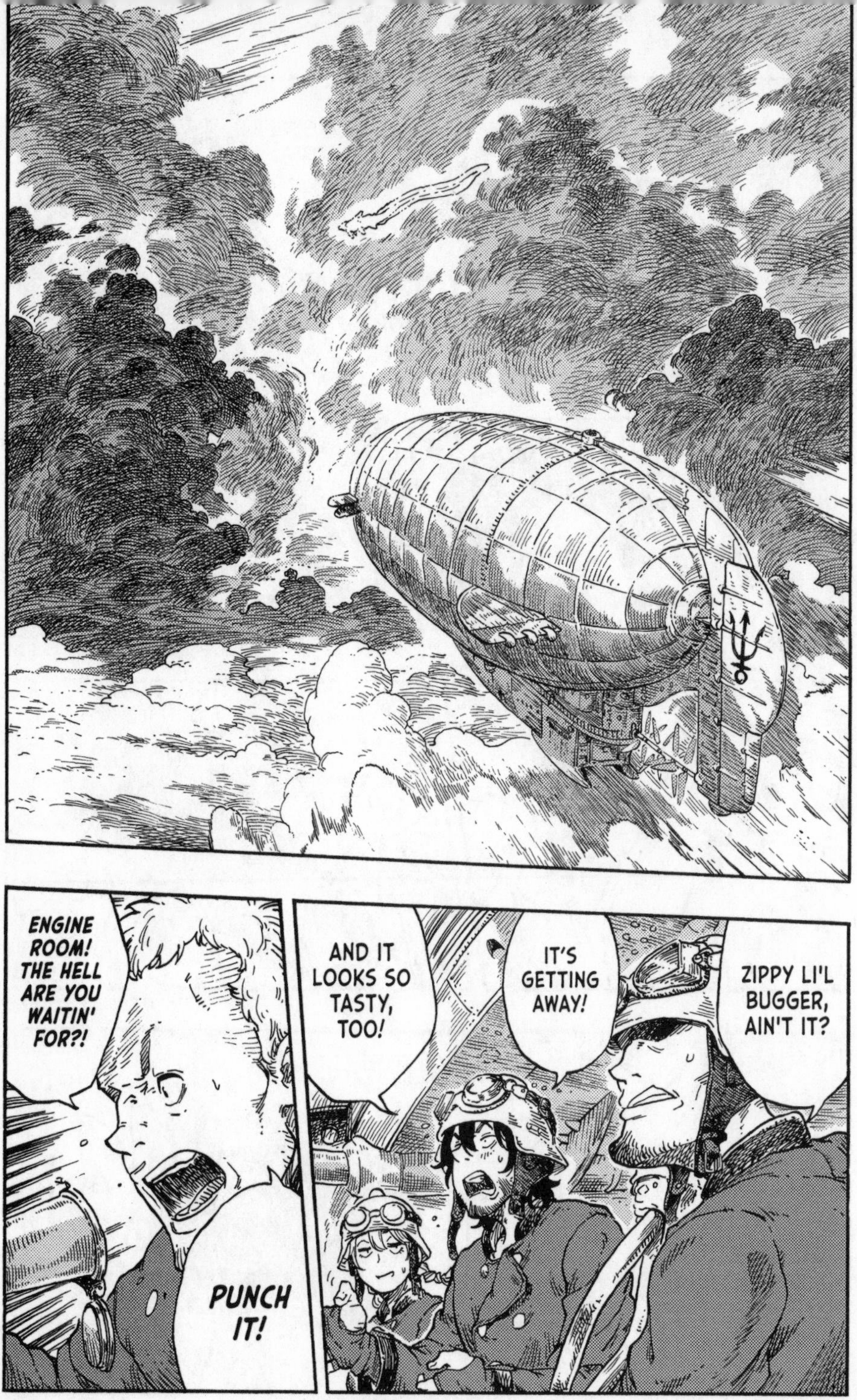
ZIPPY LI'L BUGGER, AIN'T IT?
IT'S GETTING AWAY!
AND IT LOOKS SO TASTY, TOO!
ENGINE ROOM! THE HELL ARE YOU WAITIN' FOR?!
PUNCH IT!

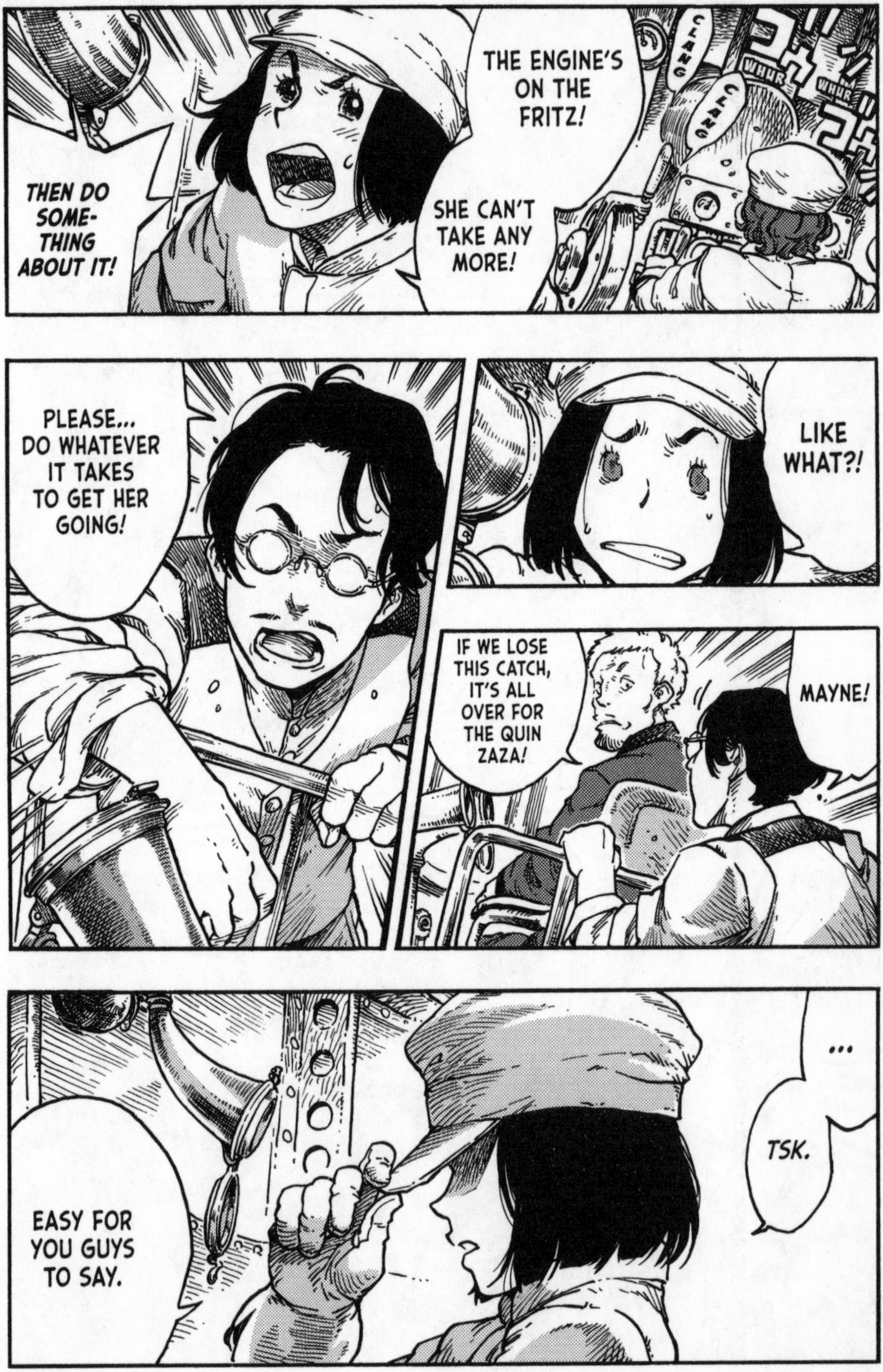
WHHR
WHHR
CLANG
CLANG
THE ENGINE'S ON THE FRITZ!
SHE CAN'T TAKE ANY MORE!
THEN DO SOME-THING ABOUT IT!
LIKE WHAT?!
MAYNE!
IF WE LOSE THIS CATCH, IT'S ALL OVER FOR THE QUIN ZAZA!
PLEASE... DO WHATEVER IT TAKES TO GET HER GOING!
...
TSK.
EASY FOR YOU GUYS TO SAY.

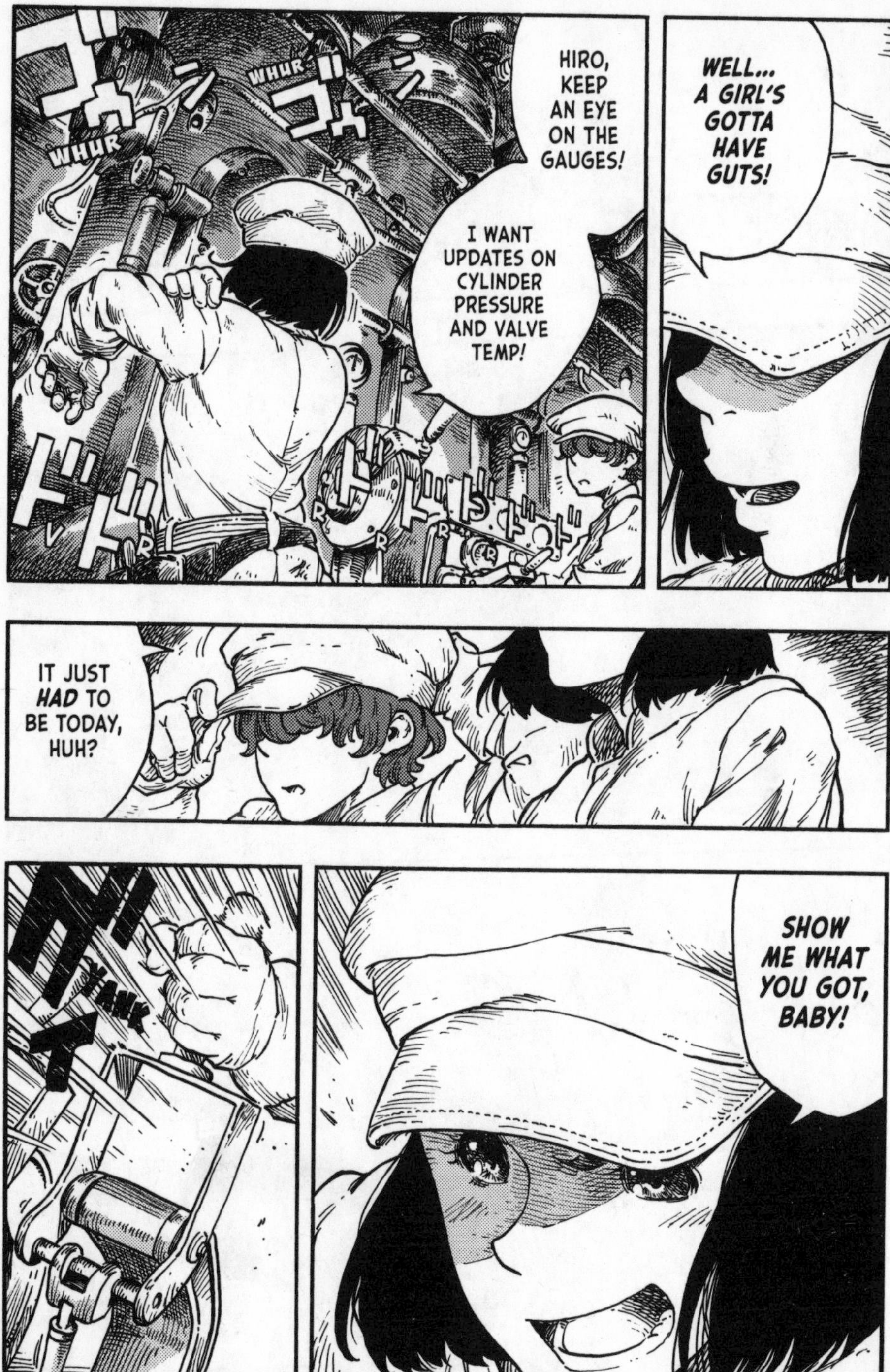
WELL... A GIRL'S GOTTA HAVE GUTS!
HIRO, KEEP AN EYE ON THE GAUGES!
I WANT UPDATES ON CYLINDER PRESSURE AND VALVE TEMP!
WHUR
WHUR
IT JUST *HAD* TO BE TODAY, HUH?
SHOW ME WHAT YOU GOT, BABY!
YANK

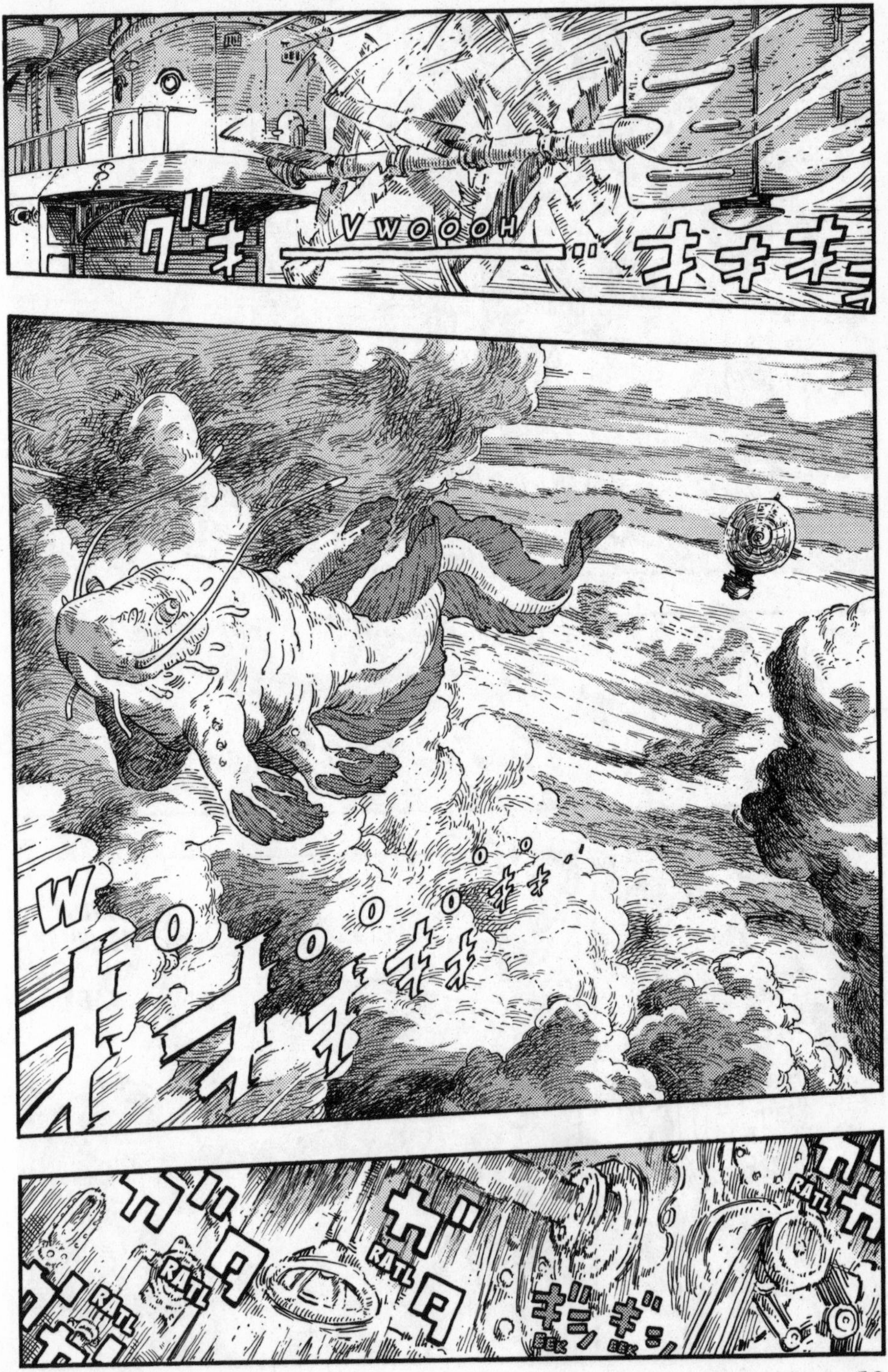
VWOOOH
WOOOOOOO
RATL
RATL
EEK
EEK
RATL
RATL
RATL

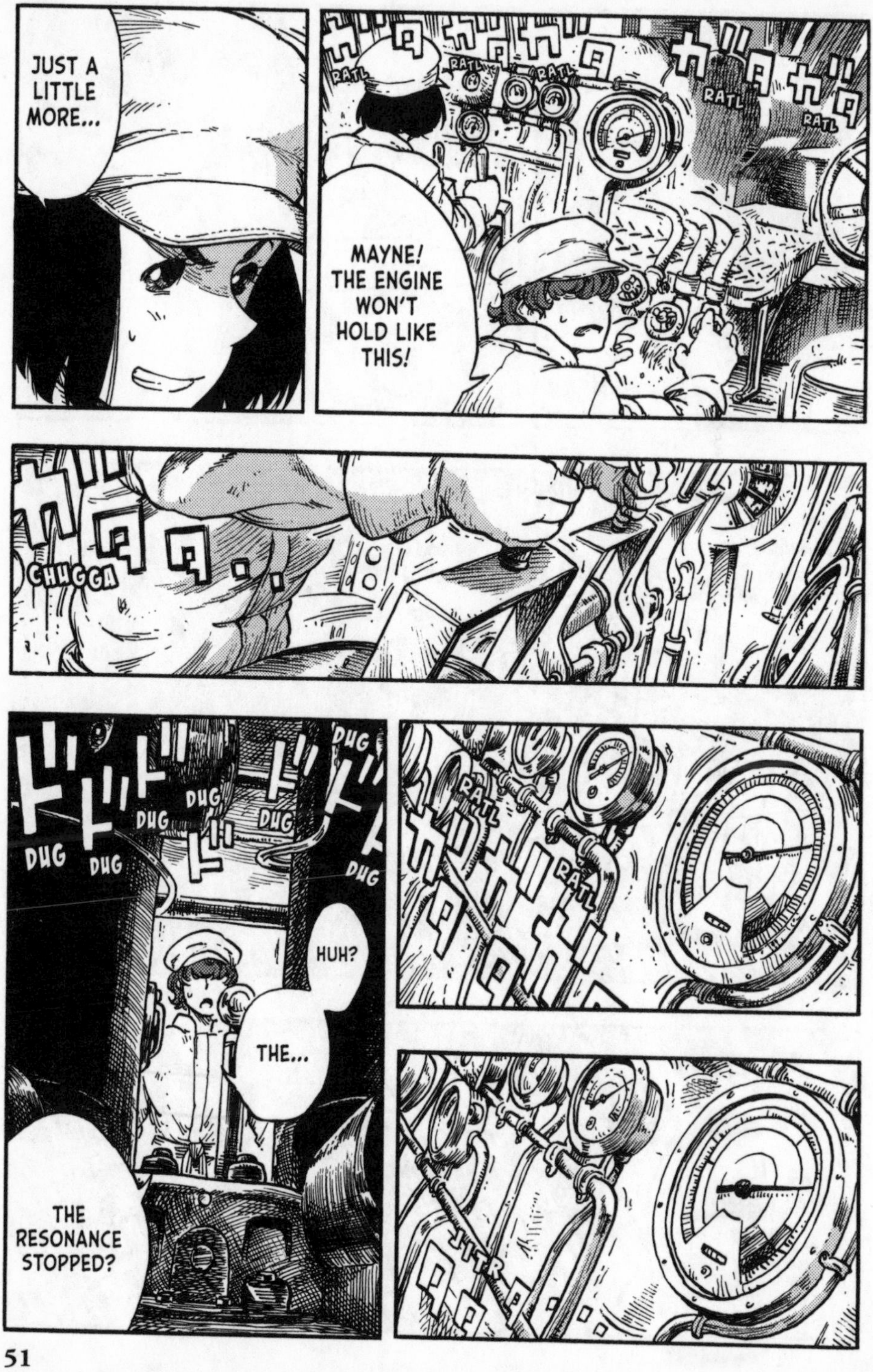

RATL
RATL
RATL
RATL
RATL
MAYNE! THE ENGINE WON'T HOLD LIKE THIS!
JUST A LITTLE MORE...
CHUGGA
RATL
RATL
JITR
DUG
DUG
DUG
DUG
DUG
DUG
DUG
HUH?
THE...
THE RESONANCE STOPPED?

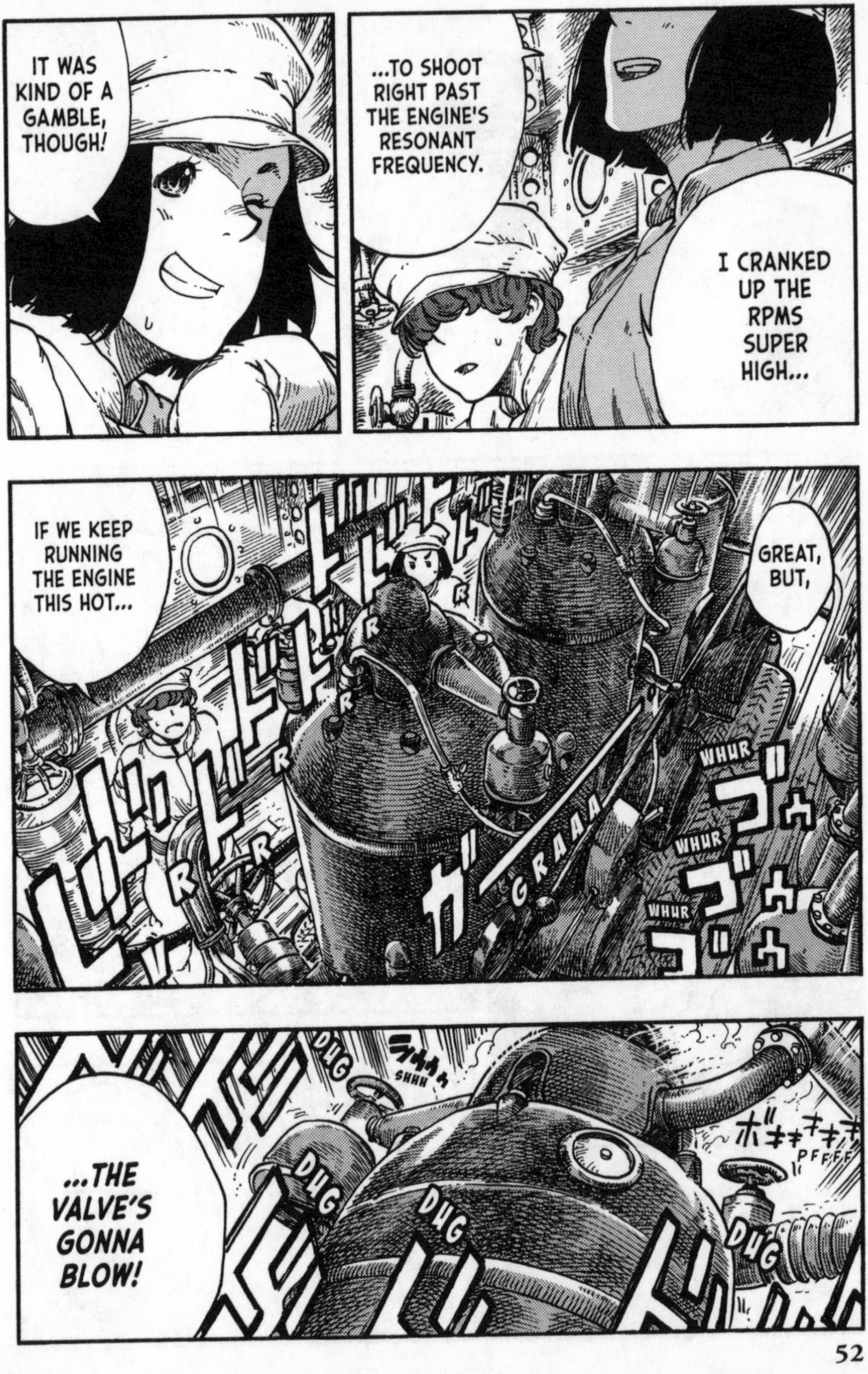
I CRANKED UP THE RPMS SUPER HIGH...
...TO SHOOT RIGHT PAST THE ENGINE'S RESONANT FREQUENCY.
IT WAS KIND OF A GAMBLE, THOUGH!
GREAT, BUT,
WHUR
WHUR
WHUR
GRAAA
R
R
R
R
R
R
IF WE KEEP RUNNING THE ENGINE THIS HOT...
PFFFF
DUG
SHHH
DUG
DUG
DUG
...THE VALVE'S GONNA BLOW!

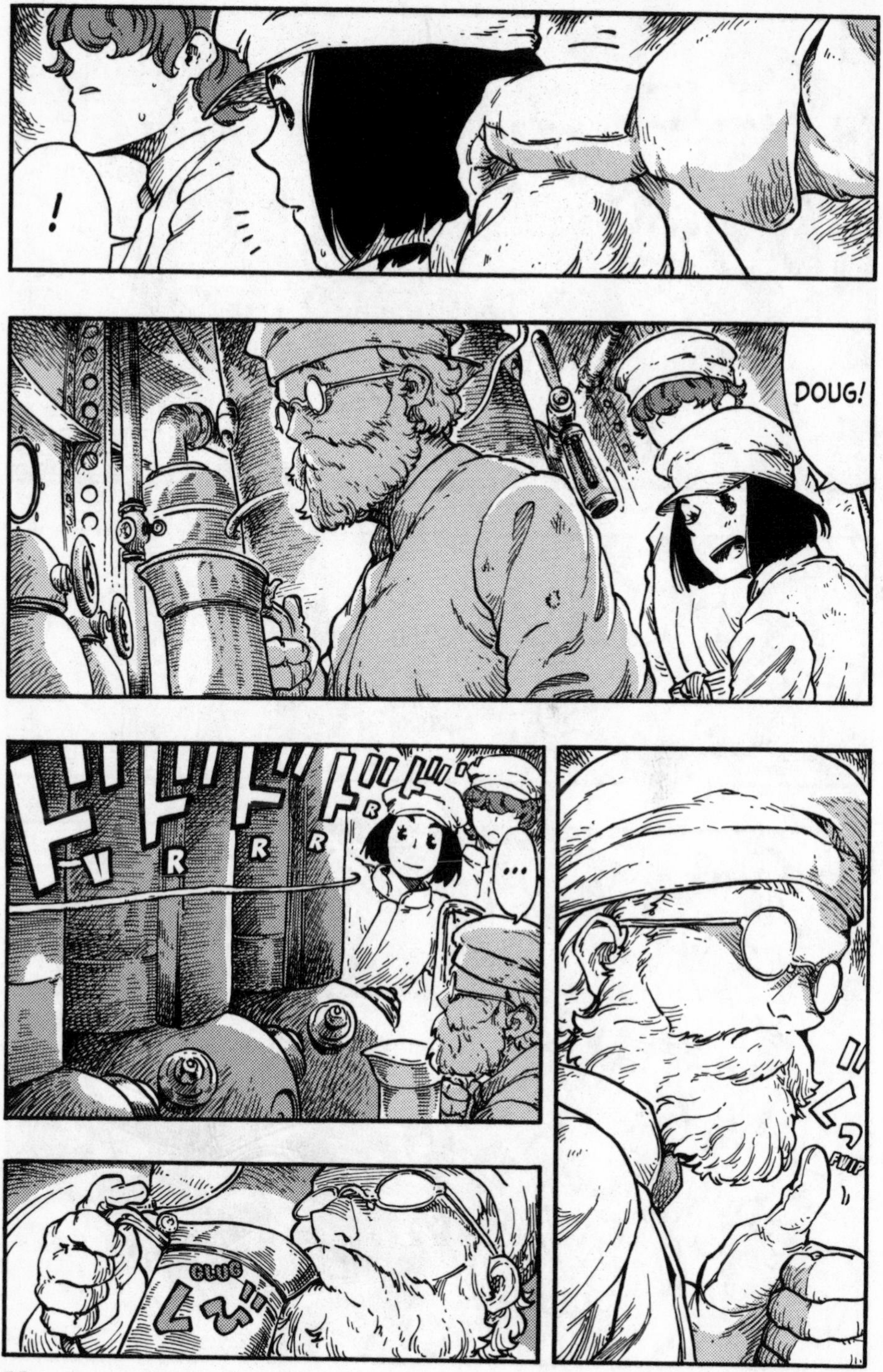
!
DOUG!
FWIP
VRRRR
...
CLUG

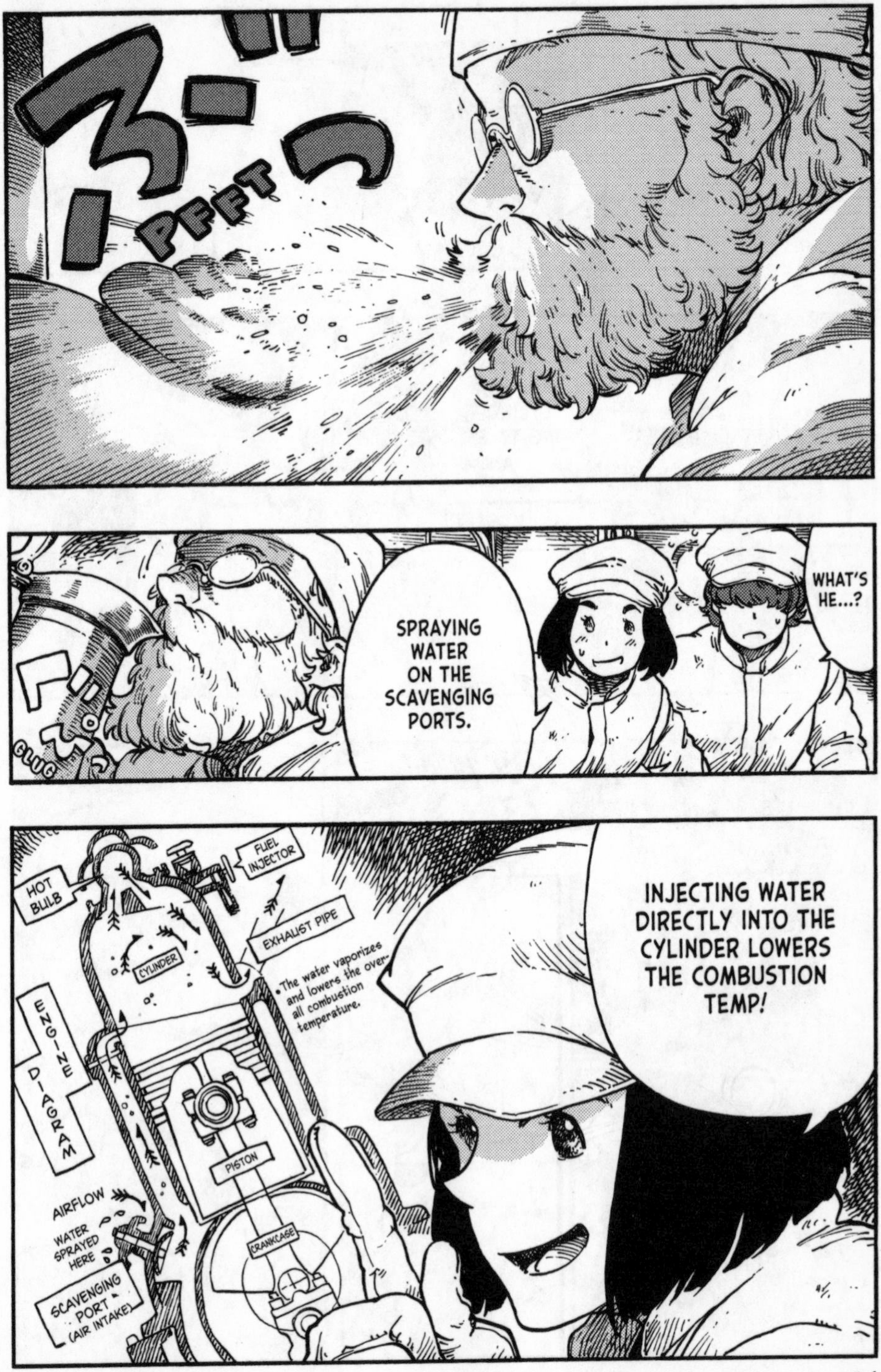
PFFT
WHAT'S HE...?
SPRAYING WATER ON THE SCAVENGING PORTS.
GLUG
INJECTING WATER DIRECTLY INTO THE CYLINDER LOWERS THE COMBUSTION TEMP!
FUEL INJECTOR
HOT BULB
EXHAUST PIPE
CYLINDER
• The water vaporizes and lowers the overall combustion temperature.
ENGINE DIAGRAM
PISTON
AIRFLOW
WATER SPRAYED HERE
CRANKCASE
SCAVENGING PORT (AIR INTAKE)

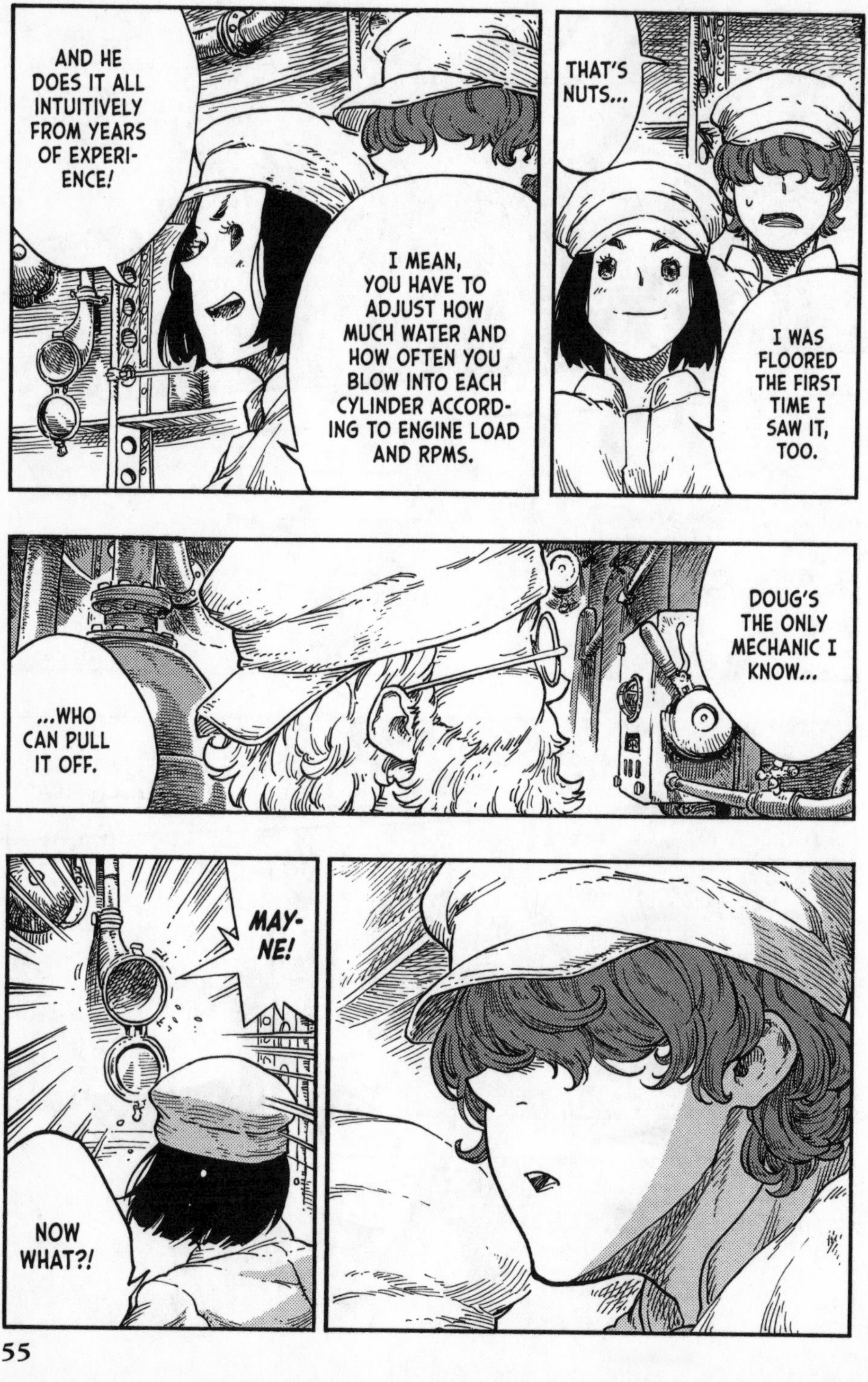
THAT'S NUTS...
I WAS FLOORED THE FIRST TIME I SAW IT, TOO.
AND HE DOES IT ALL INTUITIVELY FROM YEARS OF EXPERI- ENCE!
I MEAN, YOU HAVE TO ADJUST HOW MUCH WATER AND HOW OFTEN YOU BLOW INTO EACH CYLINDER ACCORD- ING TO ENGINE LOAD AND RPMS.
DOUG'S THE ONLY MECHANIC I KNOW...
...WHO CAN PULL IT OFF.
MAY- NE!
NOW WHAT?!

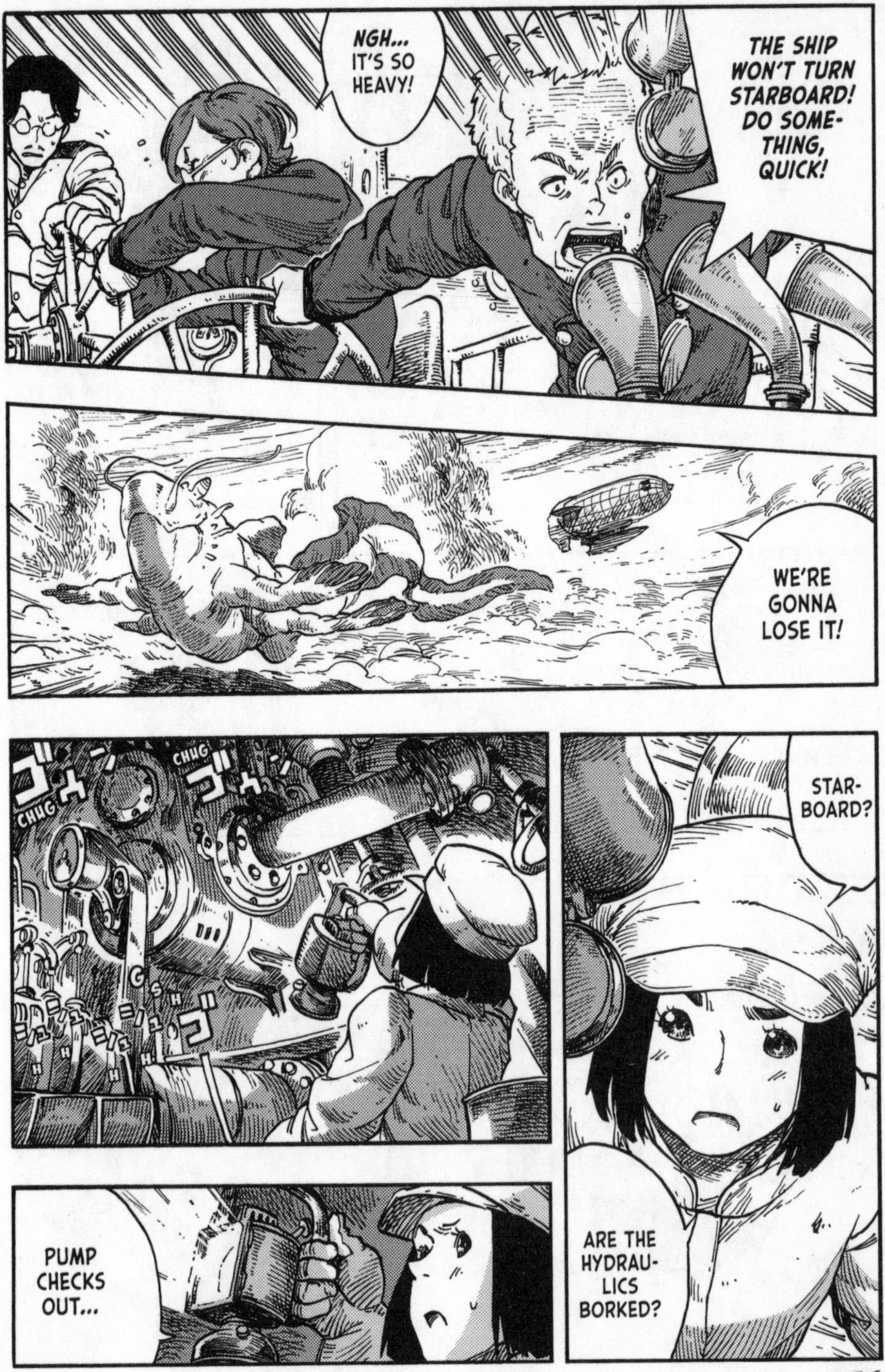
THE SHIP WON'T TURN STARBOARD! DO SOMETHING, QUICK!
NGH... IT'S SO HEAVY!
WE'RE GONNA LOSE IT!
STARBOARD?
ARE THE HYDRAULICS BORKED?
CHUG
CHUG
PUMP CHECKS OUT...

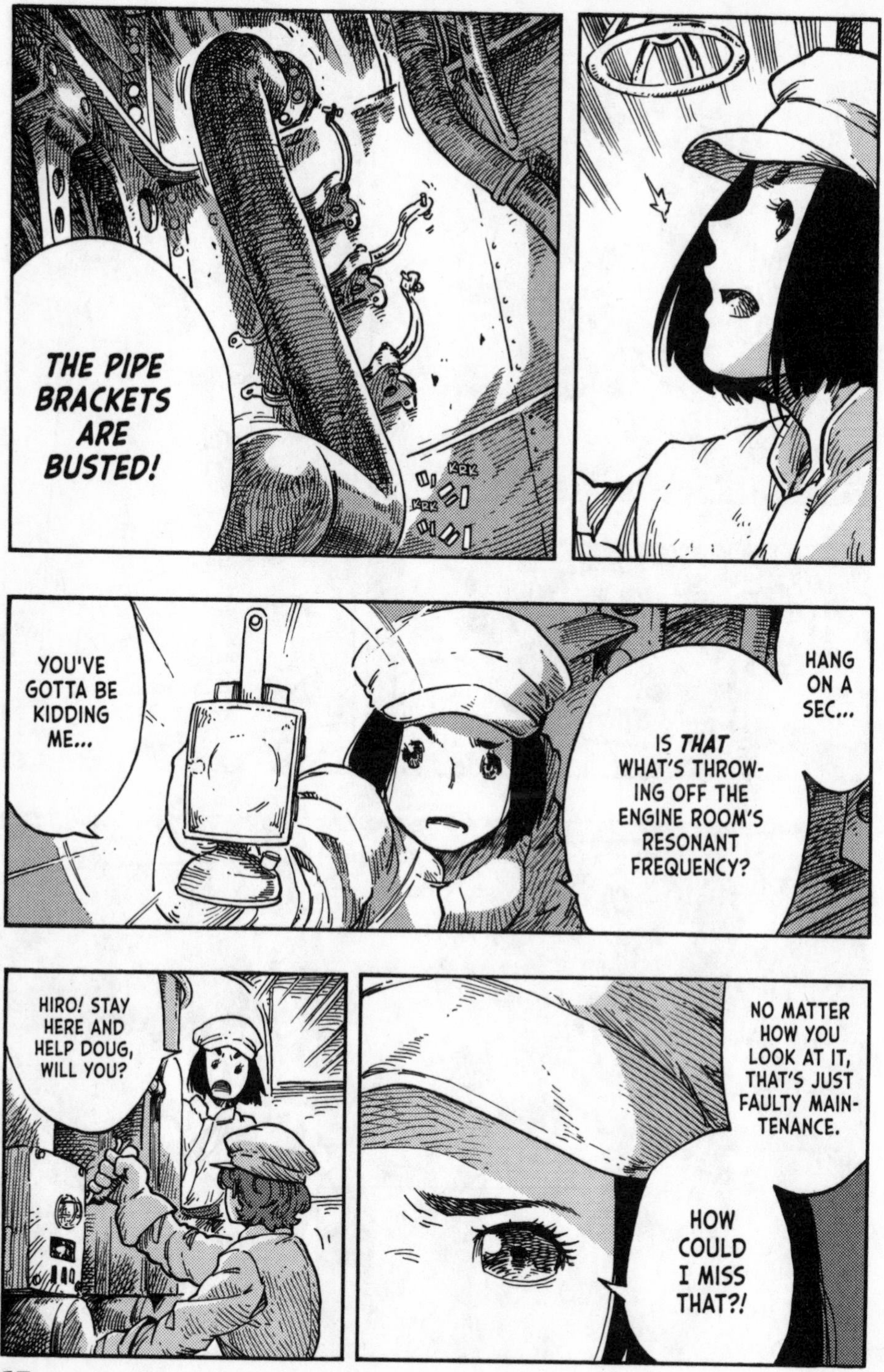
THE PIPE BRACKETS ARE BUSTED!
KRK
KRK
HANG ON A SEC...
IS THAT WHAT'S THROWING-ING OFF THE ENGINE ROOM'S RESONANT FREQUENCY?
YOU'VE GOTTA BE KIDDING ME...
NO MATTER HOW YOU LOOK AT IT, THAT'S JUST FAULTY MAIN-TENANCE.
HOW COULD I MISS THAT?!
HIRO! STAY HERE AND HELP DOUG, WILL YOU?

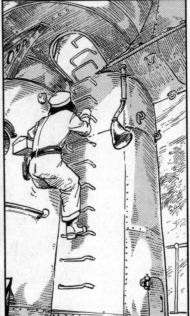

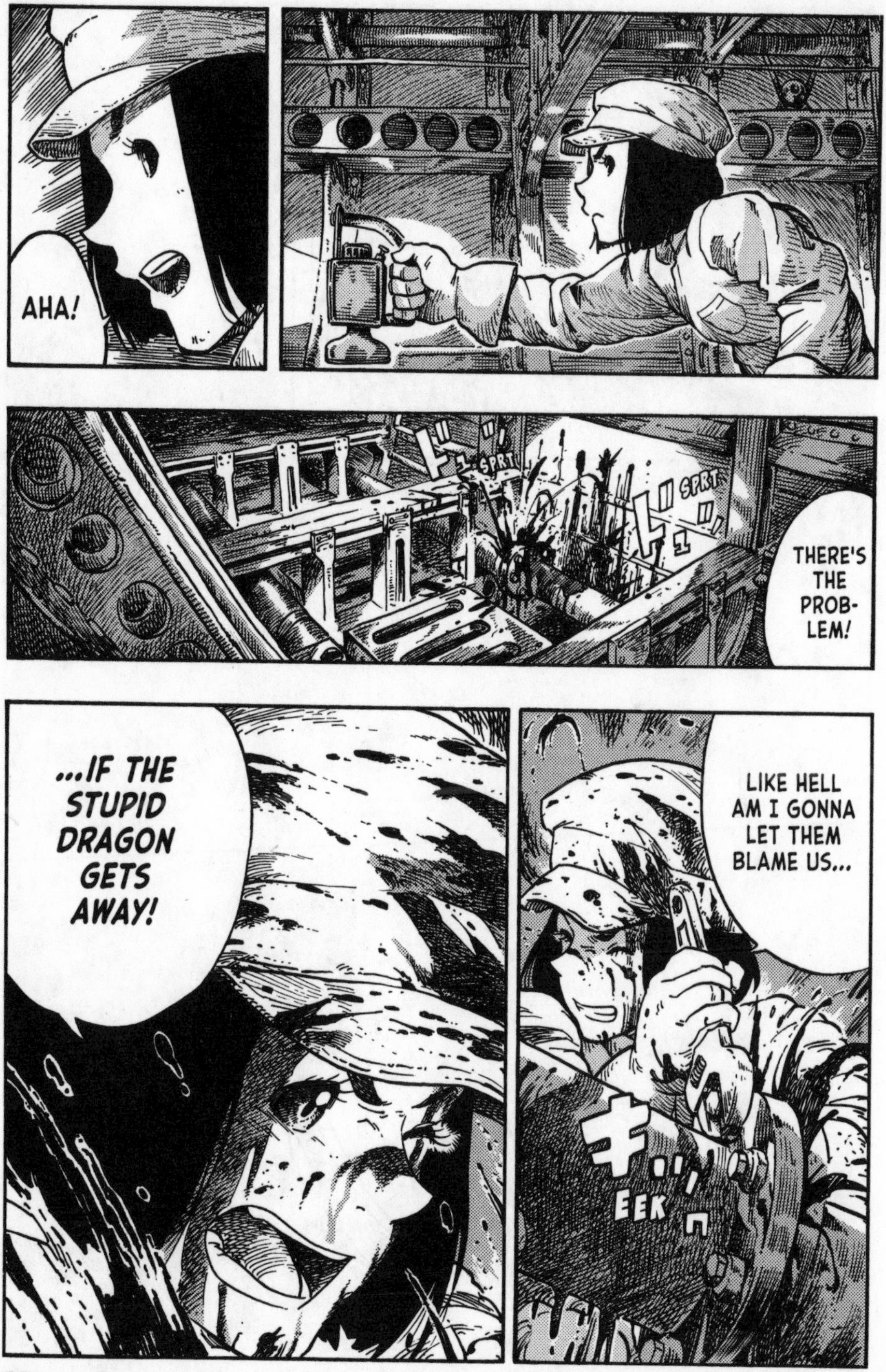
AHA!
SPRT
SPRT
THERE'S THE PROB-LEM!
LIKE HELL AM I GONNA LET THEM BLAME US...
EEK
...IF THE STUPID DRAGON GETS AWAY!

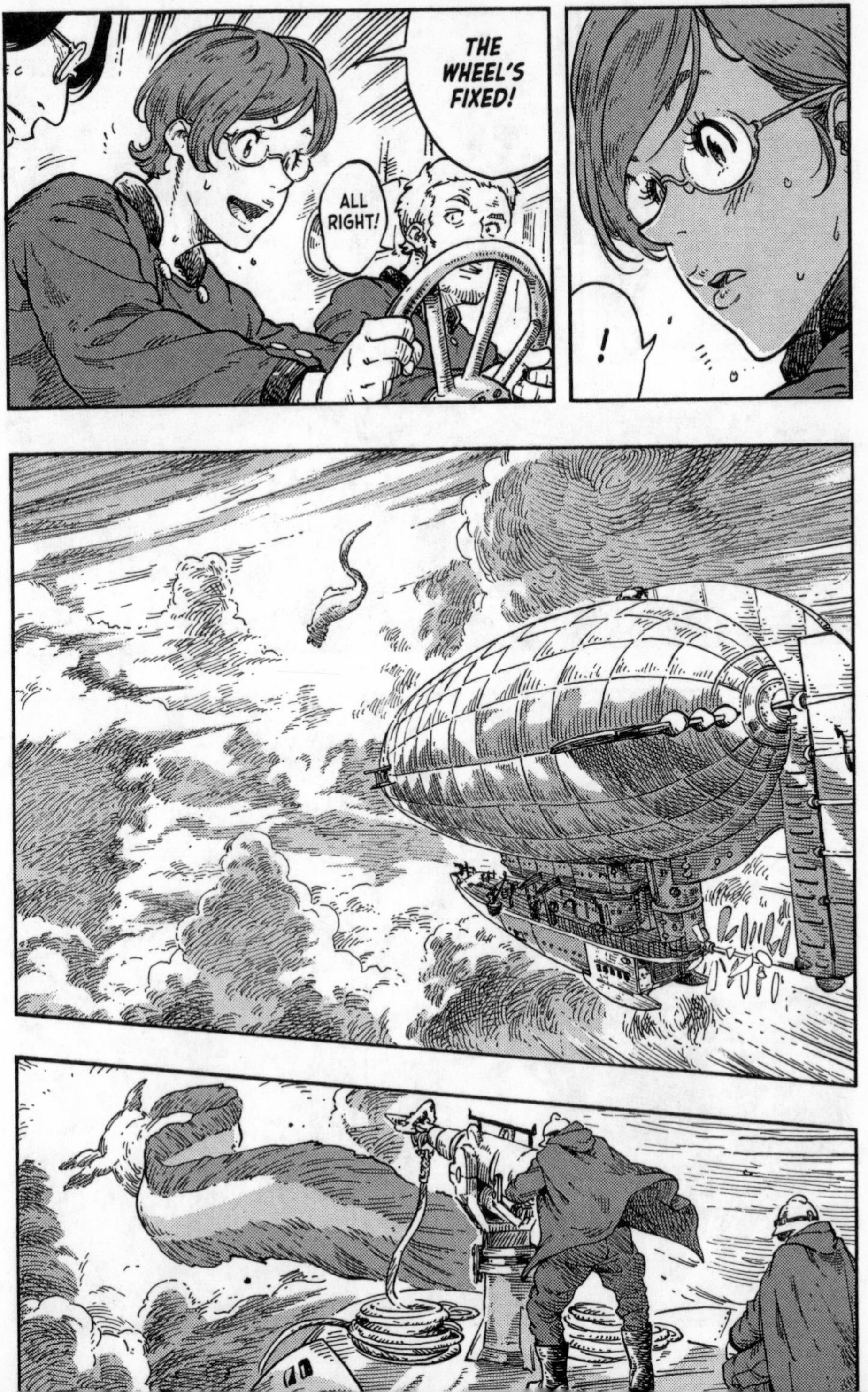
!
THE WHEEL'S FIXED!
ALL RIGHT!

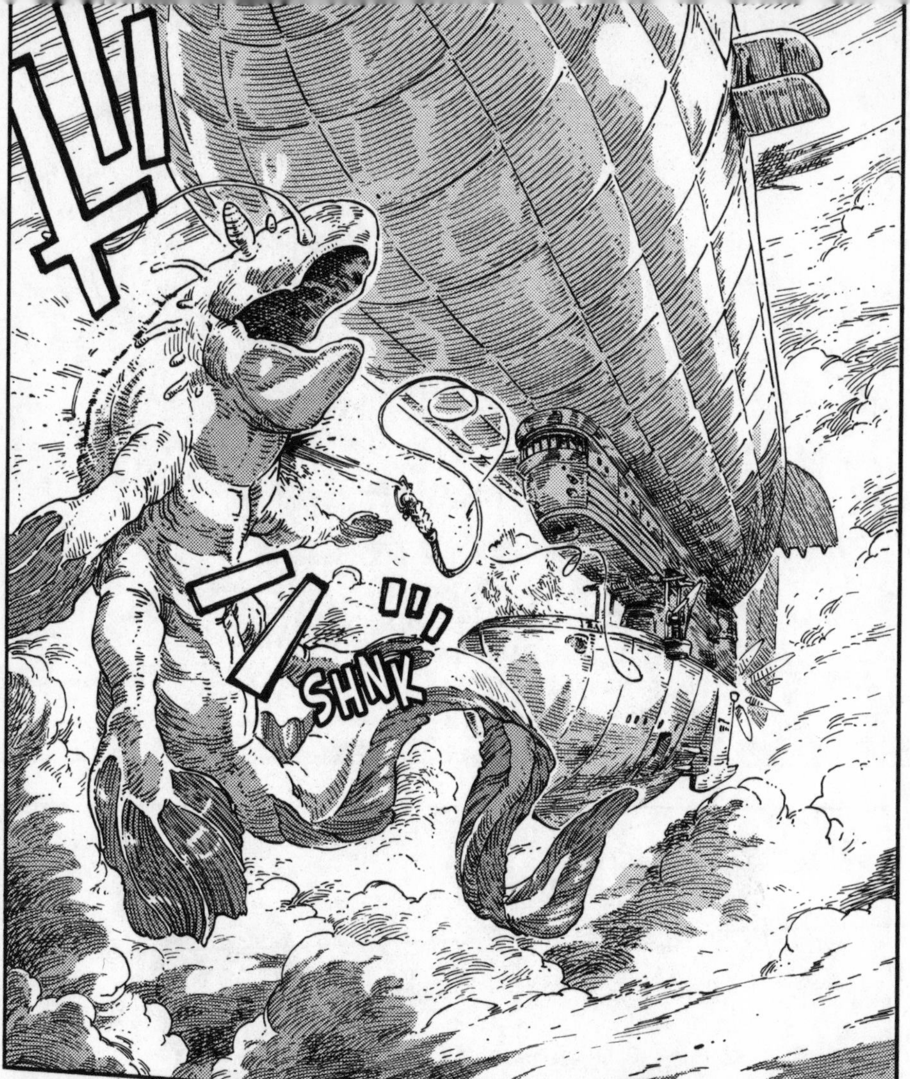
SHNK
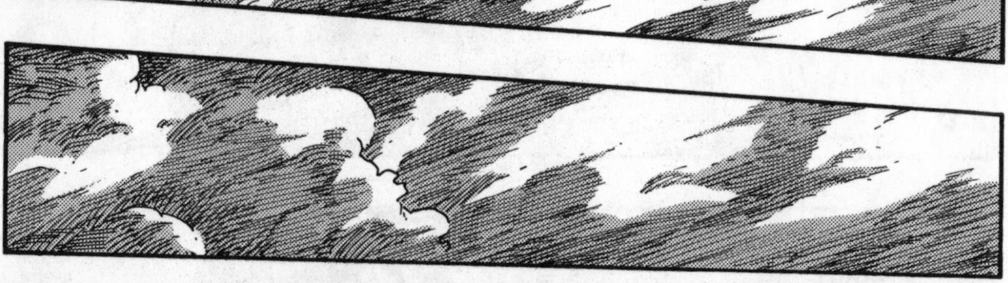
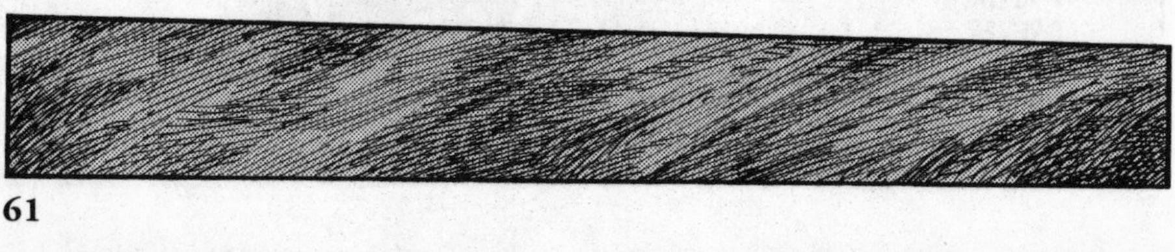

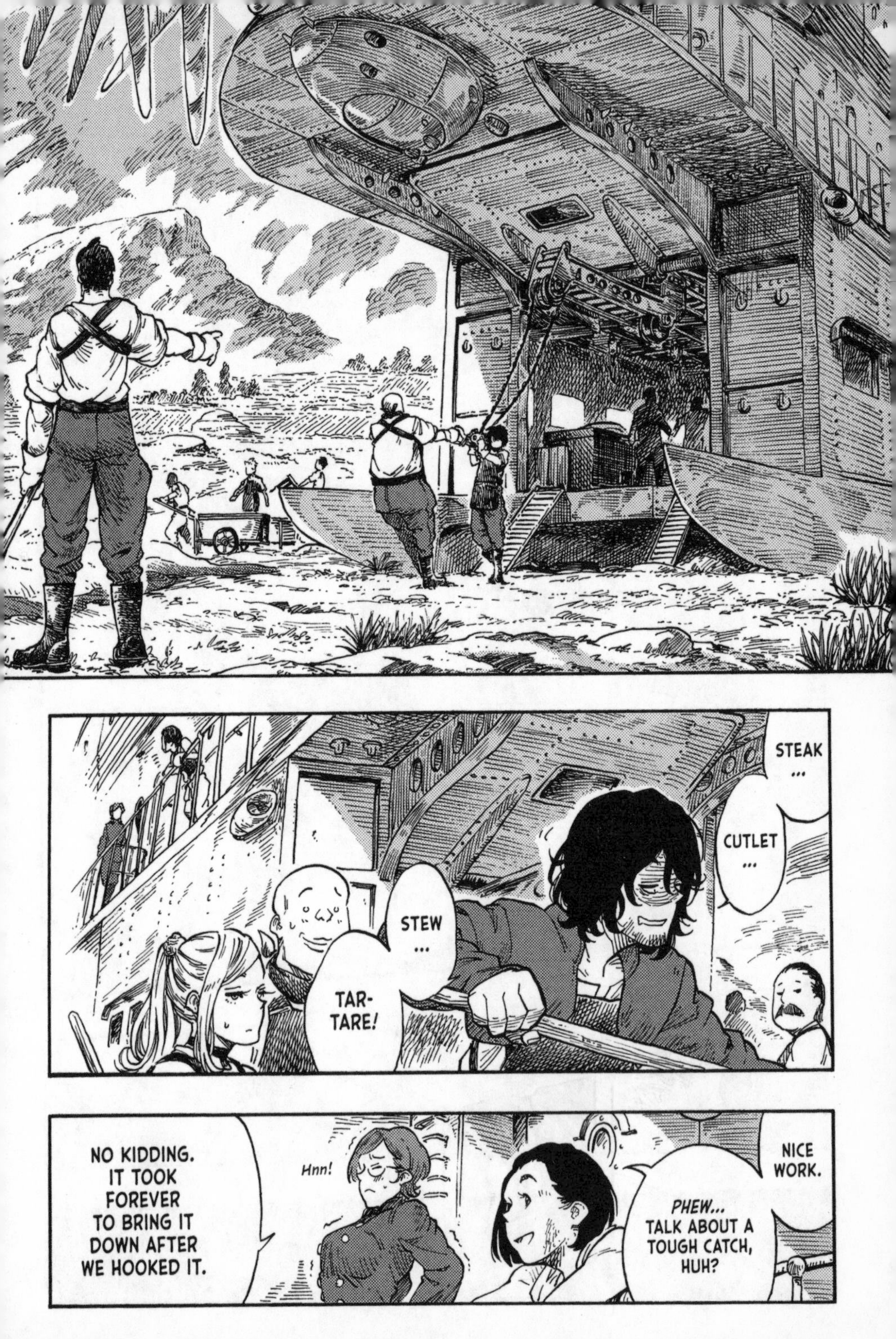
STEAK...
CUTLET...
STEW...
TAR-TARE!
NICE WORK.
PHEW... TALK ABOUT A TOUGH CATCH, HUH?
Hnn!
NO KIDDING. IT TOOK FOREVER TO BRING IT DOWN AFTER WE HOOKED IT.

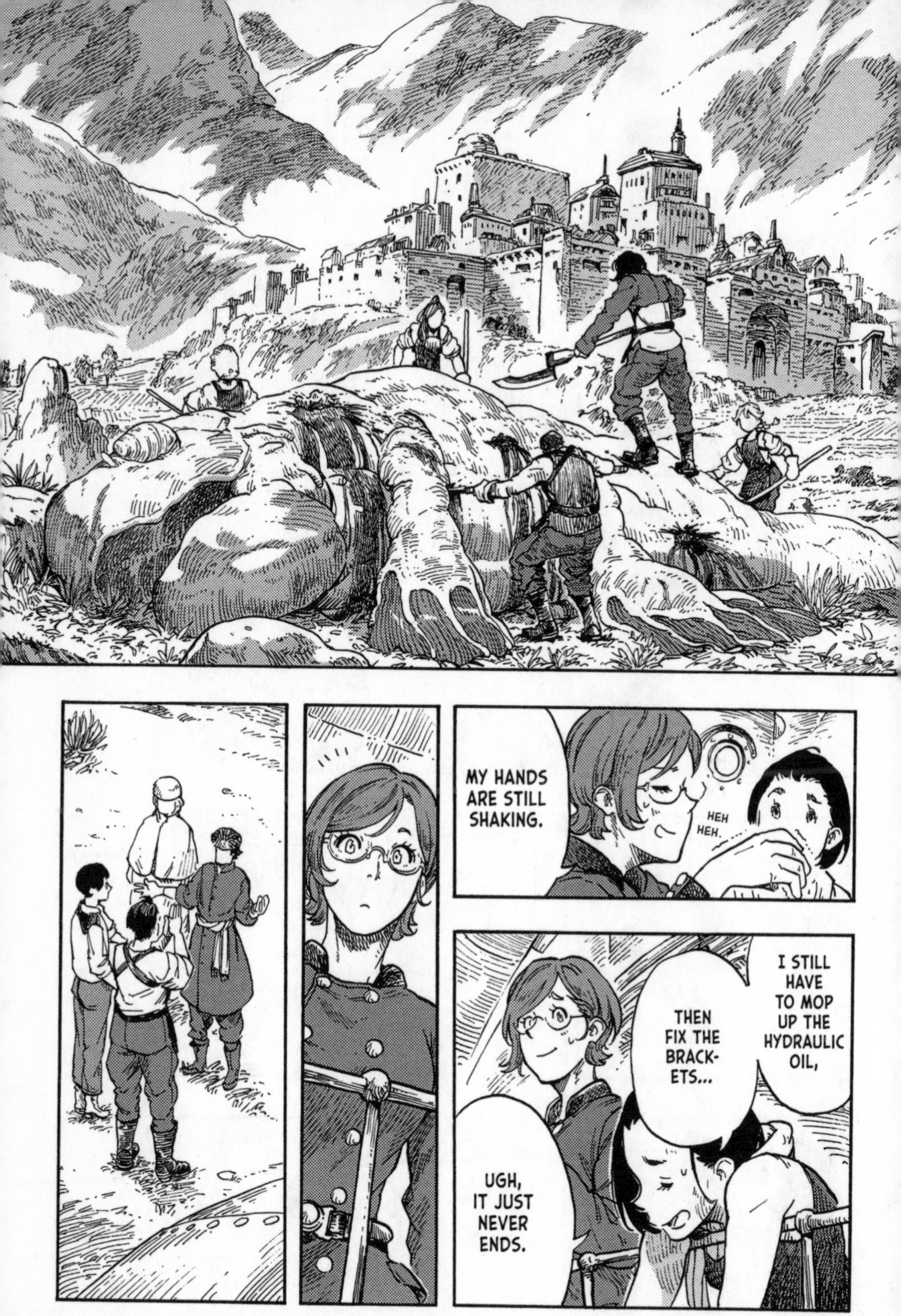
MY HANDS ARE STILL SHAKING.
HEH HEH.
I STILL HAVE TO MOP UP THE HYDRAULIC OIL,
THEN FIX THE BRACK-ETS...
UGH, IT JUST NEVER ENDS.

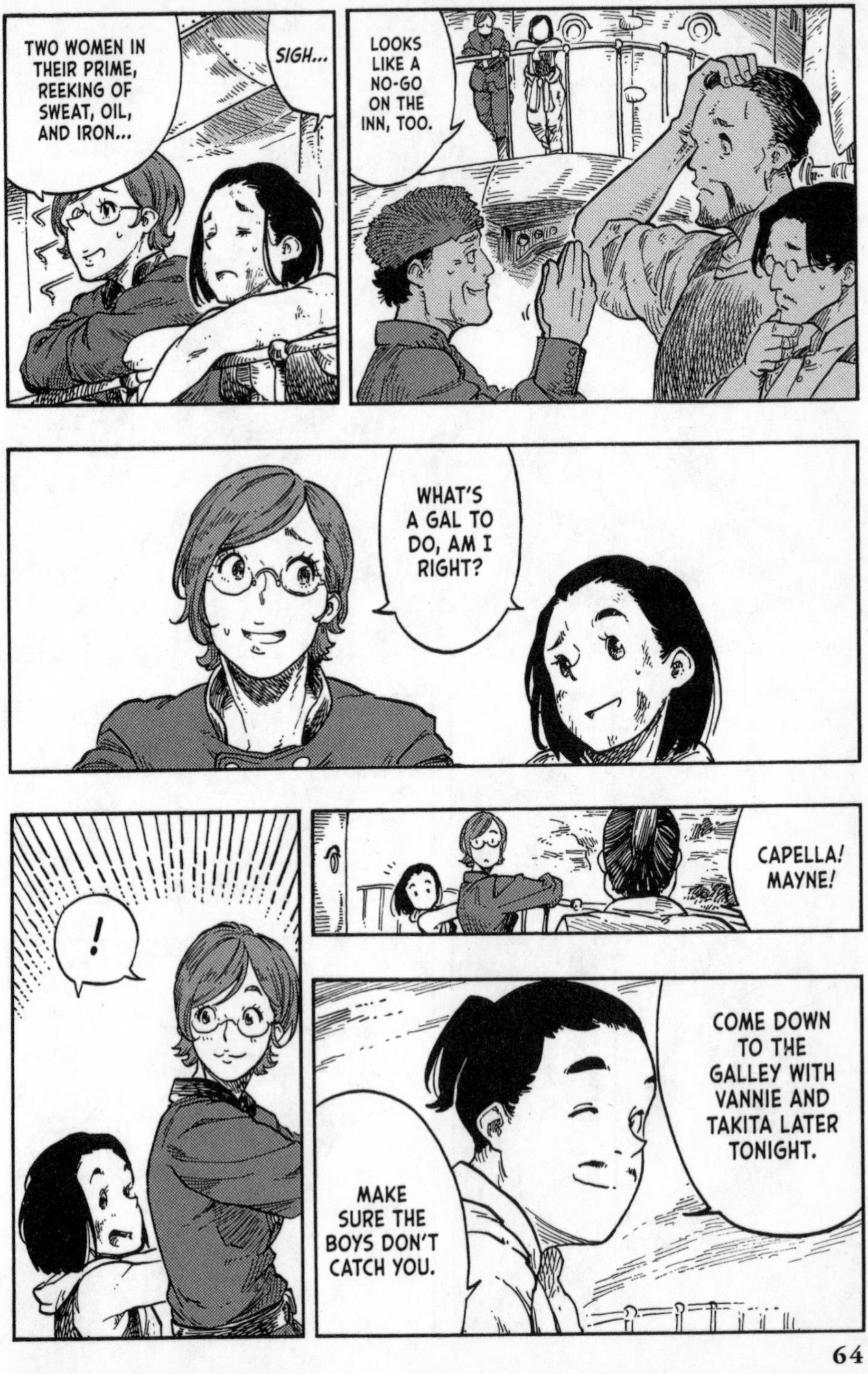
LOOKS LIKE A NO-GO ON THE INN, TOO.
SIGH...
TWO WOMEN IN THEIR PRIME, REEKING OF SWEAT, OIL, AND IRON...
WHAT'S A GAL TO DO, AM I RIGHT?
CAPELLA! MAYNE!
COME DOWN TO THE GALLEY WITH VANNIE AND TAKITA LATER TONIGHT.
MAKE SURE THE BOYS DON'T CATCH YOU.
!

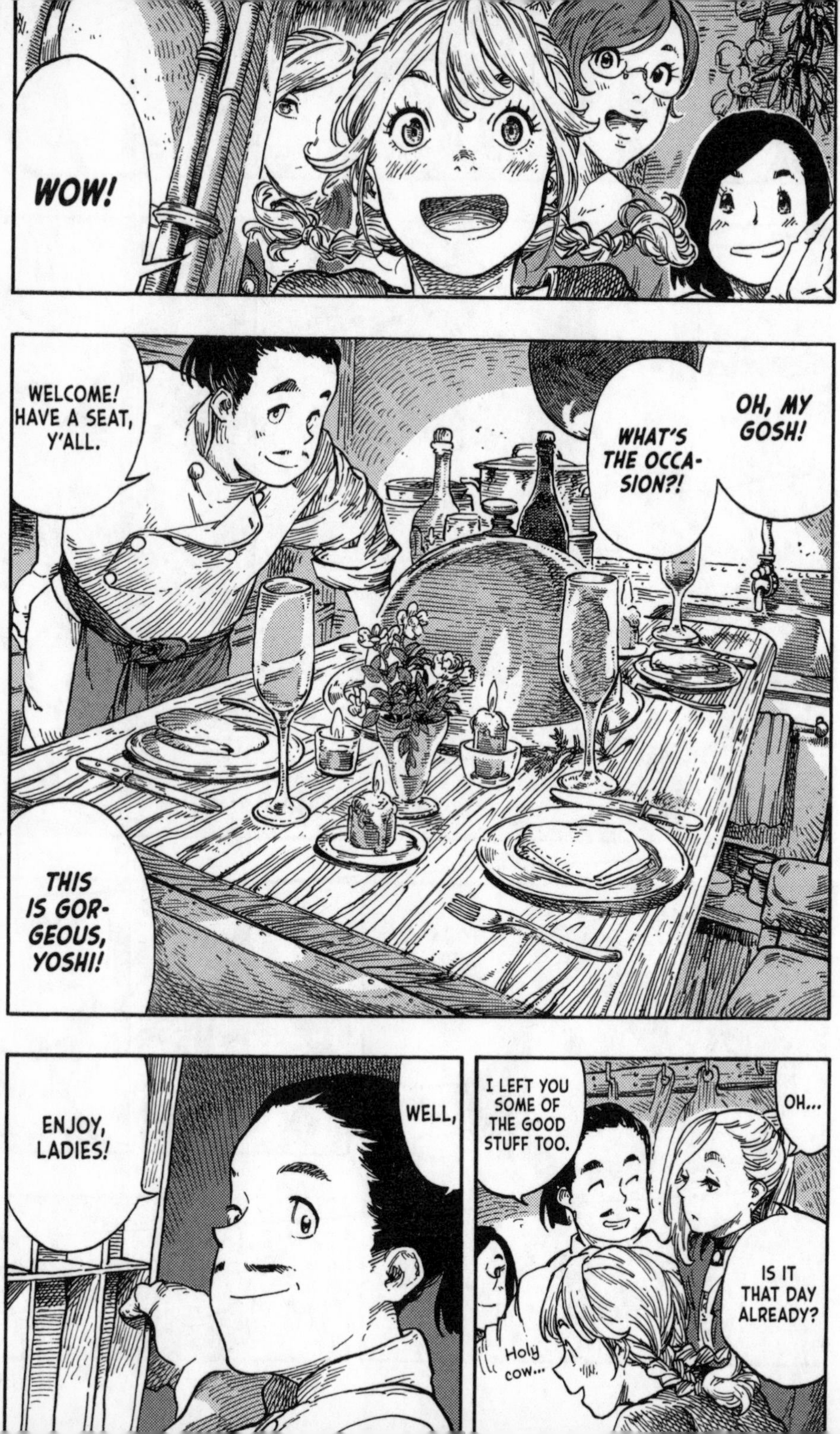
WOW!
OH, MY GOSH!
WHAT'S THE OCCASION?!
WELCOME! HAVE A SEAT, Y'ALL.
THIS IS GORGEOUS, YOSHI!
OH...
I LEFT YOU SOME OF THE GOOD STUFF TOO.
IS IT THAT DAY ALREADY?
Holy cow...
WELL,
ENJOY, LADIES!

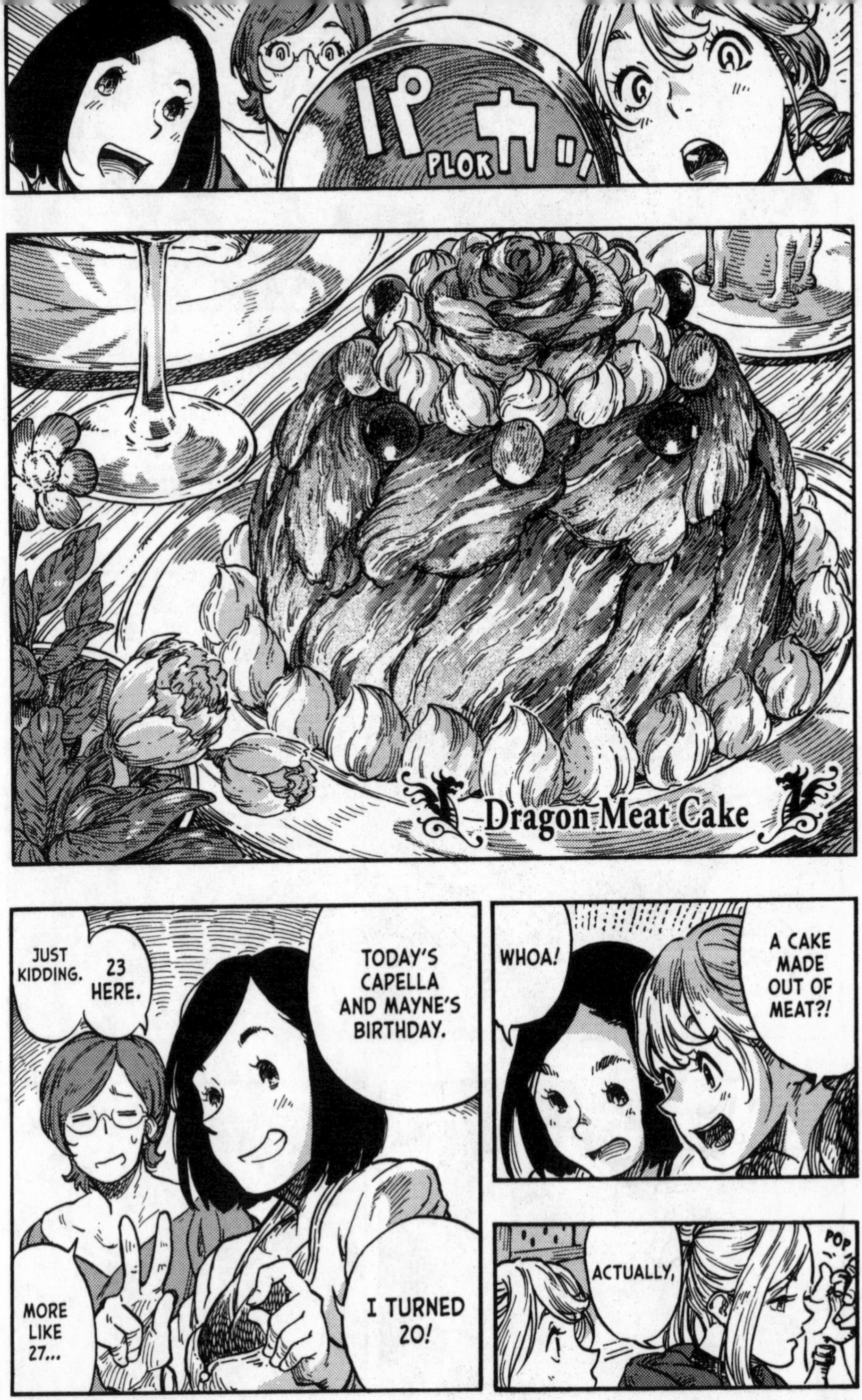
パカッ
PLOK
Dragon Meat Cake
A CAKE MADE OUT OF MEAT?!
WHOA!
POP
ACTUALLY,
TODAY'S CAPELLA AND MAYNE'S BIRTHDAY.
JUST KIDDING. 23 HERE.
I TURNED 20!
MORE LIKE 27...

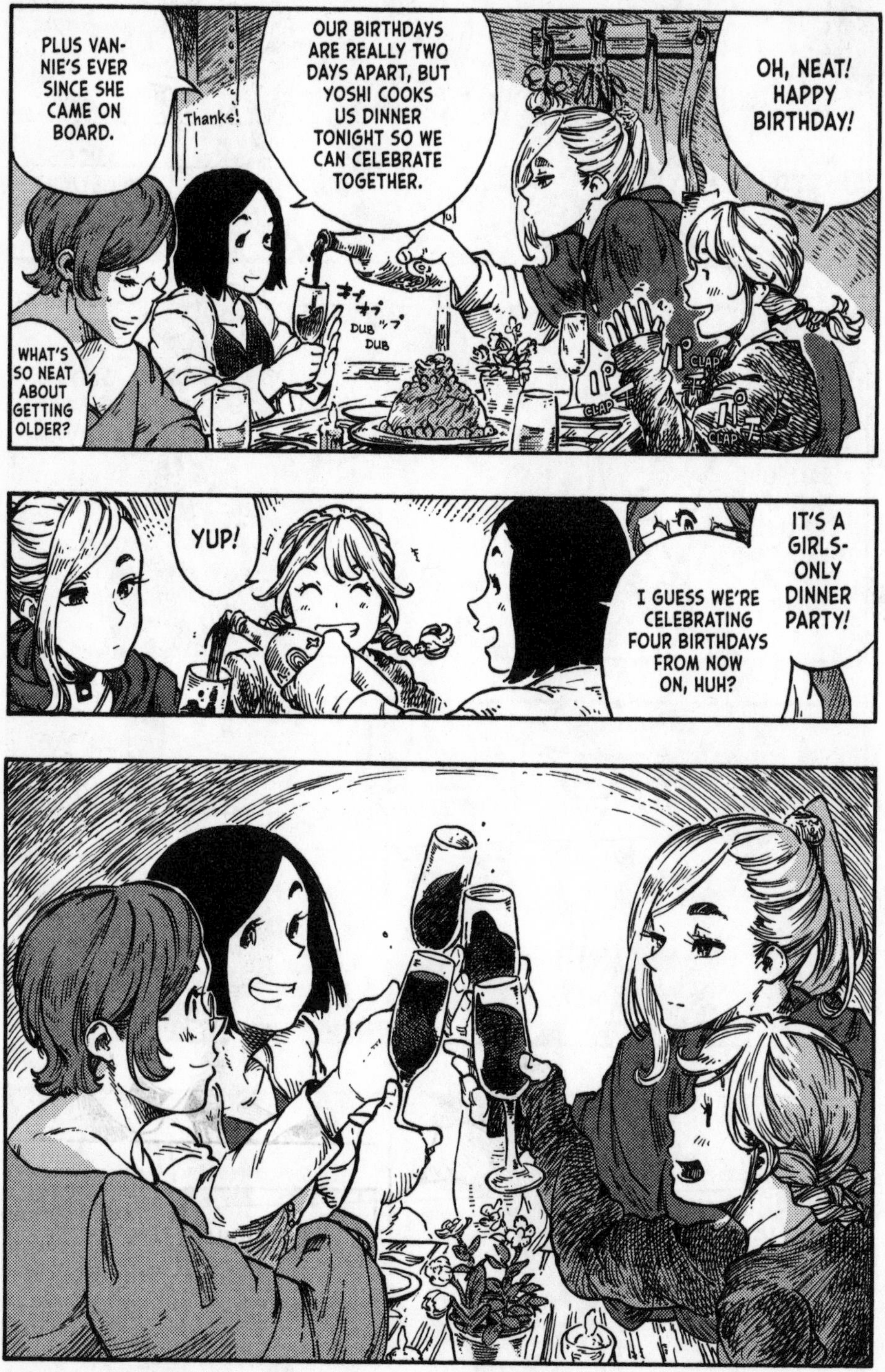
OH, NEAT! HAPPY BIRTHDAY!
CLAP
CLAP
CLAP
OUR BIRTHDAYS ARE REALLY TWO DAYS APART, BUT YOSHI COOKS US DINNER TONIGHT SO WE CAN CELEBRATE TOGETHER.
DUB DUB
Thanks!
PLUS VAN-NIE'S EVER SINCE SHE CAME ON BOARD.
WHAT'S SO NEAT ABOUT GETTING OLDER?
IT'S A GIRLS-ONLY DINNER PARTY!
I GUESS WE'RE CELEBRATING FOUR BIRTHDAYS FROM NOW ON, HUH?
YUP!

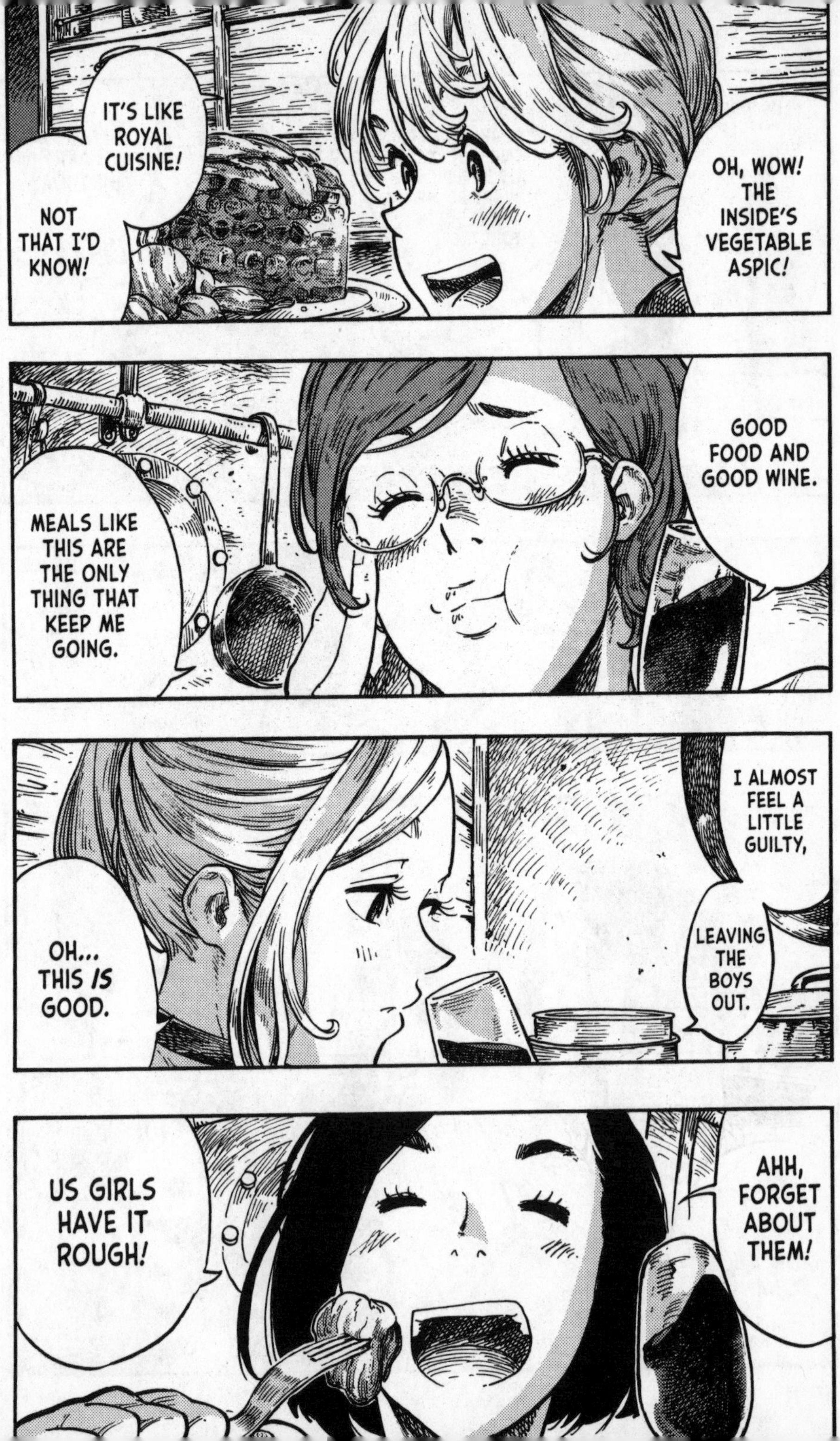
OH, WOW! THE INSIDE'S VEGETABLE ASPIC!
IT'S LIKE ROYAL CUISINE!
NOT THAT I'D KNOW!
GOOD FOOD AND GOOD WINE.
MEALS LIKE THIS ARE THE ONLY THING THAT KEEP ME GOING.
I ALMOST FEEL A LITTLE GUILTY,
LEAVING THE BOYS OUT.
OH... THIS *IS* GOOD.
AHH, FORGET ABOUT THEM!
US GIRLS HAVE IT ROUGH!

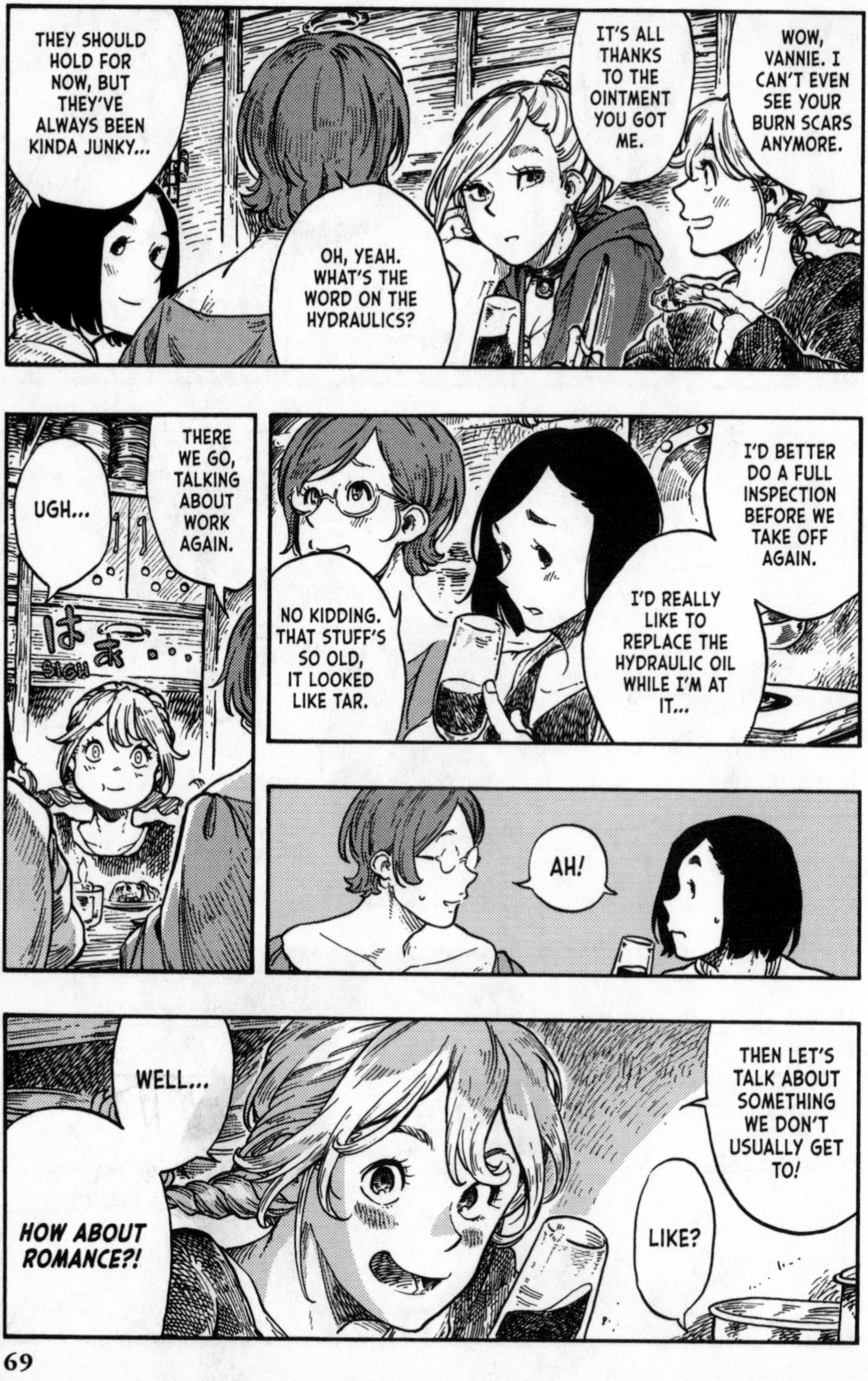
WOW, VANNIE. I CAN'T EVEN SEE YOUR BURN SCARS ANYMORE.
IT'S ALL THANKS TO THE OINTMENT YOU GOT ME.
OH, YEAH. WHAT'S THE WORD ON THE HYDRAULICS?
THEY SHOULD HOLD FOR NOW, BUT THEY'VE ALWAYS BEEN KINDA JUNKY...
I'D BETTER DO A FULL INSPECTION BEFORE WE TAKE OFF AGAIN.
I'D REALLY LIKE TO REPLACE THE HYDRAULIC OIL WHILE I'M AT IT...
NO KIDDING. THAT STUFF'S SO OLD, IT LOOKED LIKE TAR.
AH!
THERE WE GO, TALKING ABOUT WORK AGAIN.
UGH...
はぁ...
SIGH
THEN LET'S TALK ABOUT SOMETHING WE DON'T USUALLY GET TO!
LIKE?
WELL...
HOW ABOUT ROMANCE?!

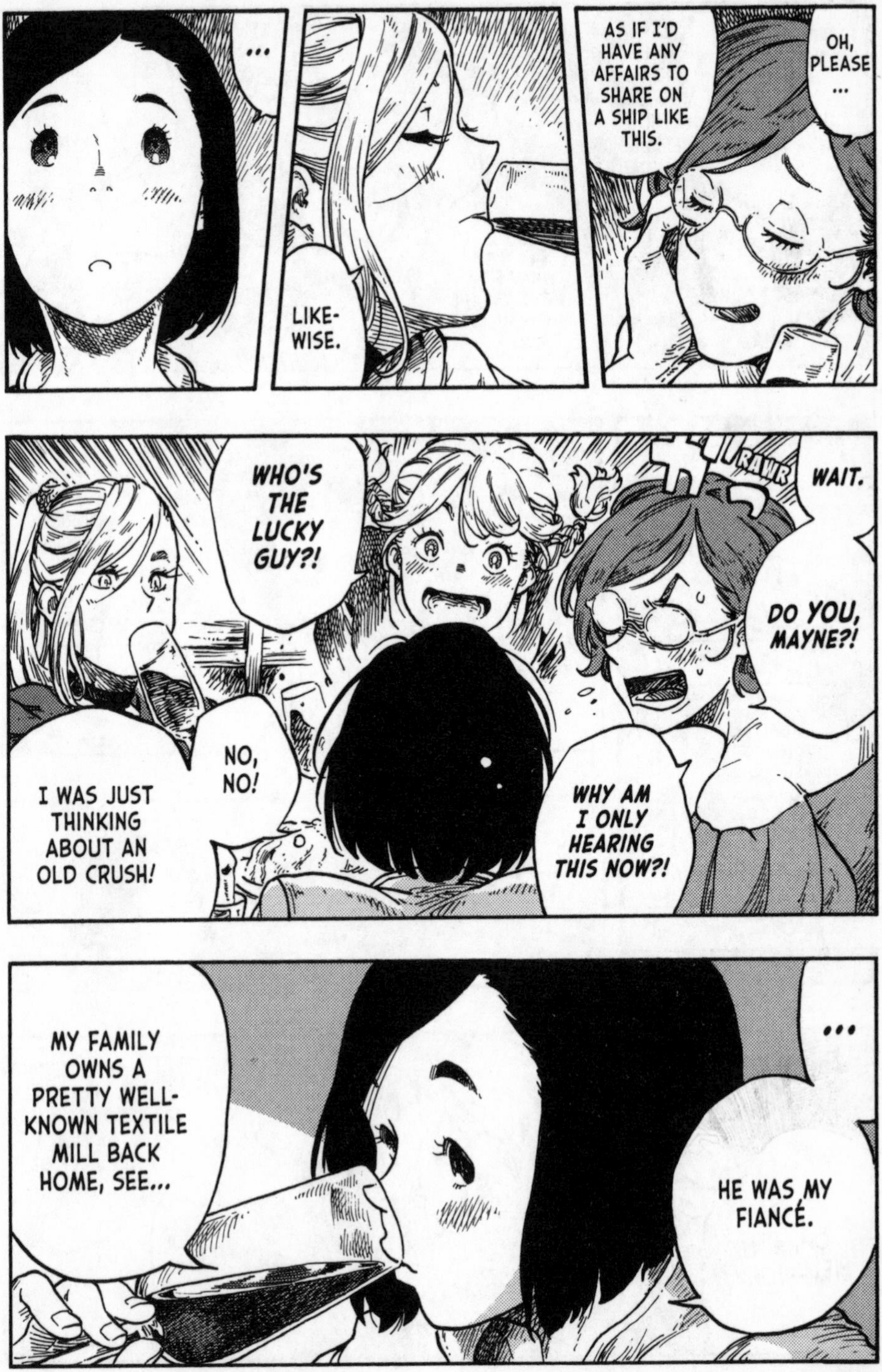
OH, PLEASE ...
AS IF I'D HAVE ANY AFFAIRS TO SHARE ON A SHIP LIKE THIS.
LIKE-WISE.
...
RAWR
WAIT.
DO YOU, MAYNE?!
WHY AM I ONLY HEARING THIS NOW?!
WHO'S THE LUCKY GUY?!
NO, NO!
I WAS JUST THINKING ABOUT AN OLD CRUSH!
...
HE WAS MY FIANCÉ.
MY FAMILY OWNS A PRETTY WELL-KNOWN TEXTILE MILL BACK HOME, SEE...

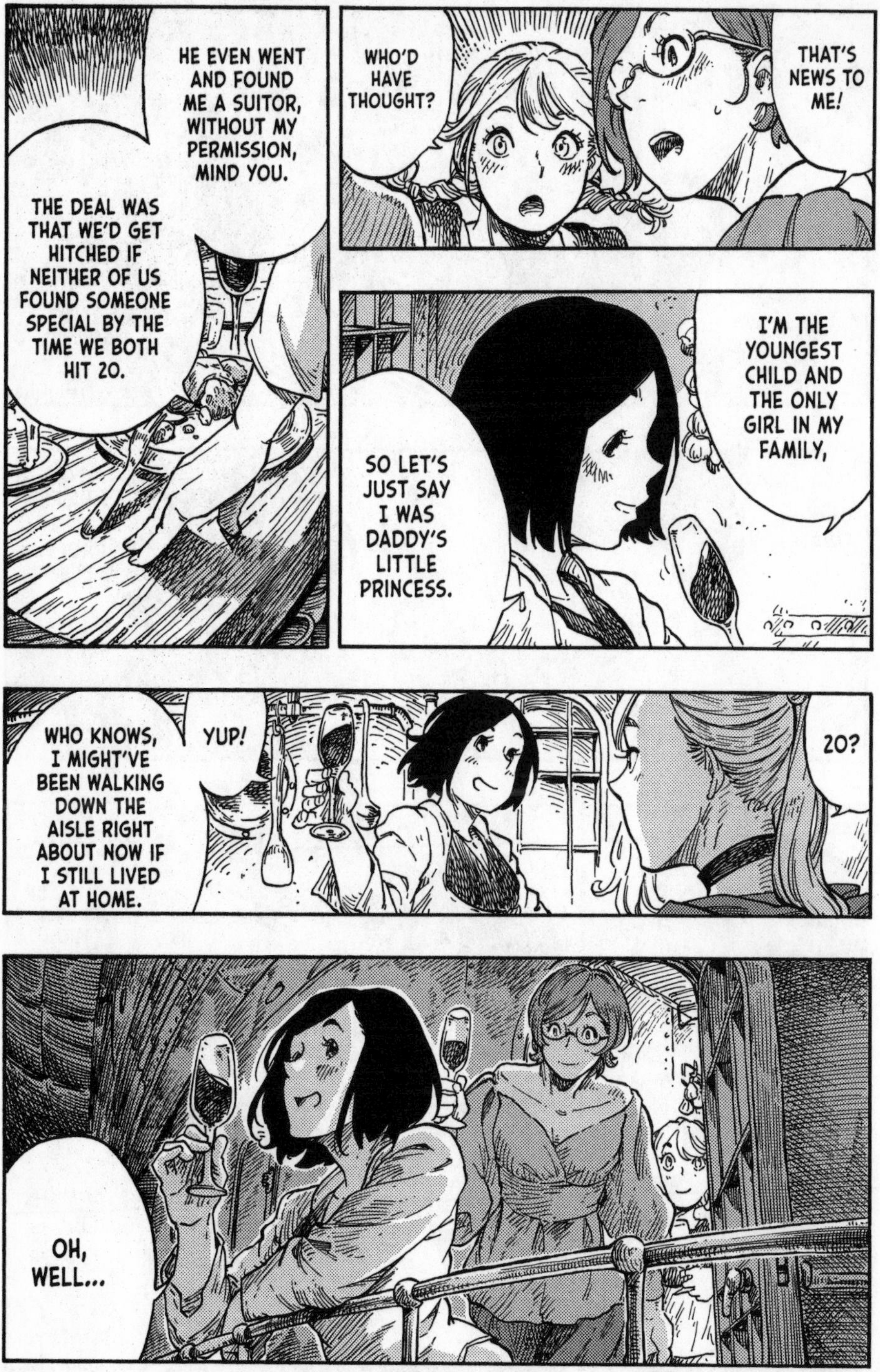
THAT'S NEWS TO ME!
WHO'D HAVE THOUGHT?
I'M THE YOUNGEST CHILD AND THE ONLY GIRL IN MY FAMILY,
SO LET'S JUST SAY I WAS DADDY'S LITTLE PRINCESS.
HE EVEN WENT AND FOUND ME A SUITOR, WITHOUT MY PERMISSION, MIND YOU.
THE DEAL WAS THAT WE'D GET HITCHED IF NEITHER OF US FOUND SOMEONE SPECIAL BY THE TIME WE BOTH HIT 20.
20?
YUP!
WHO KNOWS, I MIGHT'VE BEEN WALKING DOWN THE AISLE RIGHT ABOUT NOW IF I STILL LIVED AT HOME.
OH, WELL...

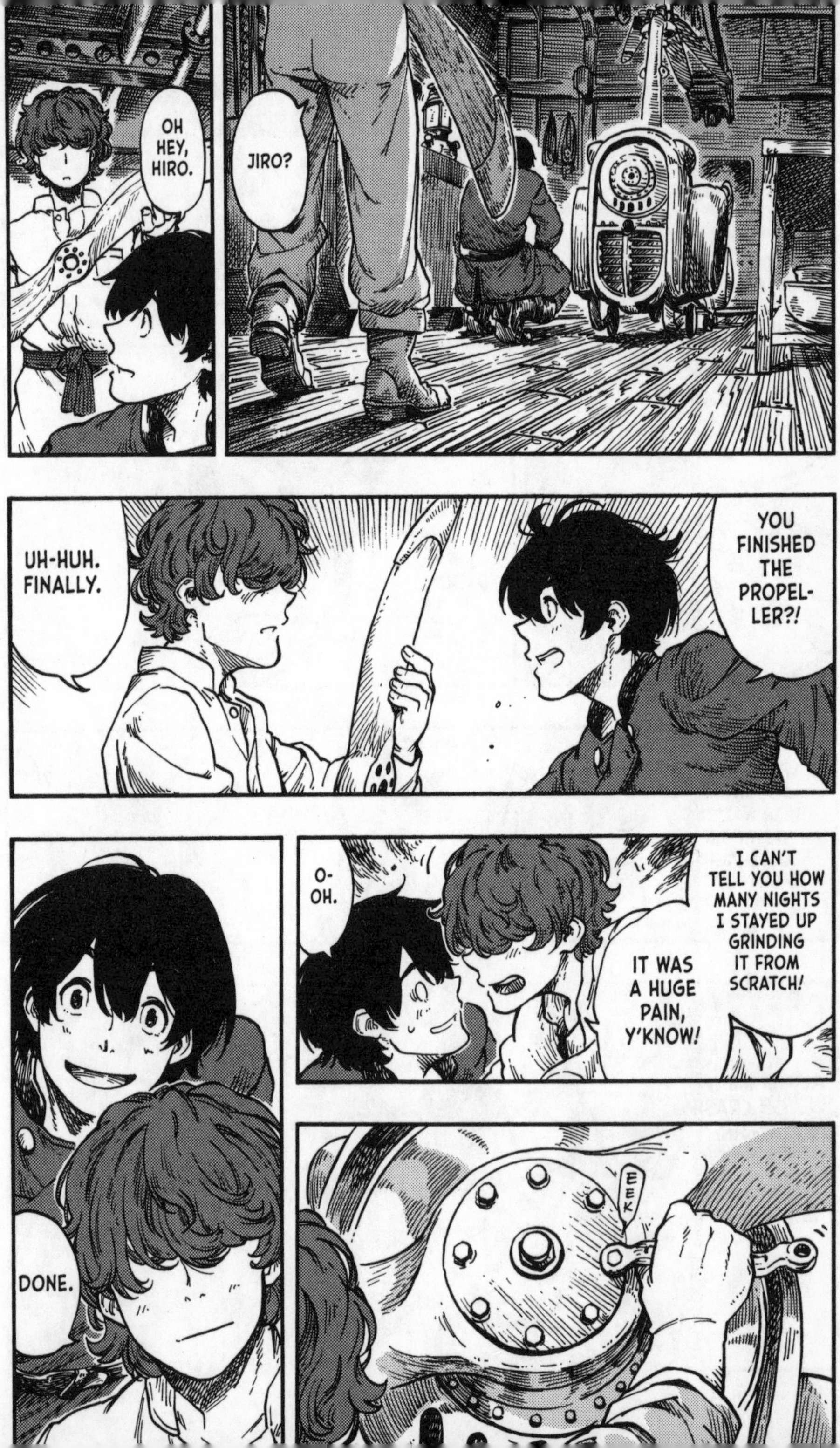
JIRO?
OH HEY, HIRO.
YOU FINISHED THE PROPELLER?!
UH-HUH. FINALLY.
I CAN'T TELL YOU HOW MANY NIGHTS I STAYED UP GRINDING IT FROM SCRATCH!
IT WAS A HUGE PAIN, Y'KNOW!
O-OH.
EEK
DONE.

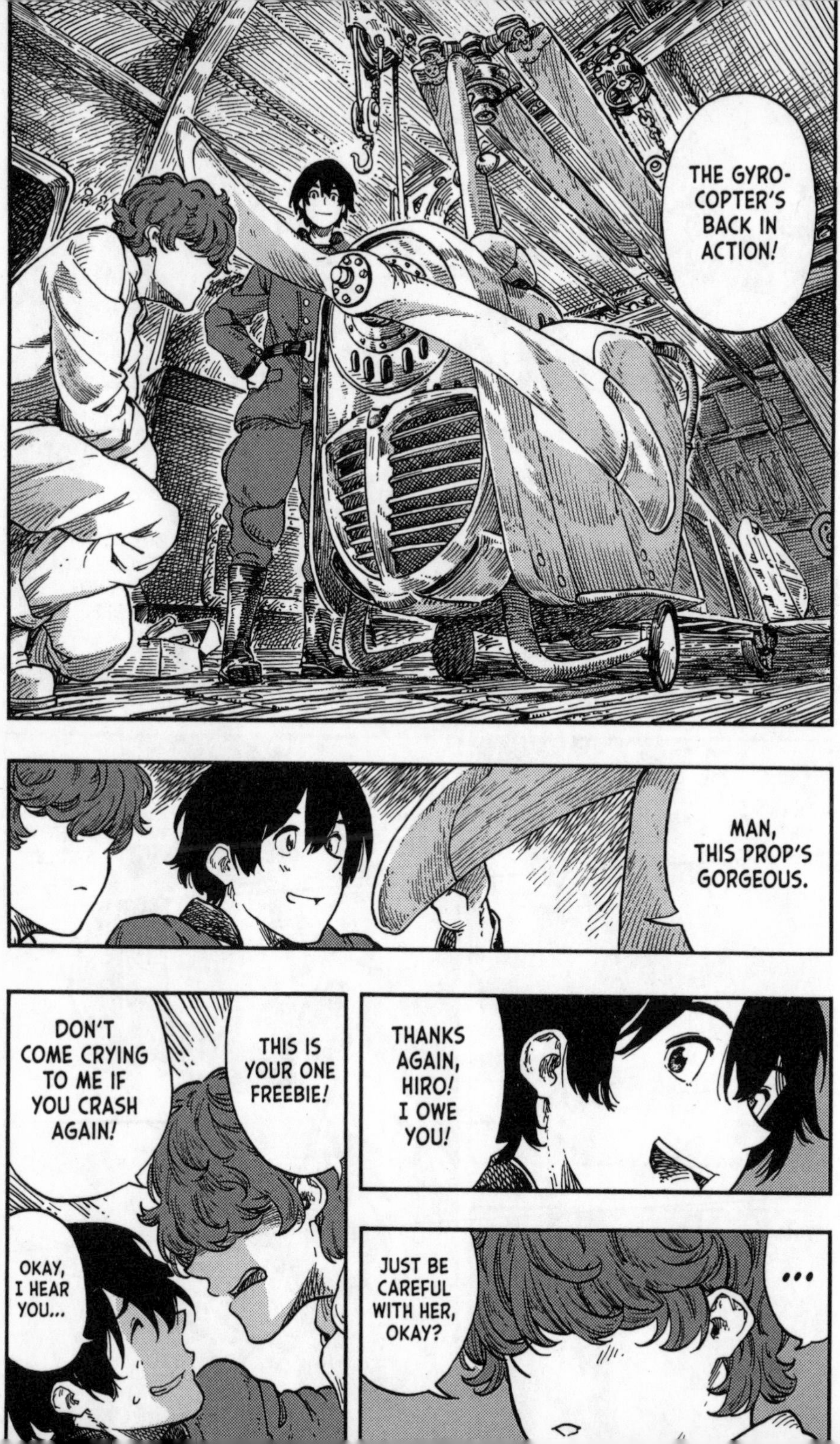
THE GYRO-COPTER'S BACK IN ACTION!
MAN, THIS PROP'S GORGEOUS.
THANKS AGAIN, HIRO! I OWE YOU!
...
JUST BE CAREFUL WITH HER, OKAY?
THIS IS YOUR ONE FREEBIE!
DON'T COME CRYING TO ME IF YOU CRASH AGAIN!
OKAY, I HEAR YOU...

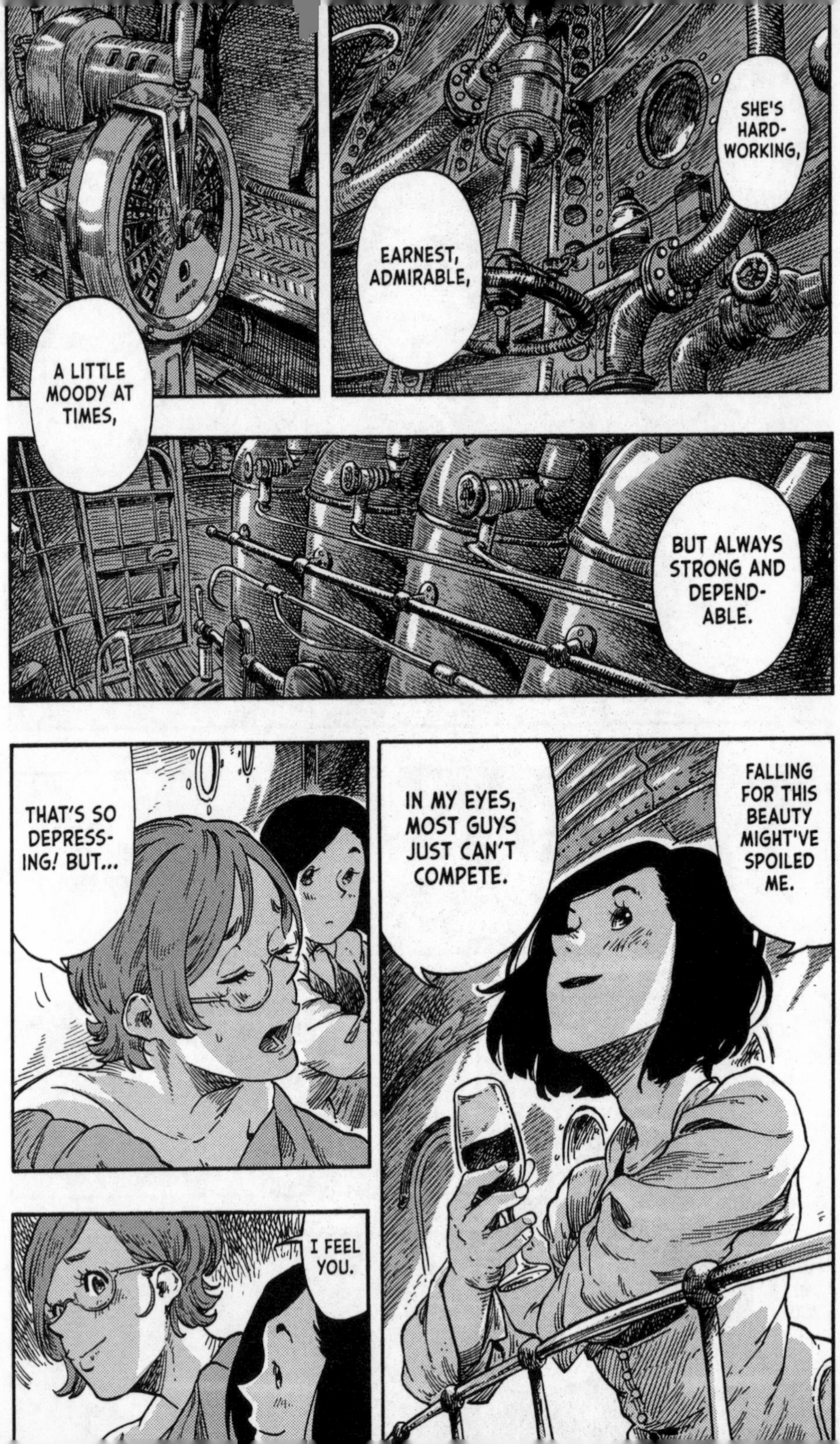
SHE'S HARD-WORKING,
EARNEST, ADMIRABLE,
A LITTLE MOODY AT TIMES,
BUT ALWAYS STRONG AND DEPEND-ABLE.
FALLING FOR THIS BEAUTY MIGHT'VE SPOILED ME.
IN MY EYES, MOST GUYS JUST CAN'T COMPETE.
THAT'S SO DEPRESS-ING! BUT...
I FEEL YOU.

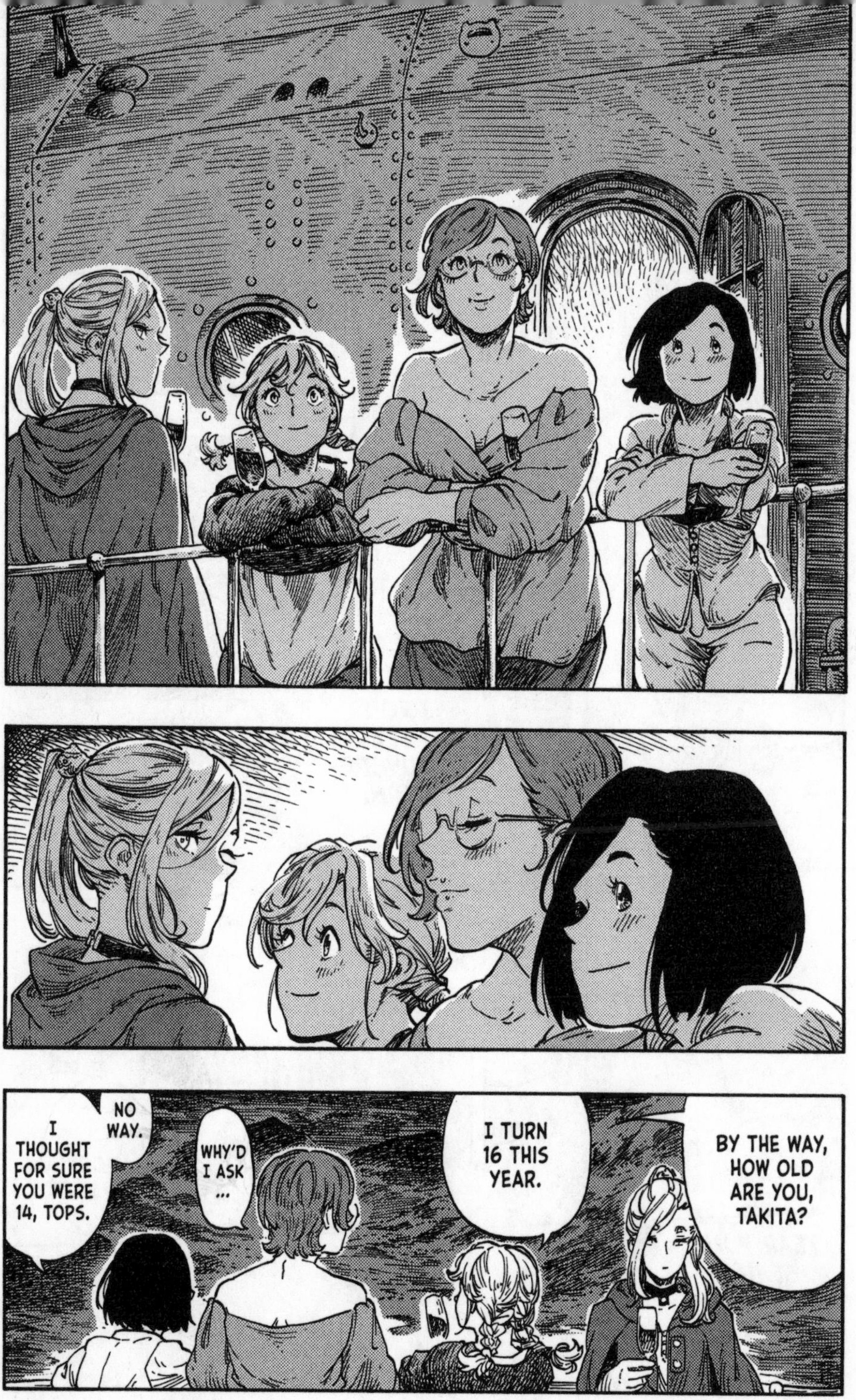
BY THE WAY, HOW OLD ARE YOU, TAKITA?
I TURN 16 THIS YEAR.
WHY'D I ASK ...
NO WAY.
I THOUGHT FOR SURE YOU WERE 14, TOPS.

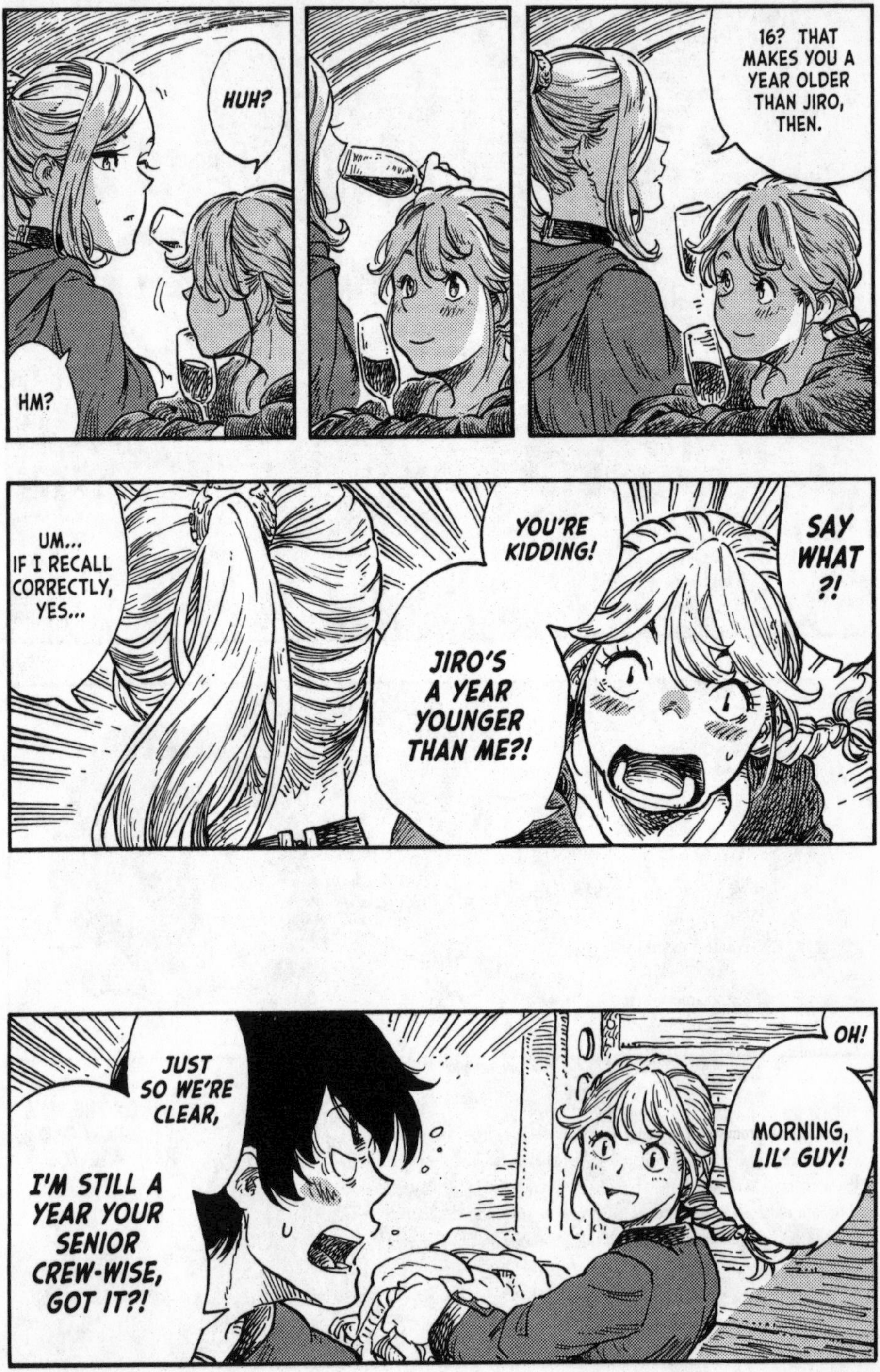
16? THAT MAKES YOU A YEAR OLDER THAN JIRO, THEN.
HUH?
HM?
SAY WHAT?!
YOU'RE KIDDING!
JIRO'S A YEAR YOUNGER THAN ME?!
UM... IF I RECALL CORRECTLY, YES...
OH!
MORNING, LIL' GUY!
JUST SO WE'RE CLEAR,
I'M STILL A YEAR YOUR SENIOR CREW-WISE, GOT IT?!

Dragon Meat Cake

Ingredients (Serves 4)
✦ Bell pepper (red/yellow): 1 each
✦ Black olives (pitted): 10
✦ Green beans: 5 ✦ Celery: ½ a stalk
✦ Consommé: 700 cc (2 ½ cups) ✦ Gelatin: 20 g
✦ Dragon sirloin: 700 g
✦ Olive oil: 1 tbsp ✦ Medium-sized potato: 2-3
✦ Horseradish: 1 small root ✦ Milk: 80 cc (⅓ cup)
✦ Heavy cream: 1 tbsp ✦ Salt & Pepper: to taste
✦ Butter: 1 tbsp
✦ Garnish with additional olives or other vegetables

01
Remove the fibrous strings from celery and chop into 1 cm pieces. Remove seeds and ribs from bell peppers and chop into 1.5 cm pieces. Slice black olives in half. Chop green beans into 1 cm pieces.

02
Bring a pot of water to a boil and season with a pinch of salt. Add celery to the pot and boil until tender. Add green beans and peppers and boil until cooked through. Strain the vegetables and place in a container lined with a clean kitchen towel and leave to steam dry.

03
In a pot, bring consommé to a near boil. Remove the pot from the heat, add powdered gelatin and mix until fully dissolved. Transfer the pot to a container or pan filled with water and let cool, stirring occasionally.

04
In a dome-shaped mold or bowl, neatly layer bell pepper, celery, black olives, and green beans. Gently pour thickened consommé over the vegetables and leave somewhere cool to set for 6-12 hours.

05
Preheat oven to 140° C / 285° F. Heat oil in a pan over medium-high heat. Season dragon meat with salt and pepper and sear on both sides in the pan.

06
Transfer the meat to a baking pan and roast in the oven for 30 minutes. Remove the pan from the oven and cover the meat with a lid or aluminum foil. Allow the meat to rest for at least 20 minutes to an hour.

07
Peel potatoes, slice into 5-mm thick rounds and place in a pot. Fill the pot with water until the potatoes are just covered and boil until the potatoes are fork tender.

08
Drain the water from the pot and while the potatoes are still hot, add milk and cream to the pot and mash with a potato masher or fork over medium heat.

09
Remove the pot from the heat and mix in grated horseradish and butter. Season mashed potatoes with salt and pepper to taste.

10
Place the mold from step 4 in a container or large bowl filled with hot water to warm the sides of the mold, then flip over onto a plate. Gently shake the mold side to side to release the gelatin salad from the mold.

11
Layer the gelatin salad with thinly-sliced roast dragon meat from the top-down in a spiral pattern. If there is any meat left over, shape into decorative flowers and adorn the top of the cake with them. Place mashed potato mixture into a piping bag and decoratively pipe along the rim and top of the meat cake. Garnish the cake with olives and other vegetables and serve.

NOTHING SAYS LADIES NIGHT LIKE A PILE OF DRAGON MEAT!

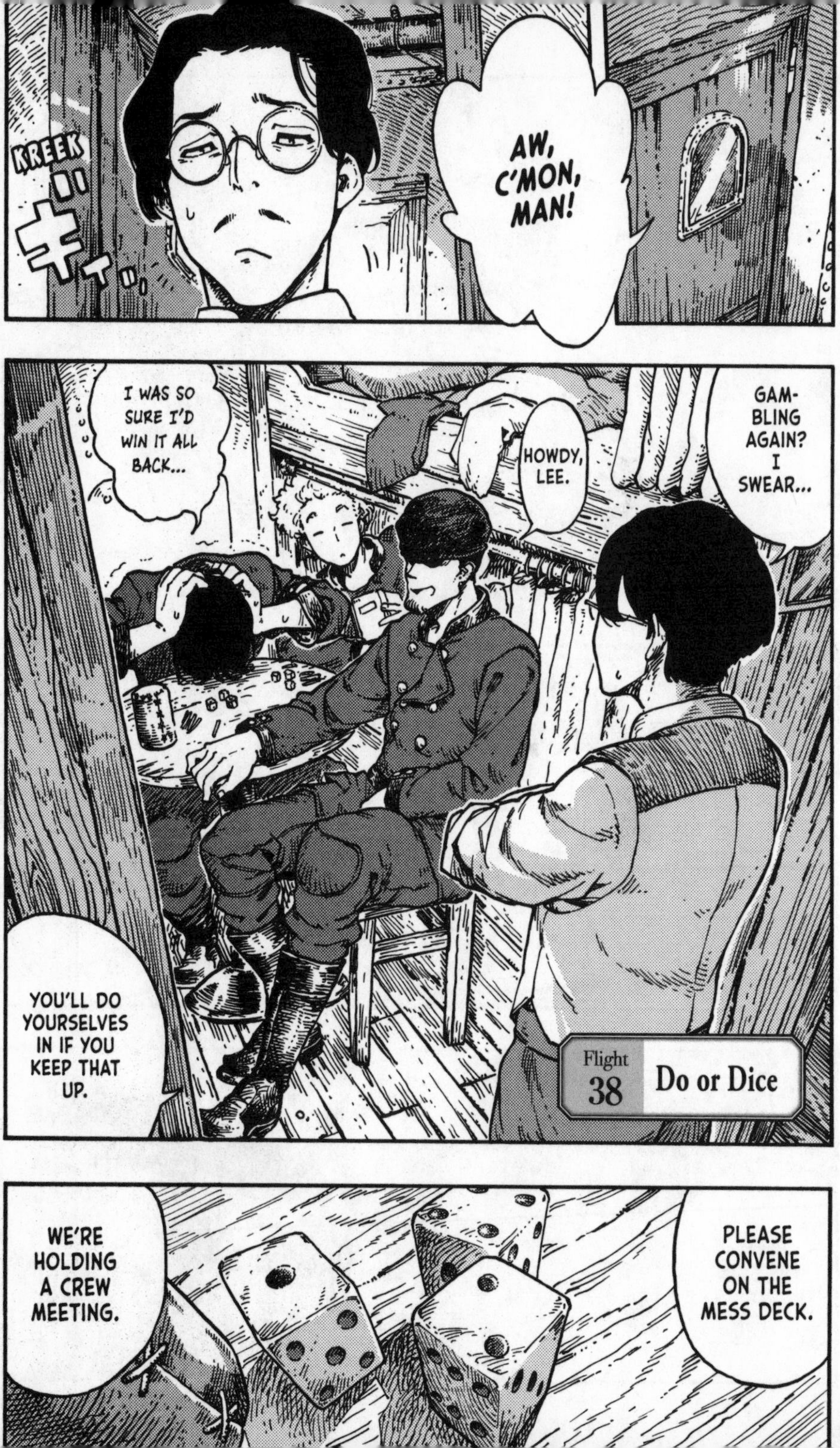
AW, C'MON, MAN!
KREEK
キィ
GAM-BLING AGAIN? I SWEAR...
HOWDY, LEE.
I WAS SO SURE I'D WIN IT ALL BACK...
YOU'LL DO YOURSELVES IN IF YOU KEEP THAT UP.
Flight 38 Do or Dice
PLEASE CONVENE ON THE MESS DECK.
WE'RE HOLDING A CREW MEETING.

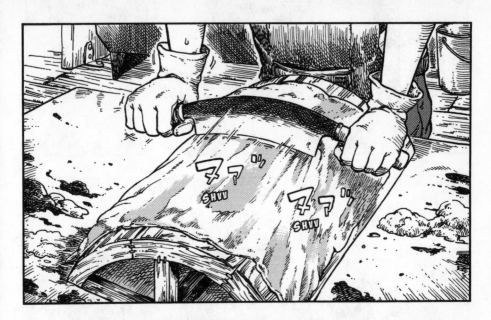

HEY, MIKA.

CAN YOU TELL ME IF THIS HIDE'S READY FOR TANNING?

HMM... SURE, LOOKS GOOD.

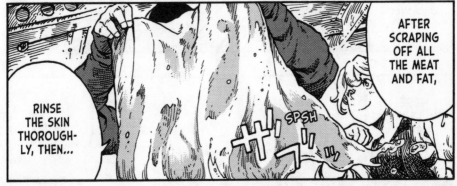

AFTER SCRAPING OFF ALL THE MEAT AND FAT,

RINSE THE SKIN THOROUGHLY, THEN...

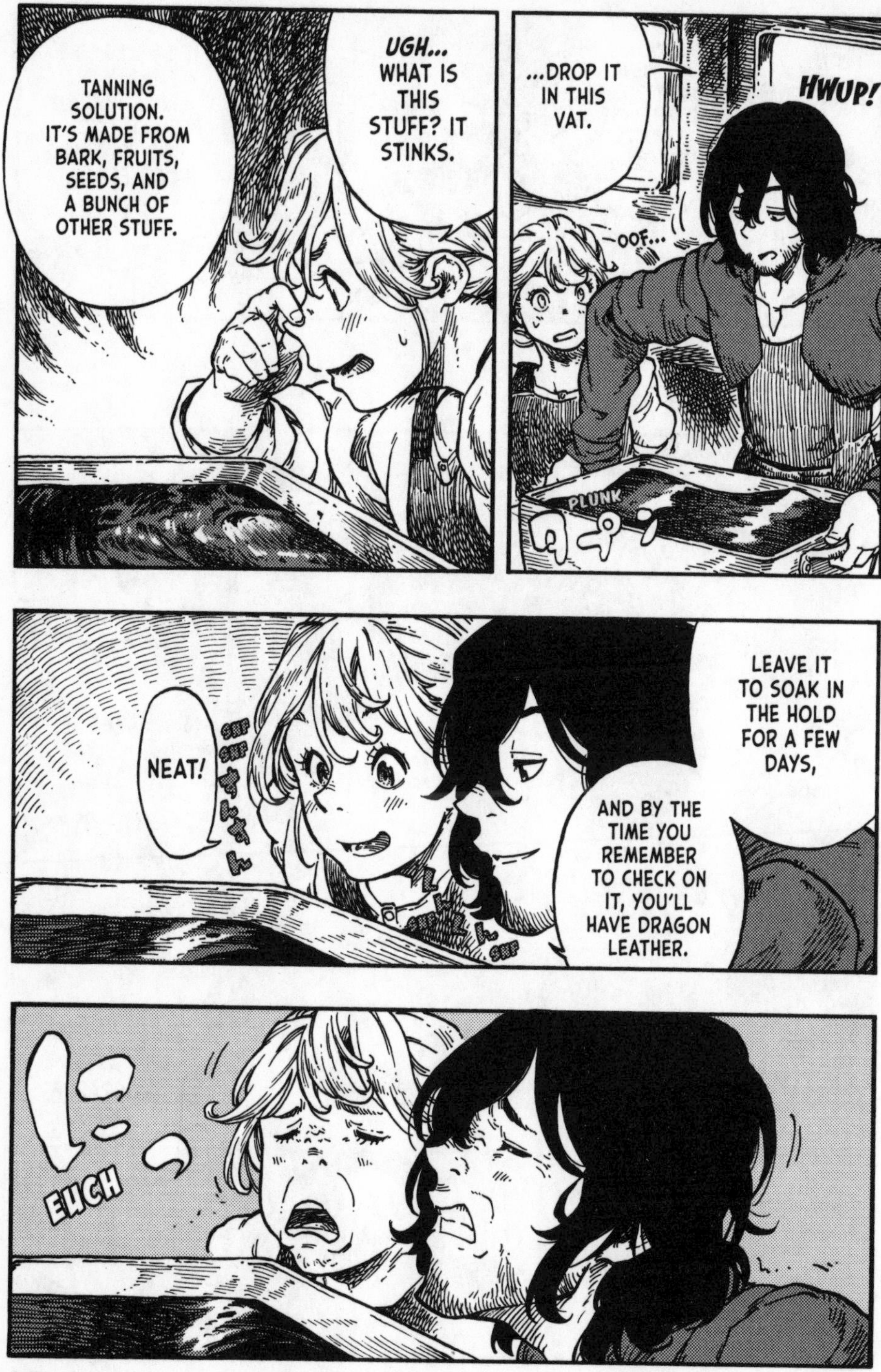
...DROP IT IN THIS VAT.
HWUP!
OOF...
PLUNK
UGH... WHAT IS THIS STUFF? IT STINKS.
TANNING SOLUTION. IT'S MADE FROM BARK, FRUITS, SEEDS, AND A BUNCH OF OTHER STUFF.
LEAVE IT TO SOAK IN THE HOLD FOR A FEW DAYS,
AND BY THE TIME YOU REMEMBER TO CHECK ON IT, YOU'LL HAVE DRAGON LEATHER.
NEAT!
EUCH

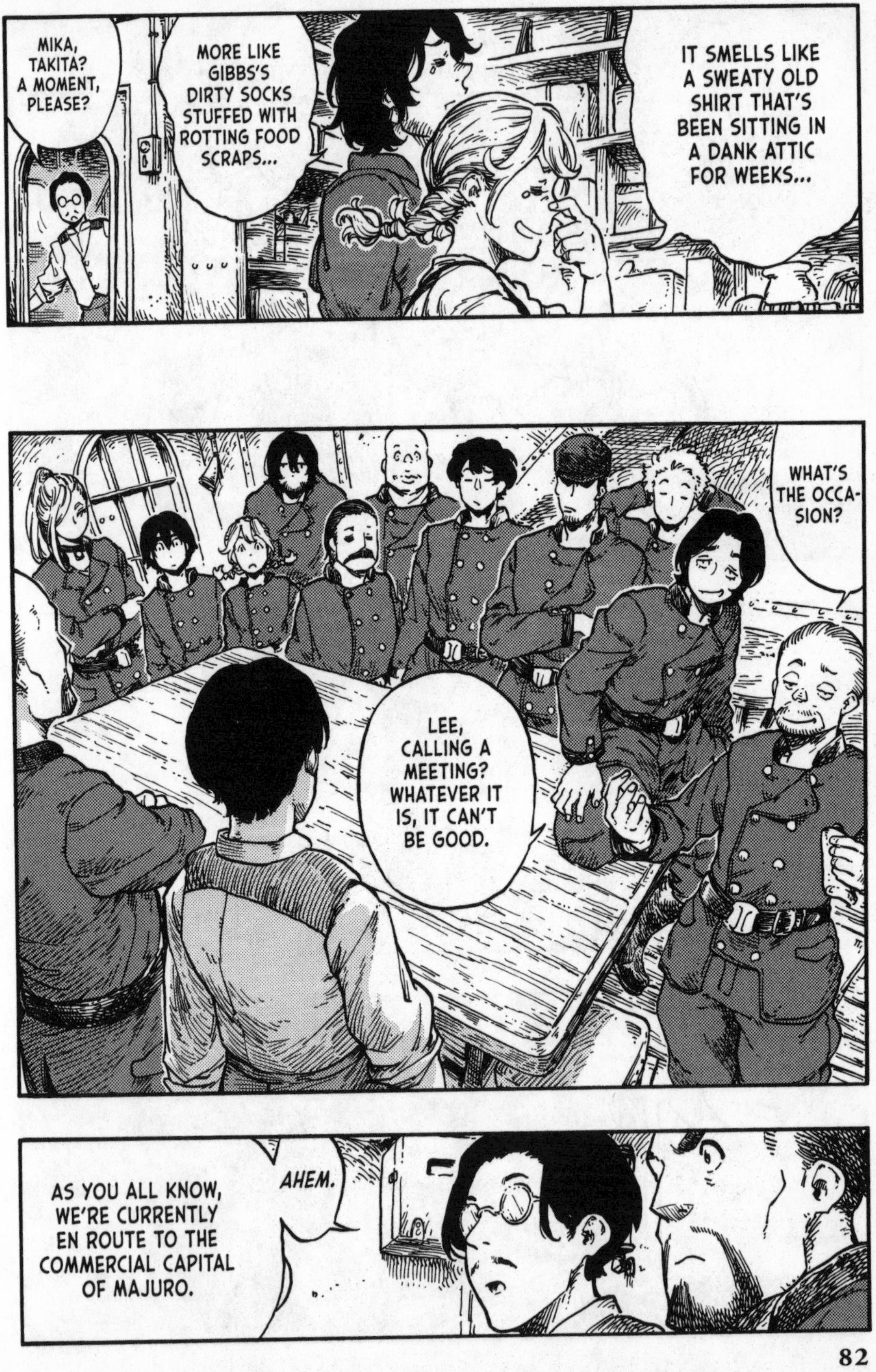
IT SMELLS LIKE A SWEATY OLD SHIRT THAT'S BEEN SITTING IN A DANK ATTIC FOR WEEKS...
MORE LIKE GIBBS'S DIRTY SOCKS STUFFED WITH ROTTING FOOD SCRAPS...
MIKA, TAKITA? A MOMENT, PLEASE?
WHAT'S THE OCCA-SION?
LEE, CALLING A MEETING? WHATEVER IT IS, IT CAN'T BE GOOD.
AHEM.
AS YOU ALL KNOW, WE'RE CURRENTLY EN ROUTE TO THE COMMERCIAL CAPITAL OF MAJURO.

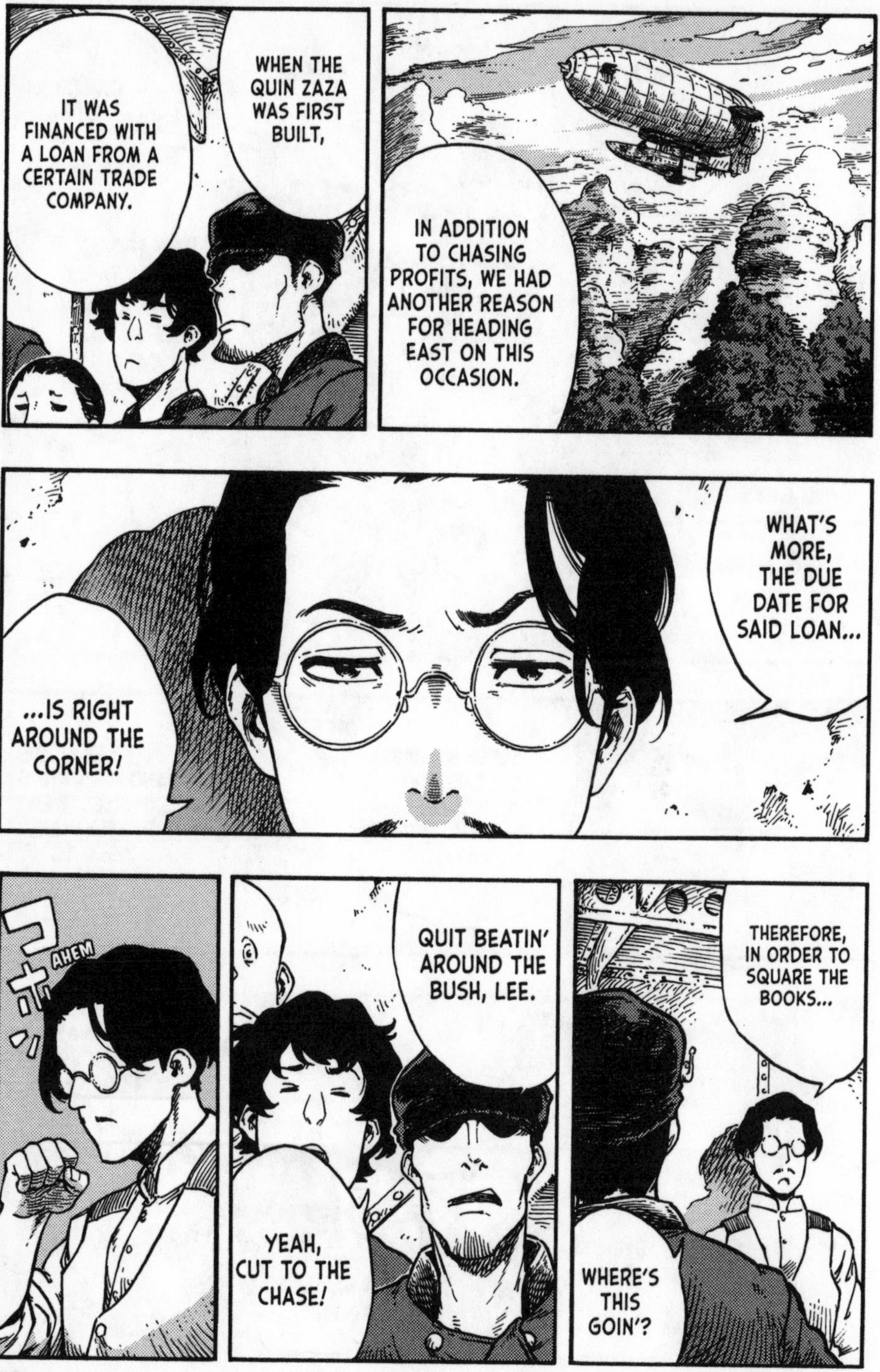
IN ADDITION TO CHASING PROFITS, WE HAD ANOTHER REASON FOR HEADING EAST ON THIS OCCASION.
WHEN THE QUIN ZAZA WAS FIRST BUILT,
IT WAS FINANCED WITH A LOAN FROM A CERTAIN TRADE COMPANY.
WHAT'S MORE, THE DUE DATE FOR SAID LOAN...
...IS RIGHT AROUND THE CORNER!
THEREFORE, IN ORDER TO SQUARE THE BOOKS...
WHERE'S THIS GOIN'?
QUIT BEATIN' AROUND THE BUSH, LEE.
YEAH, CUT TO THE CHASE!
コホッ
AHEM

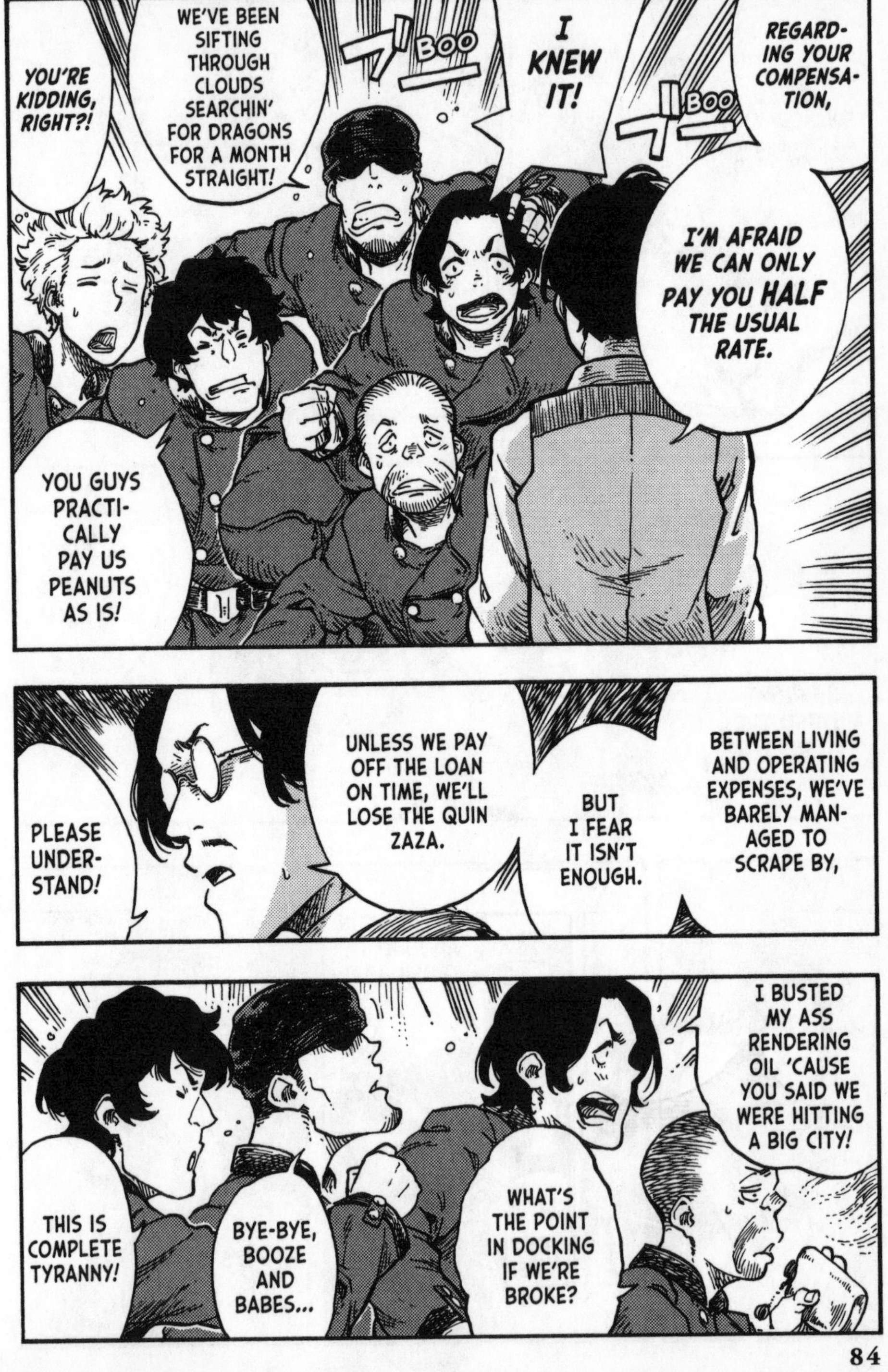
REGARDING YOUR COMPENSATION,
I'M AFRAID WE CAN ONLY PAY YOU **HALF** THE USUAL RATE.
BOO
I KNEW IT!
BOO
WE'VE BEEN SIFTING THROUGH CLOUDS SEARCHIN' FOR DRAGONS FOR A MONTH STRAIGHT!
YOU'RE KIDDING, RIGHT?!
YOU GUYS PRACTICALLY PAY US PEANUTS AS IS!
BETWEEN LIVING AND OPERATING EXPENSES, WE'VE BARELY MANAGED TO SCRAPE BY,
BUT I FEAR IT ISN'T ENOUGH.
UNLESS WE PAY OFF THE LOAN ON TIME, WE'LL LOSE THE QUIN ZAZA.
PLEASE UNDERSTAND!
I BUSTED MY ASS RENDERING OIL 'CAUSE YOU SAID WE WERE HITTING A BIG CITY!
WHAT'S THE POINT IN DOCKING IF WE'RE BROKE?
BYE-BYE, BOOZE AND BABES...
THIS IS COMPLETE TYRANNY!

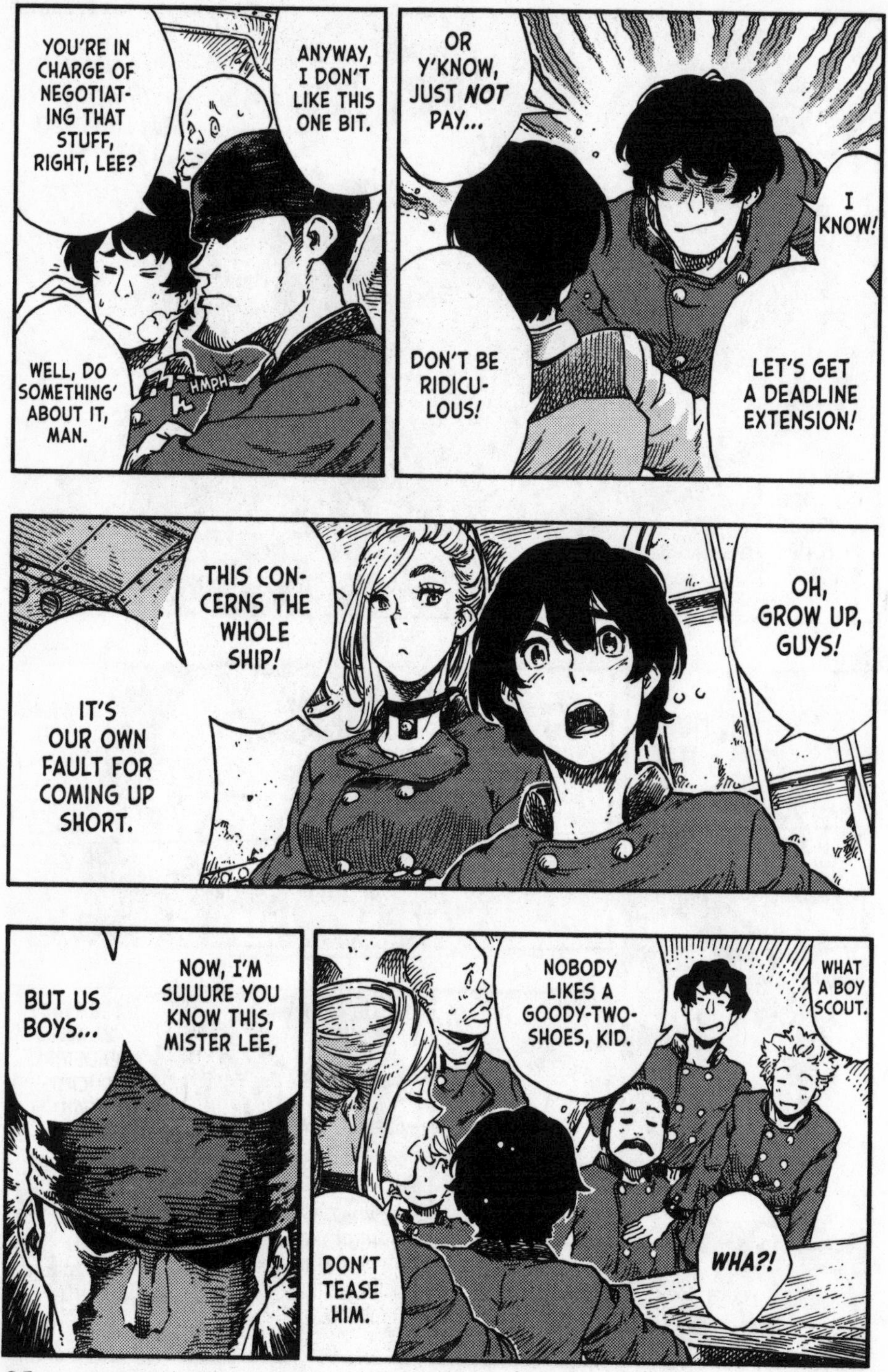
I KNOW!
LET'S GET A DEADLINE EXTENSION!
OR Y'KNOW, JUST NOT PAY...
DON'T BE RIDICULOUS!
ANYWAY, I DON'T LIKE THIS ONE BIT.
YOU'RE IN CHARGE OF NEGOTIAT-ING THAT STUFF, RIGHT, LEE?
HMPH
WELL, DO SOMETHING' ABOUT IT, MAN.
OH, GROW UP, GUYS!
THIS CON-CERNS THE WHOLE SHIP!
IT'S OUR OWN FAULT FOR COMING UP SHORT.
WHAT A BOY SCOUT.
NOBODY LIKES A GOODY-TWO-SHOES, KID.
WHA?!
DON'T TEASE HIM.
NOW, I'M SUUURE YOU KNOW THIS, MISTER LEE,
BUT US BOYS...

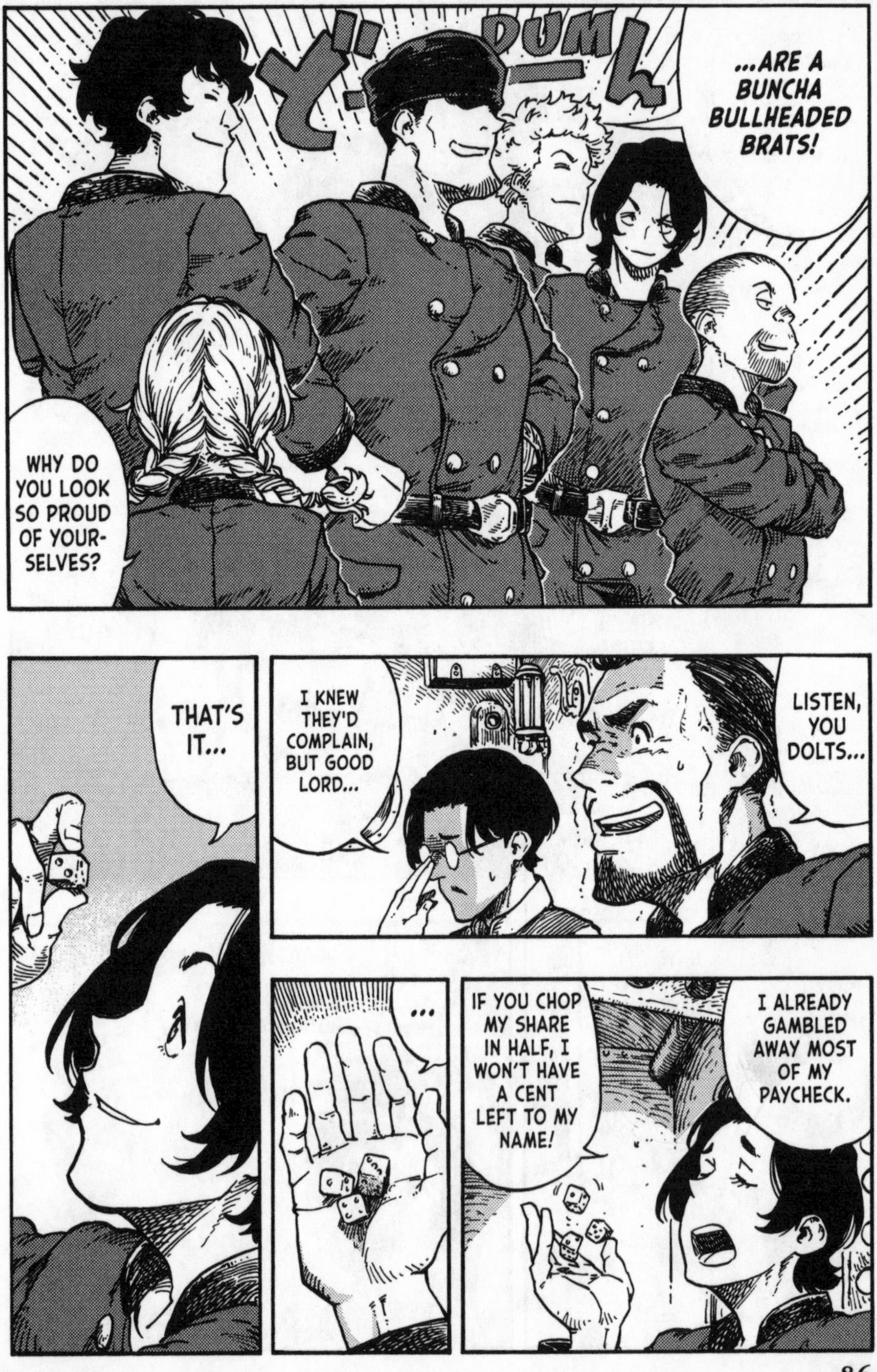
...ARE A BUNCHA BULLHEADED BRATS!
DUM
ずーん
WHY DO YOU LOOK SO PROUD OF YOUR-SELVES?
LISTEN, YOU DOLTS...
I KNEW THEY'D COMPLAIN, BUT GOOD LORD...
I ALREADY GAMBLED AWAY MOST OF MY PAYCHECK.
IF YOU CHOP MY SHARE IN HALF, I WON'T HAVE A CENT LEFT TO MY NAME!
...
THAT'S IT...

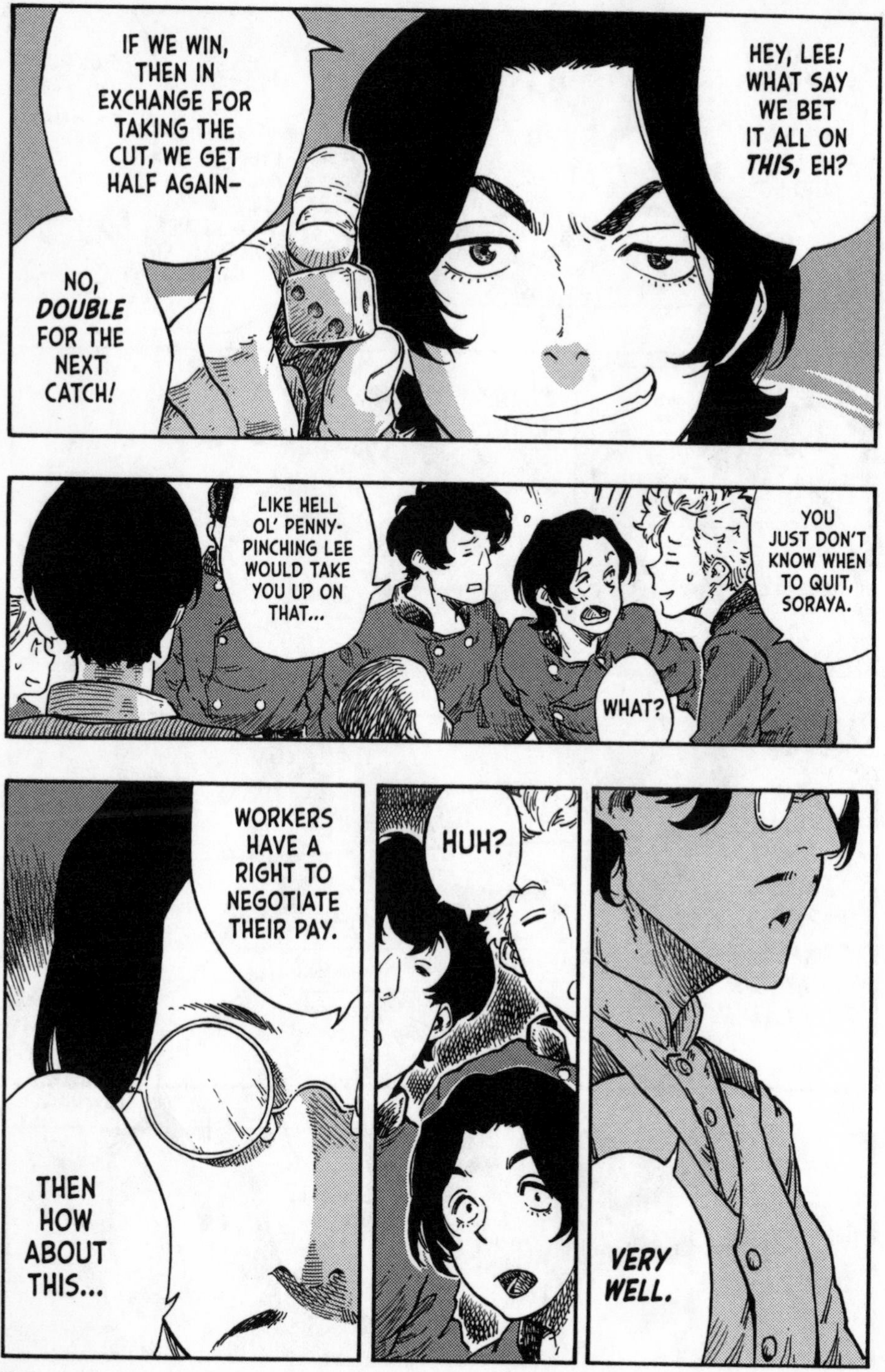
HEY, LEE! WHAT SAY WE BET IT ALL ON *THIS,* EH?
IF WE WIN, THEN IN EXCHANGE FOR TAKING THE CUT, WE GET HALF AGAIN–
NO, *DOUBLE* FOR THE NEXT CATCH!
YOU JUST DON'T KNOW WHEN TO QUIT, SORAYA.
WHAT?
LIKE HELL OL' PENNY-PINCHING LEE WOULD TAKE YOU UP ON THAT...
VERY WELL.
HUH?
WORKERS HAVE A RIGHT TO NEGOTIATE THEIR PAY.
THEN HOW ABOUT THIS...

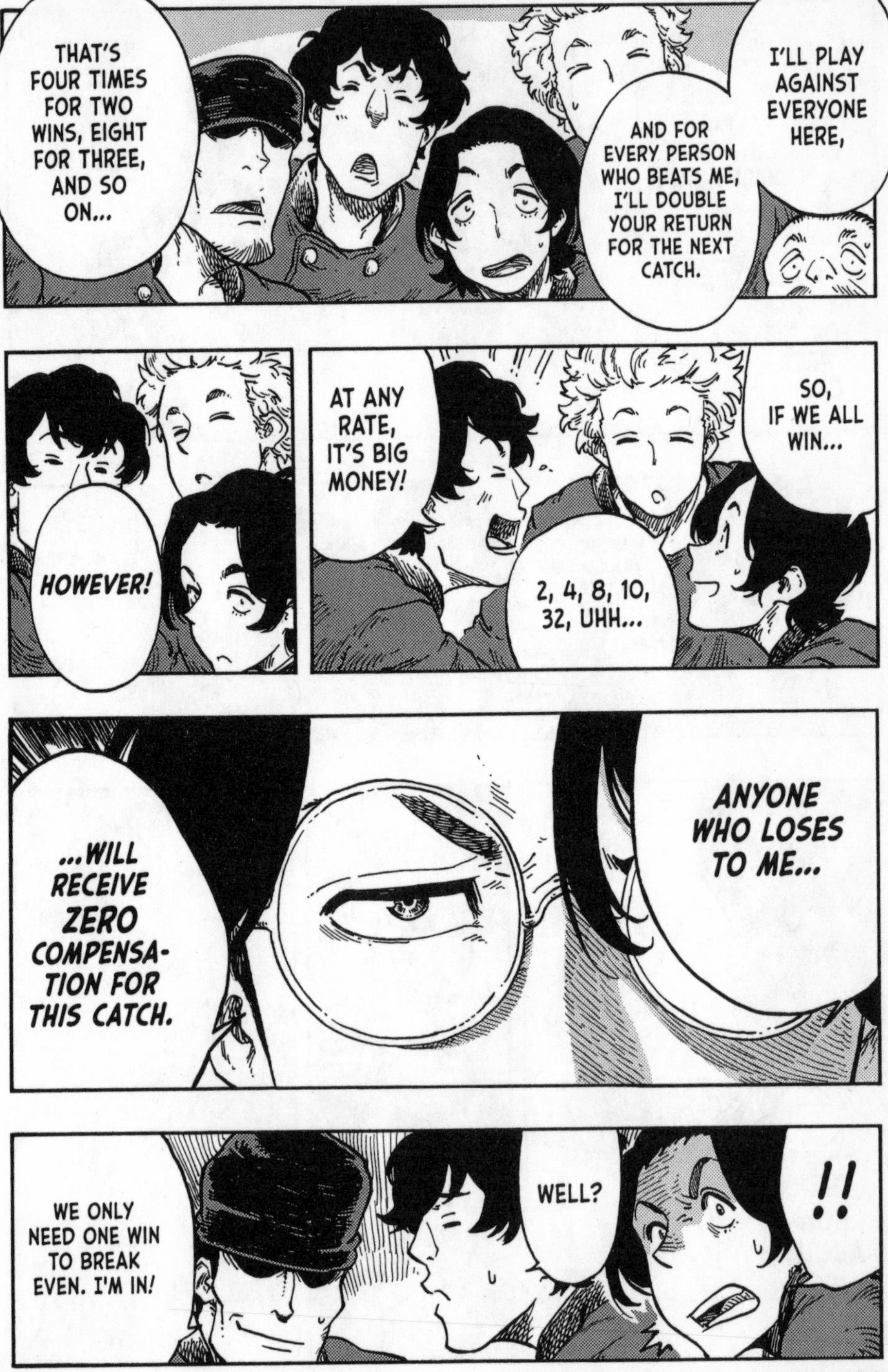

I'LL PLAY AGAINST EVERYONE HERE,
AND FOR EVERY PERSON WHO BEATS ME, I'LL DOUBLE YOUR RETURN FOR THE NEXT CATCH.
THAT'S FOUR TIMES FOR TWO WINS, EIGHT FOR THREE, AND SO ON...
SO, IF WE ALL WIN...
AT ANY RATE, IT'S BIG MONEY!
2, 4, 8, 10, 32, UHH...
HOWEVER!
ANYONE WHO LOSES TO ME...
...WILL RECEIVE ZERO COMPENSA-TION FOR THIS CATCH.
!!
WELL?
WE ONLY NEED ONE WIN TO BREAK EVEN. I'M IN!

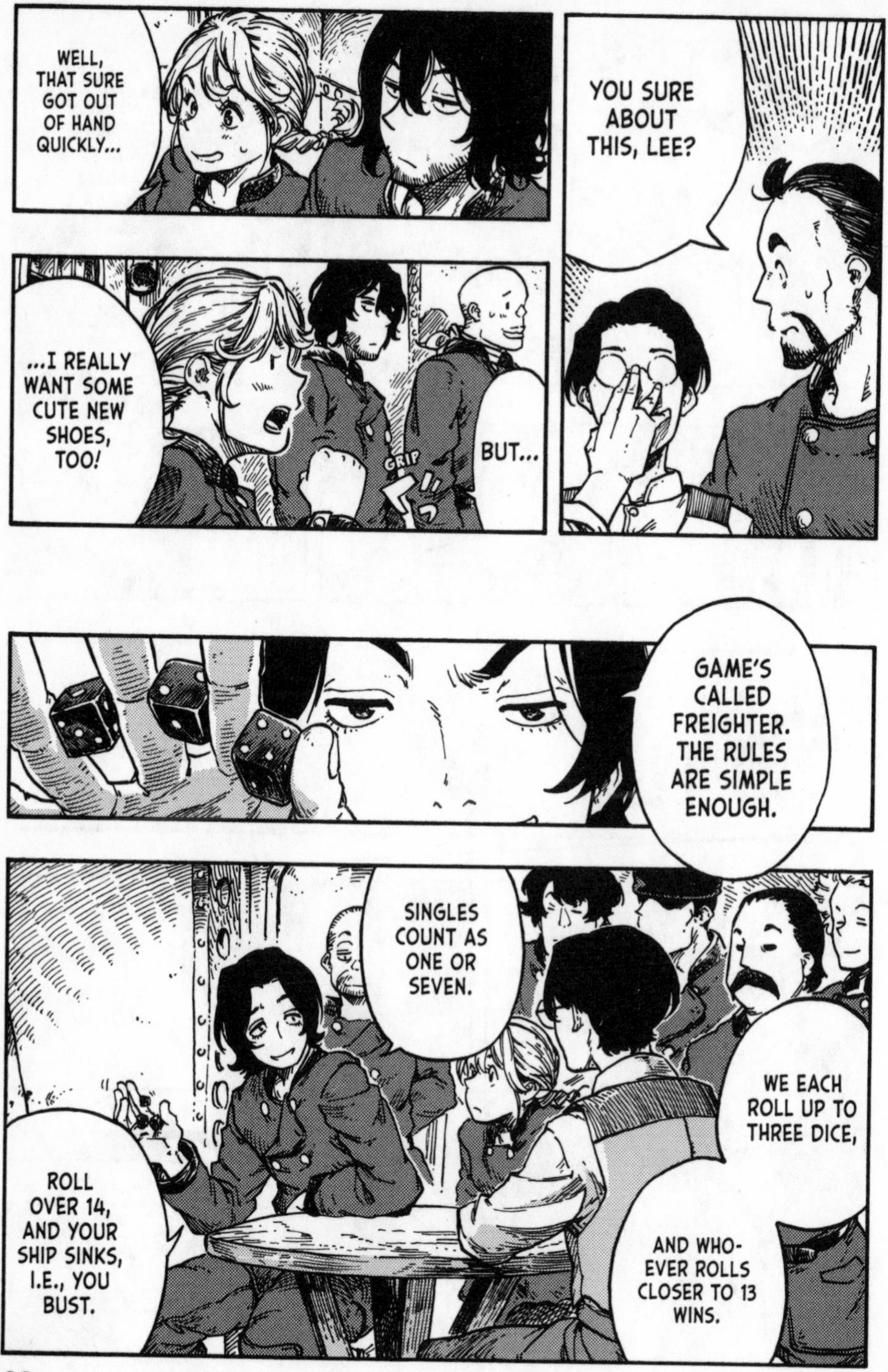
YOU SURE ABOUT THIS, LEE?
WELL, THAT SURE GOT OUT OF HAND QUICKLY...
BUT...
GRIP
...I REALLY WANT SOME CUTE NEW SHOES, TOO!
GAME'S CALLED FREIGHTER. THE RULES ARE SIMPLE ENOUGH.
SINGLES COUNT AS ONE OR SEVEN.
WE EACH ROLL UP TO THREE DICE,
AND WHO-EVER ROLLS CLOSER TO 13 WINS.
ROLL OVER 14, AND YOUR SHIP SINKS, I.E., YOU BUST.

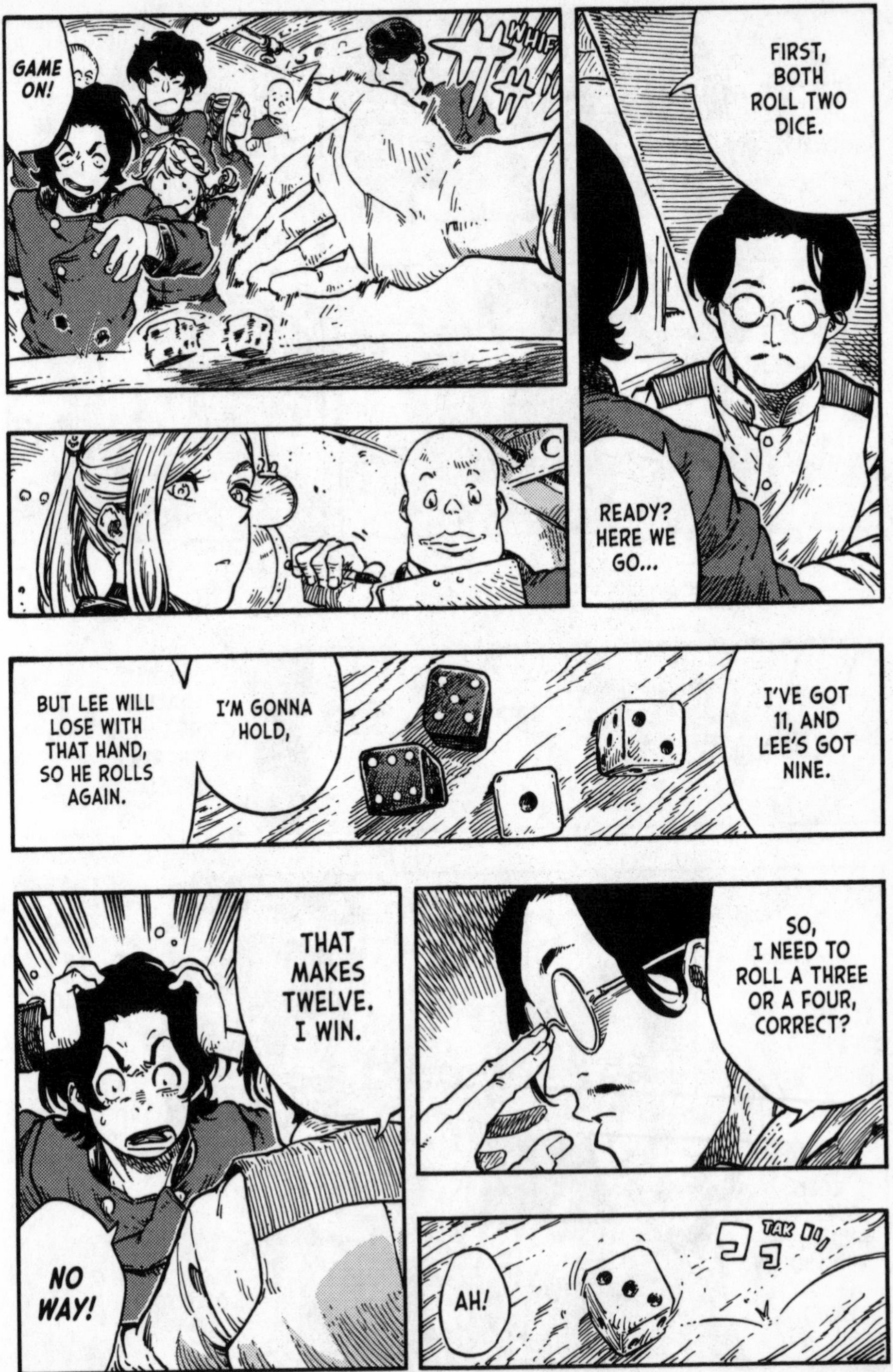
FIRST, BOTH ROLL TWO DICE.
READY? HERE WE GO...
GAME ON!
WHIF
I'VE GOT 11, AND LEE'S GOT NINE.
I'M GONNA HOLD,
BUT LEE WILL LOSE WITH THAT HAND, SO HE ROLLS AGAIN.
SO, I NEED TO ROLL A THREE OR A FOUR, CORRECT?
TAK
AH!
THAT MAKES TWELVE. I WIN.
NO WAY!

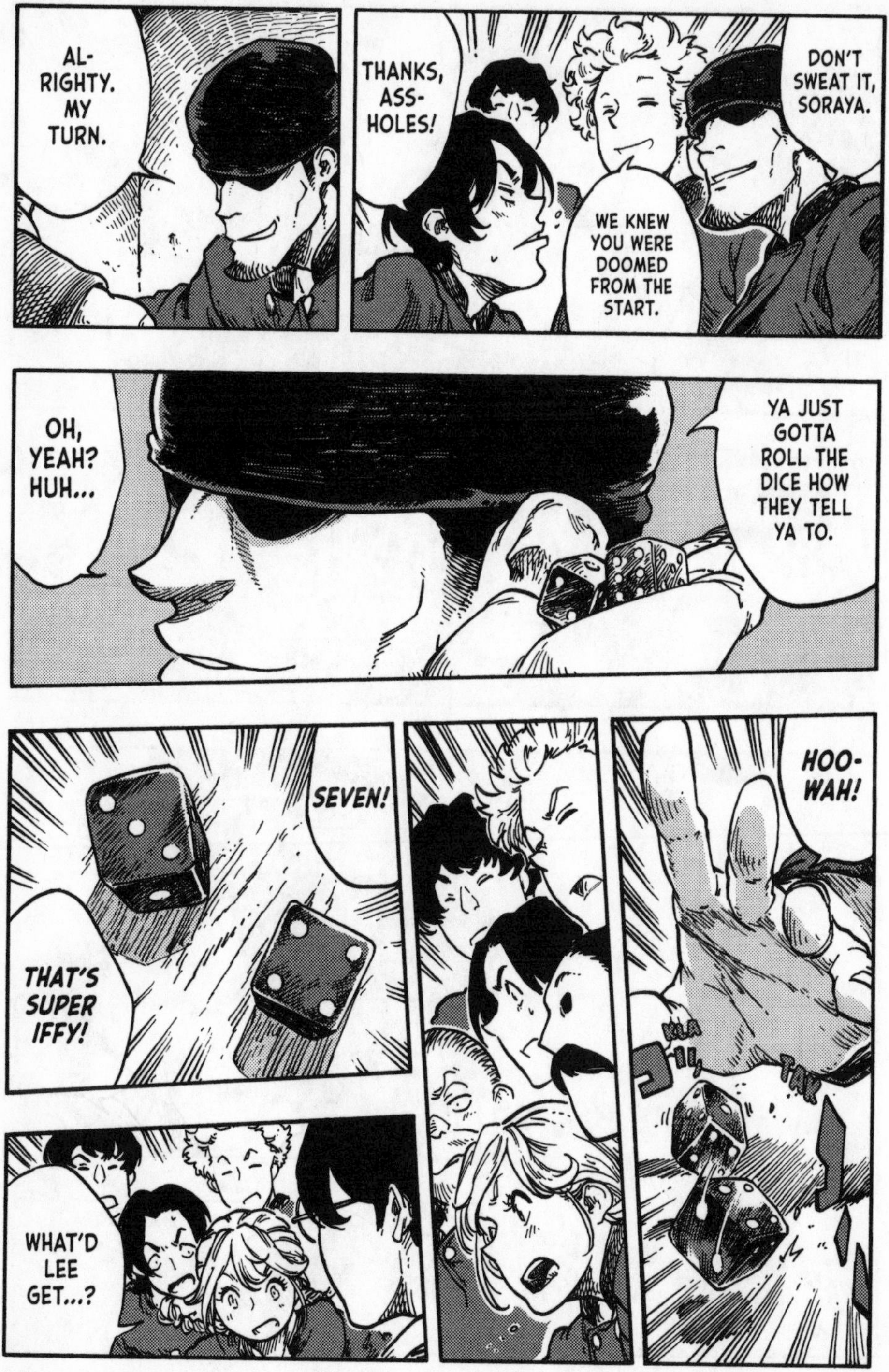
DON'T SWEAT IT, SORAYA.
WE KNEW YOU WERE DOOMED FROM THE START.
THANKS, ASS-HOLES!
AL-RIGHTY. MY TURN.
YA JUST GOTTA ROLL THE DICE HOW THEY TELL YA TO.
OH, YEAH? HUH...
HOO-WAH!
SEVEN!
THAT'S SUPER IFFY!
WHAT'D LEE GET...?

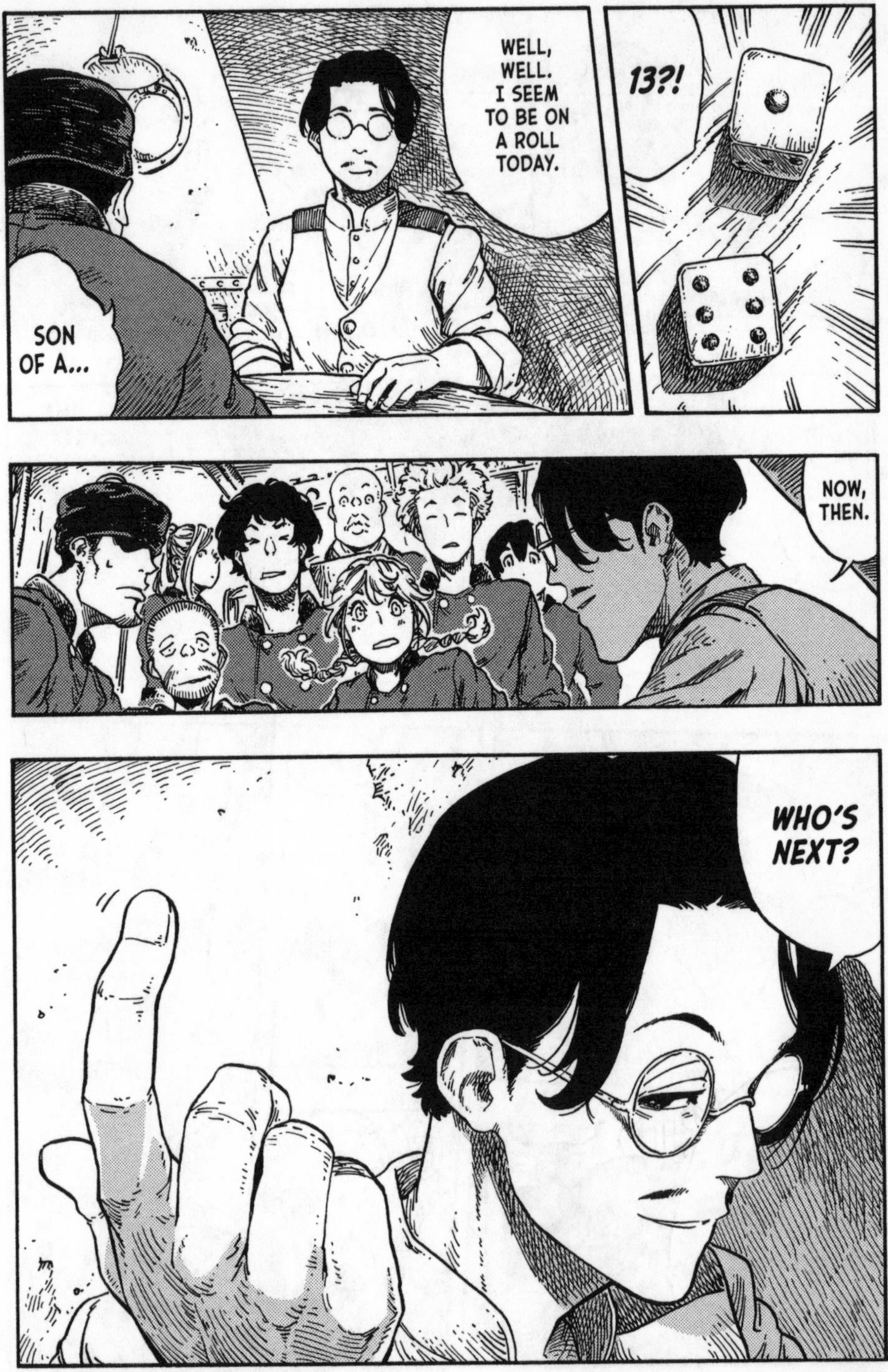
13?!
WELL, WELL. I SEEM TO BE ON A ROLL TODAY.
SON OF A...
NOW, THEN.
WHO'S NEXT?

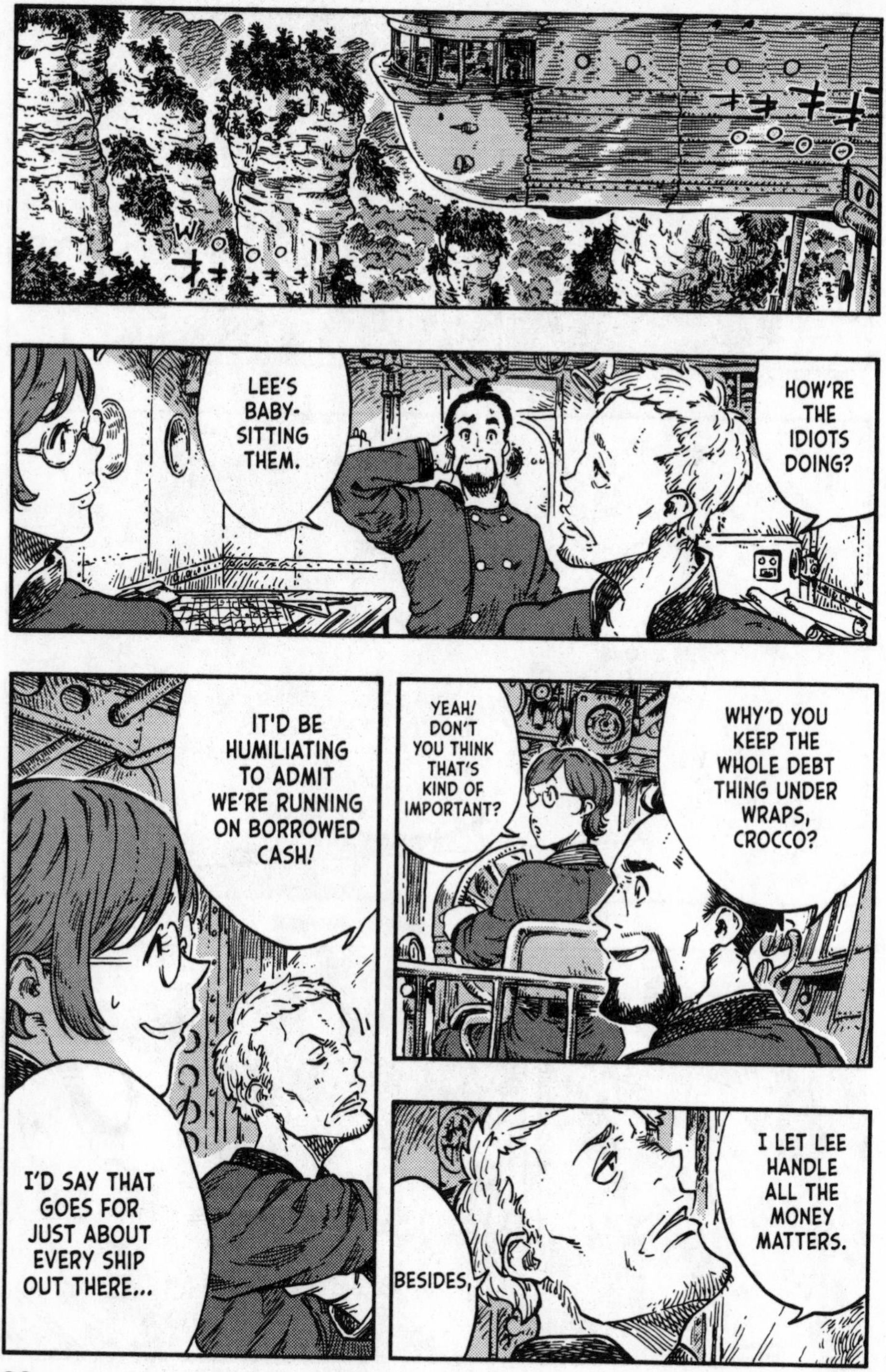
HOW'RE THE IDIOTS DOING?
LEE'S BABY-SITTING THEM.
WHY'D YOU KEEP THE WHOLE DEBT THING UNDER WRAPS, CROCCO?
YEAH! DON'T YOU THINK THAT'S KIND OF IMPORTANT?
I LET LEE HANDLE ALL THE MONEY MATTERS.
BESIDES,
IT'D BE HUMILIATING TO ADMIT WE'RE RUNNING ON BORROWED CASH!
I'D SAY THAT GOES FOR JUST ABOUT EVERY SHIP OUT THERE...

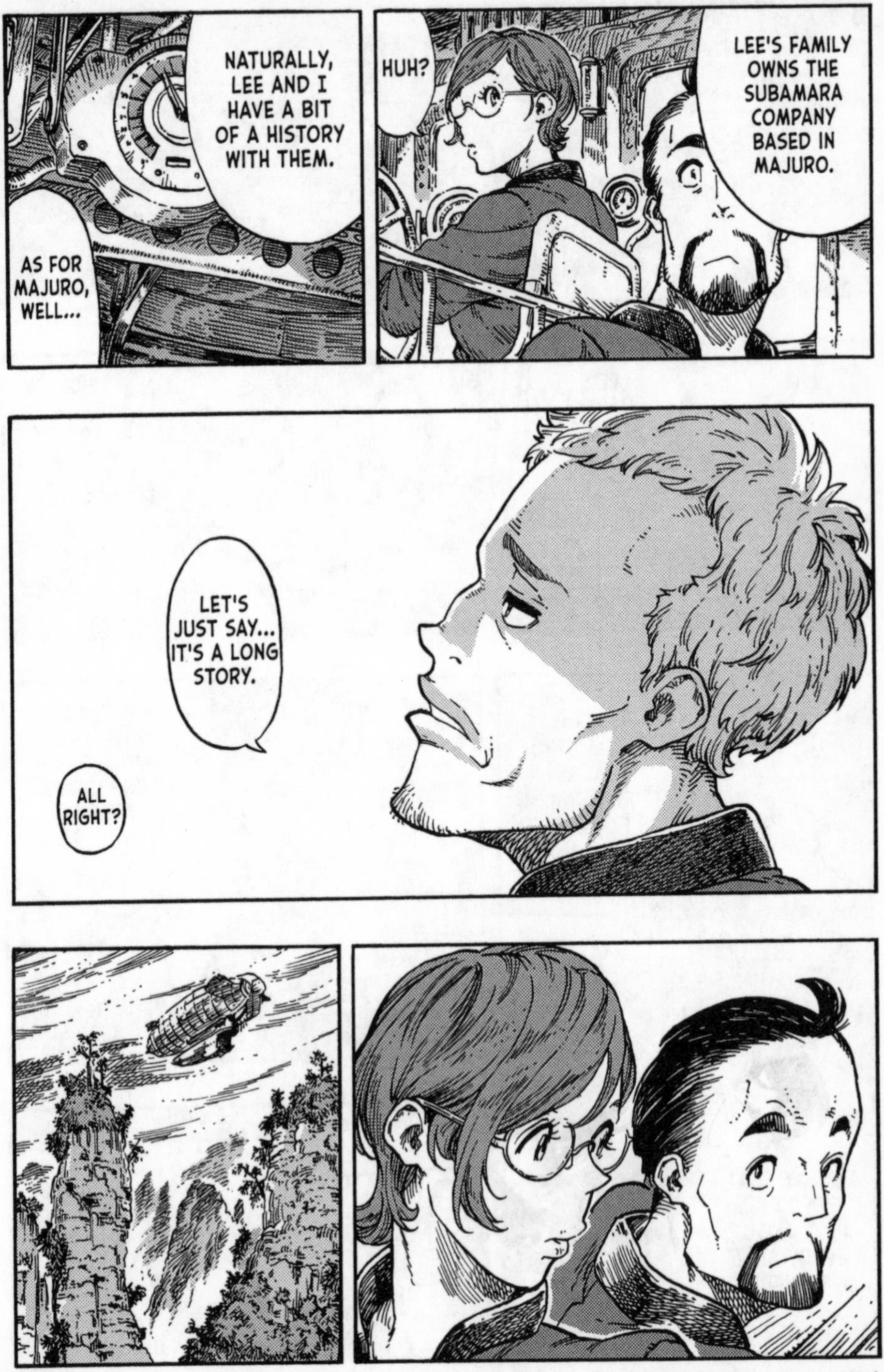
LEE'S FAMILY OWNS THE SUBAMARA COMPANY BASED IN MAJURO.
HUH?
NATURALLY, LEE AND I HAVE A BIT OF A HISTORY WITH THEM.
AS FOR MAJURO, WELL...
LET'S JUST SAY... IT'S A LONG STORY.
ALL RIGHT?

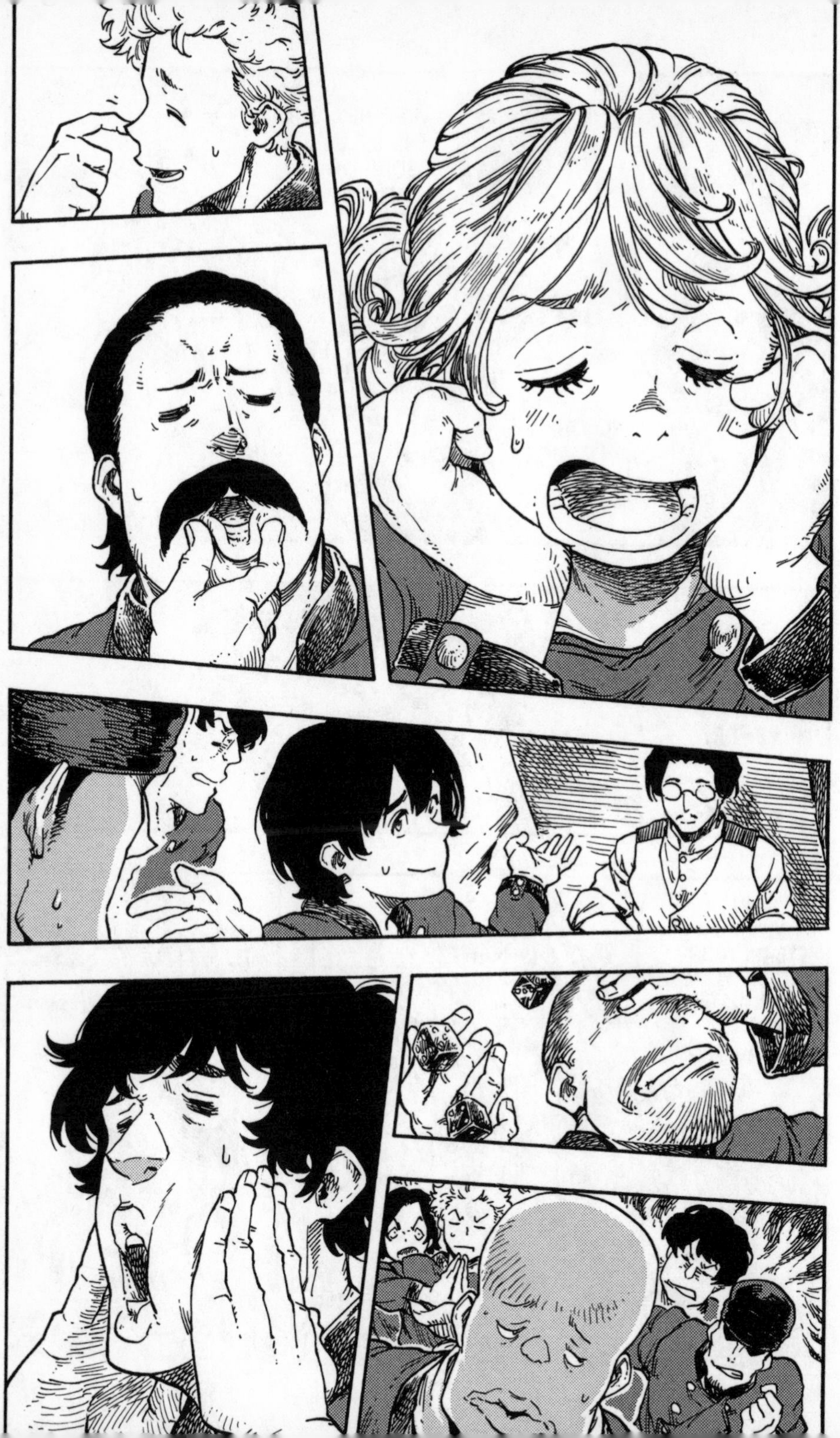

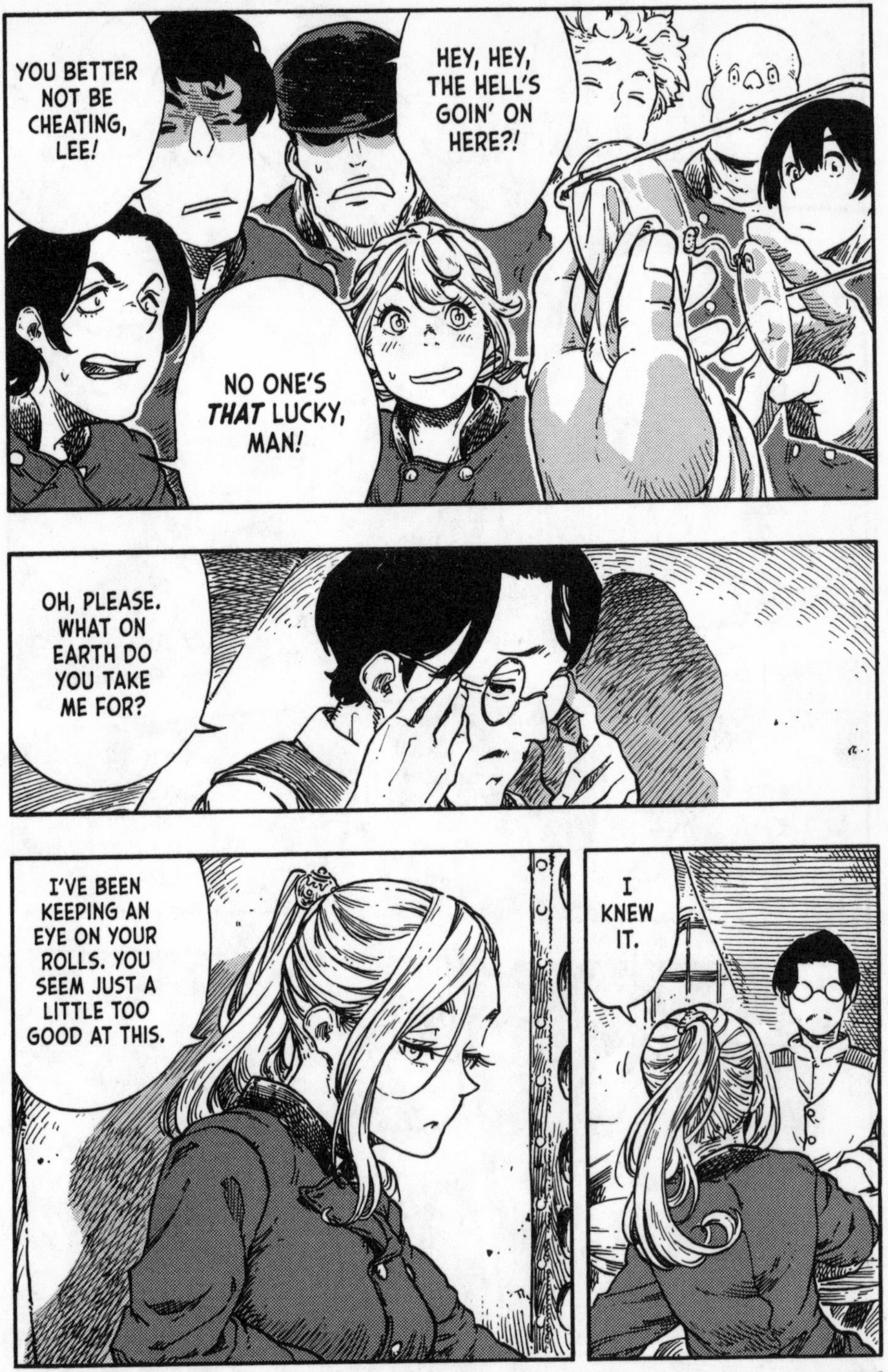
HEY, HEY, THE HELL'S GOIN' ON HERE?!
YOU BETTER NOT BE CHEATING, LEE!
NO ONE'S *THAT* LUCKY, MAN!
OH, PLEASE. WHAT ON EARTH DO YOU TAKE ME FOR?
I KNEW IT.
I'VE BEEN KEEPING AN EYE ON YOUR ROLLS. YOU SEEM JUST A LITTLE TOO GOOD AT THIS.

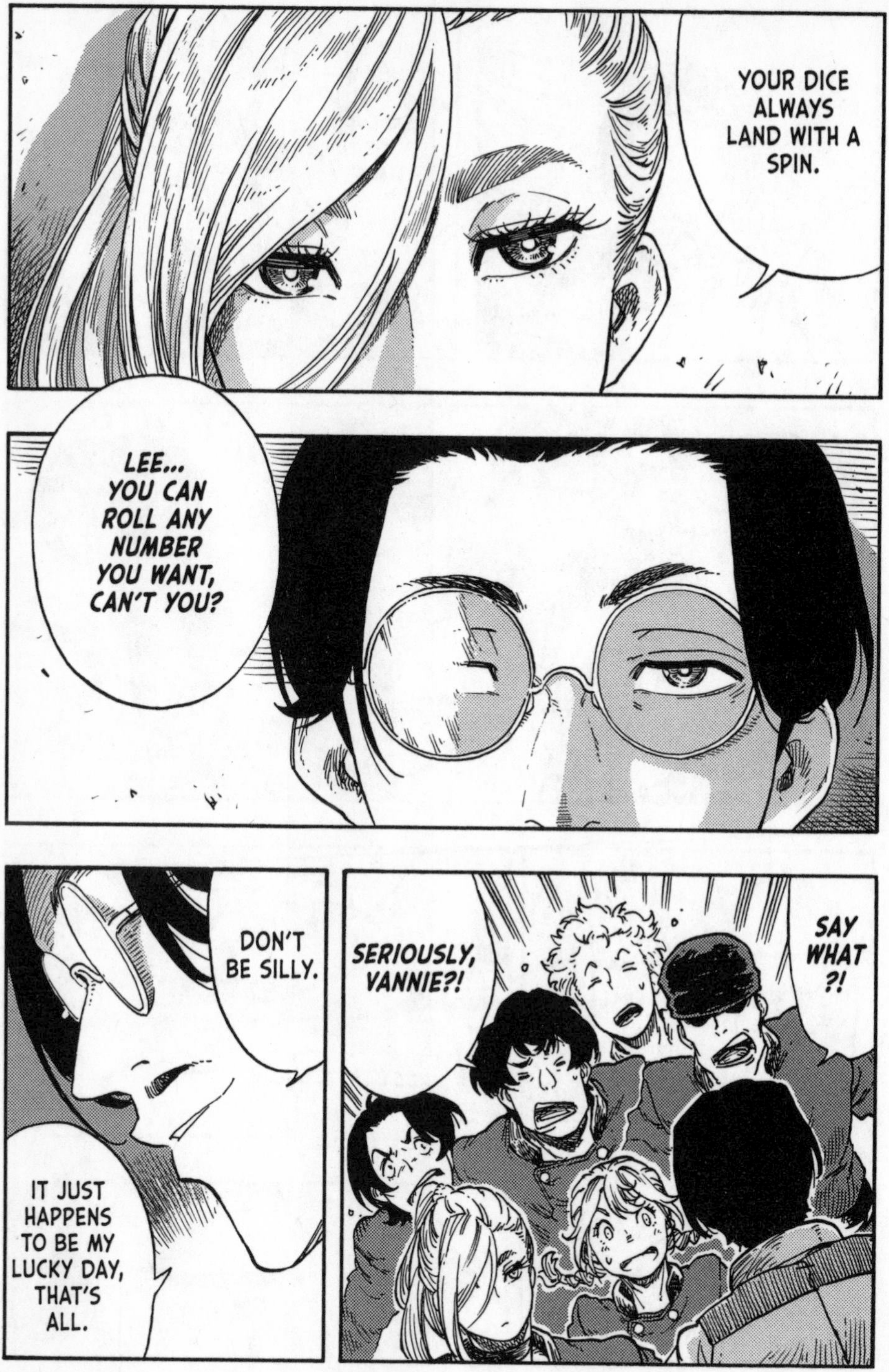
YOUR DICE ALWAYS LAND WITH A SPIN.
LEE... YOU CAN ROLL ANY NUMBER YOU WANT, CAN'T YOU?
SAY WHAT?!
SERIOUSLY, VANNIE?!
DON'T BE SILLY.
IT JUST HAPPENS TO BE MY LUCKY DAY, THAT'S ALL.

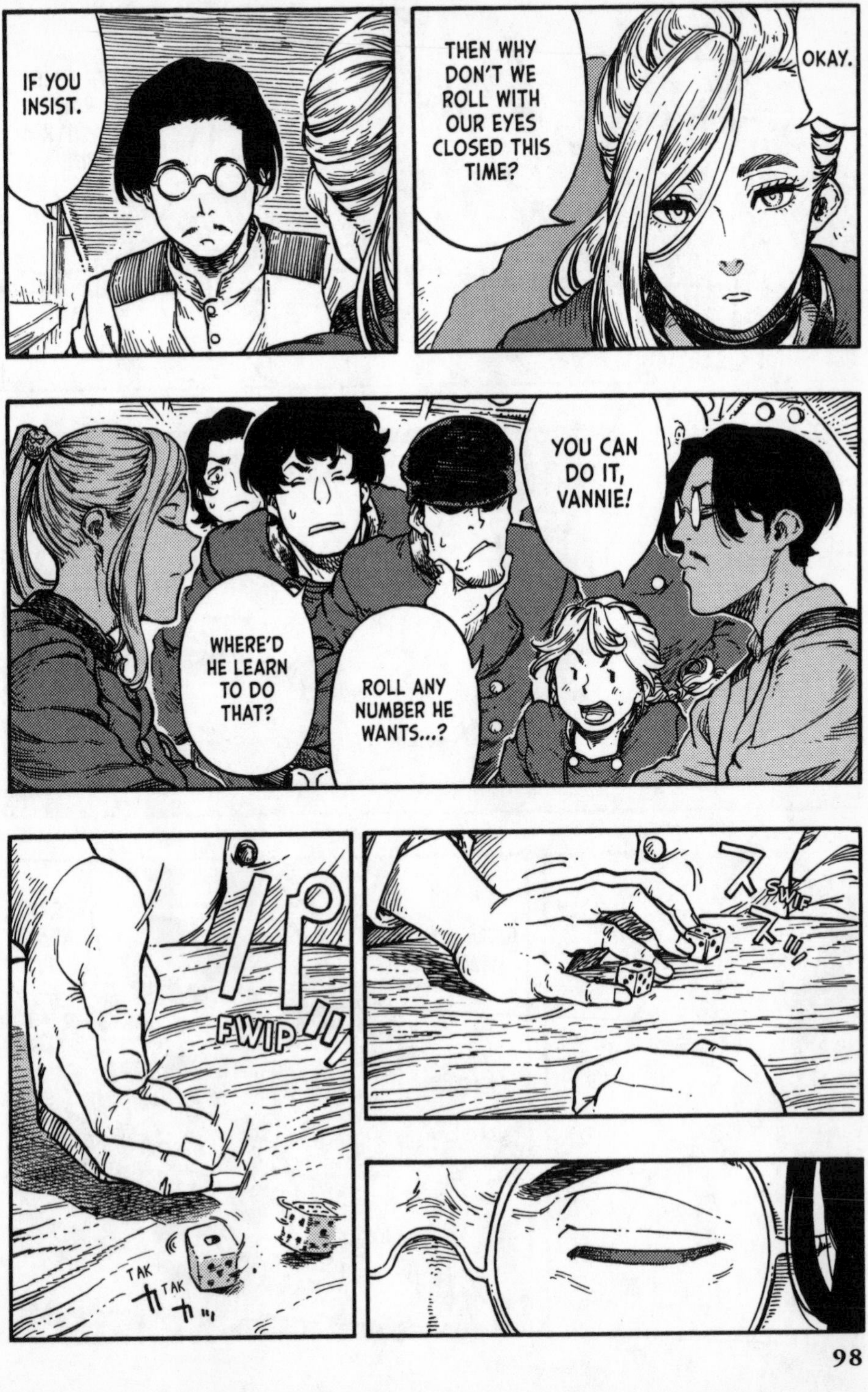
THEN WHY DON'T WE ROLL WITH OUR EYES CLOSED THIS TIME?
OKAY.
IF YOU INSIST.
YOU CAN DO IT, VANNIE!
ROLL ANY NUMBER HE WANTS...?
WHERE'D HE LEARN TO DO THAT?
SWIF
FWIP
TAK
TAK

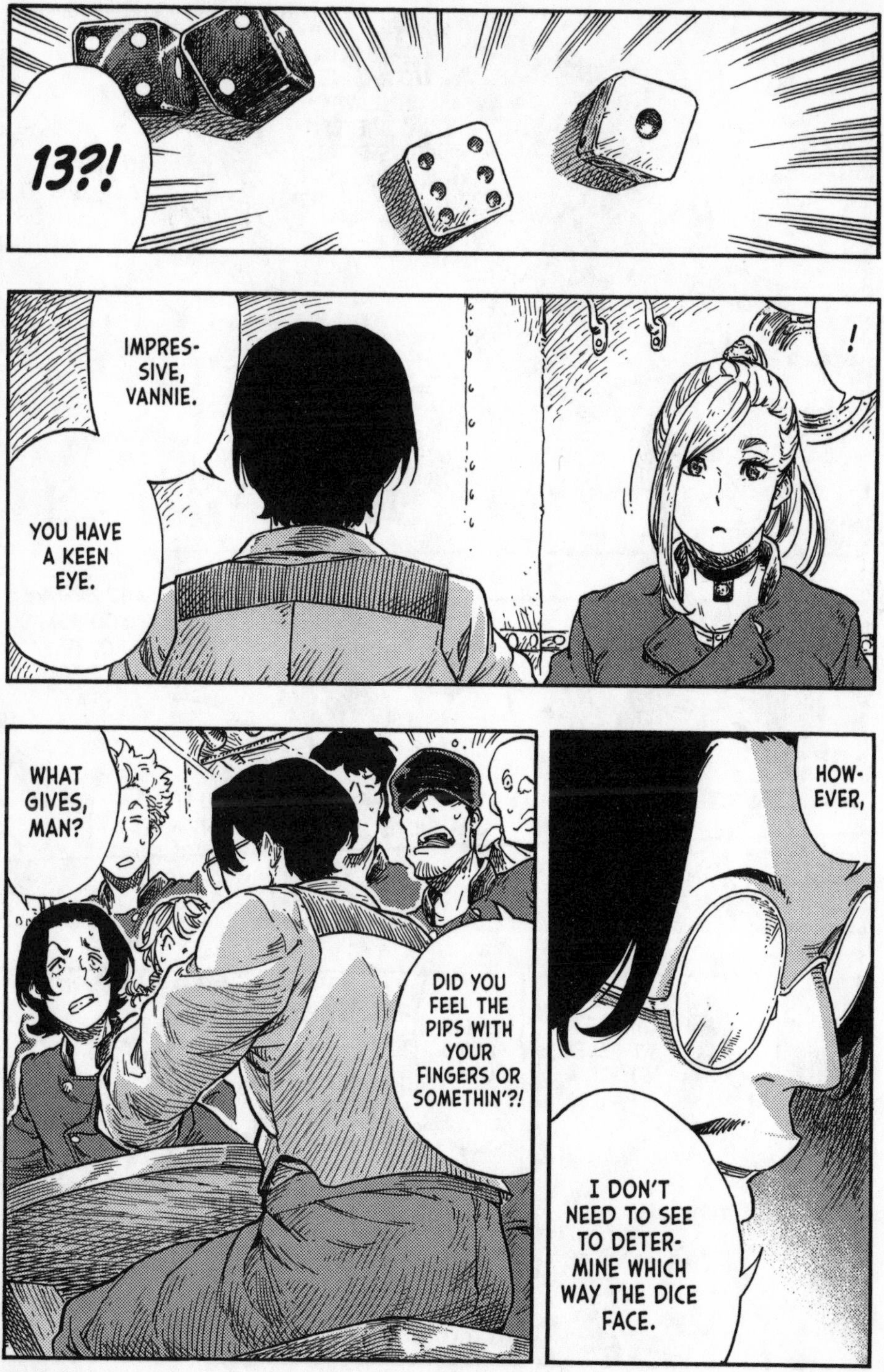
13?!
!
IMPRES-SIVE, VANNIE.
YOU HAVE A KEEN EYE.
HOW-EVER,
I DON'T NEED TO SEE TO DETER-MINE WHICH WAY THE DICE FACE.
WHAT GIVES, MAN?
DID YOU FEEL THE PIPS WITH YOUR FINGERS OR SOMETHIN'?!

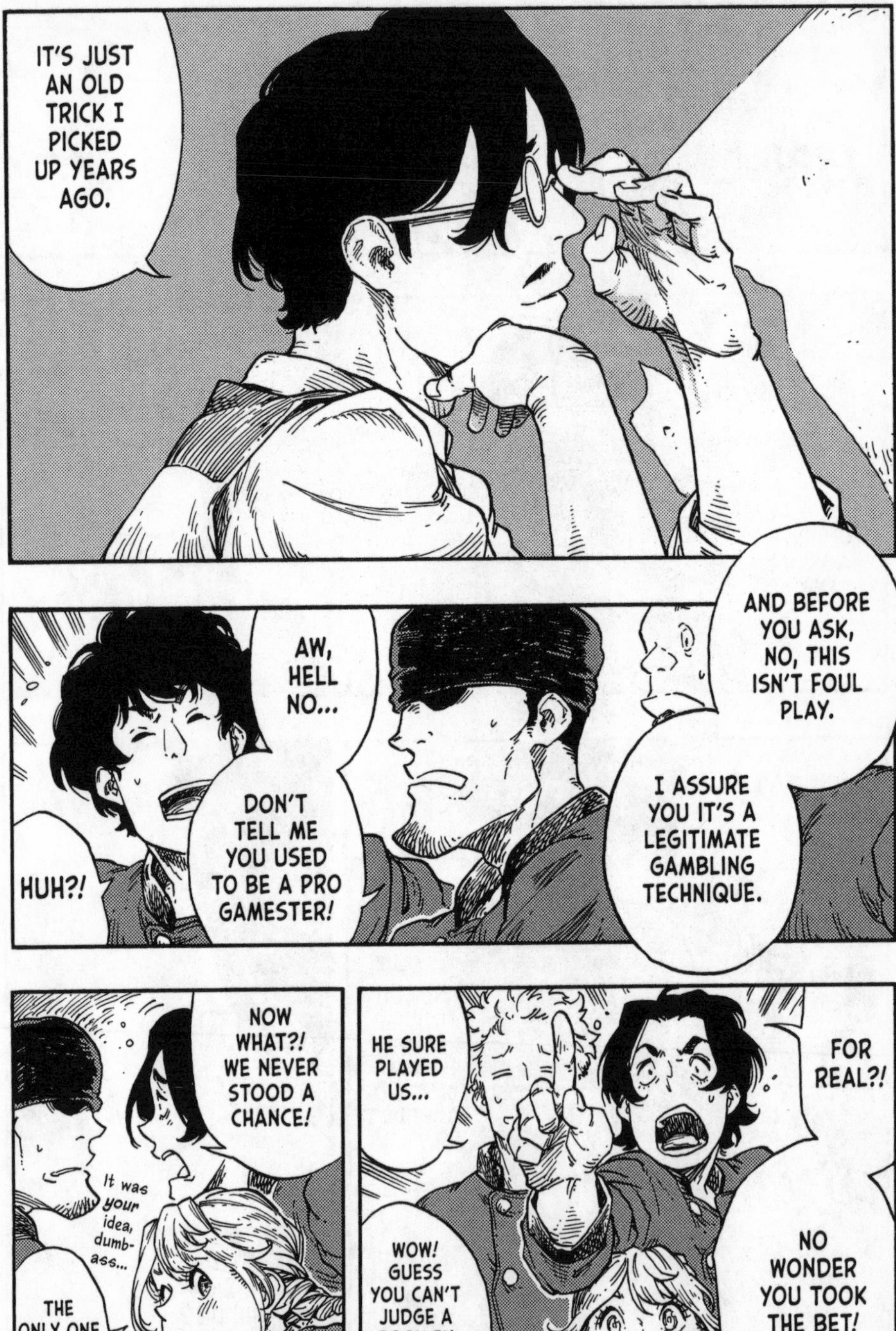
IT'S JUST AN OLD TRICK I PICKED UP YEARS AGO.
AND BEFORE YOU ASK, NO, THIS ISN'T FOUL PLAY.
I ASSURE YOU IT'S A LEGITIMATE GAMBLING TECHNIQUE.
AW, HELL NO...
DON'T TELL ME YOU USED TO BE A PRO GAMESTER!
HUH?!
FOR REAL?!
HE SURE PLAYED US...
NO WONDER YOU TOOK THE BET!
WOW! GUESS YOU CAN'T JUDGE A BOOK BY ITS COVER.
NOW WHAT?! WE NEVER STOOD A CHANCE!
It was *your* idea, dumb-ass...
THE ONLY ONE LEFT IS...

...WUH?

?

THIS IS THE FINAL MATCH.

ARE YOU READY?

PULL IT TOGETHER, MIKA! YOU'RE OUR ONLY HOPE!

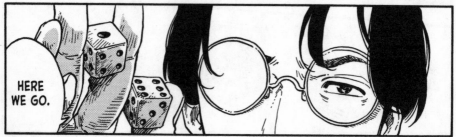

HERE WE GO.

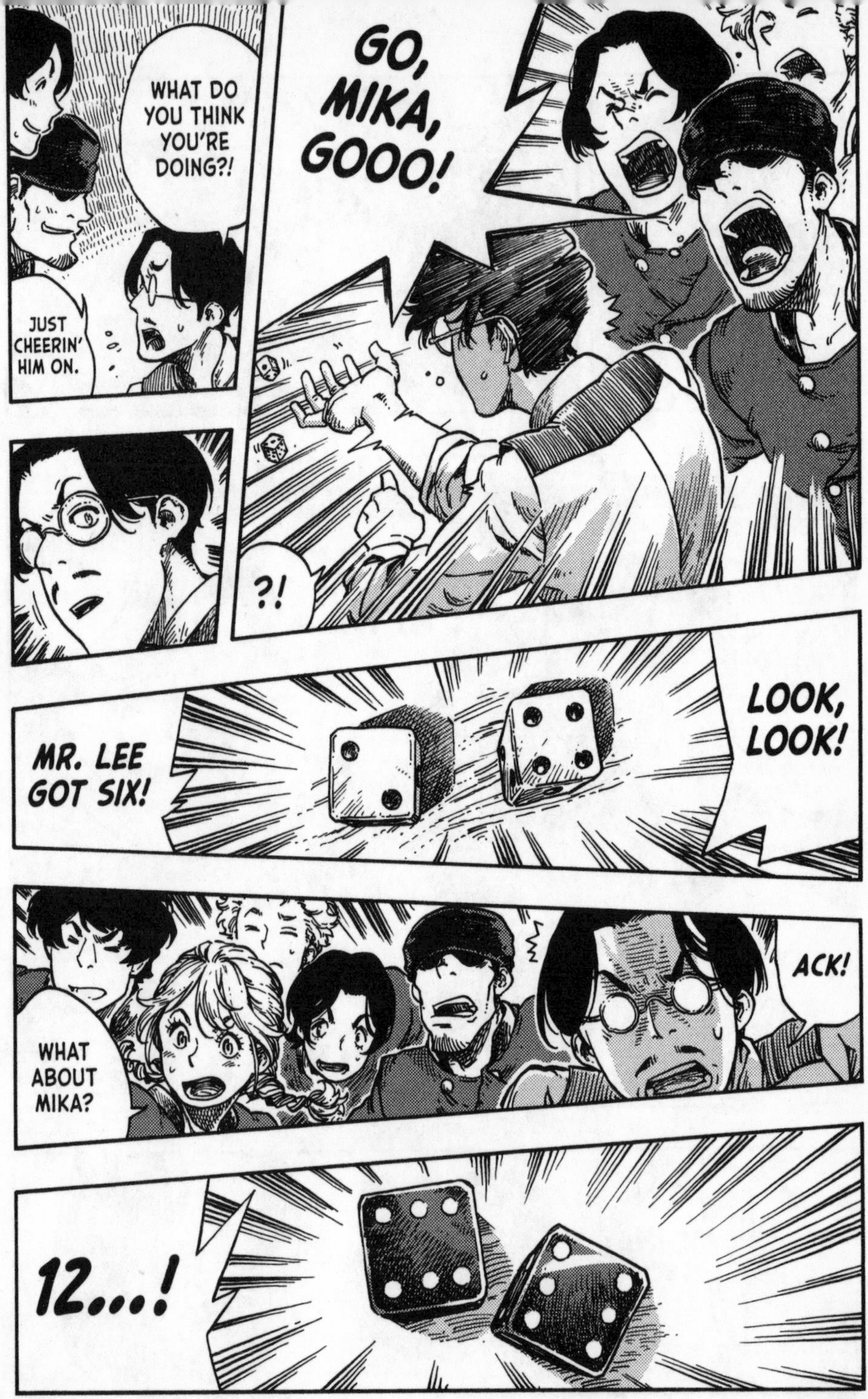

GO, MIKA, GOOO!
?!
WHAT DO YOU THINK YOU'RE DOING?!
JUST CHEERIN' HIM ON.
LOOK, LOOK!
MR. LEE GOT SIX!
ACK!
WHAT ABOUT MIKA?
12...!

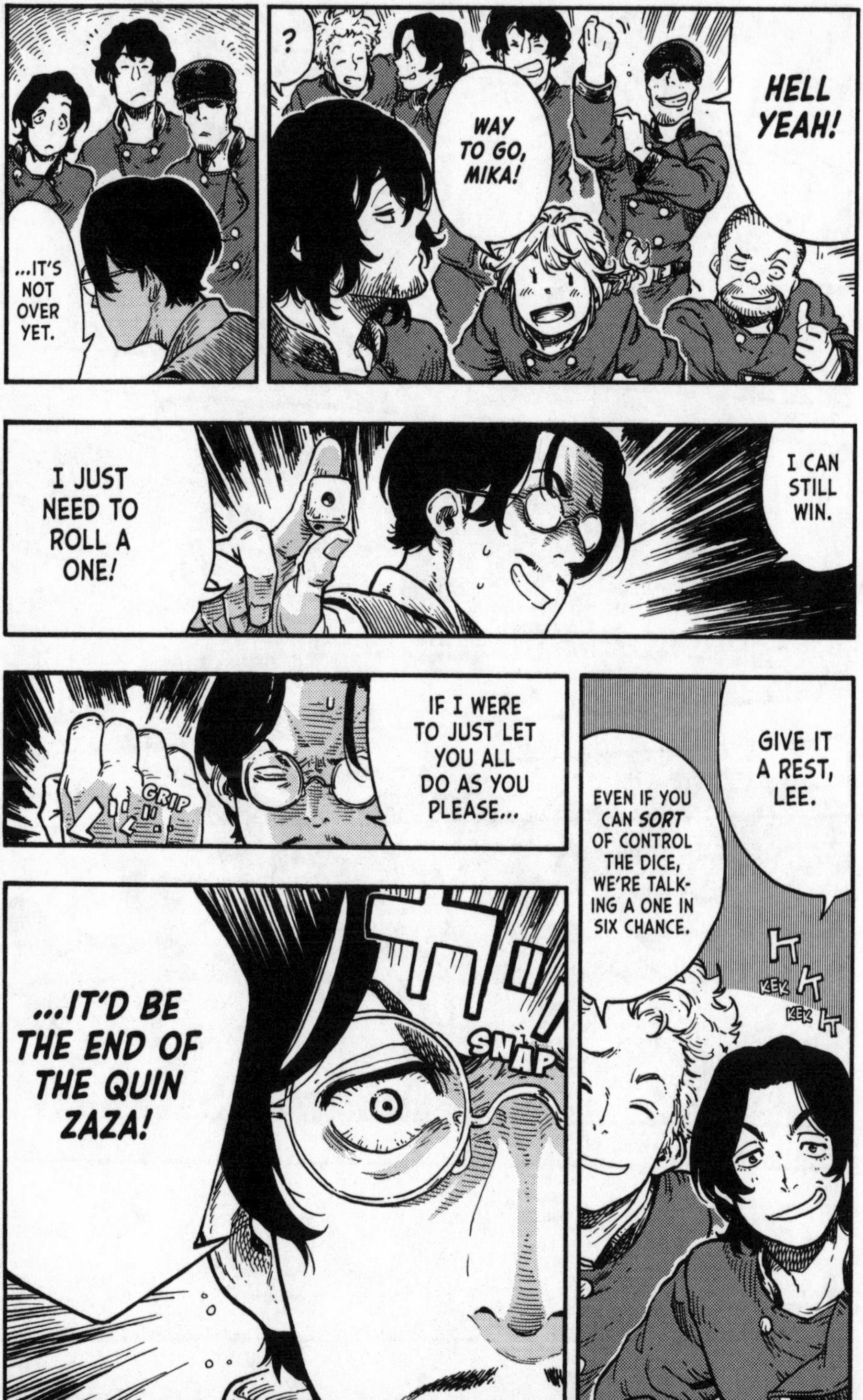
HELL YEAH!
WAY TO GO, MIKA!
?
...IT'S NOT OVER YET.
I CAN STILL WIN.
I JUST NEED TO ROLL A ONE!
GIVE IT A REST, LEE.
EVEN IF YOU CAN SORT OF CONTROL THE DICE, WE'RE TALKING A ONE IN SIX CHANCE.
KEK KEK
IF I WERE TO JUST LET YOU ALL DO AS YOU PLEASE...
GRIP
SNAP
...IT'D BE THE END OF THE QUIN ZAZA!

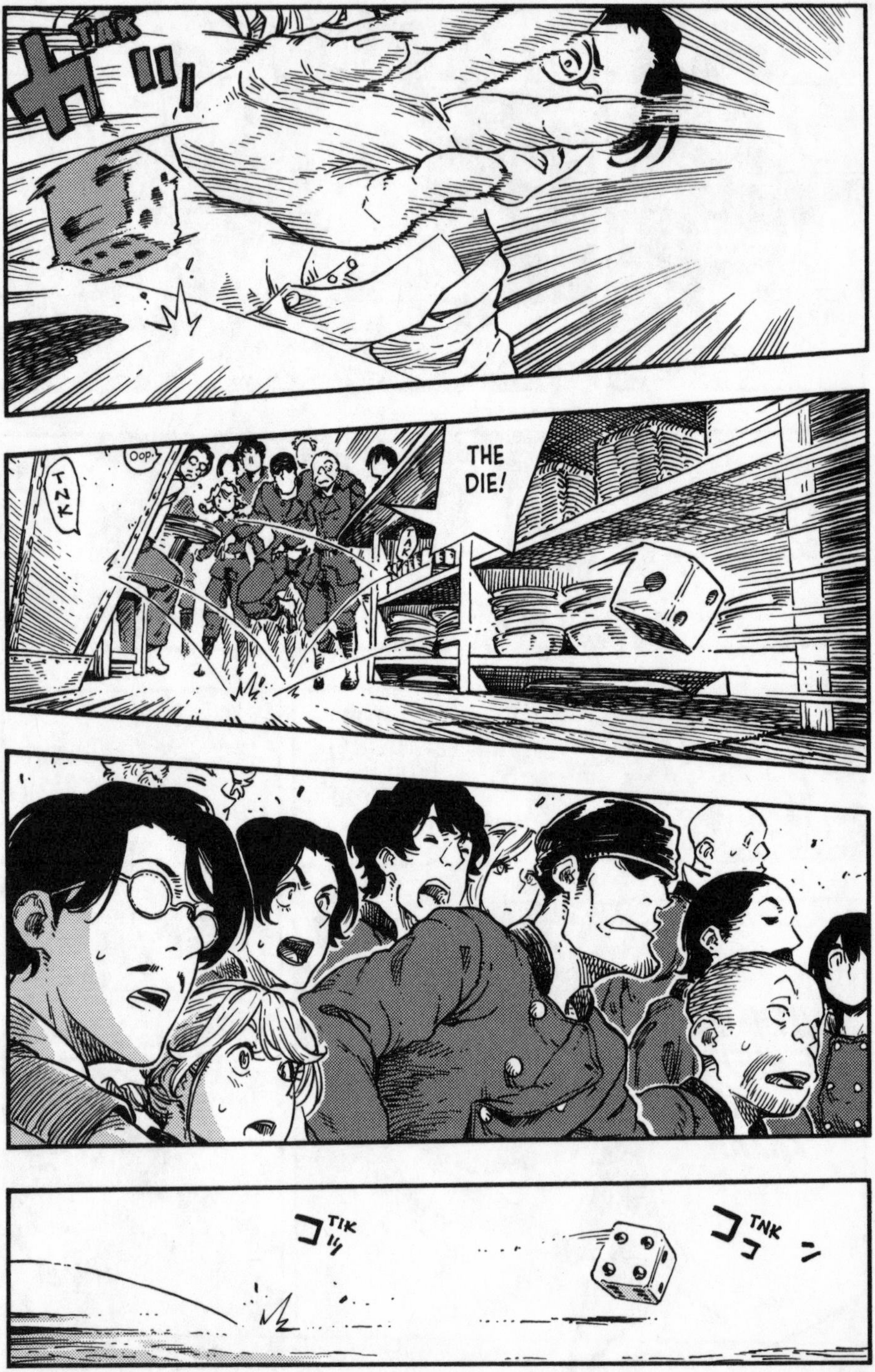
TAK
THE DIE!
Oop.
TNK
TIK
TNK

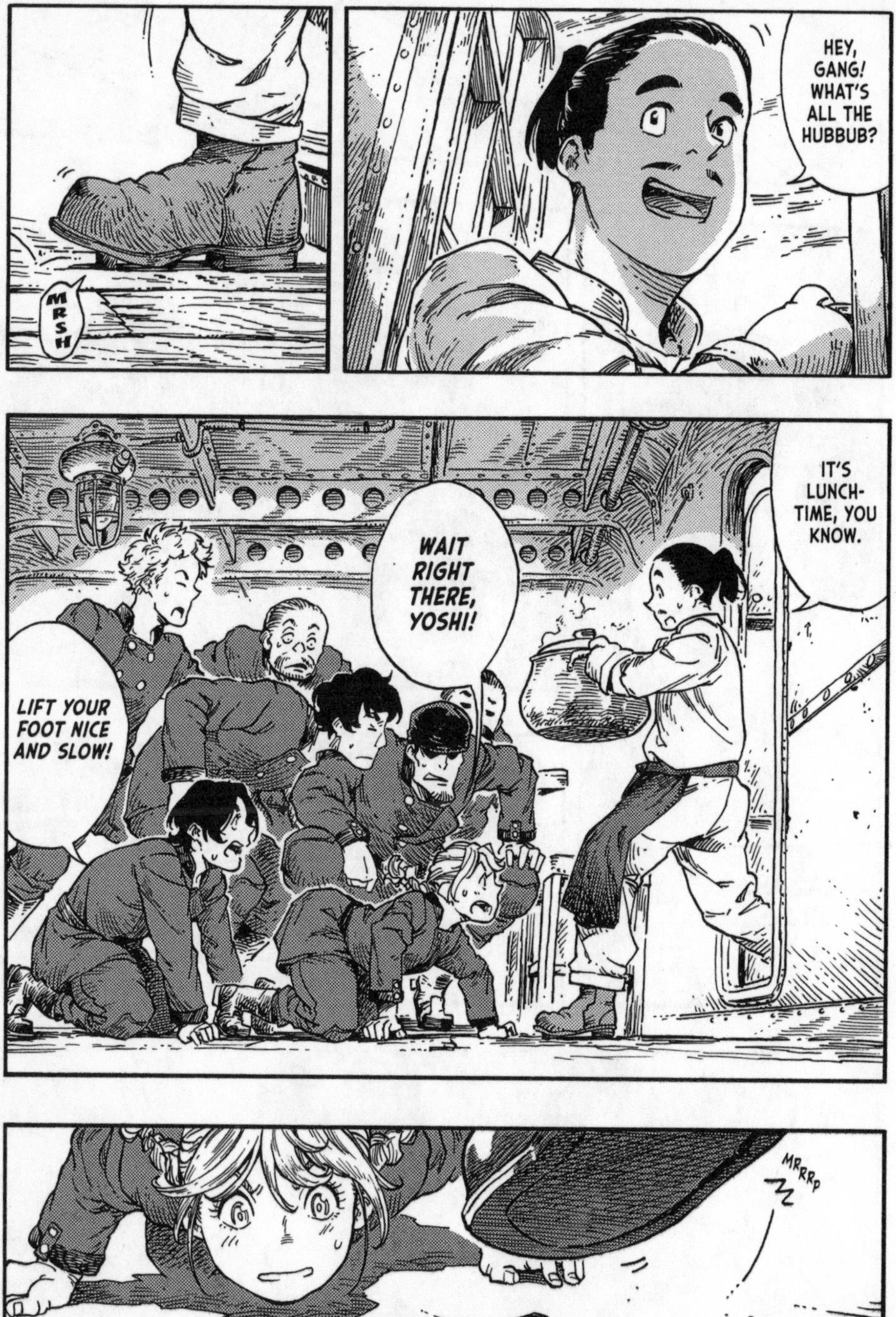
HEY, GANG! WHAT'S ALL THE HUBBUB?
MRSH
IT'S LUNCH-TIME, YOU KNOW.
WAIT RIGHT THERE, YOSHI!
LIFT YOUR FOOT NICE AND SLOW!
MRRRP

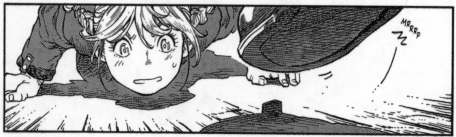

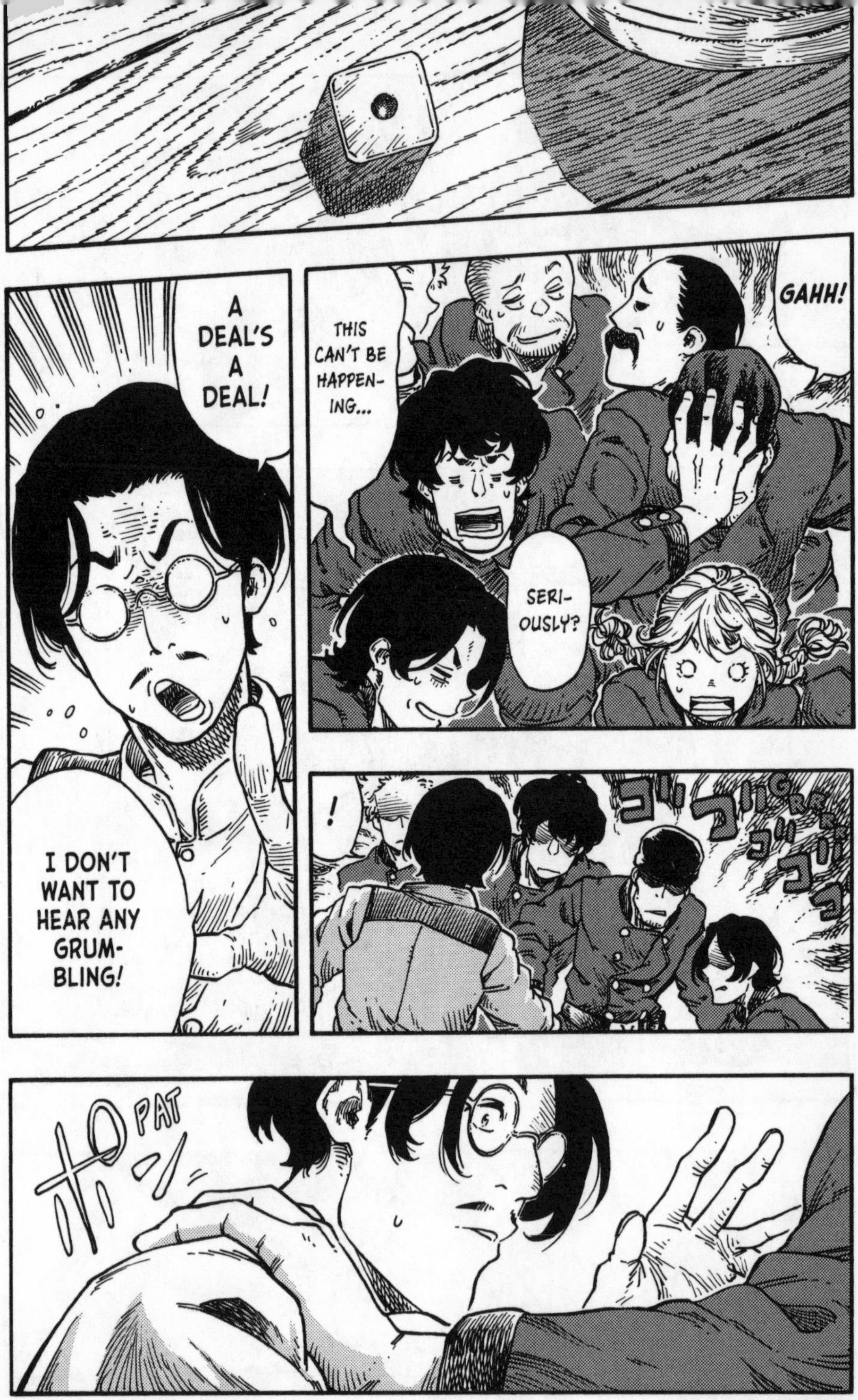
GAHH!
THIS CAN'T BE HAPPEN-ING...
SERI-OUSLY?
!
A DEAL'S A DEAL!
I DON'T WANT TO HEAR ANY GRUM-BLING!
PAT

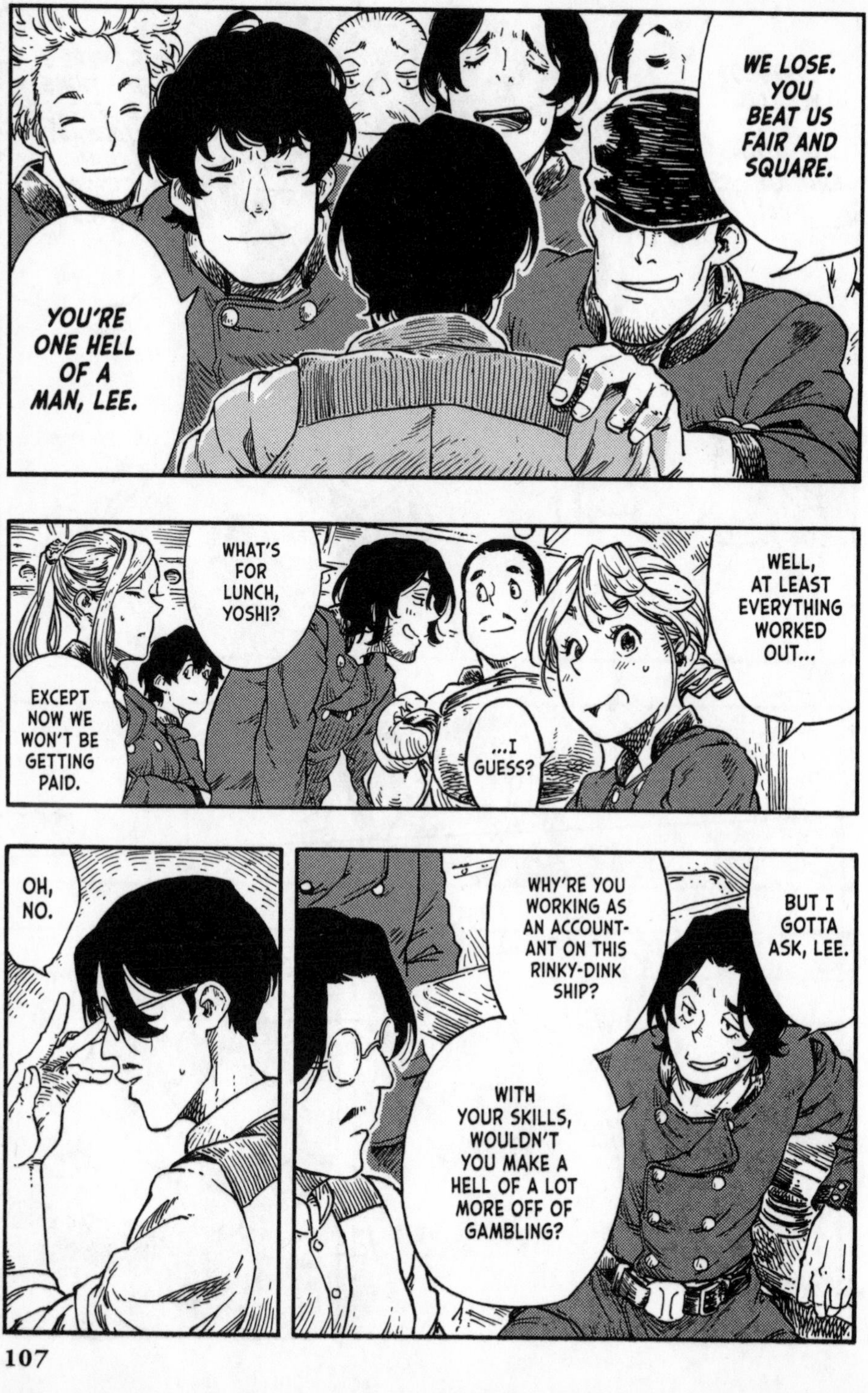
WE LOSE. YOU BEAT US FAIR AND SQUARE.
YOU'RE ONE HELL OF A MAN, LEE.
WELL, AT LEAST EVERYTHING WORKED OUT...
...I GUESS?
WHAT'S FOR LUNCH, YOSHI?
EXCEPT NOW WE WON'T BE GETTING PAID.
BUT I GOTTA ASK, LEE.
WHY'RE YOU WORKING AS AN ACCOUNT-ANT ON THIS RINKY-DINK SHIP?
WITH YOUR SKILLS, WOULDN'T YOU MAKE A HELL OF A LOT MORE OFF OF GAMBLING?
OH, NO.

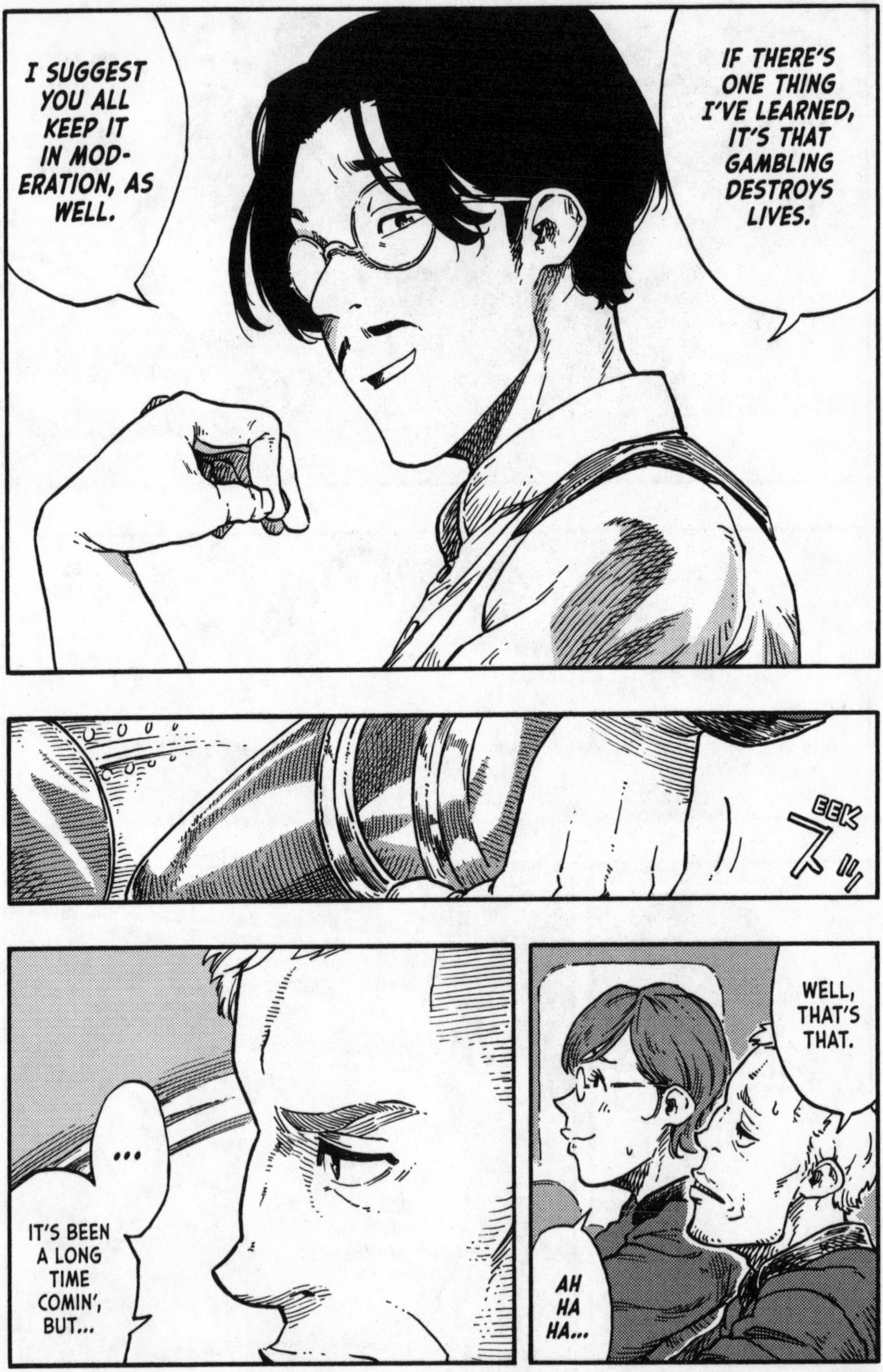
IF THERE'S ONE THING I'VE LEARNED, IT'S THAT GAMBLING DESTROYS LIVES.
I SUGGEST YOU ALL KEEP IT IN MOD-ERATION, AS WELL.
EEK
スッ
WELL, THAT'S THAT.
AH HA HA...
...
IT'S BEEN A LONG TIME COMIN', BUT...

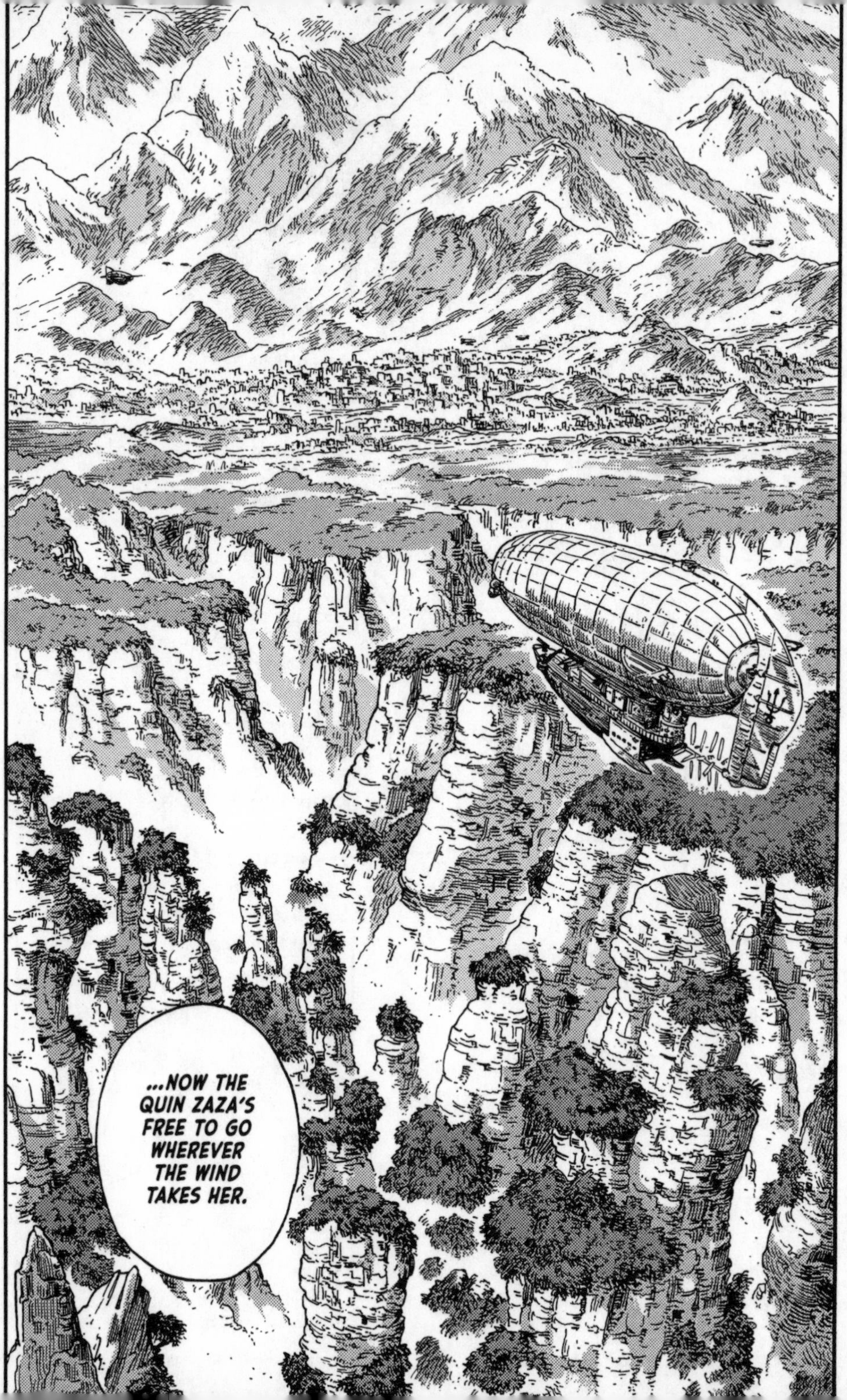
...NOW THE QUIN ZAZA'S FREE TO GO WHEREVER THE WIND TAKES HER.

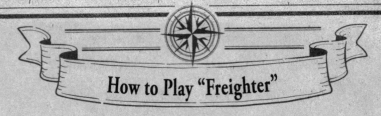

How to Play "Freighter"

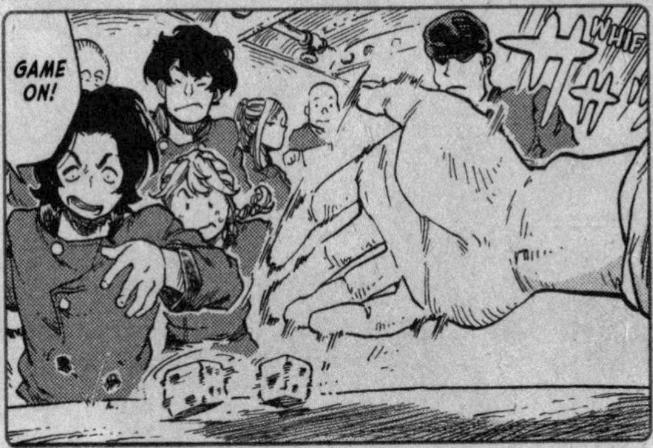
GAME ON!
WHIF

A game which uses three dice that represent freight ships. The more wares that can be moved at once, the larger the profit. However, get too greedy and your ships might sink under the weight of all that booty!

Game Progression

01 One player makes a bet which participating players must match.

02 After a rolling order has been decided, players roll the first two of three dice, one at a time. Players who roll 13 (Full Load) at this point automatically win the round.

03 Once everyone has rolled, players may choose whether or not to roll a third die and must announce so to the table. Players who do not speak up forfeit their right to roll.

04 Whoever rolls closest to 13 is declared the winner.

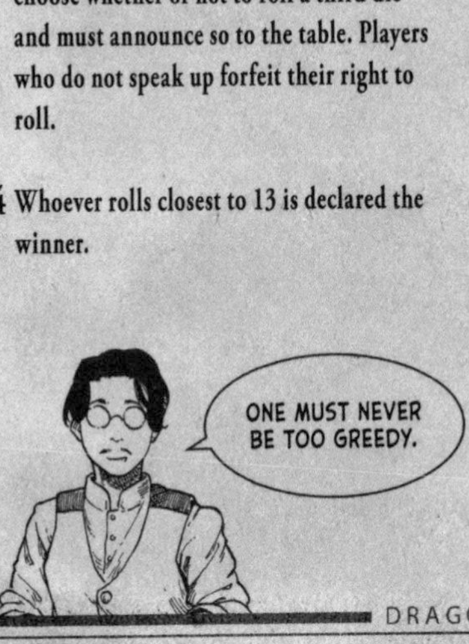
ONE MUST NEVER BE TOO GREEDY.

What You'll Need

✦ Dice (3 per player)

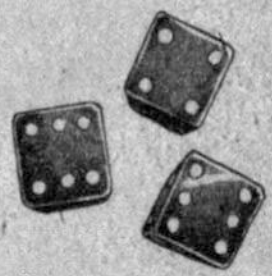

Rules

✦ A maximum of three dice can be thrown. Whoever rolls closest to 13 total (Full Load), wins.

✦ Single pips count as both 1 and 7.

✦ Rolls over 14 result in a bust (Sink).

✦ In the event of a tie or if all players sink, the round ends in a draw.

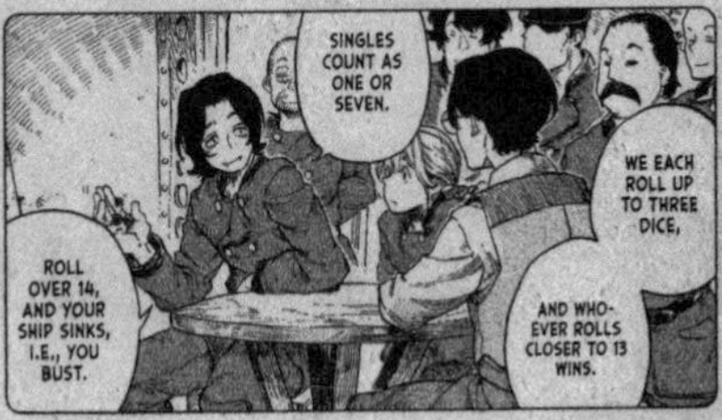
WE EACH ROLL UP TO THREE DICE,
AND WHO-EVER ROLLS CLOSER TO 13 WINS.
SINGLES COUNT AS ONE OR SEVEN.
ROLL OVER 14, AND YOUR SHIP SINKS, I.E., YOU BUST.

Payout

✦ The winner takes the pot.

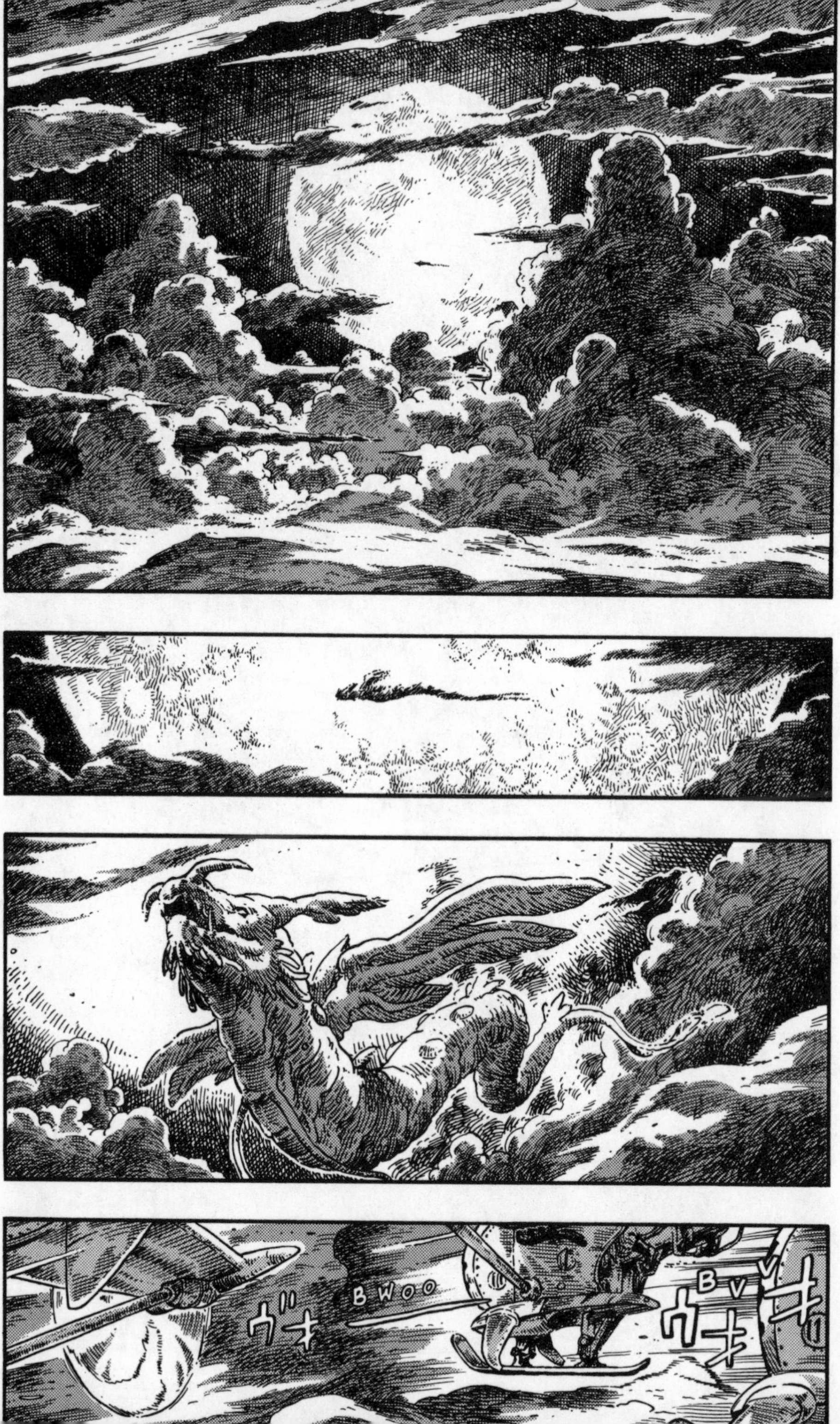
ウォオ
BVV
ヴォ
BWOO

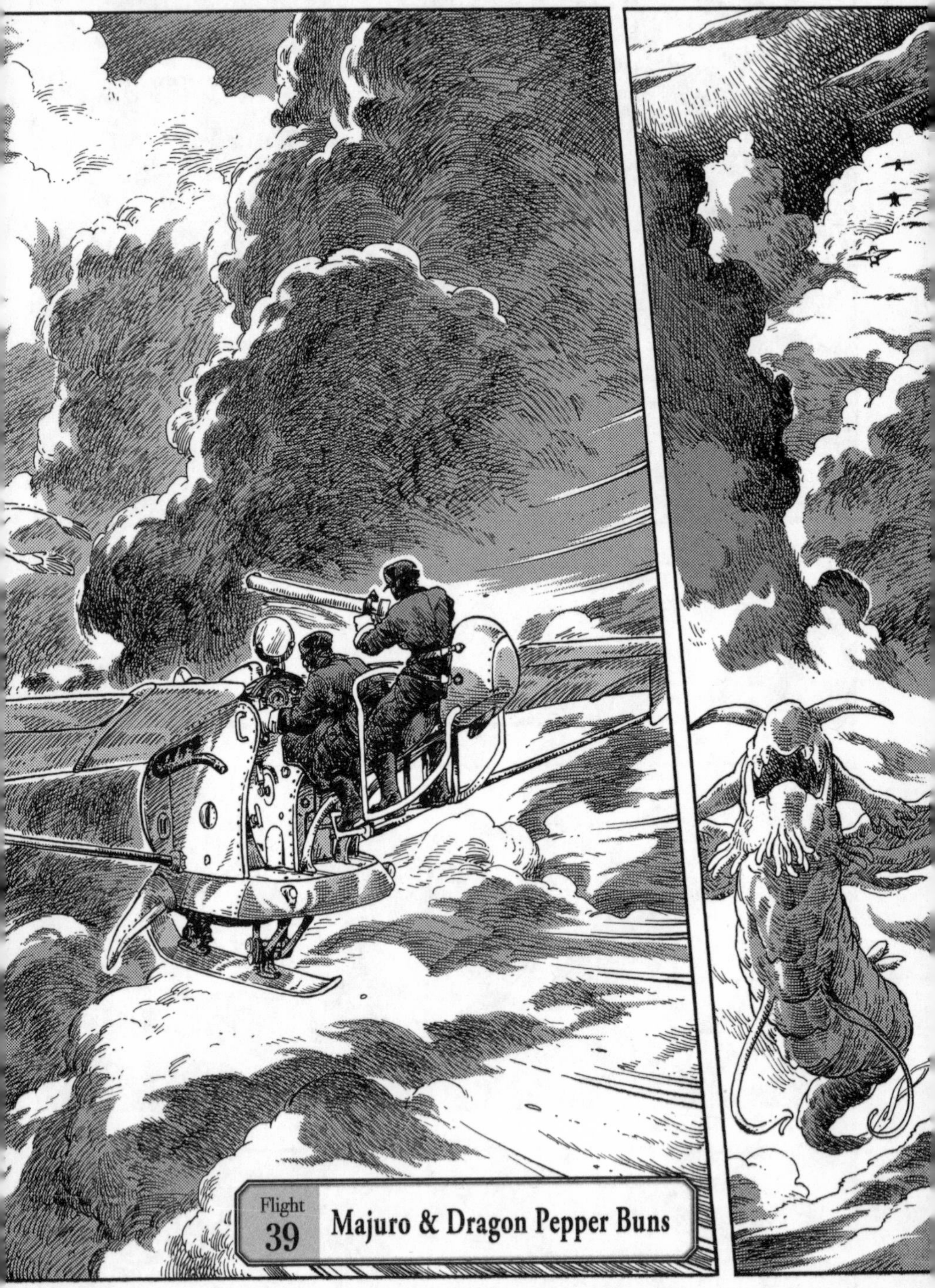
Flight 39
Majuro & Dragon Pepper Buns

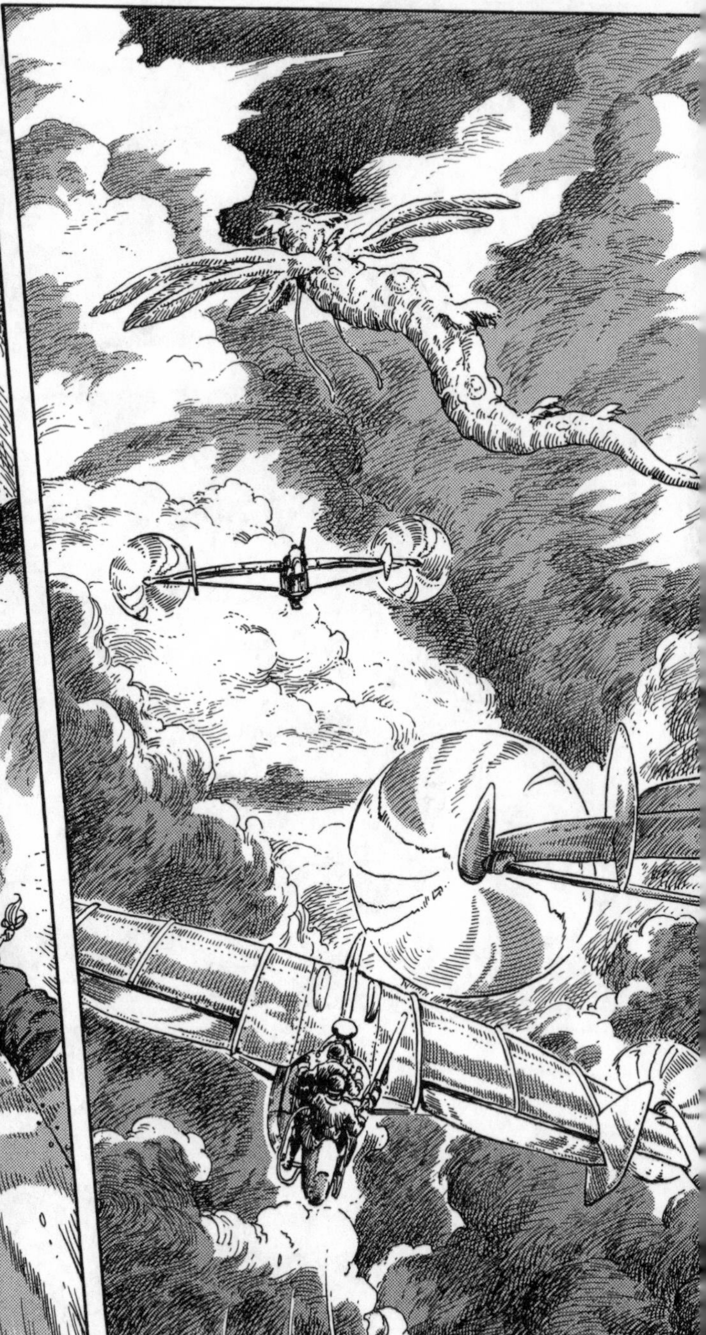

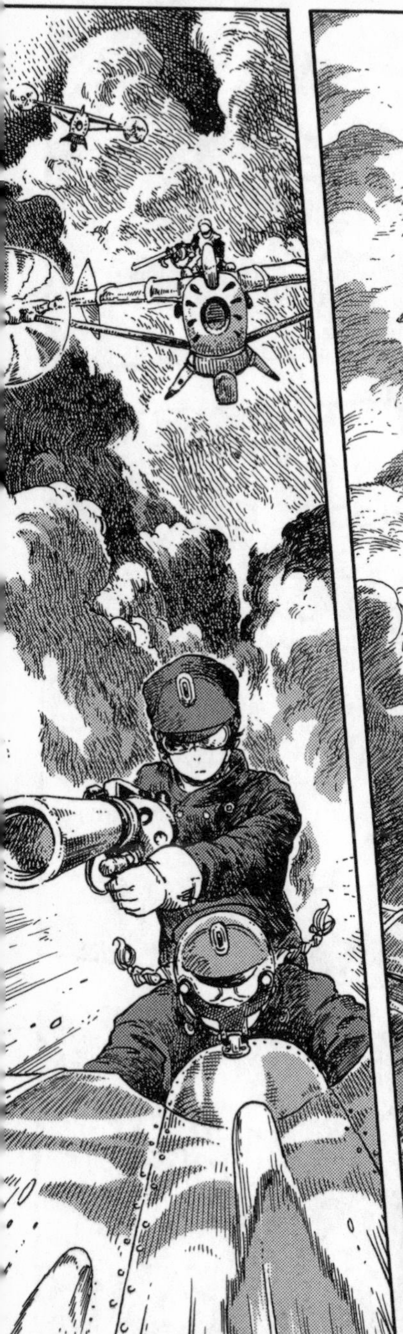

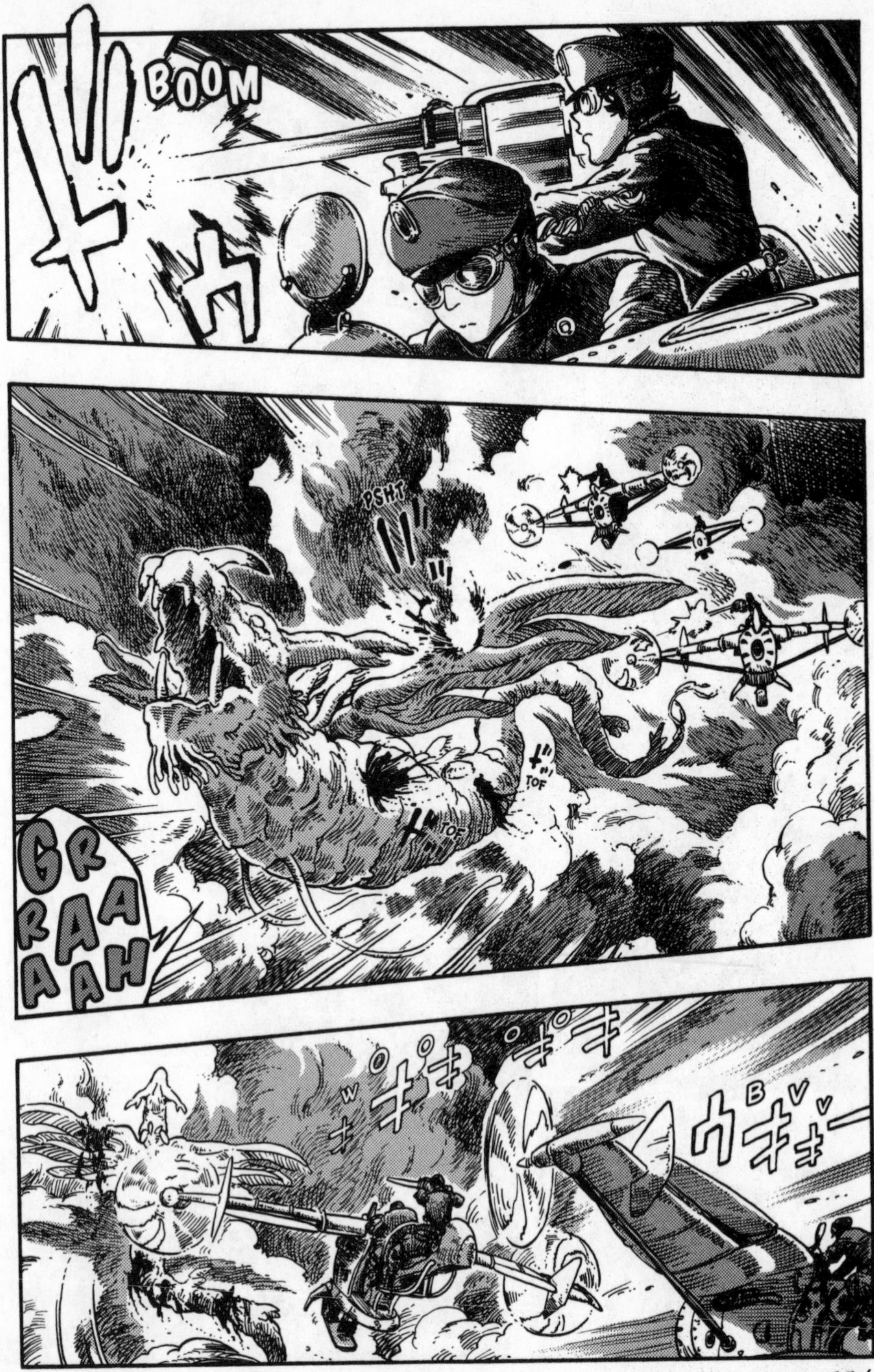
ドッ
BOOM
PSHT
TOF
TOF
GRRAAAAH

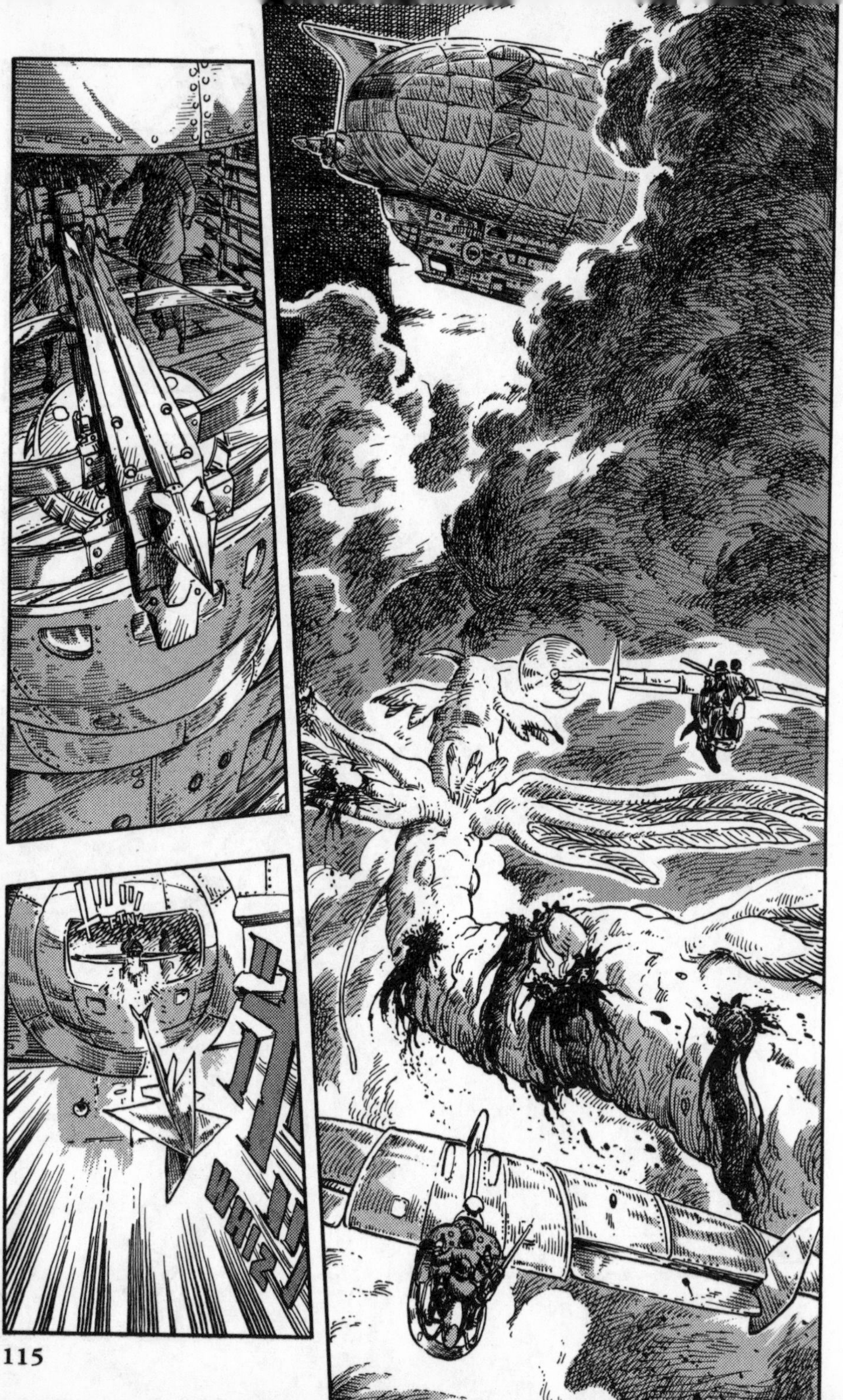
WHIZZ

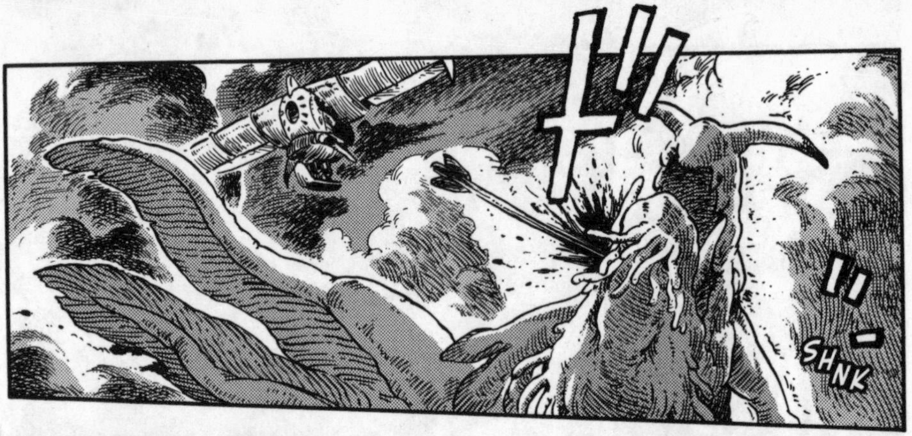
SHNK

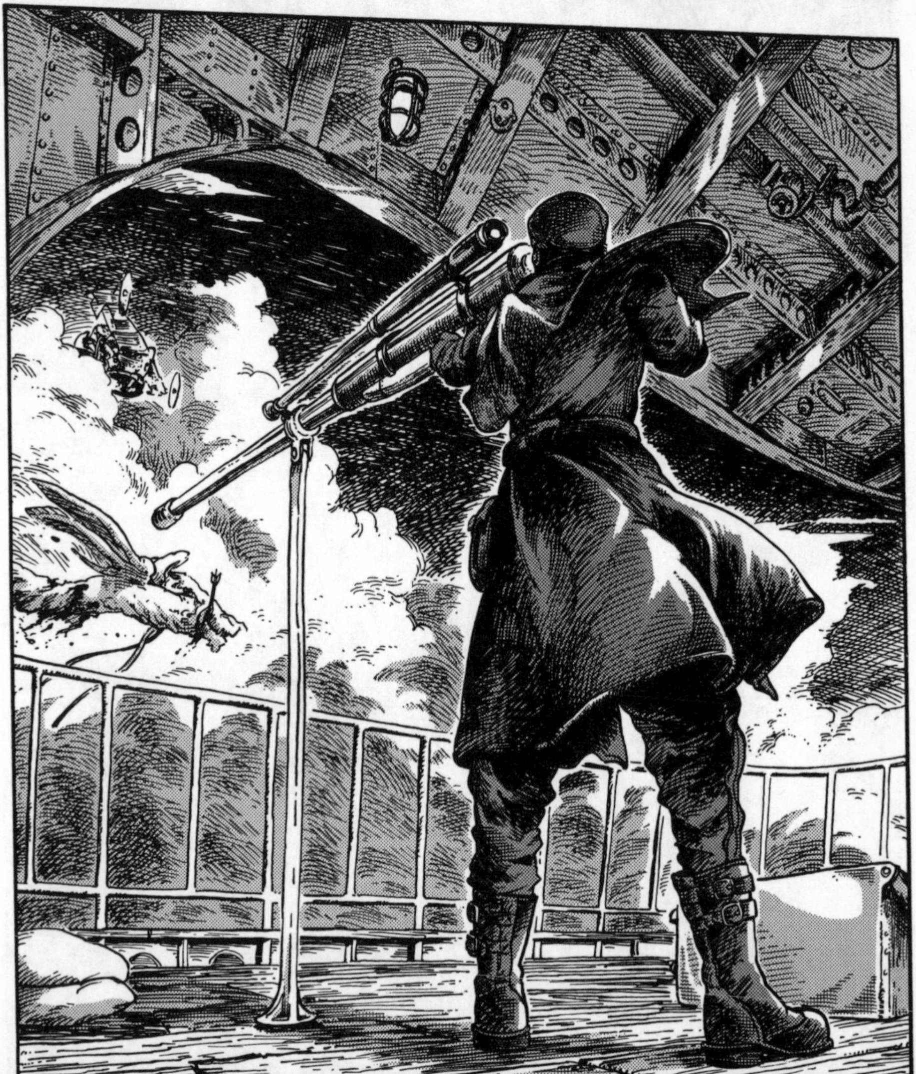

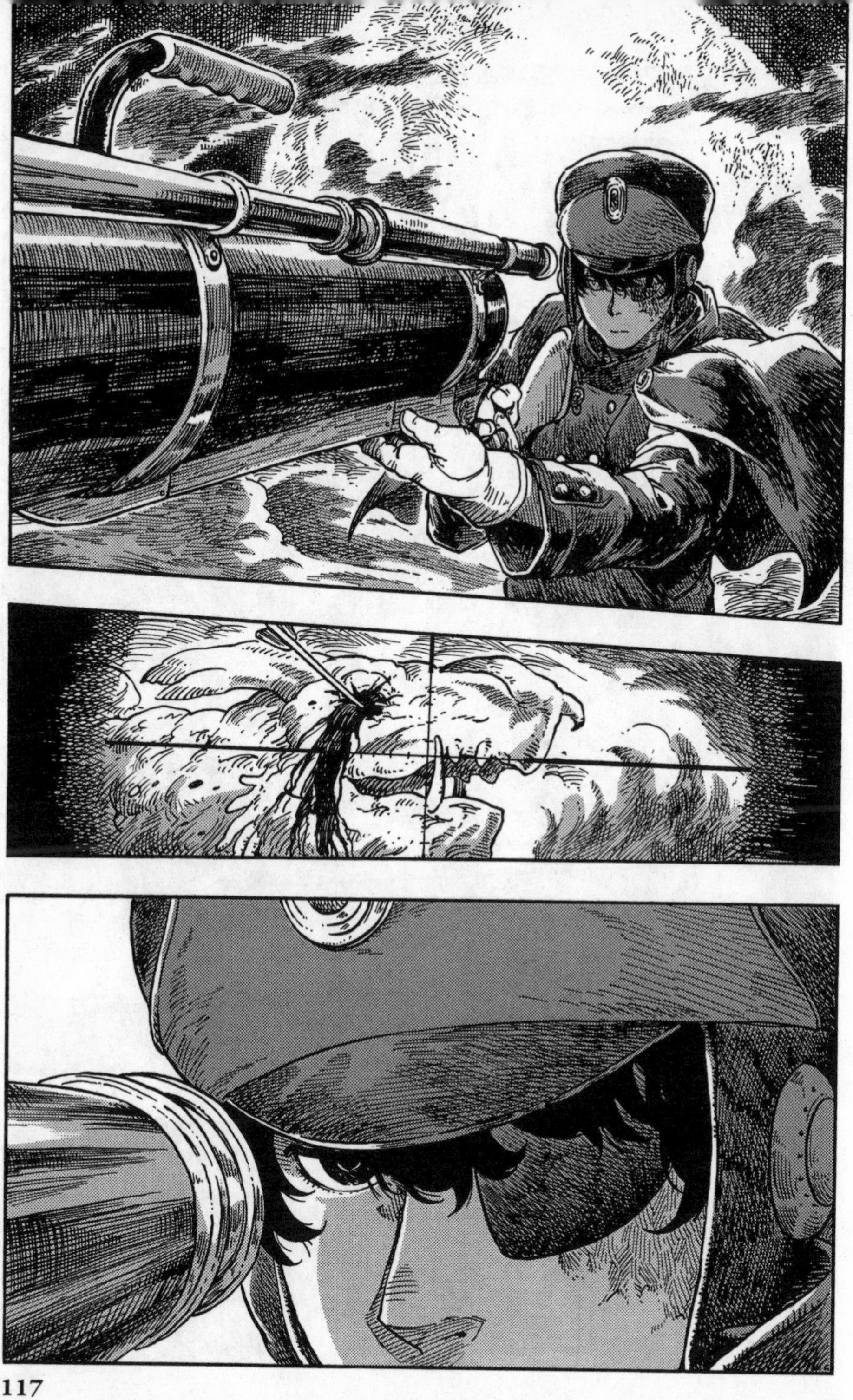

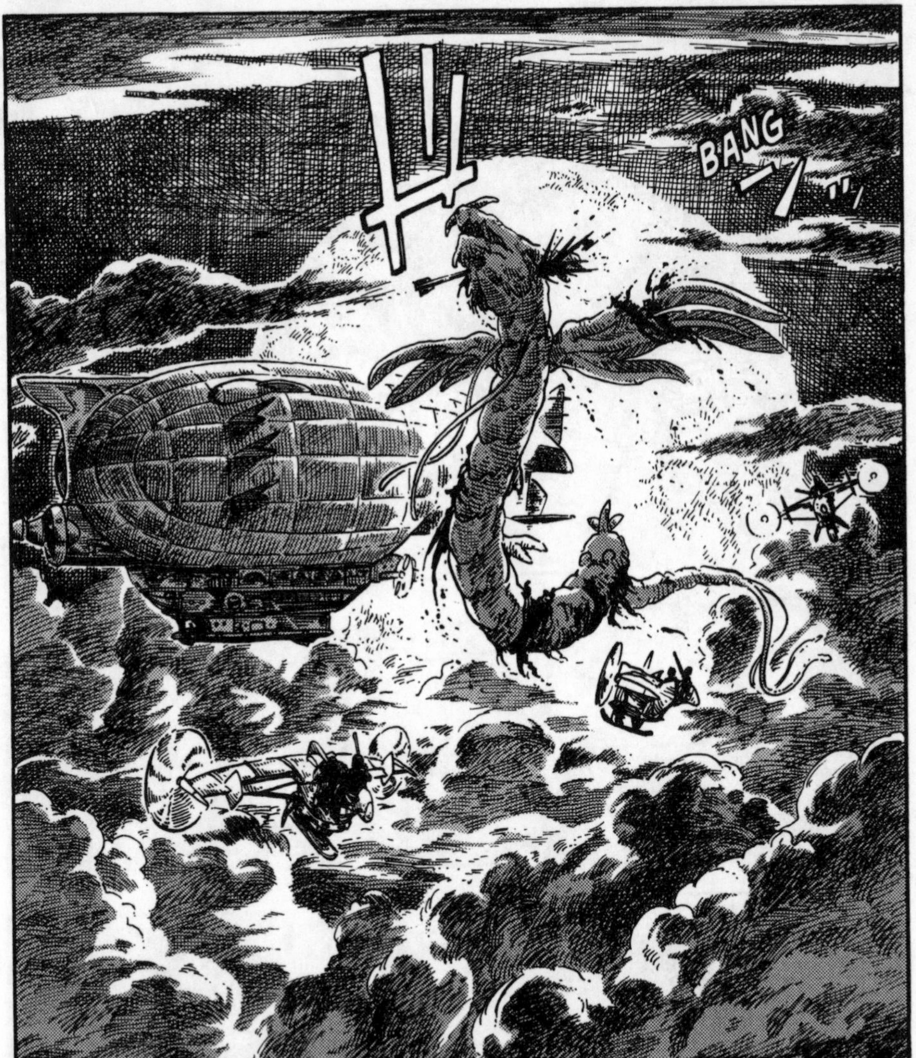
BANG
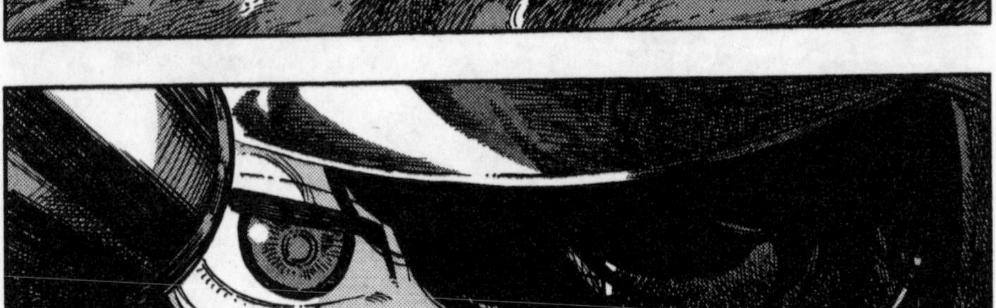

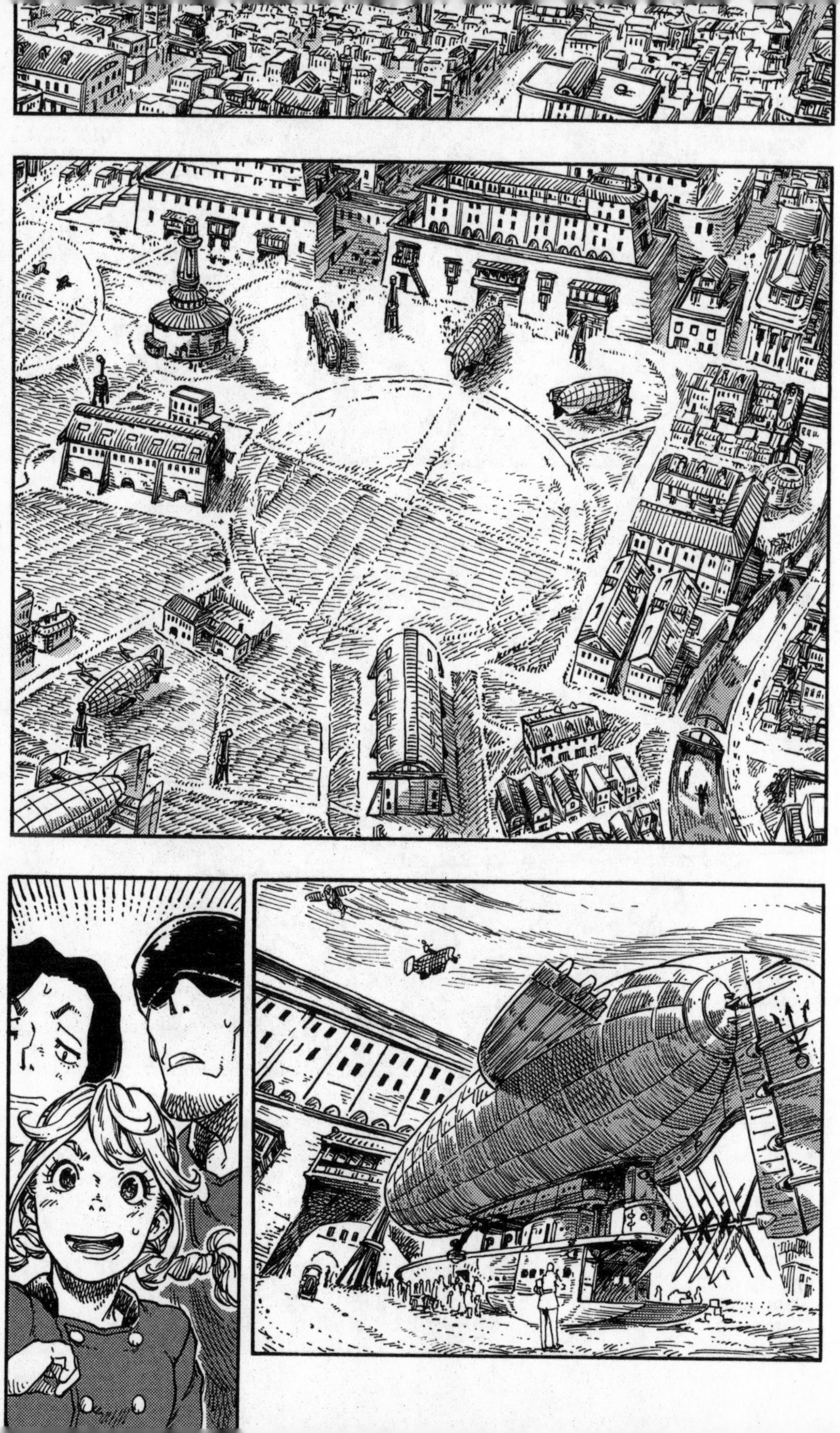

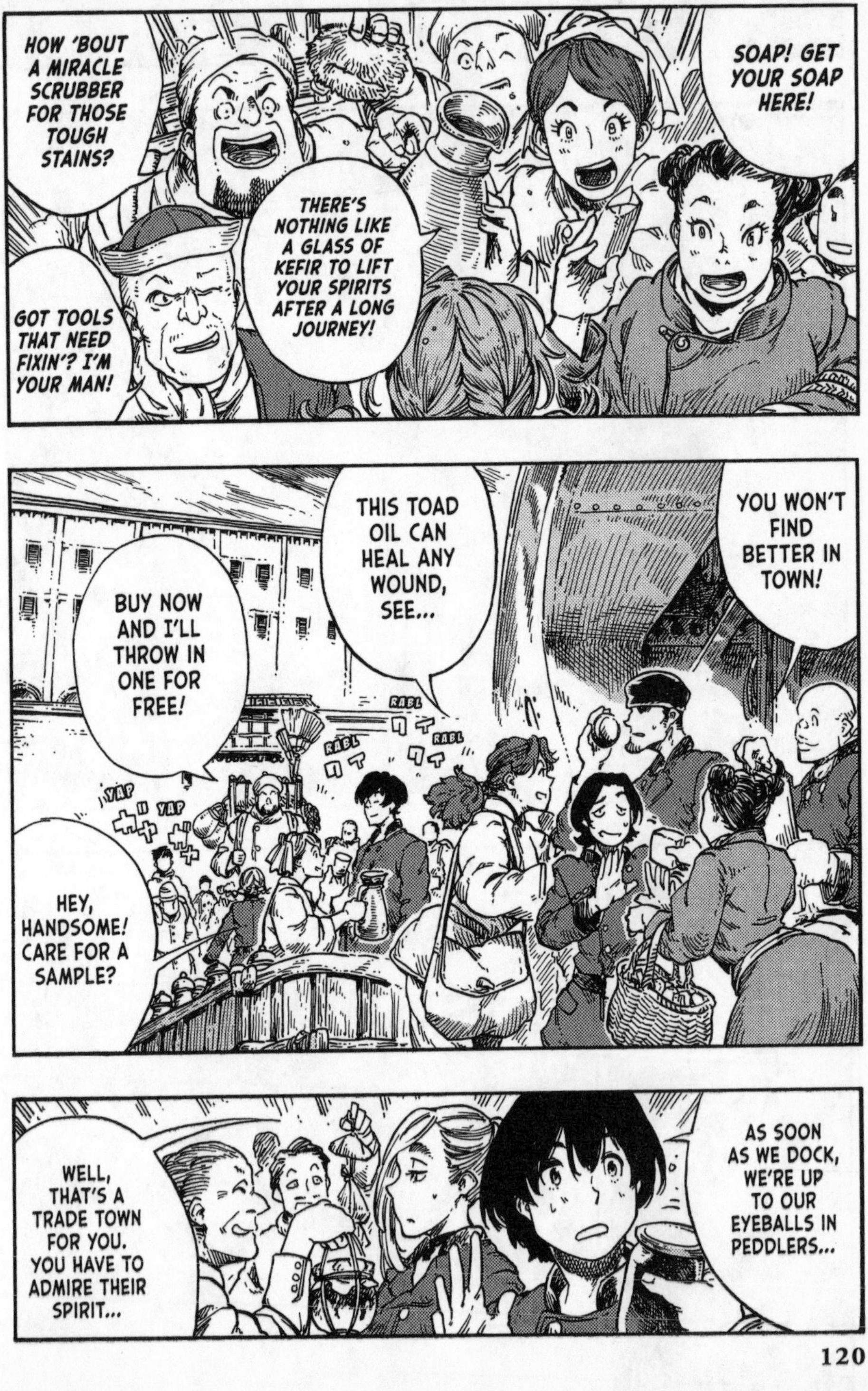

SOAP! GET YOUR SOAP HERE!
THERE'S NOTHING LIKE A GLASS OF KEFIR TO LIFT YOUR SPIRITS AFTER A LONG JOURNEY!
HOW 'BOUT A MIRACLE SCRUBBER FOR THOSE TOUGH STAINS?
GOT TOOLS THAT NEED FIXIN'? I'M YOUR MAN!
YOU WON'T FIND BETTER IN TOWN!
THIS TOAD OIL CAN HEAL ANY WOUND, SEE...
RABL
RABL
RABL
BUY NOW AND I'LL THROW IN ONE FOR FREE!
YAP
YAP
HEY, HANDSOME! CARE FOR A SAMPLE?
AS SOON AS WE DOCK, WE'RE UP TO OUR EYEBALLS IN PEDDLERS...
WELL, THAT'S A TRADE TOWN FOR YOU. YOU HAVE TO ADMIRE THEIR SPIRIT...

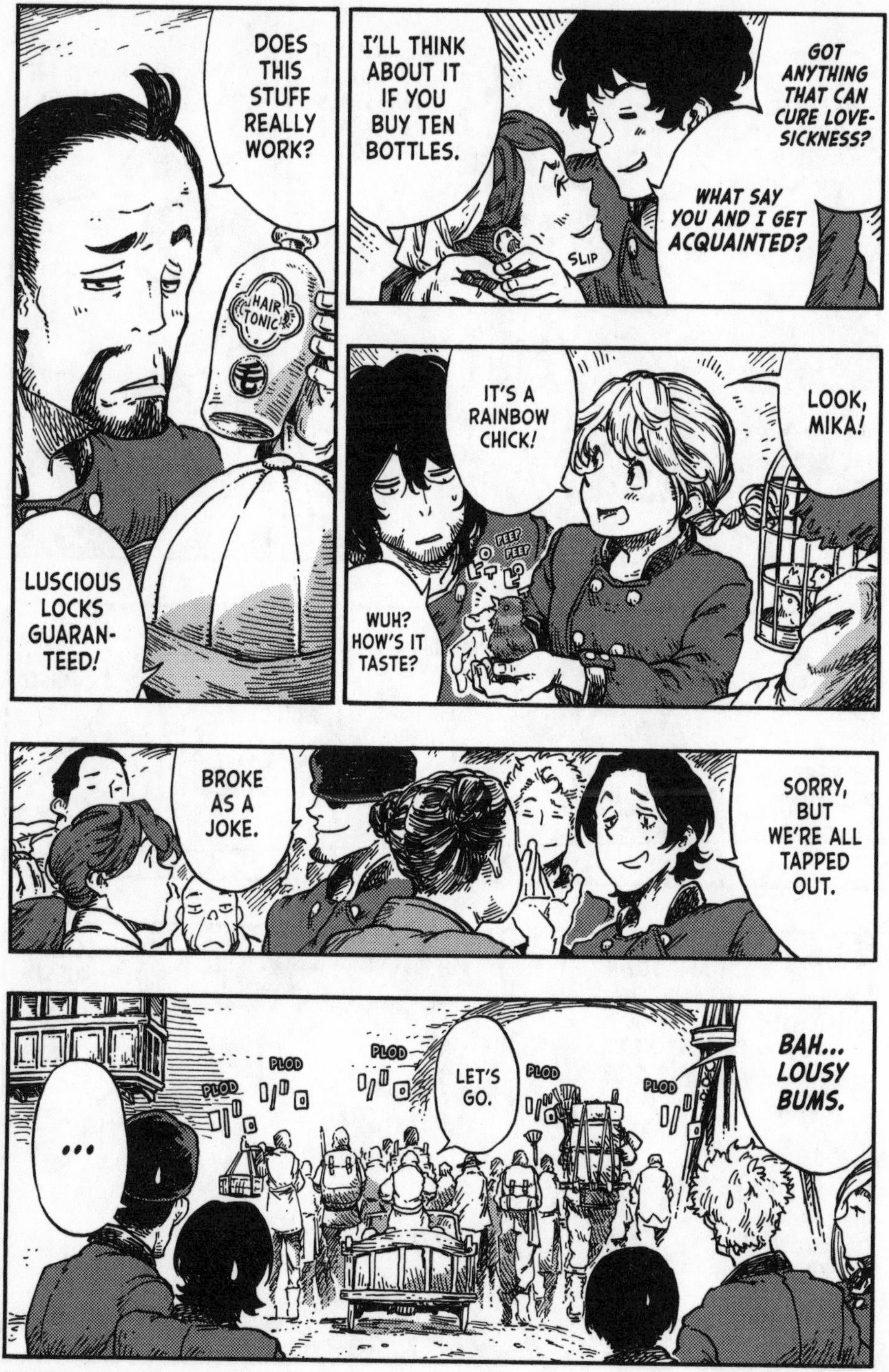
GOT ANYTHING THAT CAN CURE LOVE-SICKNESS?
WHAT SAY YOU AND I GET ACQUAINTED?
SLIP
I'LL THINK ABOUT IT IF YOU BUY TEN BOTTLES.
LOOK, MIKA!
IT'S A RAINBOW CHICK!
PEEP PEEP
WUH? HOW'S IT TASTE?
DOES THIS STUFF REALLY WORK?
HAIR TONIC!
LUSCIOUS LOCKS GUARANTEED!
SORRY, BUT WE'RE ALL TAPPED OUT.
BROKE AS A JOKE.
BAH... LOUSY BUMS.
PLOD
PLOD
LET'S GO.
PLOD
PLOD
PLOD
...

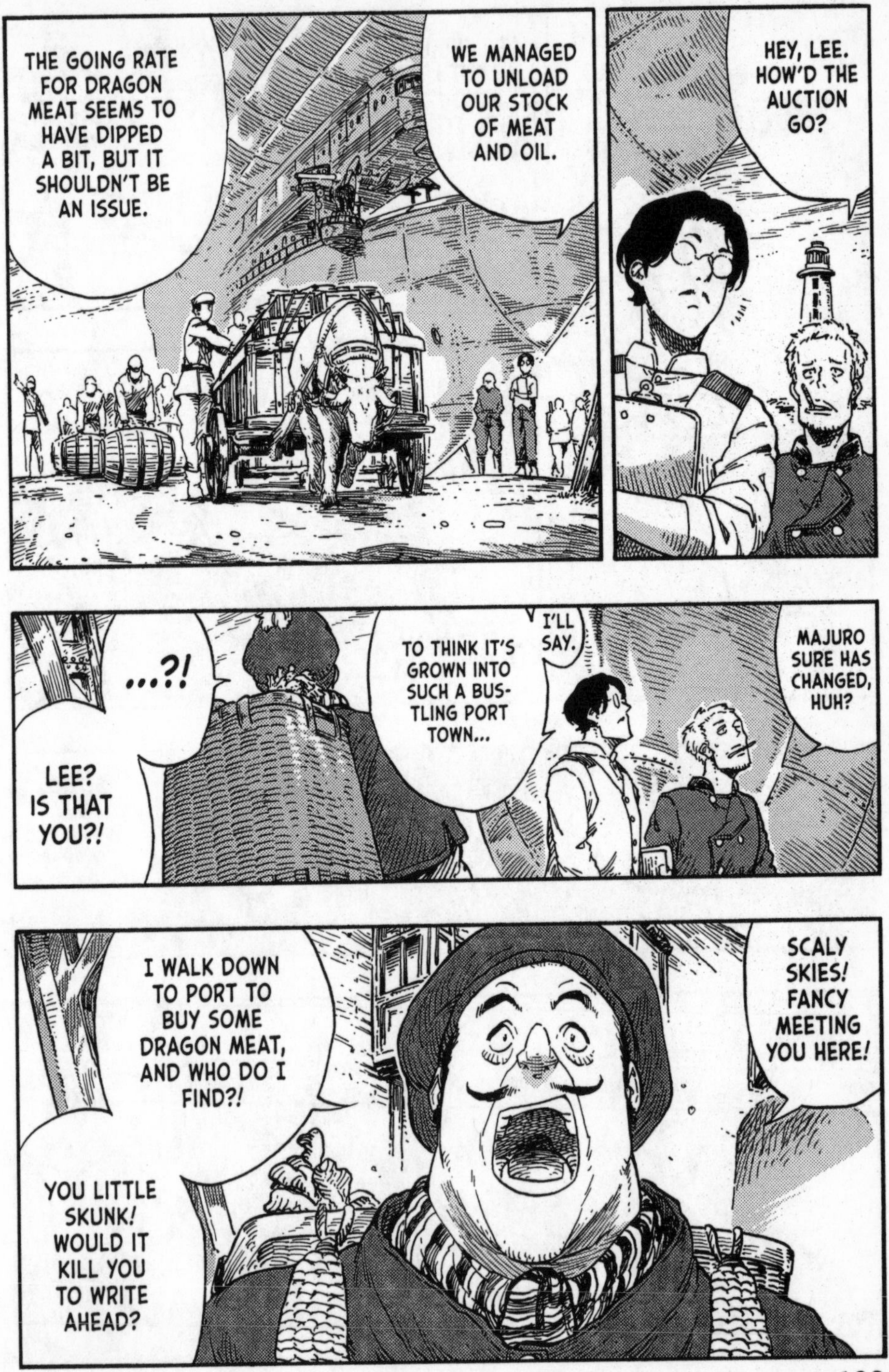
HEY, LEE. HOW'D THE AUCTION GO?
WE MANAGED TO UNLOAD OUR STOCK OF MEAT AND OIL.
THE GOING RATE FOR DRAGON MEAT SEEMS TO HAVE DIPPED A BIT, BUT IT SHOULDN'T BE AN ISSUE.
MAJURO SURE HAS CHANGED, HUH?
I'LL SAY.
TO THINK IT'S GROWN INTO SUCH A BUS-TLING PORT TOWN...
...?!
LEE? IS THAT YOU?!
SCALY SKIES! FANCY MEETING YOU HERE!
I WALK DOWN TO PORT TO BUY SOME DRAGON MEAT, AND WHO DO I FIND?!
YOU LITTLE SKUNK! WOULD IT KILL YOU TO WRITE AHEAD?

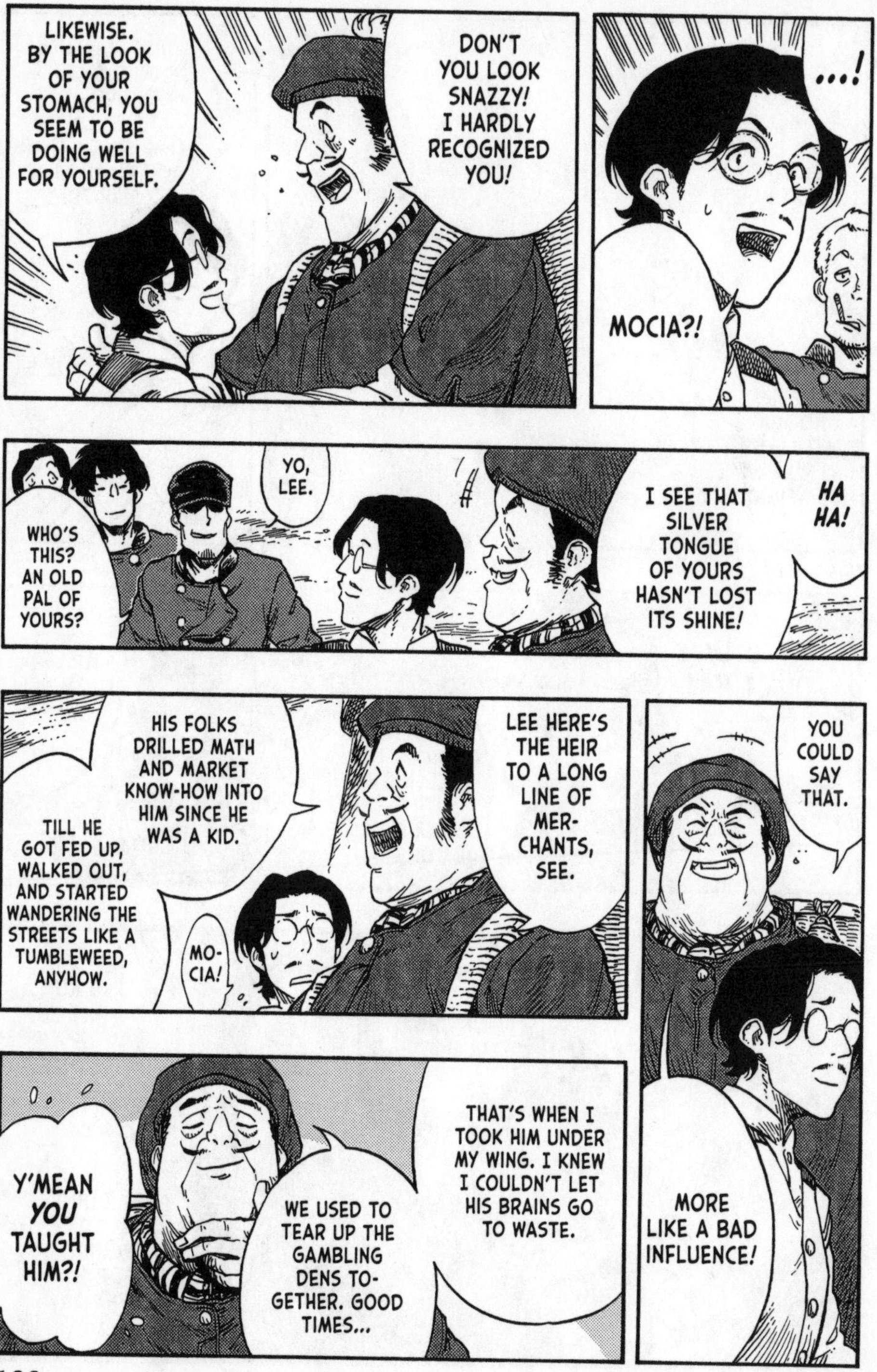

...!
MOCIA?!
DON'T YOU LOOK SNAZZY! I HARDLY RECOGNIZED YOU!
LIKEWISE. BY THE LOOK OF YOUR STOMACH, YOU SEEM TO BE DOING WELL FOR YOURSELF.
HA HA!
I SEE THAT SILVER TONGUE OF YOURS HASN'T LOST ITS SHINE!
YO, LEE.
WHO'S THIS? AN OLD PAL OF YOURS?
YOU COULD SAY THAT.
MORE LIKE A BAD INFLUENCE!
LEE HERE'S THE HEIR TO A LONG LINE OF MER-CHANTS, SEE.
HIS FOLKS DRILLED MATH AND MARKET KNOW-HOW INTO HIM SINCE HE WAS A KID.
TILL HE GOT FED UP, WALKED OUT, AND STARTED WANDERING THE STREETS LIKE A TUMBLEWEED, ANYHOW.
MO-CIA!
THAT'S WHEN I TOOK HIM UNDER MY WING. I KNEW I COULDN'T LET HIS BRAINS GO TO WASTE.
WE USED TO TEAR UP THE GAMBLING DENS TO-GETHER. GOOD TIMES...
Y'MEAN *YOU* TAUGHT HIM?!

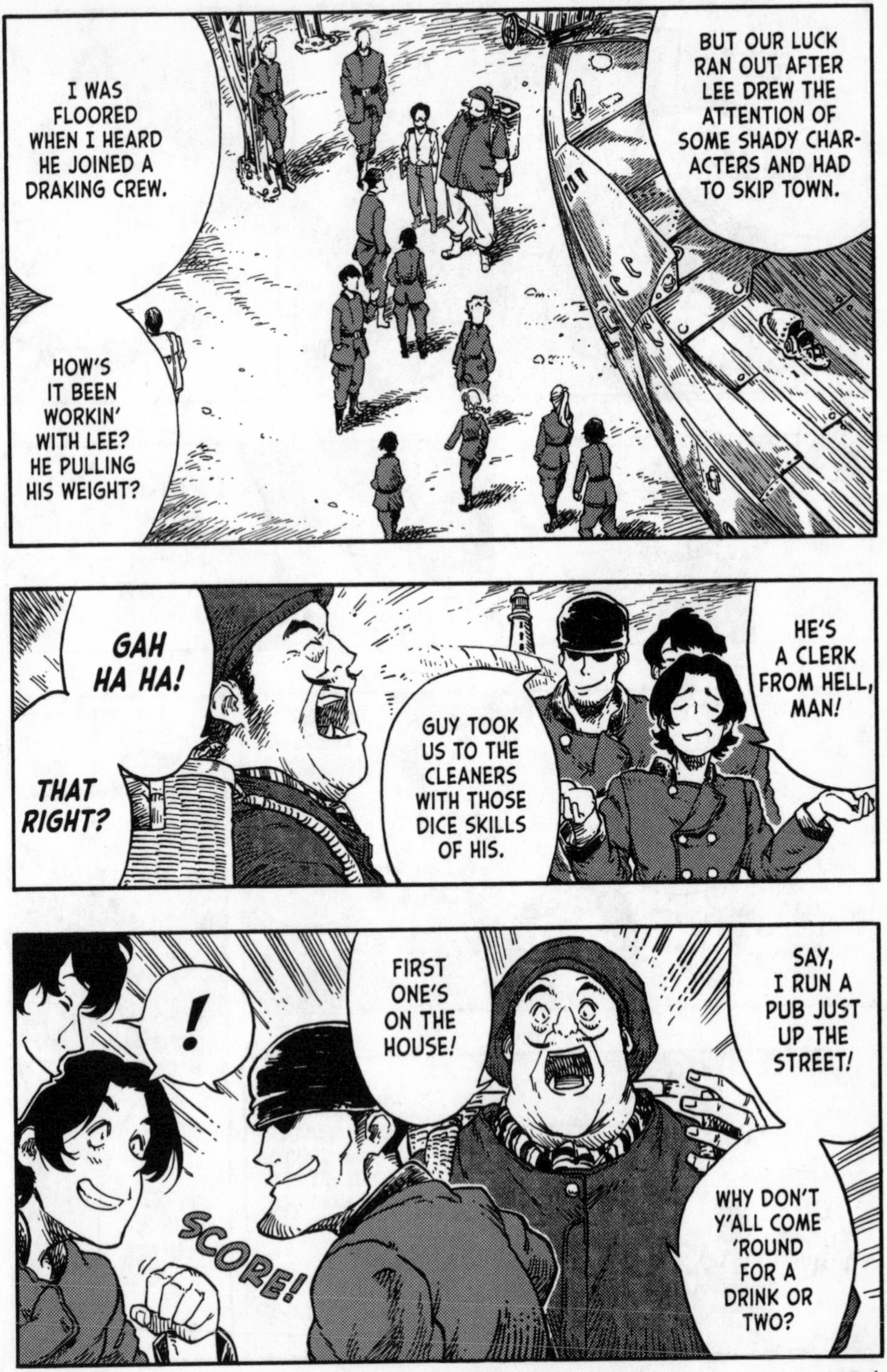
BUT OUR LUCK RAN OUT AFTER LEE DREW THE ATTENTION OF SOME SHADY CHAR-ACTERS AND HAD TO SKIP TOWN.
I WAS FLOORED WHEN I HEARD HE JOINED A DRAKING CREW.
HOW'S IT BEEN WORKIN' WITH LEE? HE PULLING HIS WEIGHT?
HE'S A CLERK FROM HELL, MAN!
GUY TOOK US TO THE CLEANERS WITH THOSE DICE SKILLS OF HIS.
GAH HA HA!
THAT RIGHT?
SAY, I RUN A PUB JUST UP THE STREET!
FIRST ONE'S ON THE HOUSE!
!
WHY DON'T Y'ALL COME 'ROUND FOR A DRINK OR TWO?
SCORE!

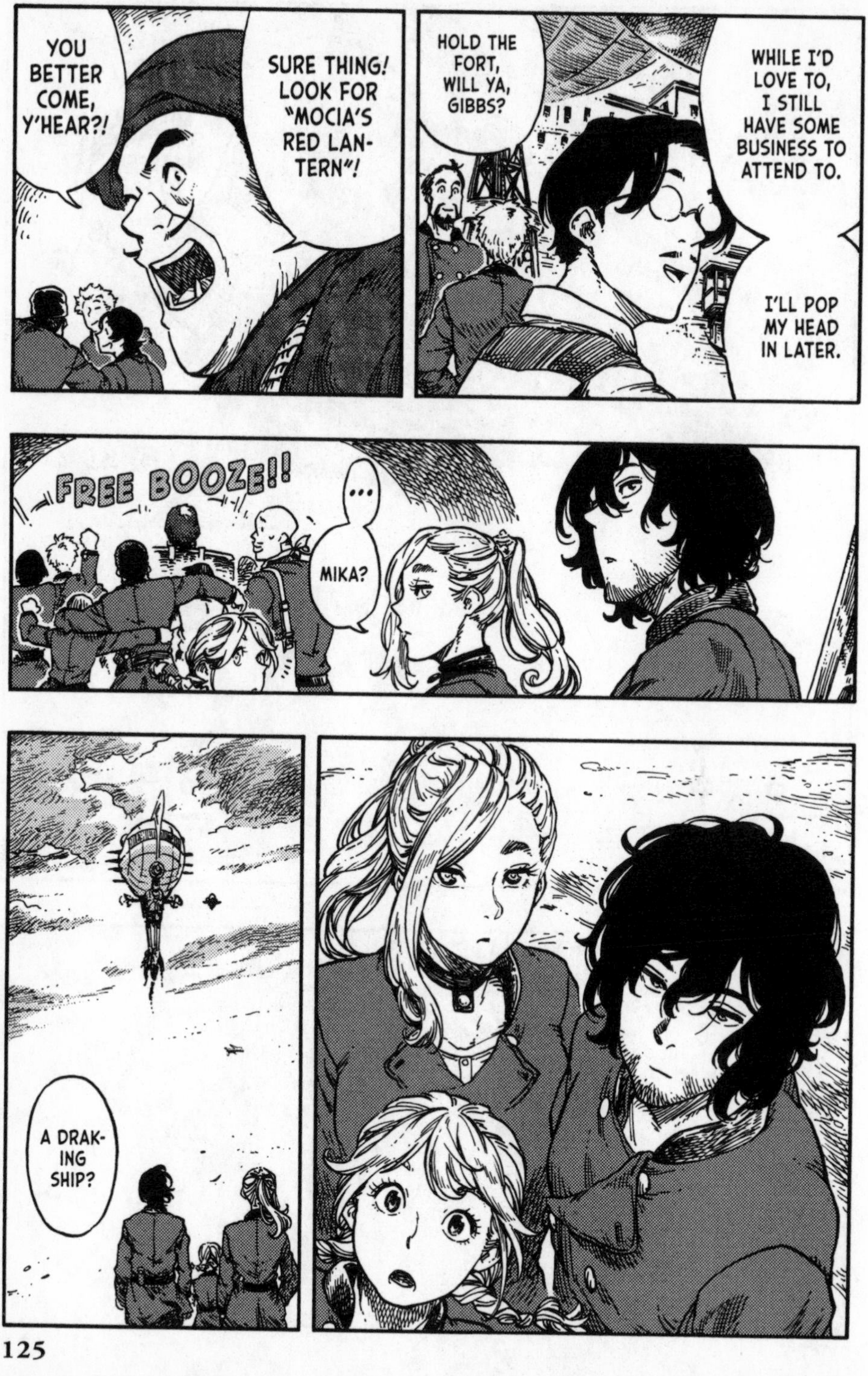
WHILE I'D LOVE TO, I STILL HAVE SOME BUSINESS TO ATTEND TO.
HOLD THE FORT, WILL YA, GIBBS?
I'LL POP MY HEAD IN LATER.
SURE THING! LOOK FOR "MOCIA'S RED LANTERN"!
YOU BETTER COME, Y'HEAR?!
MIKA?
...
FREE BOOZE!!
A DRAKING SHIP?

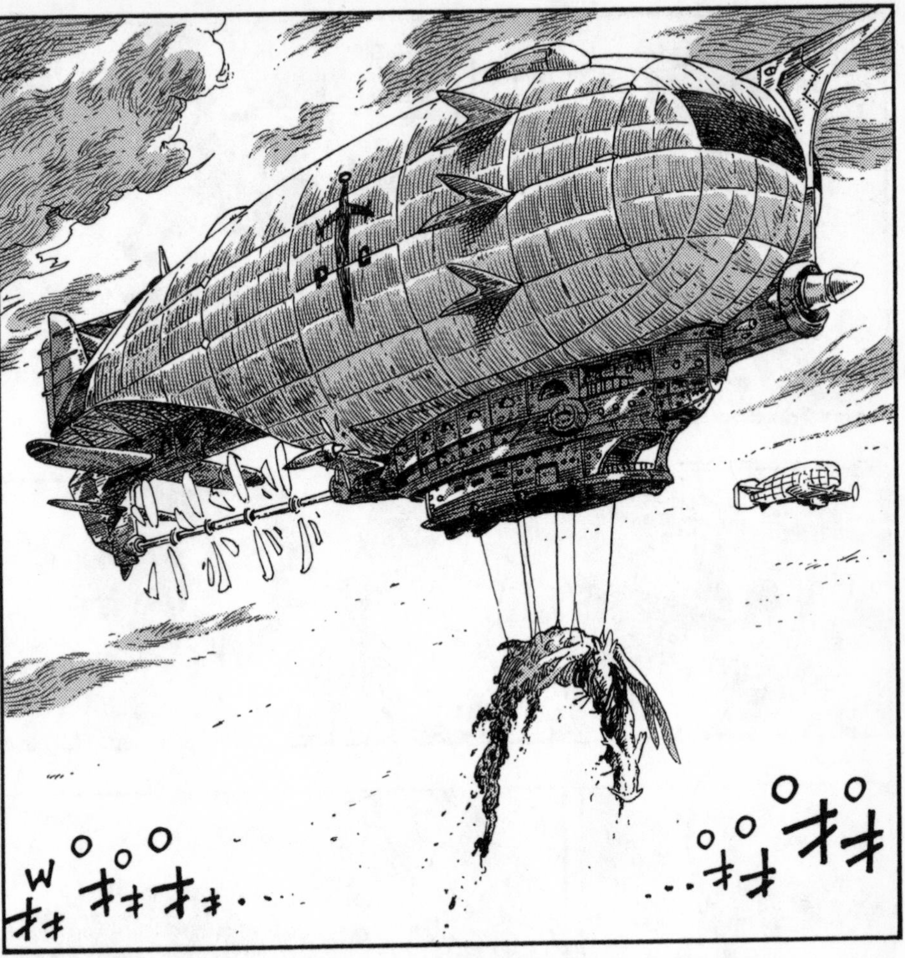
WOOO…
…OOOO

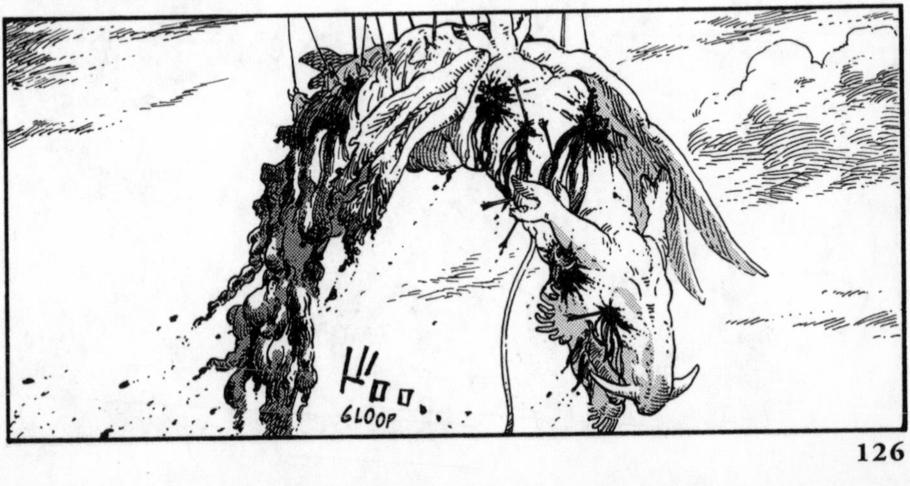
ドロロ…
GLOOP

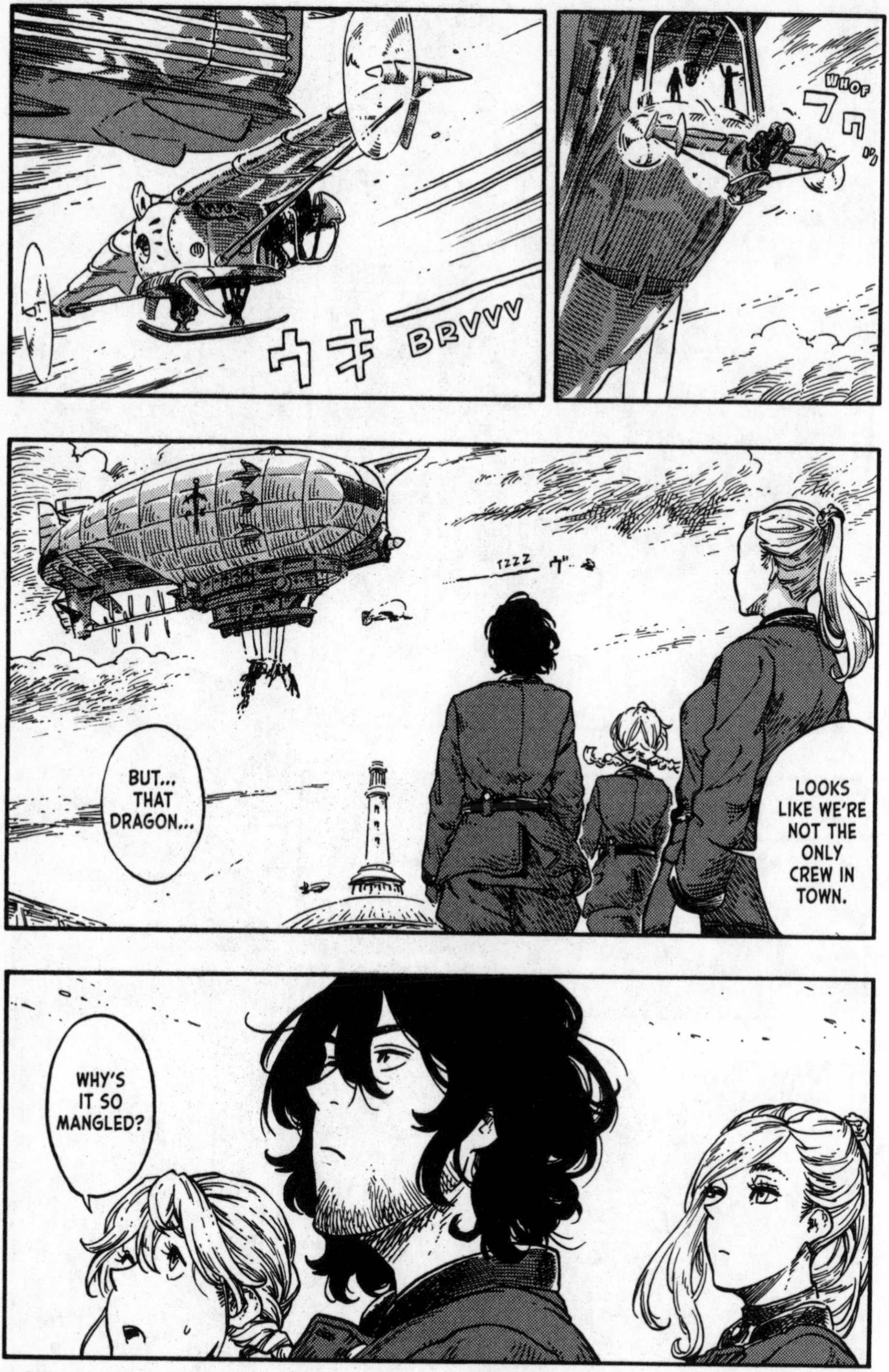
WHOF
BRVVV
LOOKS LIKE WE'RE NOT THE ONLY CREW IN TOWN.
BUT... THAT DRAGON...
WHY'S IT SO MANGLED?

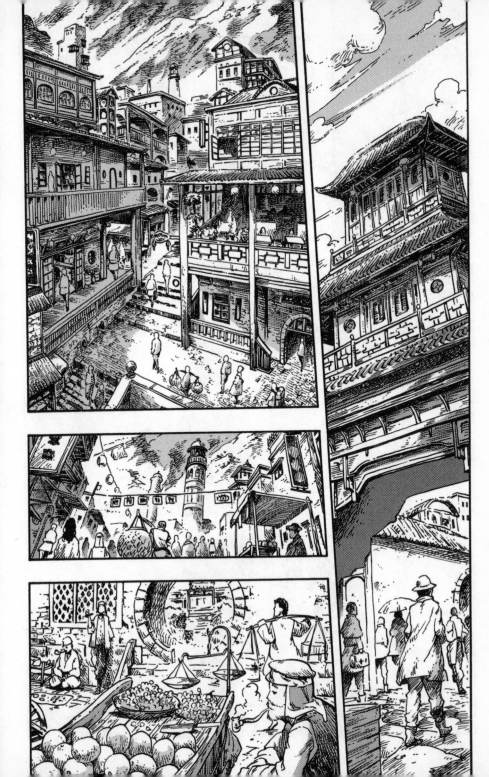

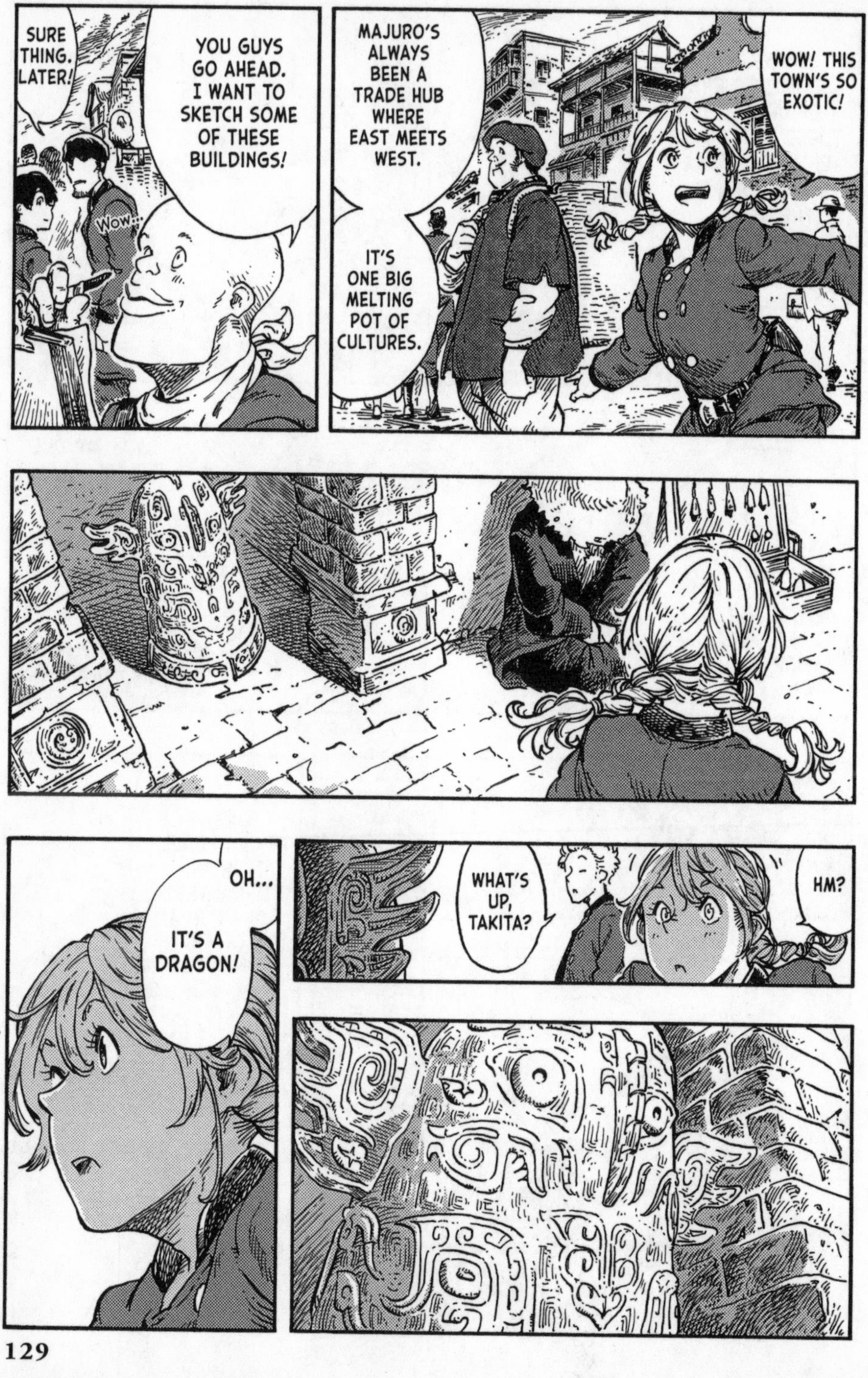
WOW! THIS TOWN'S SO EXOTIC!
MAJURO'S ALWAYS BEEN A TRADE HUB WHERE EAST MEETS WEST.
IT'S ONE BIG MELTING POT OF CULTURES.
YOU GUYS GO AHEAD. I WANT TO SKETCH SOME OF THESE BUILDINGS!
SURE THING. LATER!
Wow...
HM?
WHAT'S UP, TAKITA?
OH...
IT'S A DRAGON!

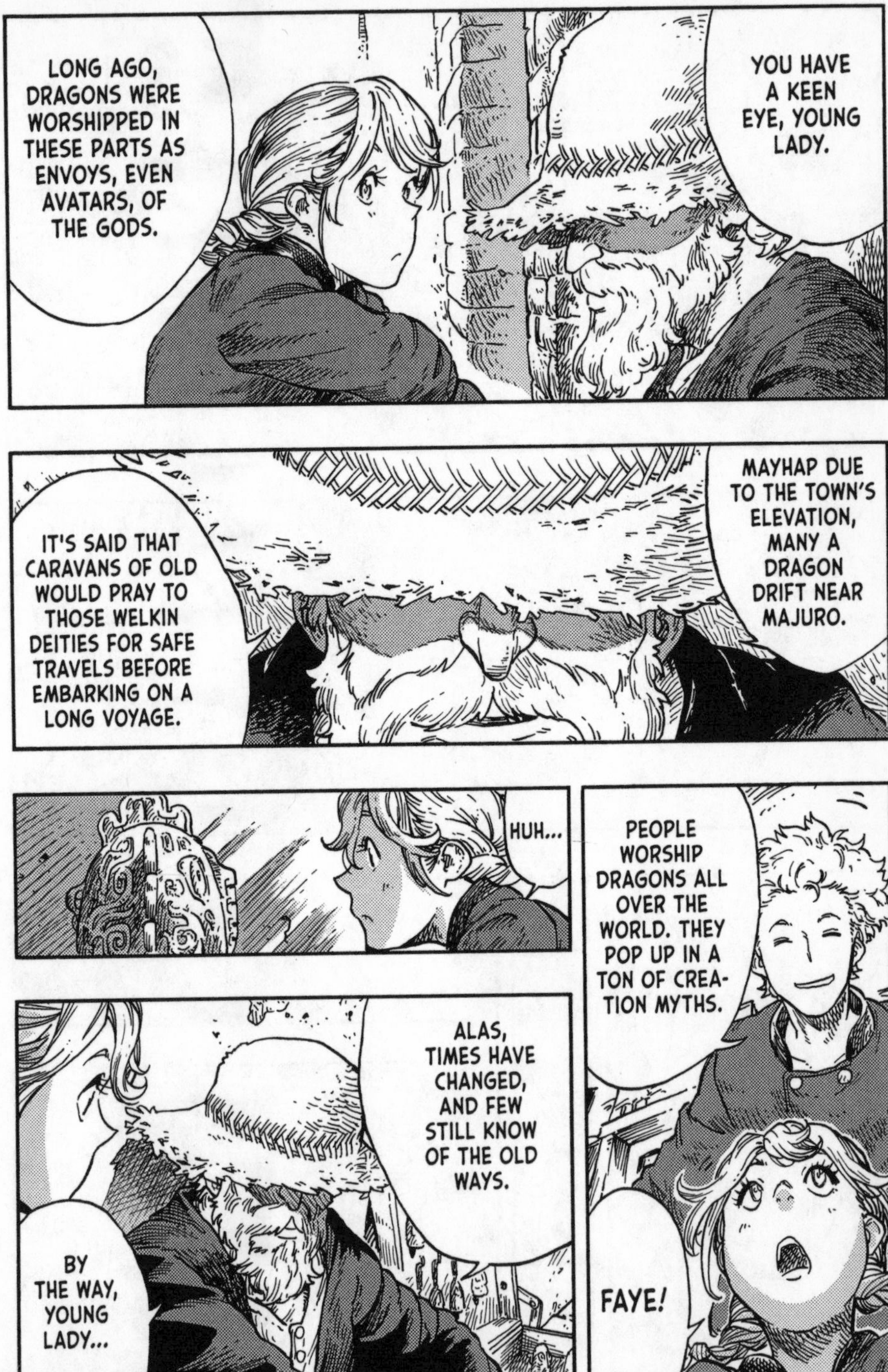
YOU HAVE A KEEN EYE, YOUNG LADY.
LONG AGO, DRAGONS WERE WORSHIPPED IN THESE PARTS AS ENVOYS, EVEN AVATARS, OF THE GODS.
MAYHAP DUE TO THE TOWN'S ELEVATION, MANY A DRAGON DRIFT NEAR MAJURO.
IT'S SAID THAT CARAVANS OF OLD WOULD PRAY TO THOSE WELKIN DEITIES FOR SAFE TRAVELS BEFORE EMBARKING ON A LONG VOYAGE.
PEOPLE WORSHIP DRAGONS ALL OVER THE WORLD. THEY POP UP IN A TON OF CREA-TION MYTHS.
FAYE!
HUH...
ALAS, TIMES HAVE CHANGED, AND FEW STILL KNOW OF THE OLD WAYS.
BY THE WAY, YOUNG LADY...

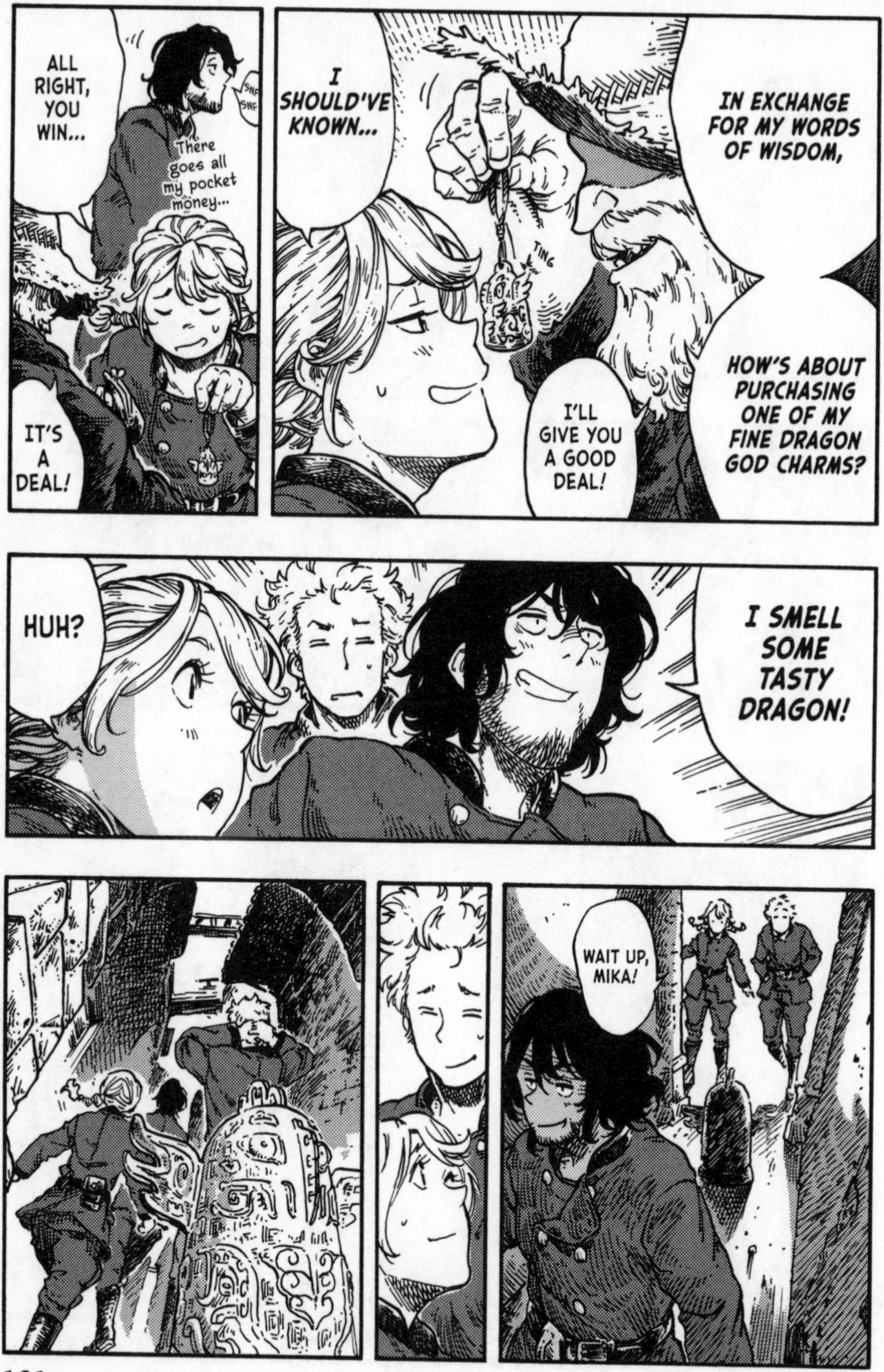
IN EXCHANGE FOR MY WORDS OF WISDOM,
HOW'S ABOUT PURCHASING ONE OF MY FINE DRAGON GOD CHARMS?
TING
I'LL GIVE YOU A GOOD DEAL!
I SHOULD'VE KNOWN...
ALL RIGHT, YOU WIN...
SNF SNF
There goes all my pocket money...
IT'S A DEAL!
I SMELL SOME TASTY DRAGON!
HUH?
WAIT UP, MIKA!

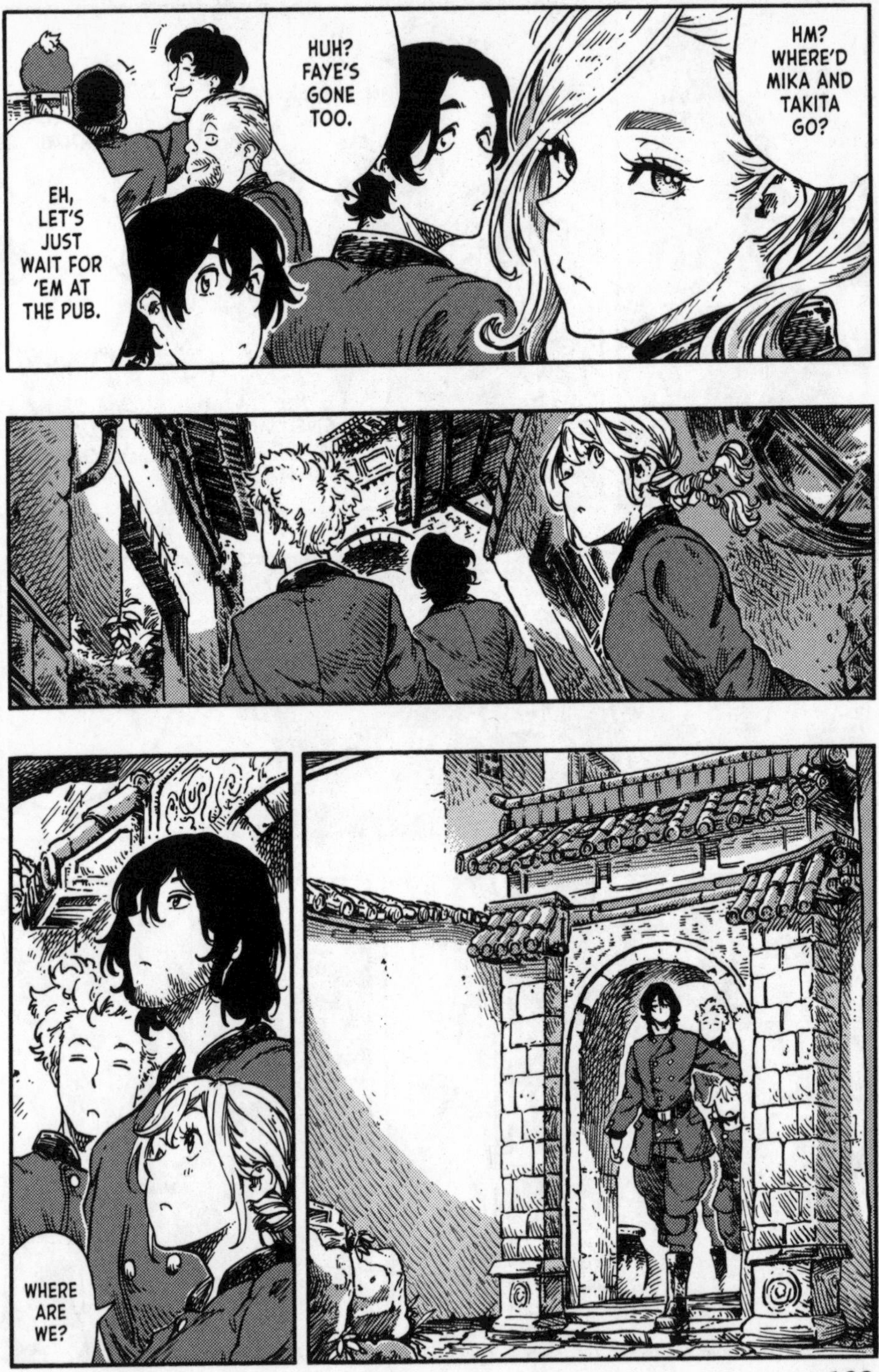
HM? WHERE'D MIKA AND TAKITA GO?
HUH? FAYE'S GONE TOO.
EH, LET'S JUST WAIT FOR 'EM AT THE PUB.
WHERE ARE WE?

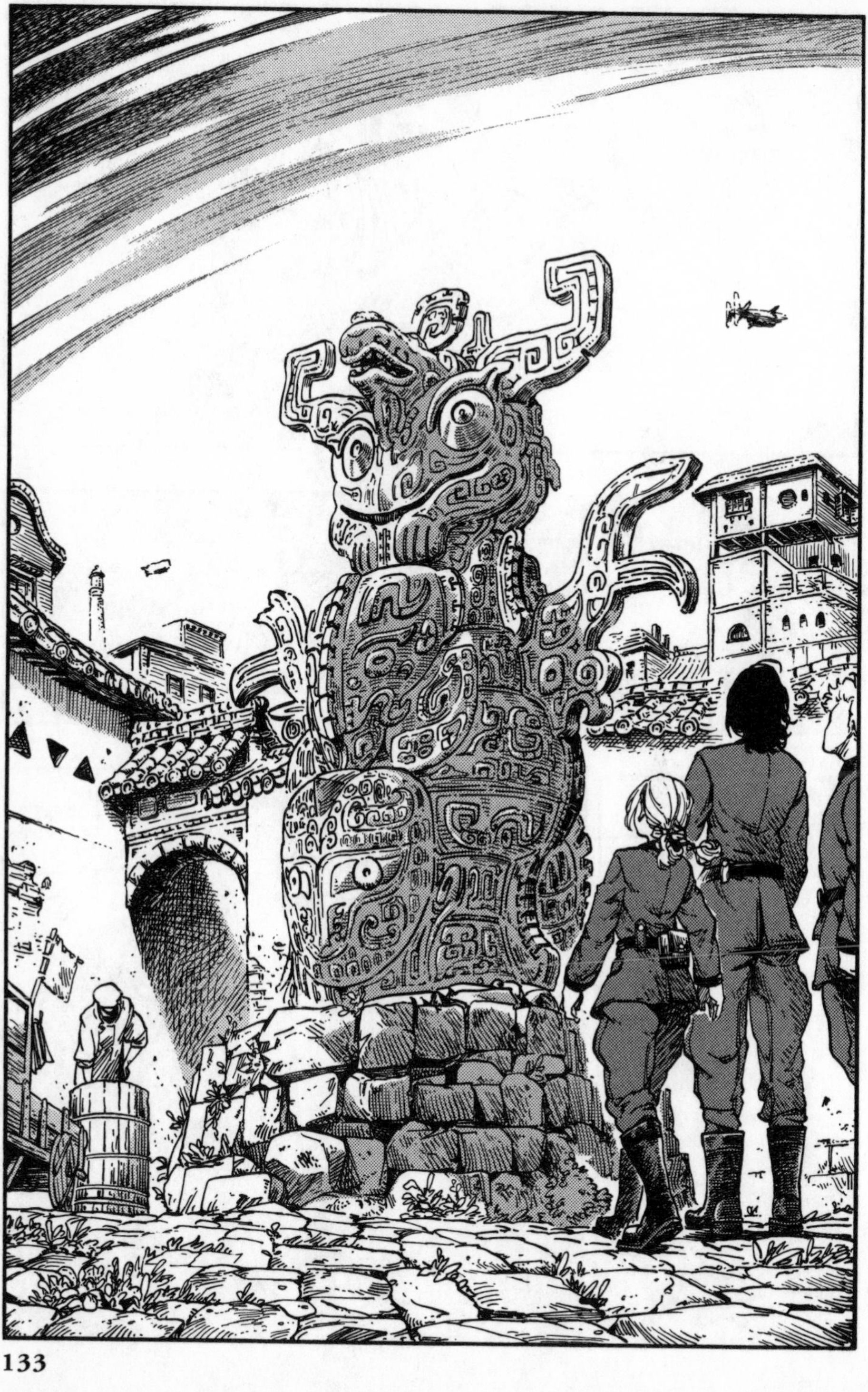

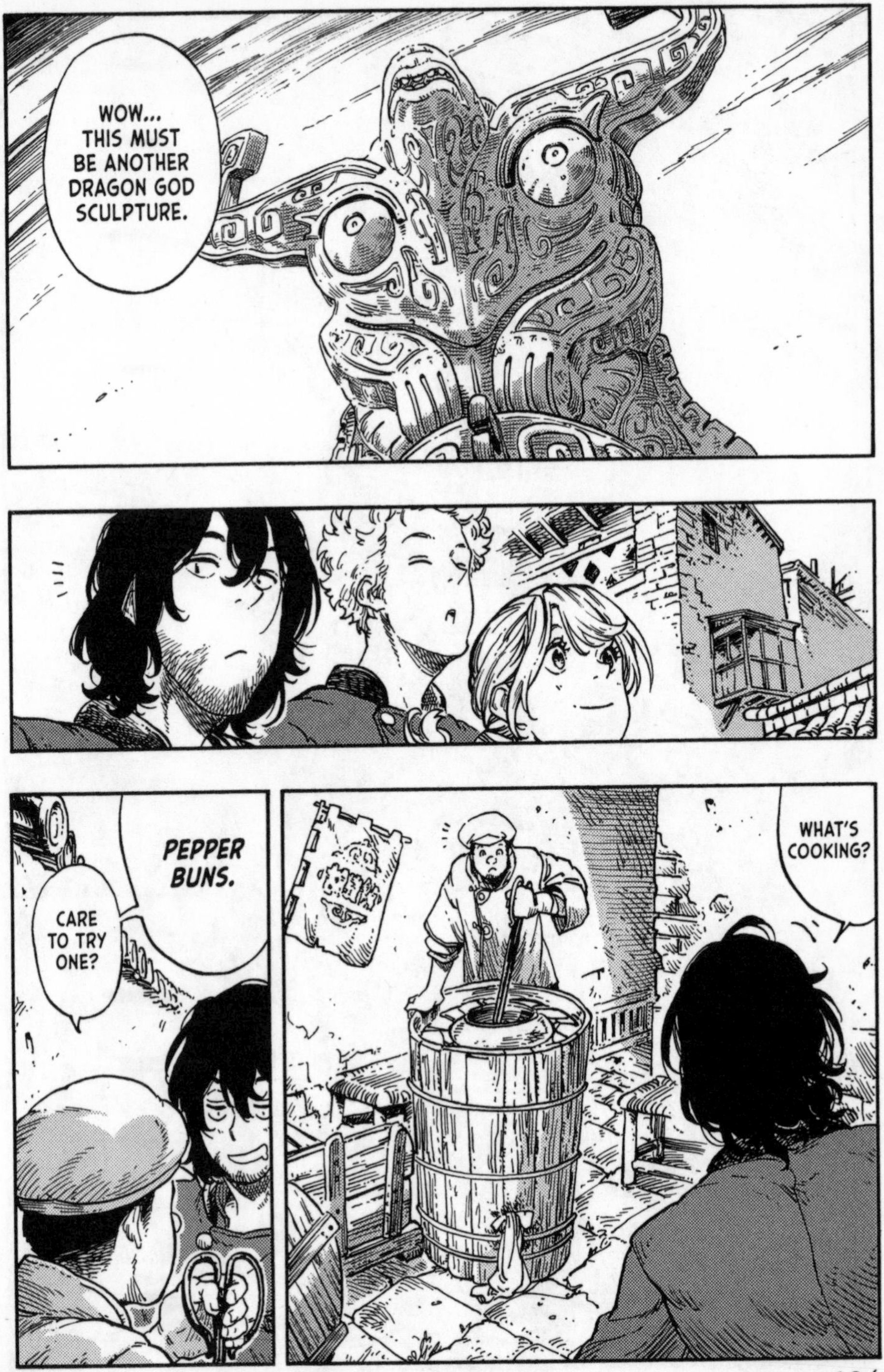
WOW... THIS MUST BE ANOTHER DRAGON GOD SCULPTURE.
WHAT'S COOKING?
PEPPER BUNS.
CARE TO TRY ONE?

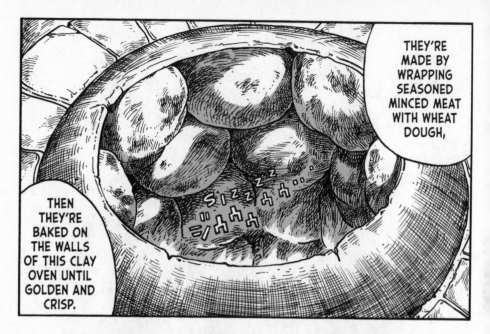

THEY'RE MADE BY WRAPPING SEASONED MINCED MEAT WITH WHEAT DOUGH,

THEN THEY'RE BAKED ON THE WALLS OF THIS CLAY OVEN UNTIL GOLDEN AND CRISP.

SiZZZ...

GOT ANY FILLED WITH DRAGON?!

SORRY, FRESH OUT. I STILL HAVE PORK AND MUTTON, THOUGH.

HUH ?!

I JUST SOLD THE LAST WITH DRAGON MEAT TO THOSE FOLKS OVER THERE.

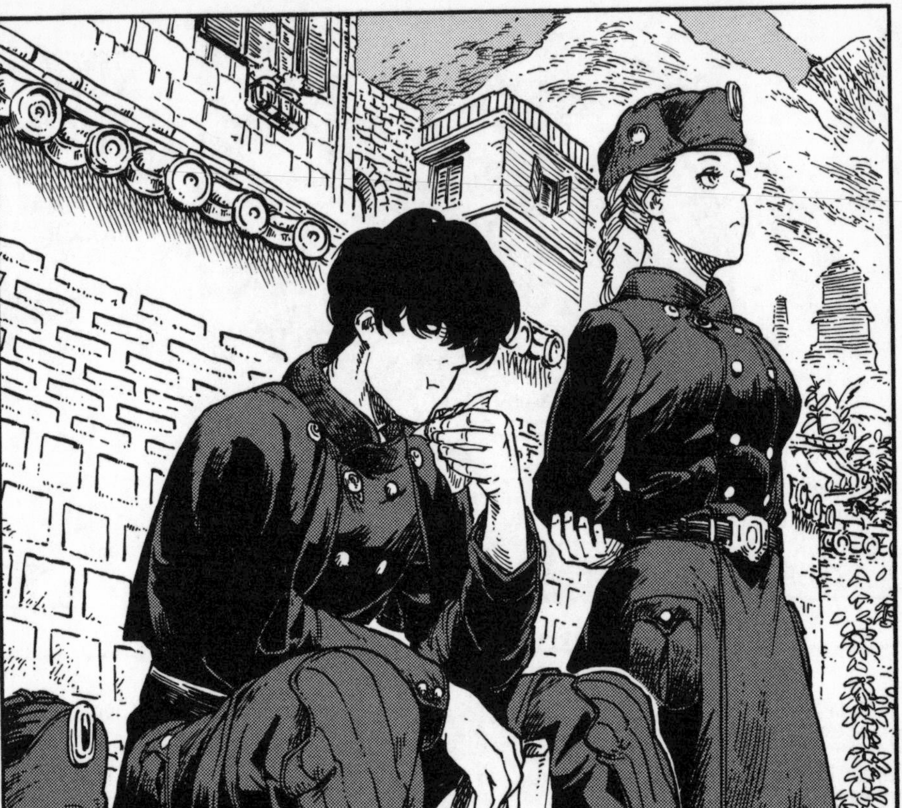

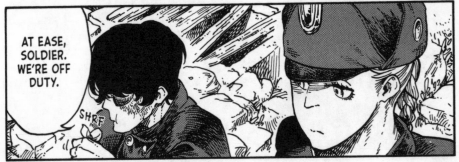

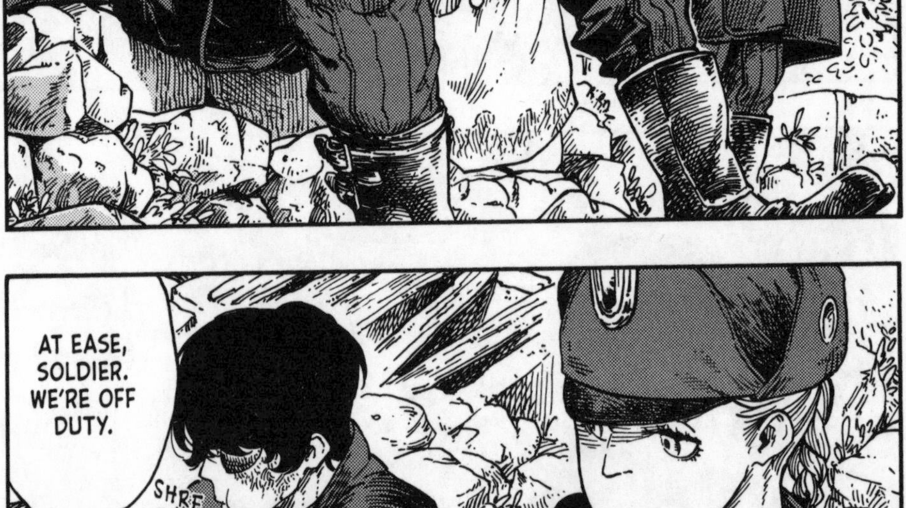
AT EASE, SOLDIER. WE'RE OFF DUTY.
SHRF

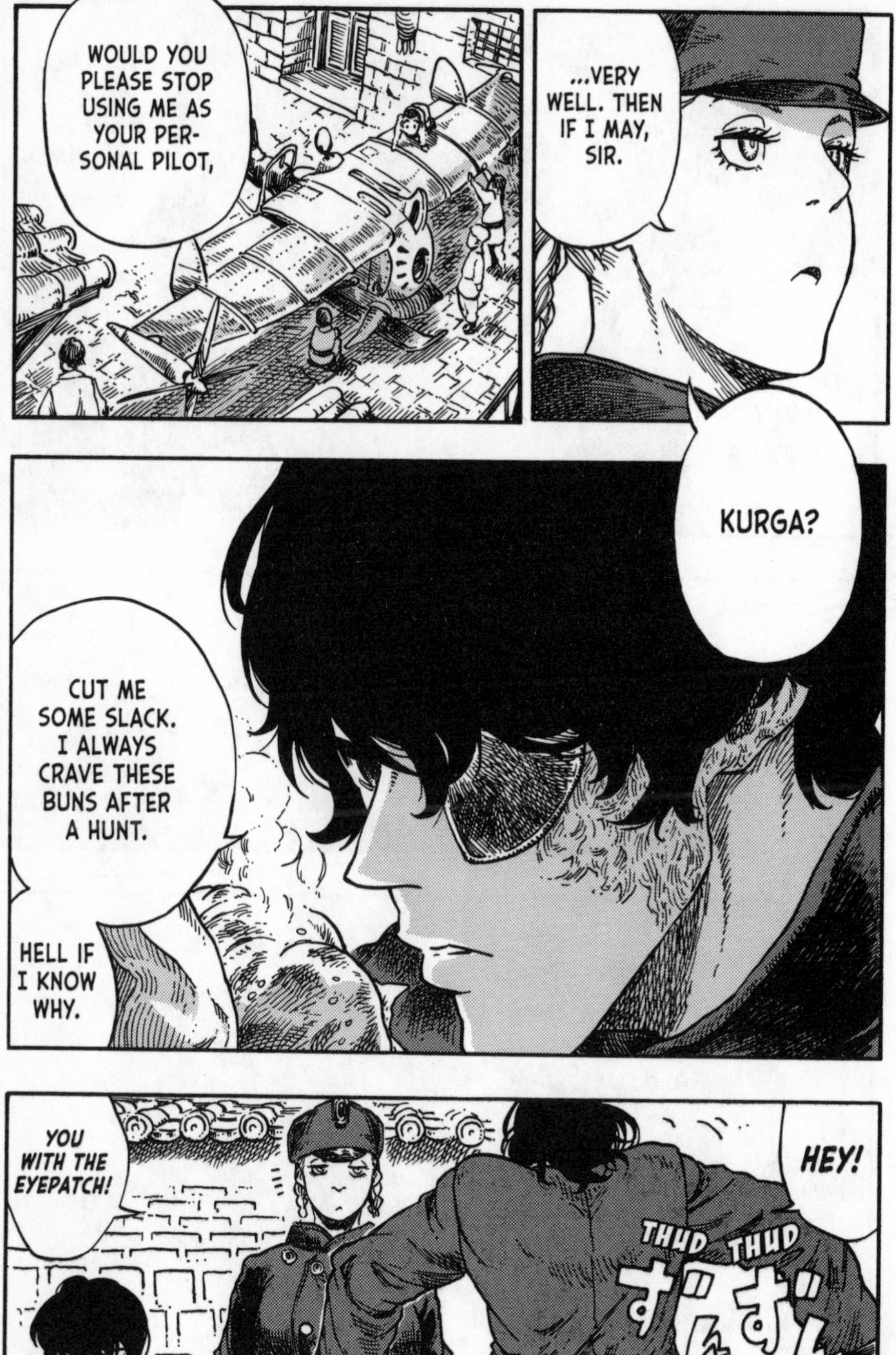
...VERY WELL. THEN IF I MAY, SIR.
WOULD YOU PLEASE STOP USING ME AS YOUR PER-SONAL PILOT,
KURGA?
CUT ME SOME SLACK. I ALWAYS CRAVE THESE BUNS AFTER A HUNT.
HELL IF I KNOW WHY.
HEY!
THUD THUD
ずんずん
YOU WITH THE EYEPATCH!

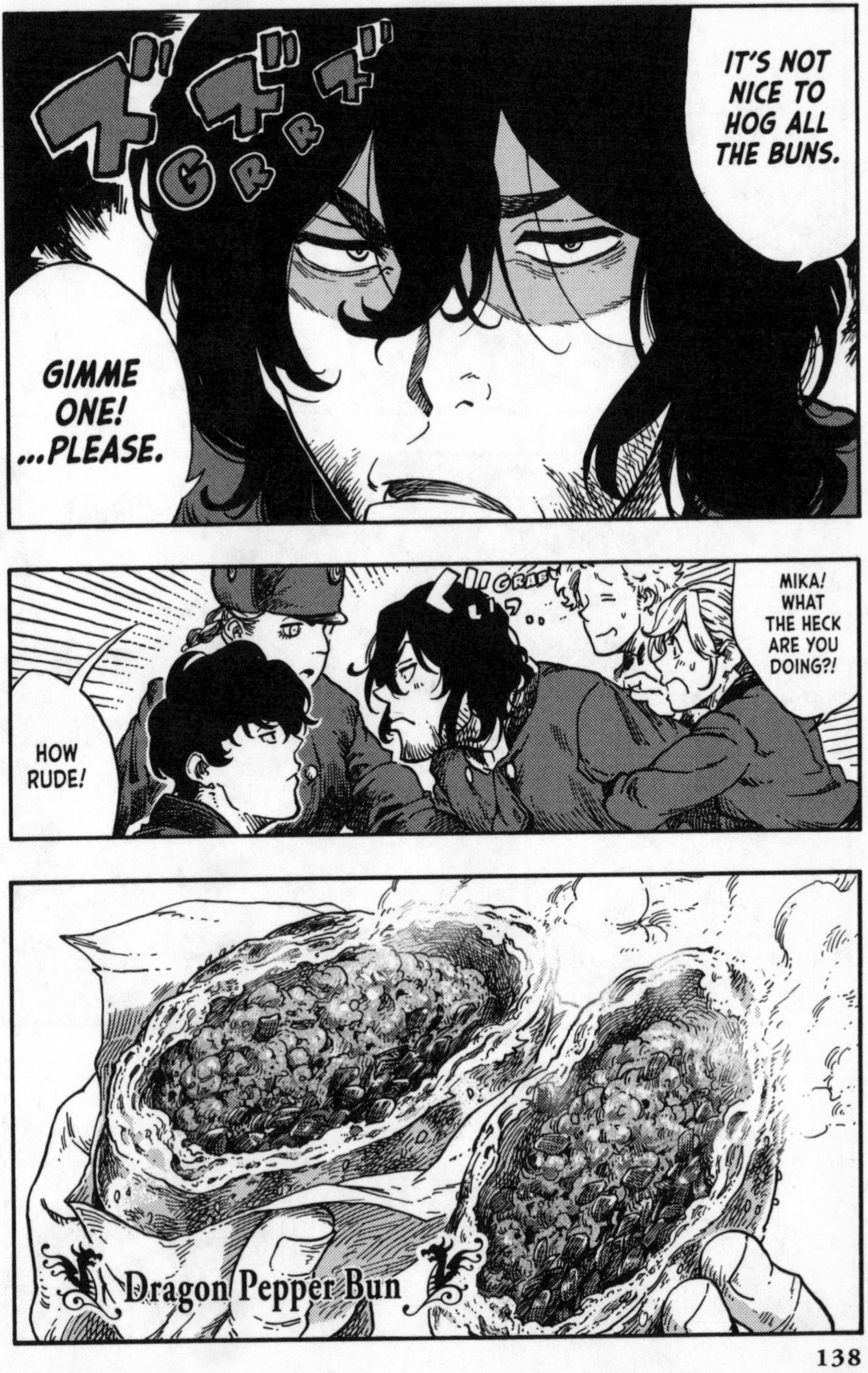
IT'S NOT NICE TO HOG ALL THE BUNS.
ズズズ
GRR
GIMME ONE! ...PLEASE.
MIKA! WHAT THE HECK ARE YOU DOING?!
GRAB
HOW RUDE!
Dragon Pepper Bun

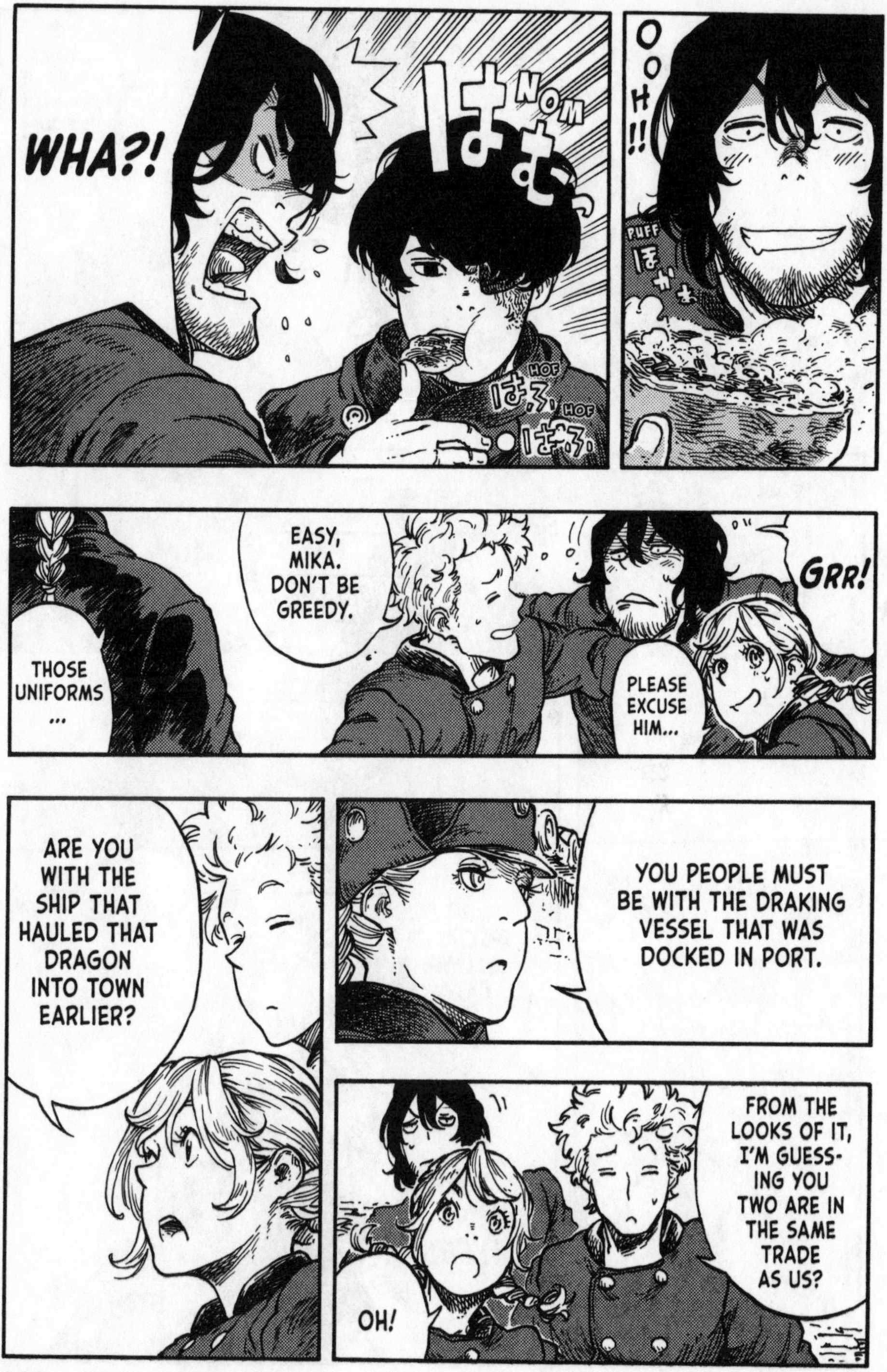
OOH!!
PUFF
NOM
WHA?!
HOF
HOF
GRR!
EASY, MIKA. DON'T BE GREEDY.
PLEASE EXCUSE HIM...
THOSE UNIFORMS ...
YOU PEOPLE MUST BE WITH THE DRAKING VESSEL THAT WAS DOCKED IN PORT.
FROM THE LOOKS OF IT, I'M GUESSING YOU TWO ARE IN THE SAME TRADE AS US?
OH!
ARE YOU WITH THE SHIP THAT HAULED THAT DRAGON INTO TOWN EARLIER?

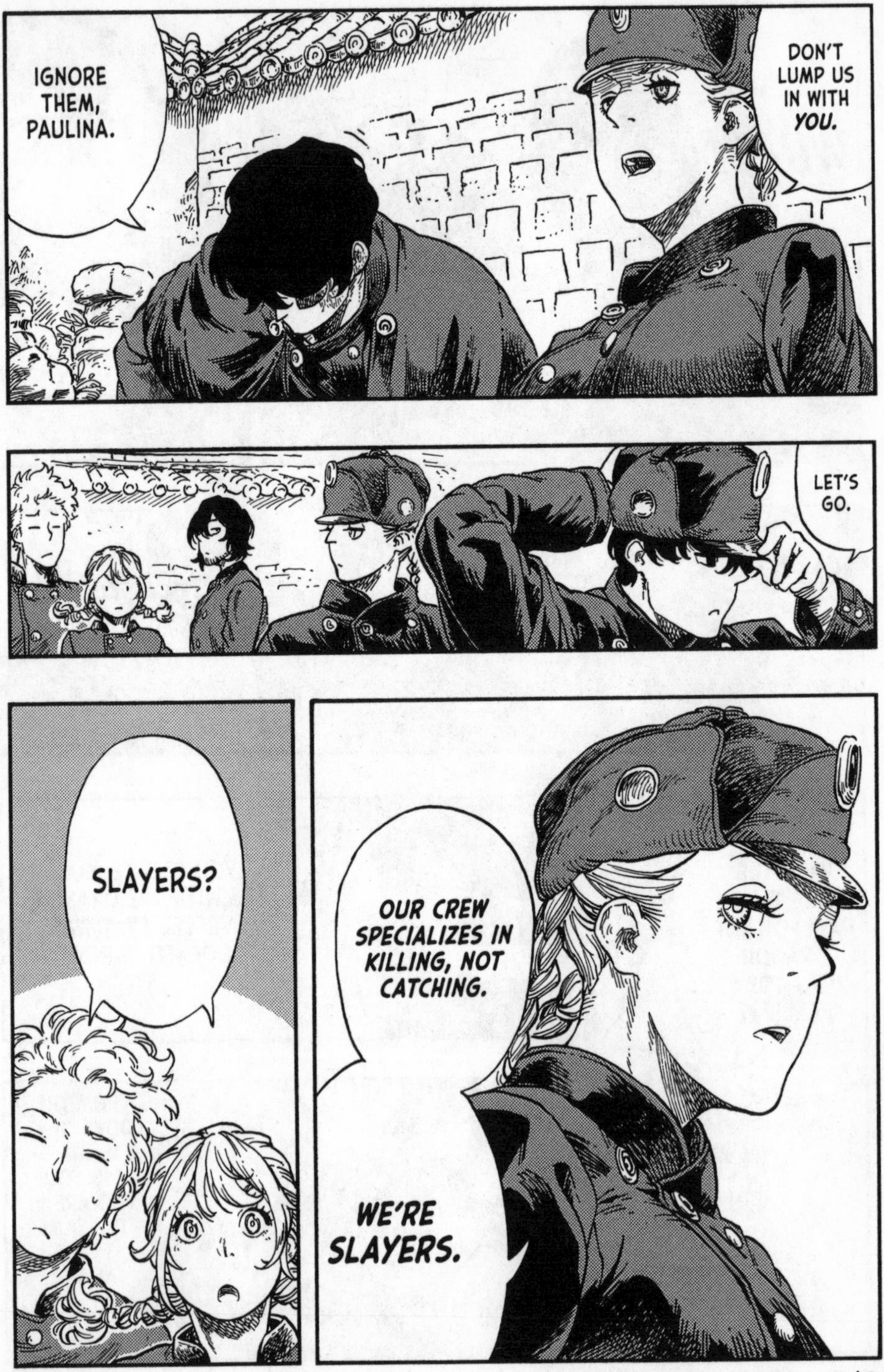
DON'T LUMP US IN WITH *YOU.*
IGNORE THEM, PAULINA.
LET'S GO.
OUR CREW SPECIALIZES IN KILLING, NOT CATCHING.
WE'RE SLAYERS.
SLAYERS?

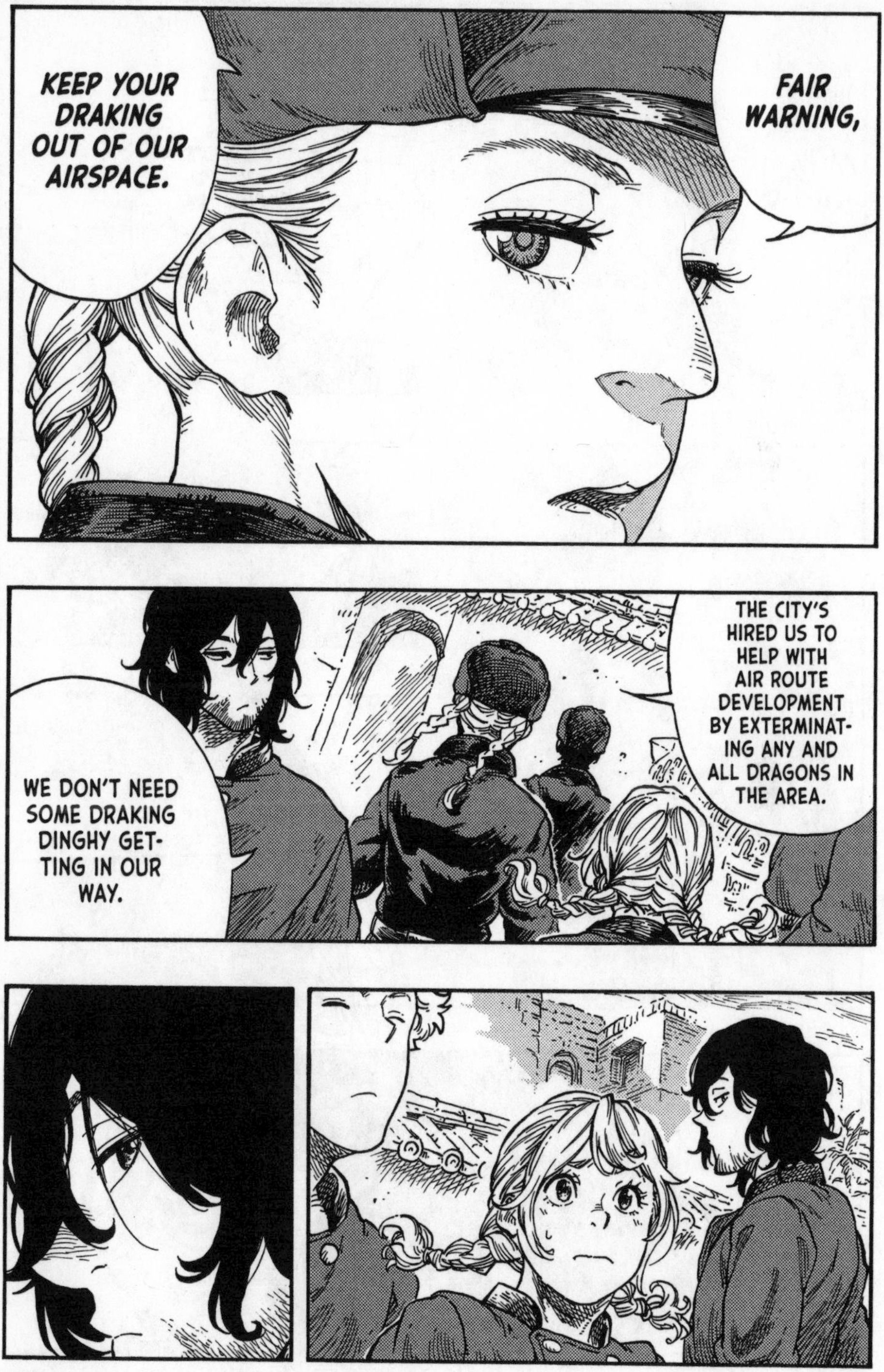
FAIR WARNING,
KEEP YOUR DRAKING OUT OF OUR AIRSPACE.
THE CITY'S HIRED US TO HELP WITH AIR ROUTE DEVELOPMENT BY EXTERMINAT-ING ANY AND ALL DRAGONS IN THE AREA.
WE DON'T NEED SOME DRAKING DINGHY GET-TING IN OUR WAY.

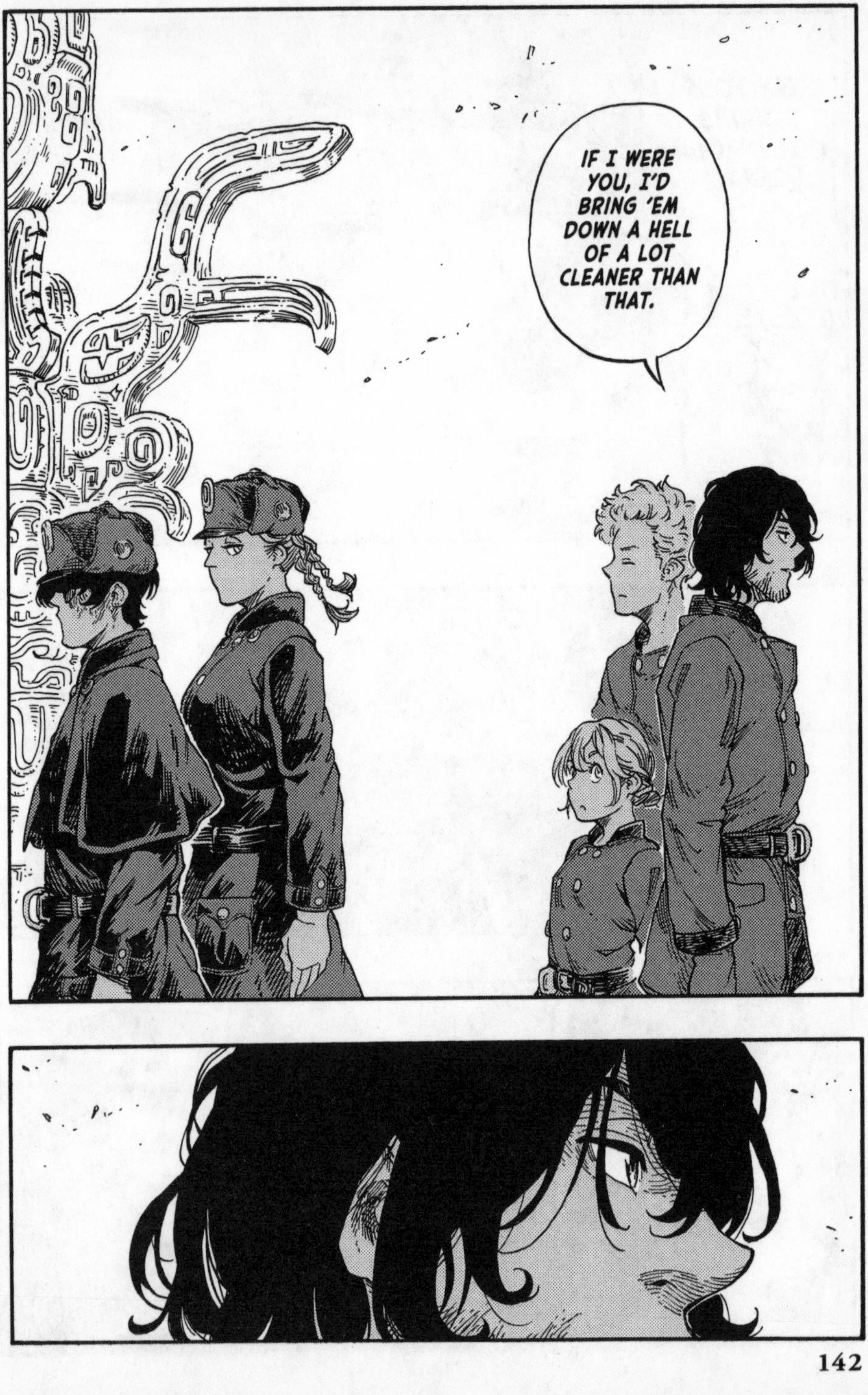
IF I WERE YOU, I'D BRING 'EM DOWN A HELL OF A LOT CLEANER THAN THAT.

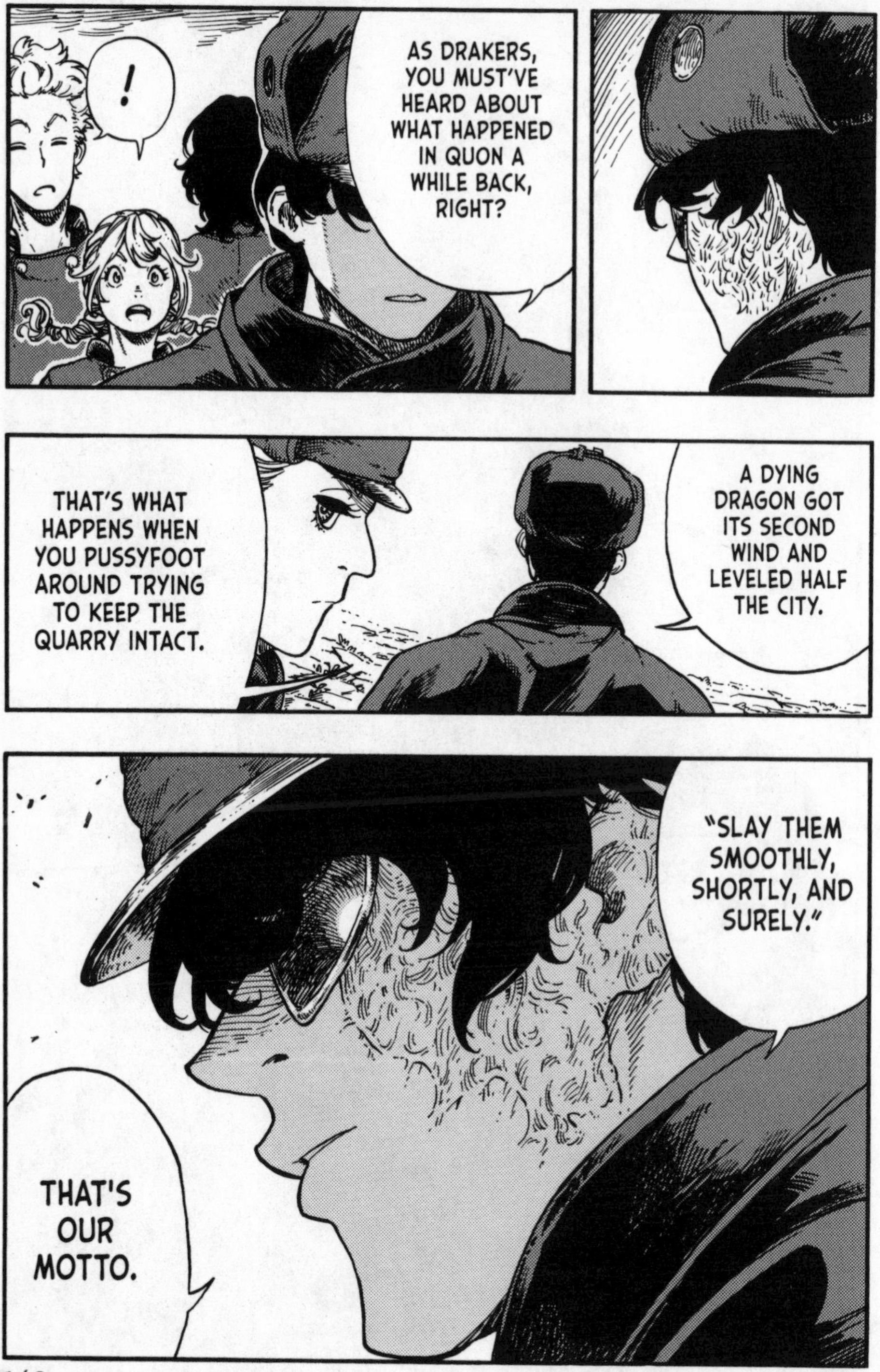
AS DRAKERS, YOU MUST'VE HEARD ABOUT WHAT HAPPENED IN QUON A WHILE BACK, RIGHT?
!
A DYING DRAGON GOT ITS SECOND WIND AND LEVELED HALF THE CITY.
THAT'S WHAT HAPPENS WHEN YOU PUSSYFOOT AROUND TRYING TO KEEP THE QUARRY INTACT.
"SLAY THEM SMOOTHLY, SHORTLY, AND SURELY."
THAT'S OUR MOTTO.

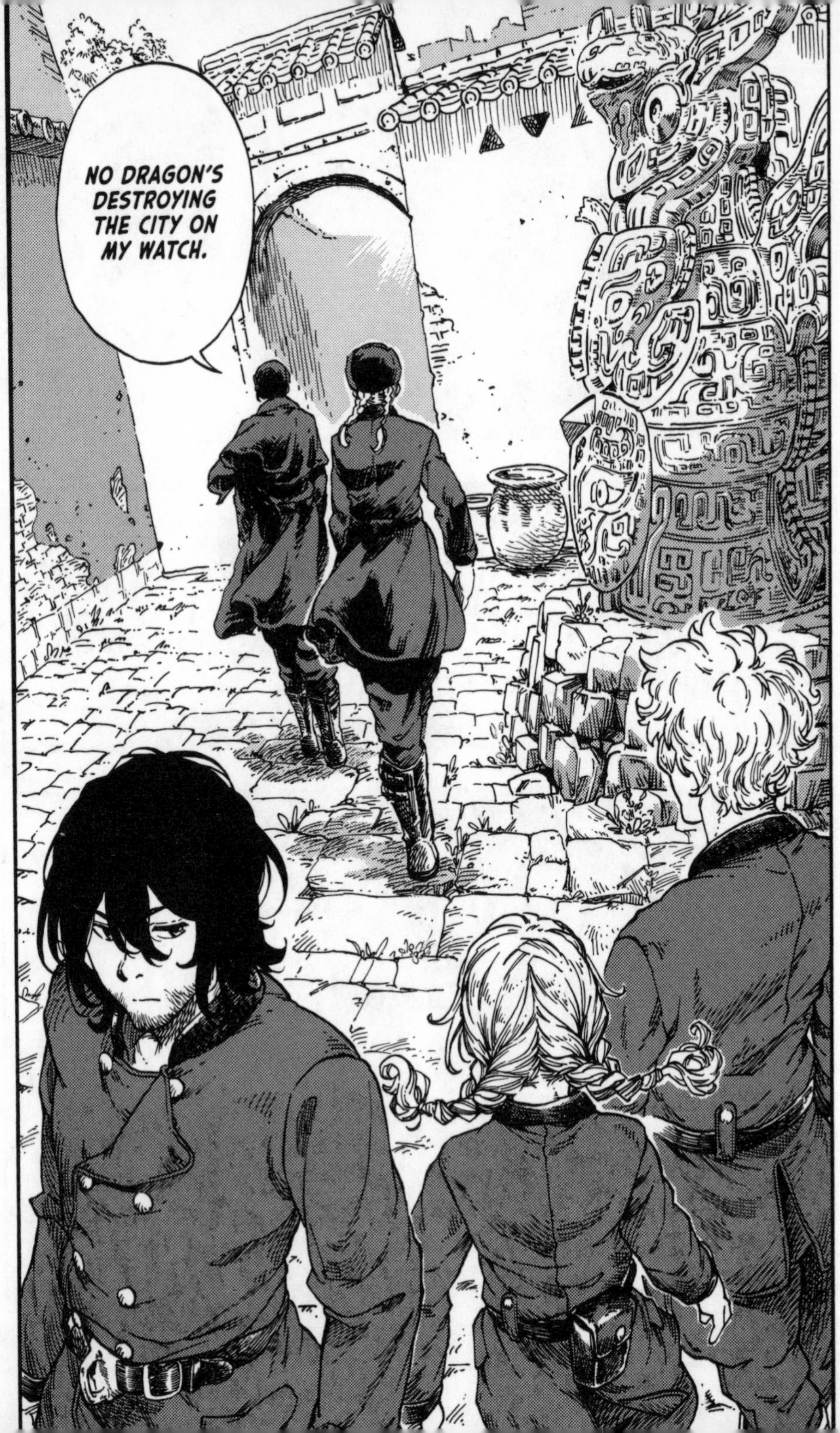
NO DRAGON'S DESTROYING THE CITY ON MY WATCH.

Dragon Pepper Buns

Ingredients (Serves 2)

★ **Dough**

Bread flour: 100 g   Cake flour: 100 g

Sugar: 20 g   Baking powder: 2 g

Water: 100 cc   Sesame oil: 1 tbsp

★ **Filling**

Ground dragon: 250 g   Green onion: 150 g

Sesame oil: 1 ½ tbsp   Ginger root (minced): ½ tbsp

Black pepper: ¾ tbsp   Sake: 1 ½ tbsp

Soy sauce: 1 tsp   Oyster sauce: 2 tsp

Sugar: ¾ tbsp   Salt: A pinch

Five spice powder: 1 ½ tbsp

White sesame seeds: As desired

01

In a large bowl, combine flours, sugar, and baking powder and mix together thoroughly with chopsticks or a whisk. Add sesame oil and loosely mix in.

02

Gradually mix in water until a tacky dough forms, then knead together with hands. If the dough is too dry, continue to knead, adding 1 tsp of water at a time.

03

Once a dough ball forms, remove from the bowl and place on a smooth surface dusted with flour and proceed to knead until the surface of the dough is smooth. Cover the dough ball with a damp kitchen towel to prevent it from drying out.

04

In a separate bowl, add ground dragon and salt and mix until smooth and sticky. Add sesame oil, ginger, black pepper, sugar, sake, five spice powder, soy sauce, and oyster sauce and mix well until thoroughly combined.

05

Chop green onion into roughly 1-cm pieces.

06

Divide the dough ball into six parts and roll into thin rounds with a rolling pin. Spoon 1/6 of the filling mixture in the middle of the disc and top with green onion. Fold the dough over and pinch the edges to seal the bun shut. If the dough tears, simply patch with excess dough. Dampen the surface of the bun with water and sprinkle with sesame seeds.

07

Using a charcoal pot oven, stick buns to the inner walls of the pot and bake for 15-20 minutes and serve hot. If using an oven, bake at 200° C (400° F).

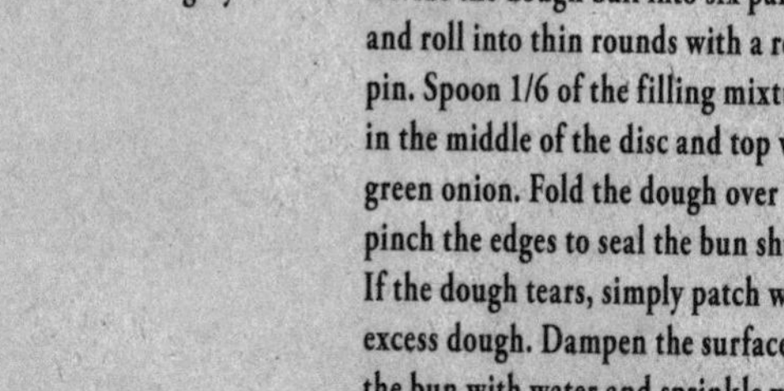

I'LL TAKE FIVE MORE.

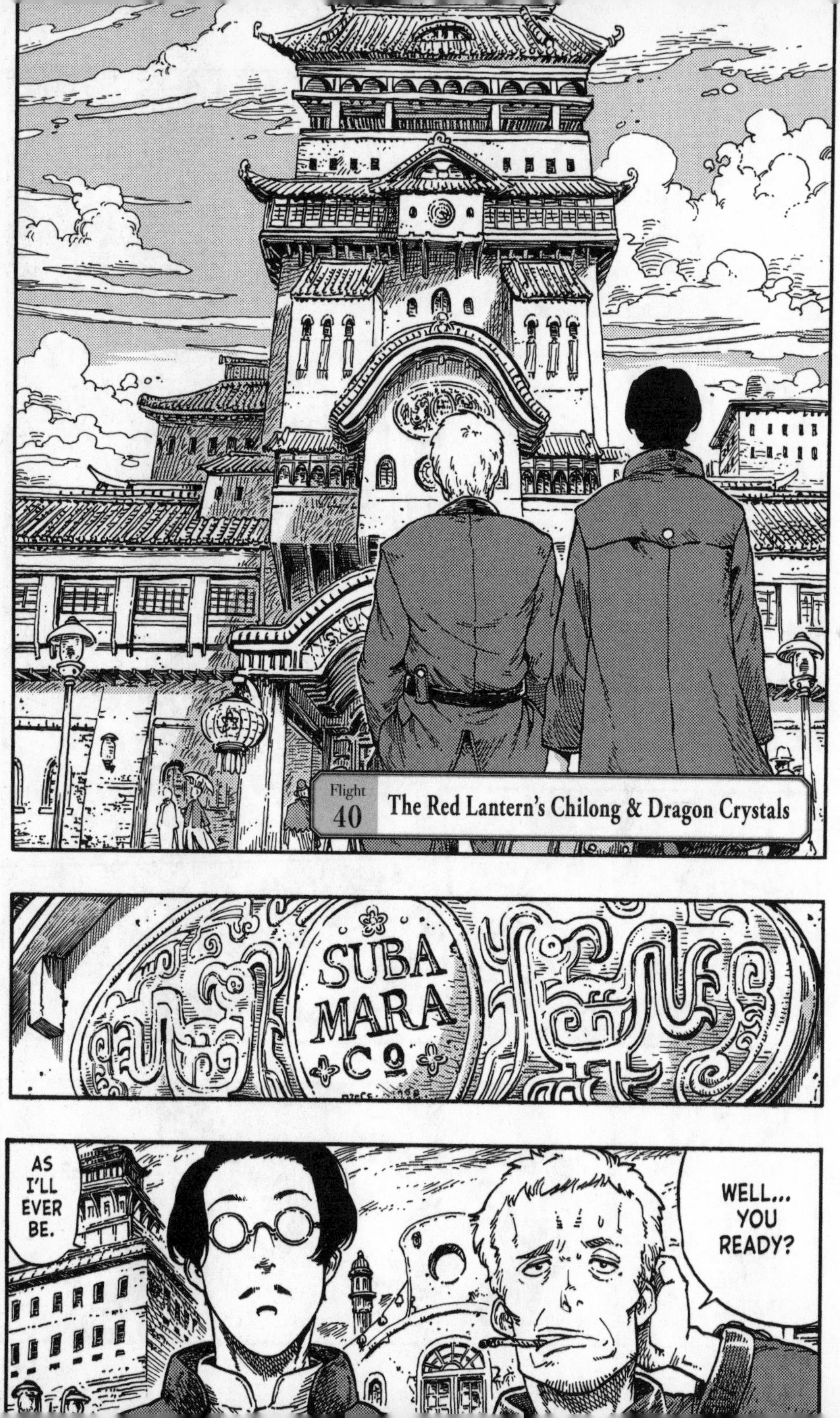
Flight 40
The Red Lantern's Chilong & Dragon Crystals
SUBA MARA CO
WELL... YOU READY?
AS I'LL EVER BE.

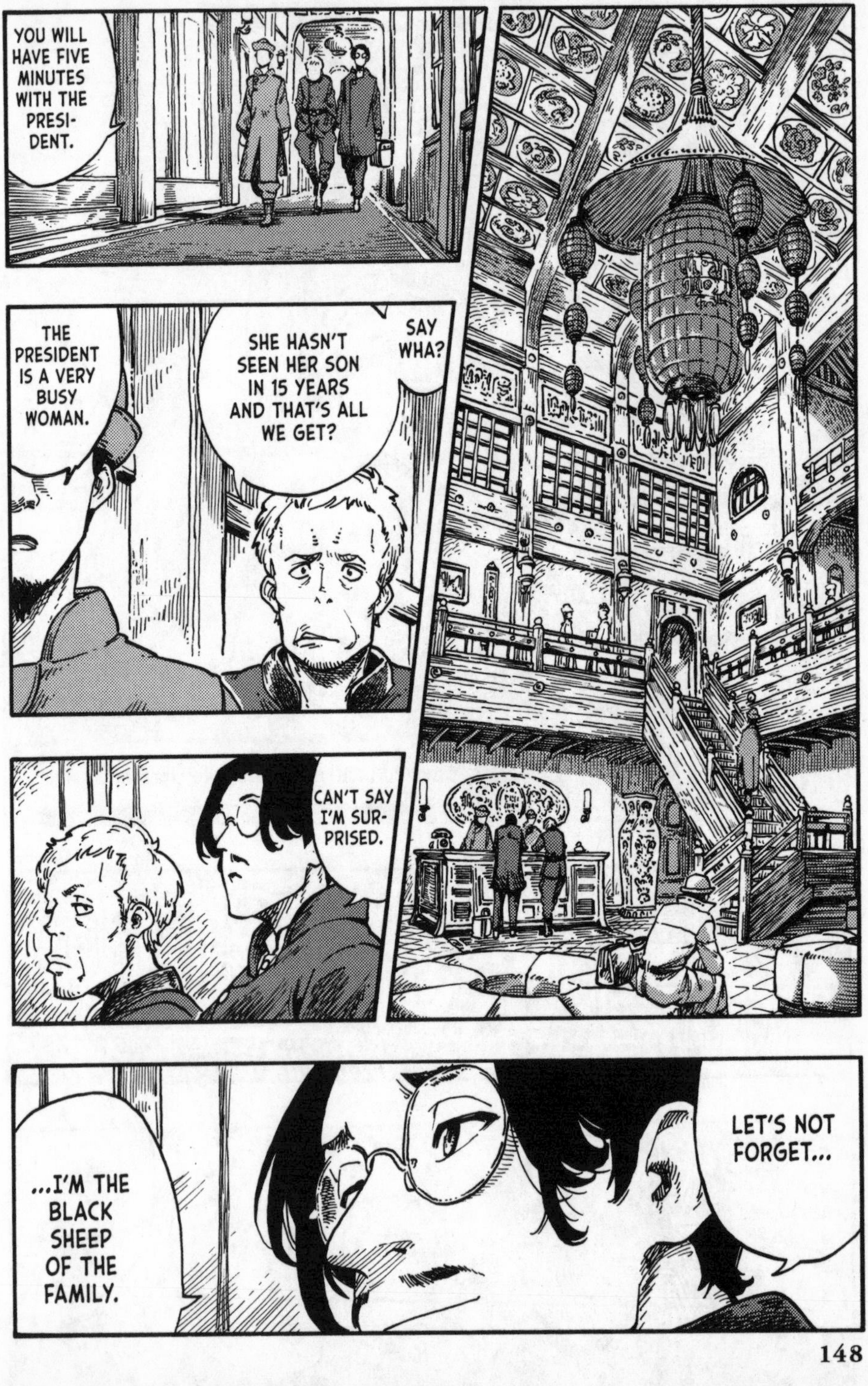
YOU WILL HAVE FIVE MINUTES WITH THE PRESIDENT.
SAY WHA?
SHE HASN'T SEEN HER SON IN 15 YEARS AND THAT'S ALL WE GET?
THE PRESIDENT IS A VERY BUSY WOMAN.
CAN'T SAY I'M SURPRISED.
LET'S NOT FORGET...
...I'M THE BLACK SHEEP OF THE FAMILY.

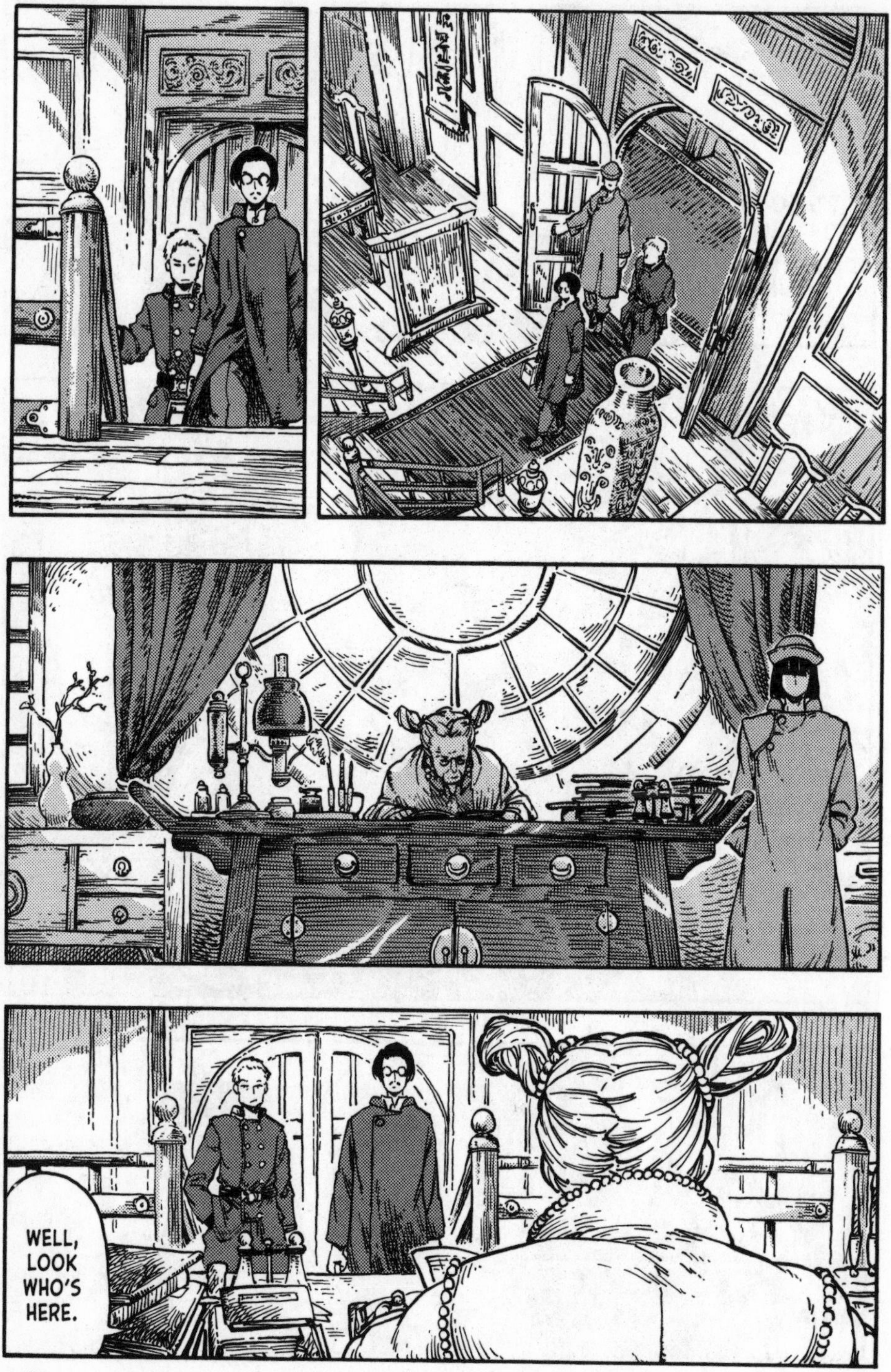
WELL, LOOK WHO'S HERE.

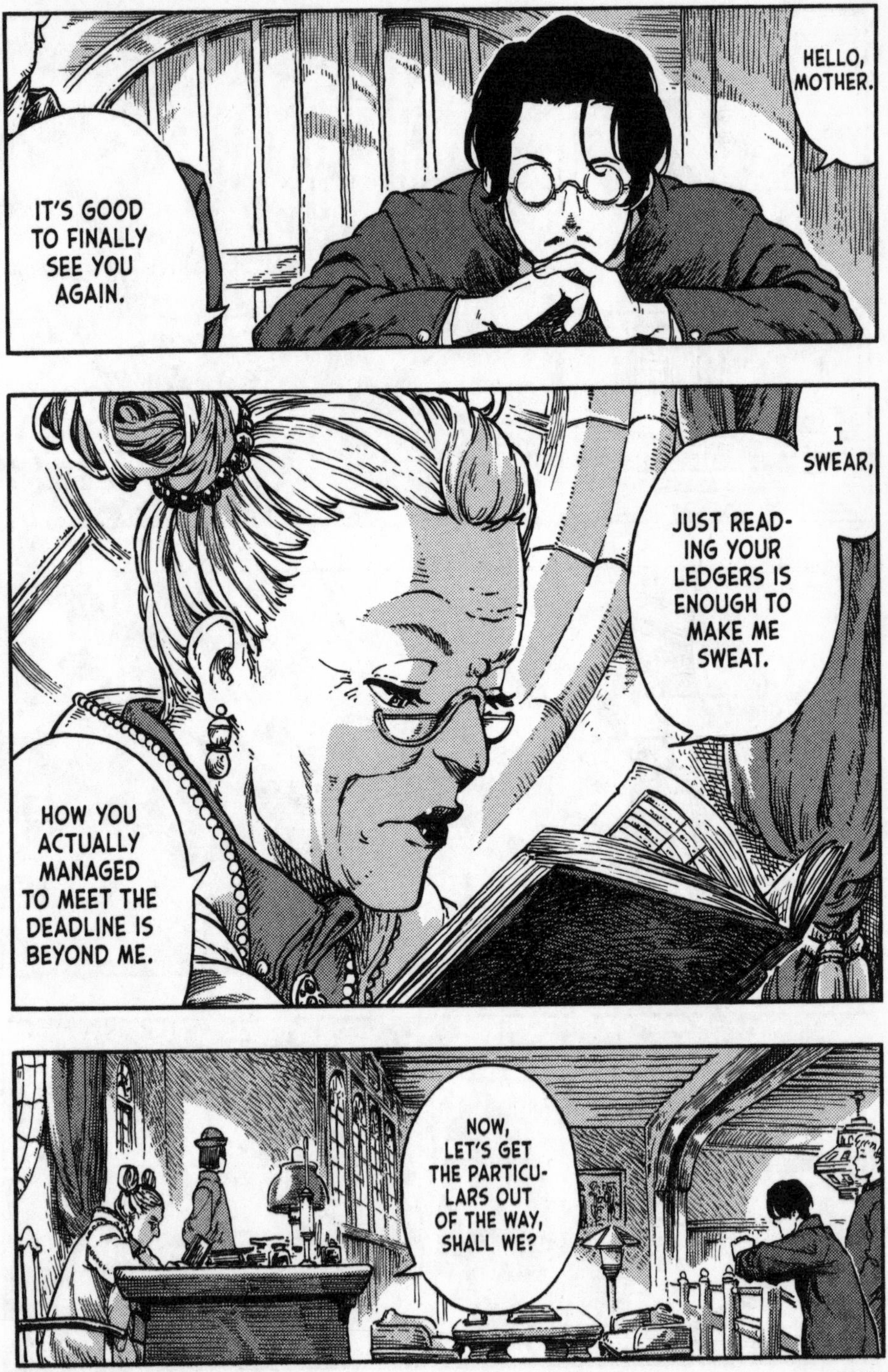
HELLO, MOTHER.
IT'S GOOD TO FINALLY SEE YOU AGAIN.
I SWEAR,
JUST READING YOUR LEDGERS IS ENOUGH TO MAKE ME SWEAT.
HOW YOU ACTUALLY MANAGED TO MEET THE DEADLINE IS BEYOND ME.
NOW, LET'S GET THE PARTICULARS OUT OF THE WAY, SHALL WE?

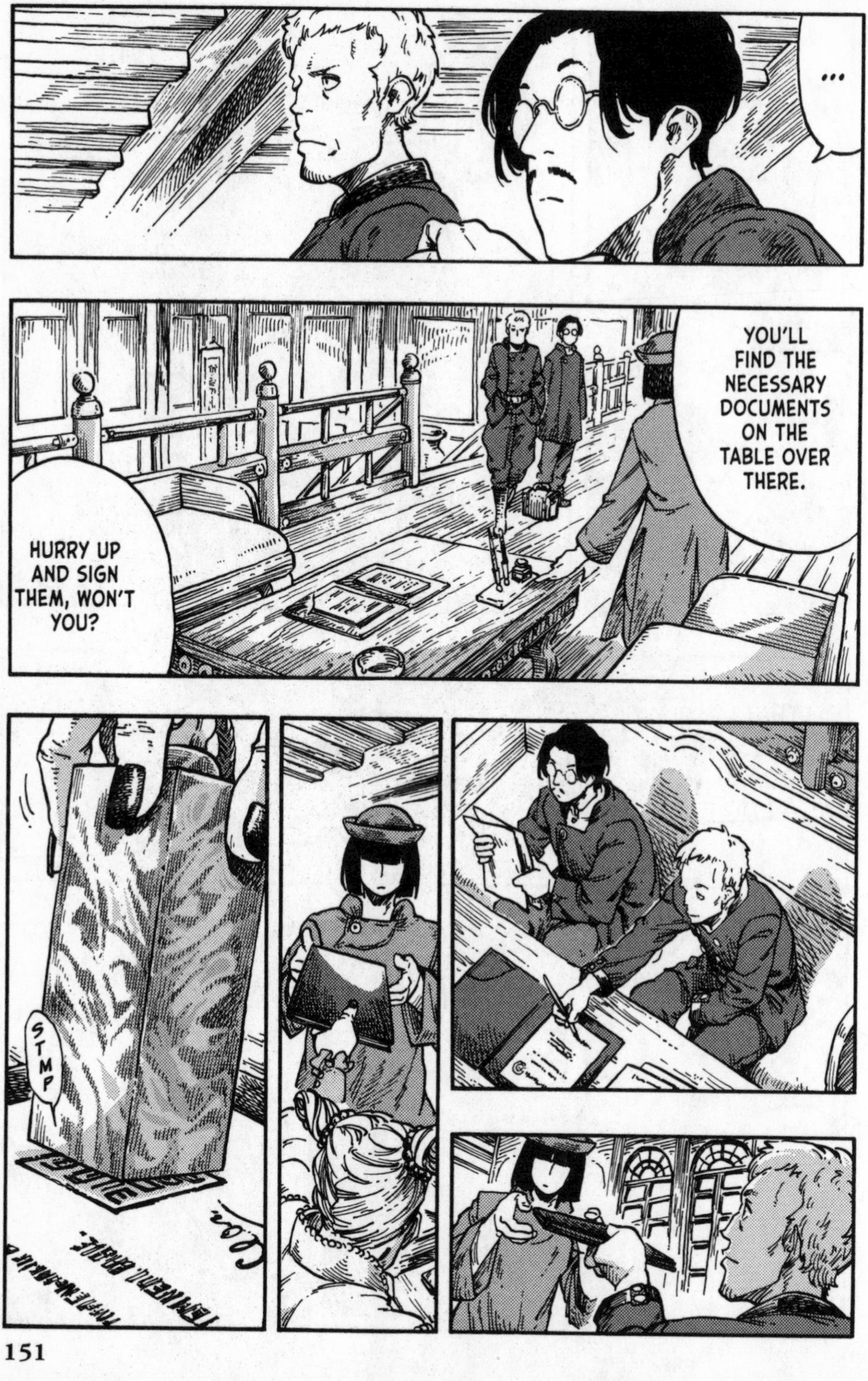
...
YOU'LL FIND THE NECESSARY DOCUMENTS ON THE TABLE OVER THERE.
HURRY UP AND SIGN THEM, WON'T YOU?
STMP

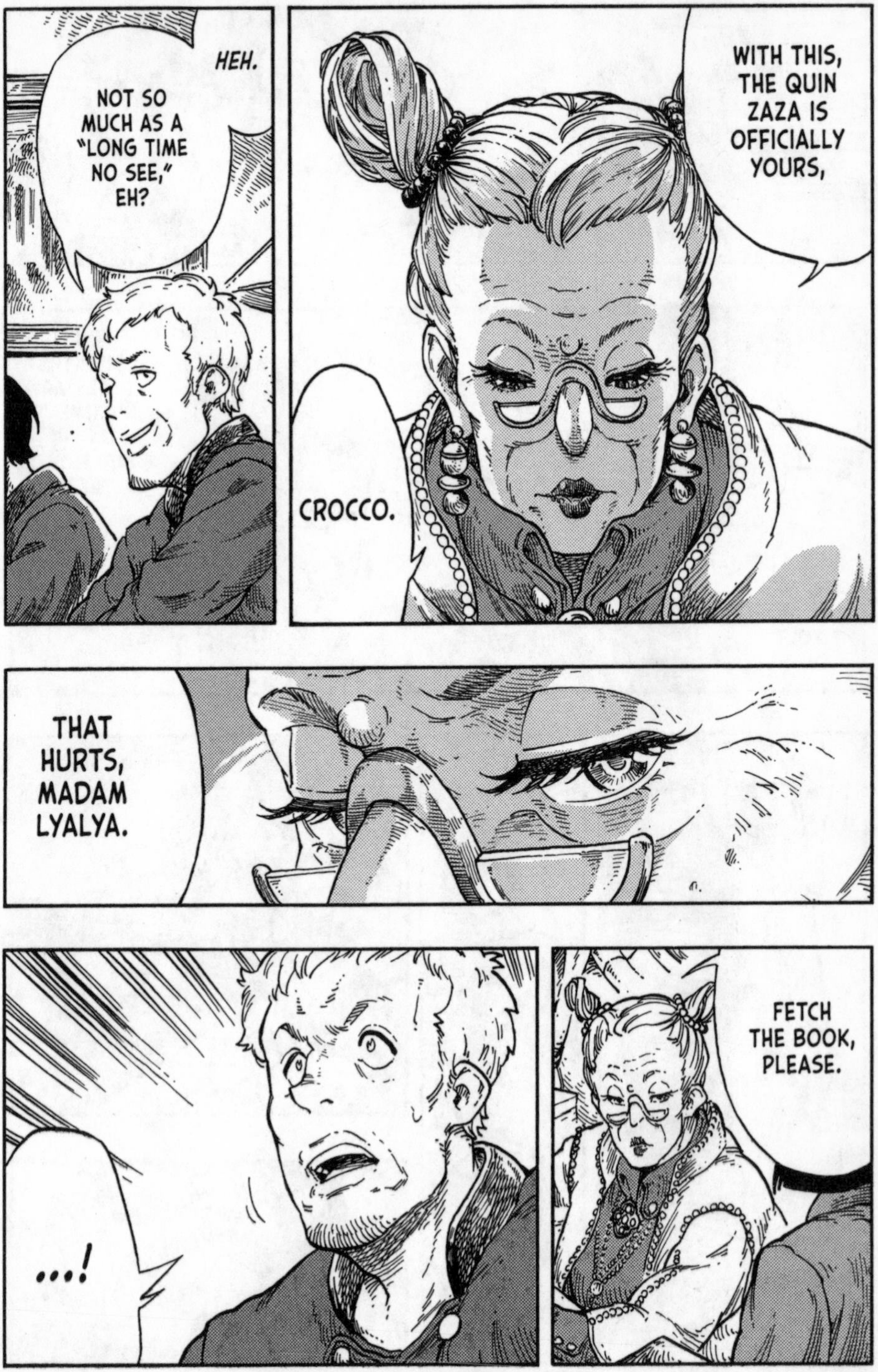
WITH THIS, THE QUIN ZAZA IS OFFICIALLY YOURS,
CROCCO.
HEH.
NOT SO MUCH AS A "LONG TIME NO SEE," EH?
THAT HURTS, MADAM LYALYA.
FETCH THE BOOK, PLEASE.
...!

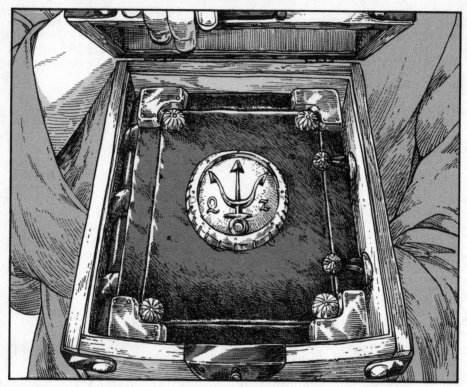

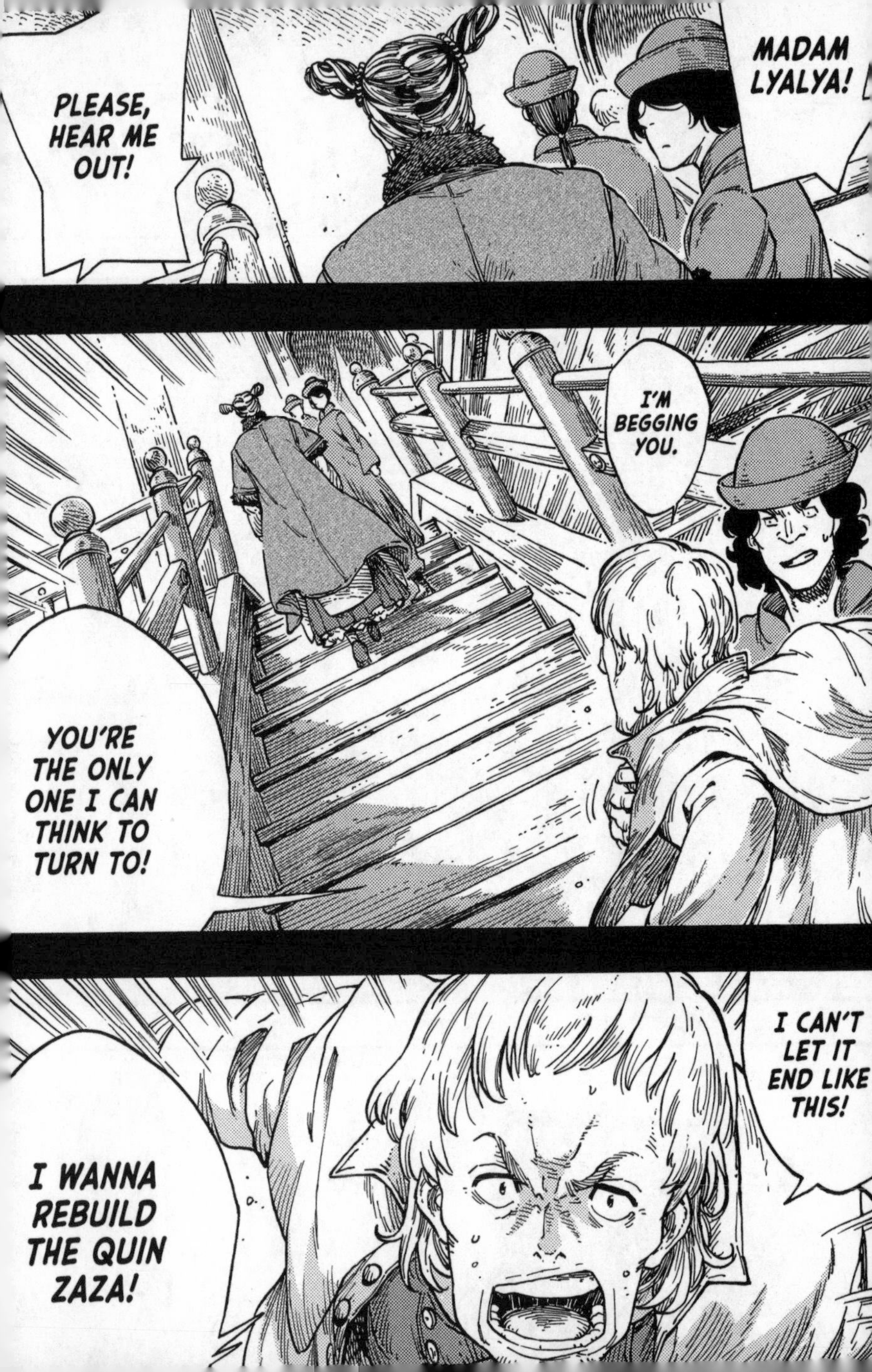
MADAM LYALYA!
PLEASE, HEAR ME OUT!
I'M BEGGING YOU.
YOU'RE THE ONLY ONE I CAN THINK TO TURN TO!
I CAN'T LET IT END LIKE THIS!
I WANNA REBUILD THE QUIN ZAZA!

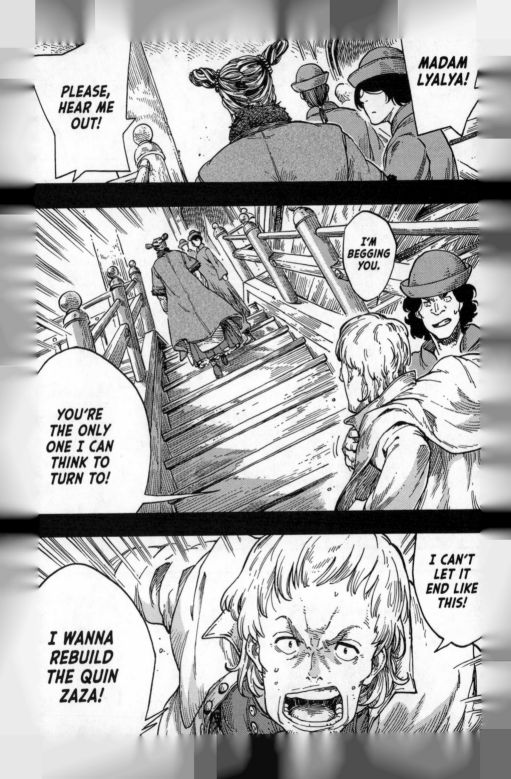

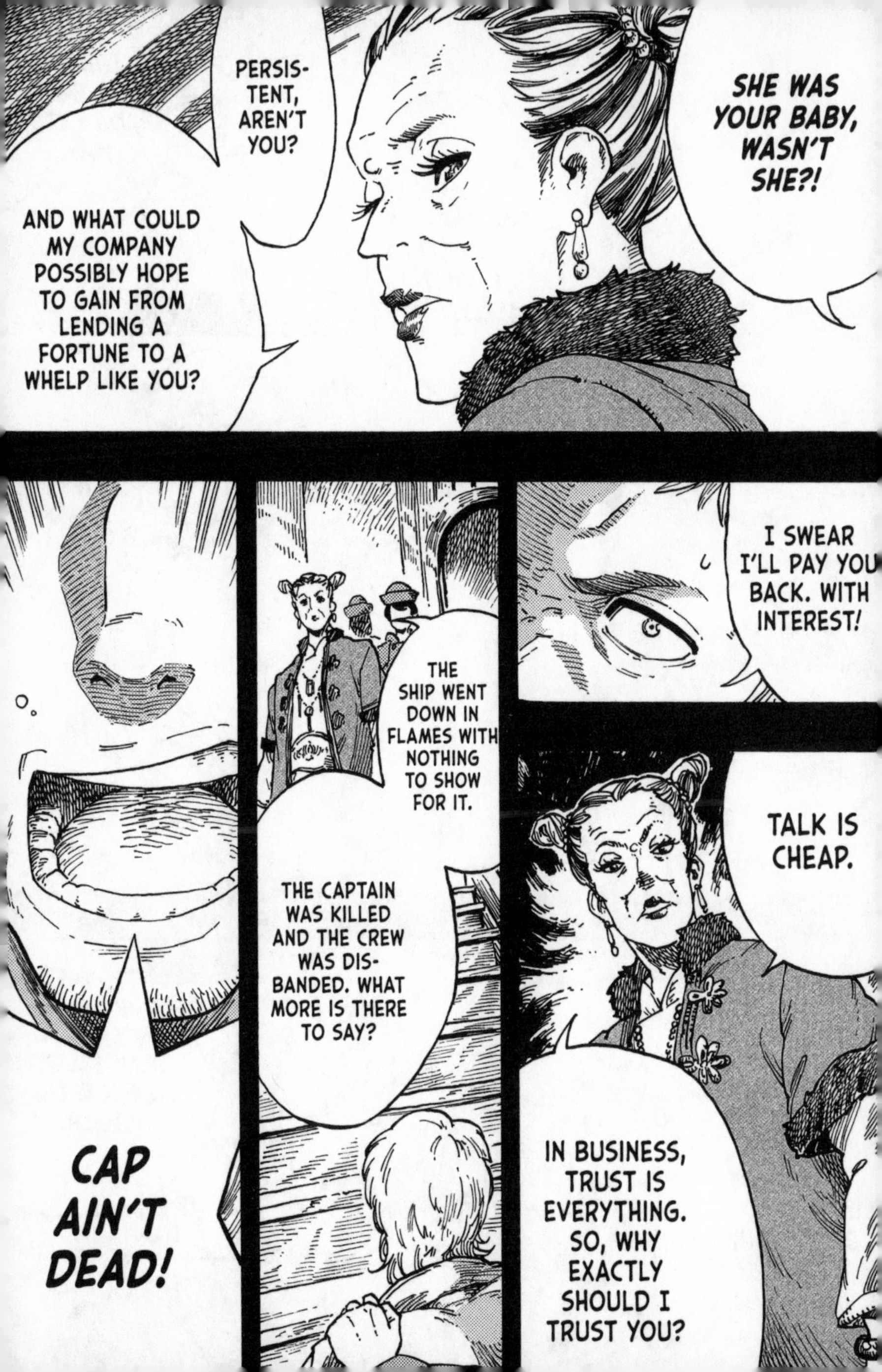
SHE WAS YOUR BABY, WASN'T SHE?!
PERSIS-TENT, AREN'T YOU?
AND WHAT COULD MY COMPANY POSSIBLY HOPE TO GAIN FROM LENDING A FORTUNE TO A WHELP LIKE YOU?
I SWEAR I'LL PAY YOU BACK. WITH INTEREST!
TALK IS CHEAP.
IN BUSINESS, TRUST IS EVERYTHING. SO, WHY EXACTLY SHOULD I TRUST YOU?
THE SHIP WENT DOWN IN FLAMES WITH NOTHING TO SHOW FOR IT.
THE CAPTAIN WAS KILLED AND THE CREW WAS DIS-BANDED. WHAT MORE IS THERE TO SAY?
CAP AIN'T DEAD!

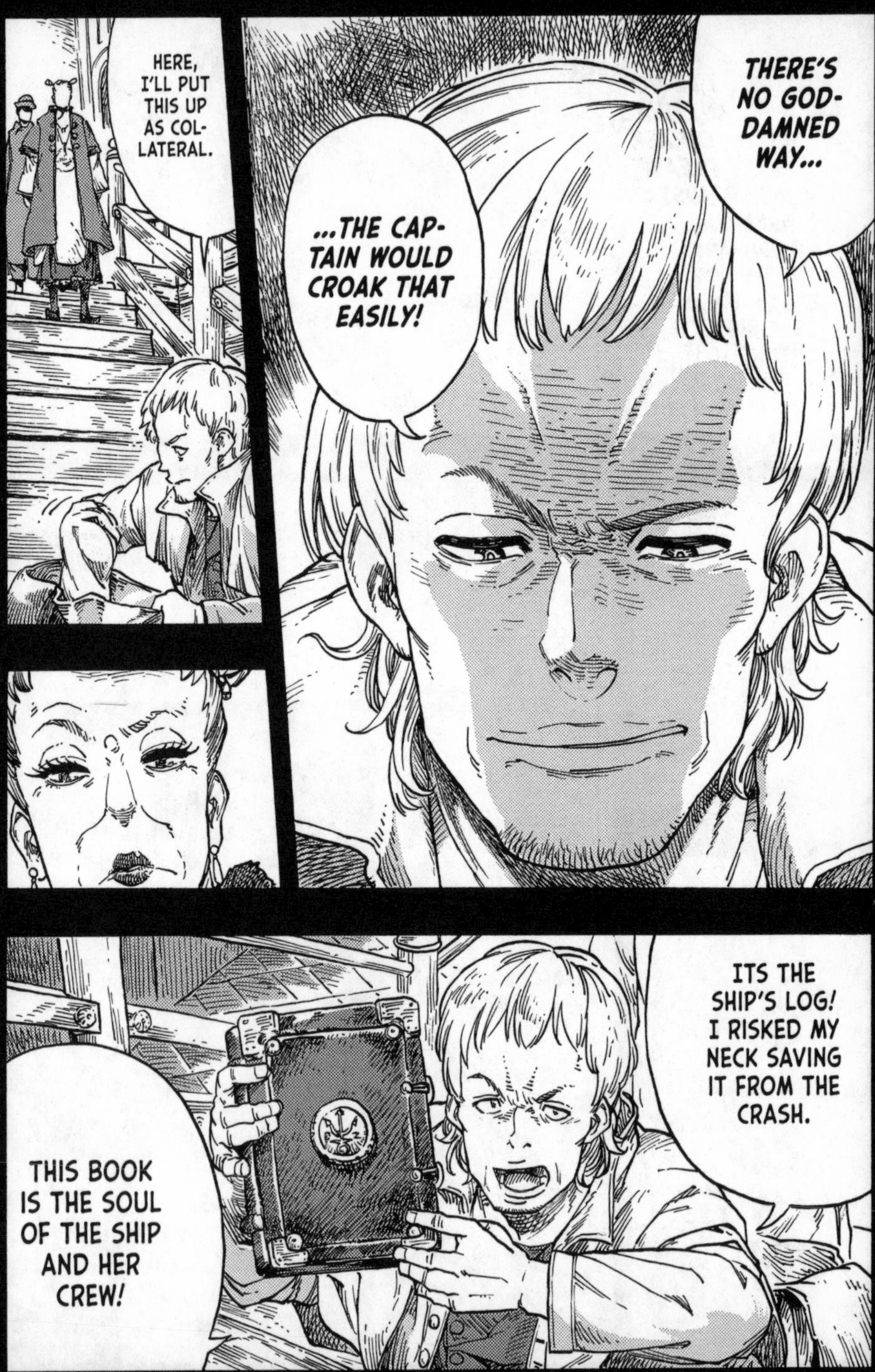
THERE'S NO GOD-DAMNED WAY...
...THE CAP-TAIN WOULD CROAK THAT EASILY!
HERE, I'LL PUT THIS UP AS COL-LATERAL.
ITS THE SHIP'S LOG! I RISKED MY NECK SAVING IT FROM THE CRASH.
THIS BOOK IS THE SOUL OF THE SHIP AND HER CREW!

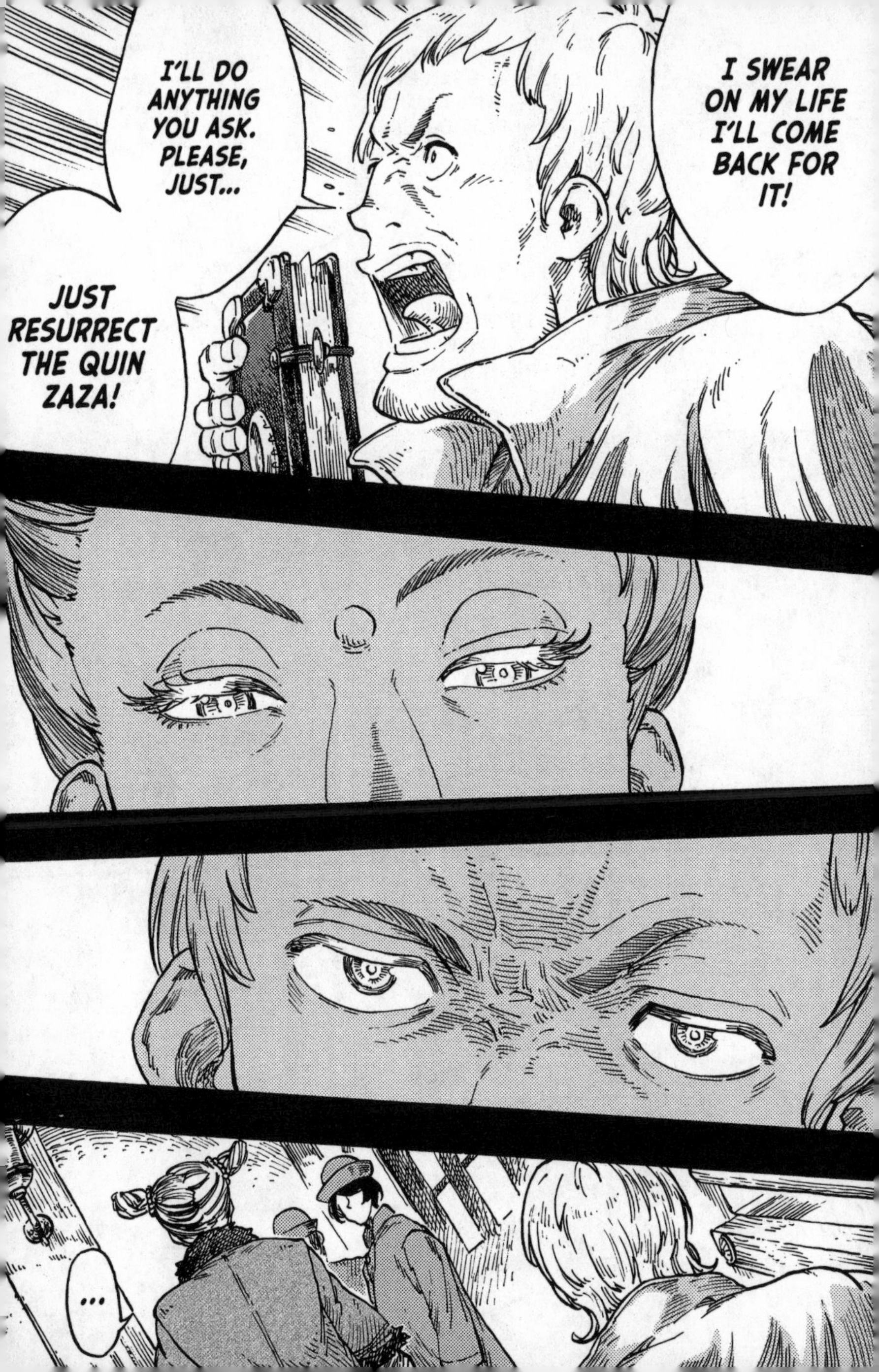
I SWEAR ON MY LIFE I'LL COME BACK FOR IT!
I'LL DO ANYTHING YOU ASK. PLEASE, JUST...
JUST RESURRECT THE QUIN ZAZA!
...

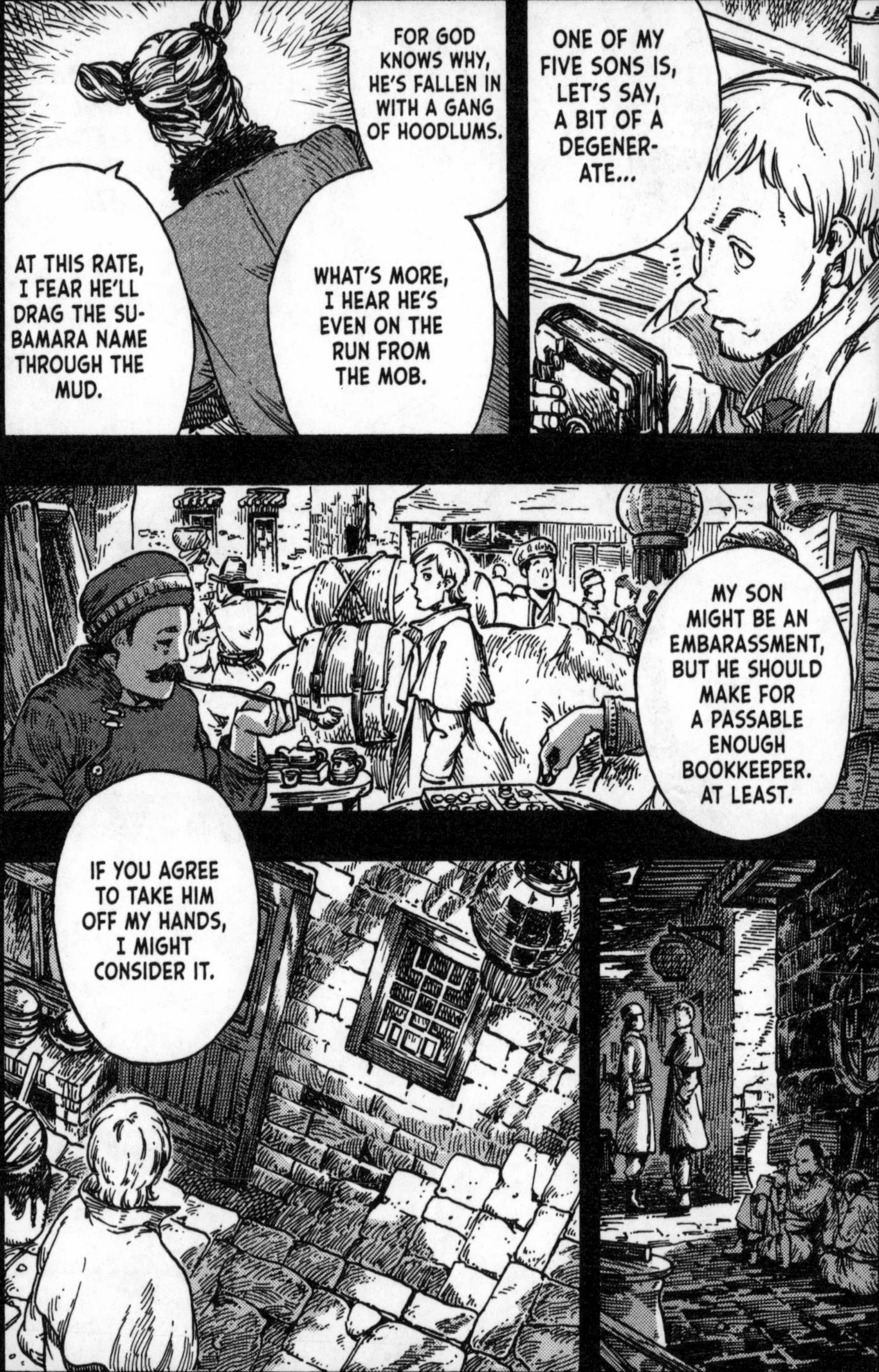
ONE OF MY FIVE SONS IS, LET'S SAY, A BIT OF A DEGENER-ATE...
FOR GOD KNOWS WHY, HE'S FALLEN IN WITH A GANG OF HOODLUMS.
WHAT'S MORE, I HEAR HE'S EVEN ON THE RUN FROM THE MOB.
AT THIS RATE, I FEAR HE'LL DRAG THE SU-BAMARA NAME THROUGH THE MUD.
MY SON MIGHT BE AN EMBARASSMENT, BUT HE SHOULD MAKE FOR A PASSABLE ENOUGH BOOKKEEPER. AT LEAST.
IF YOU AGREE TO TAKE HIM OFF MY HANDS, I MIGHT CONSIDER IT.

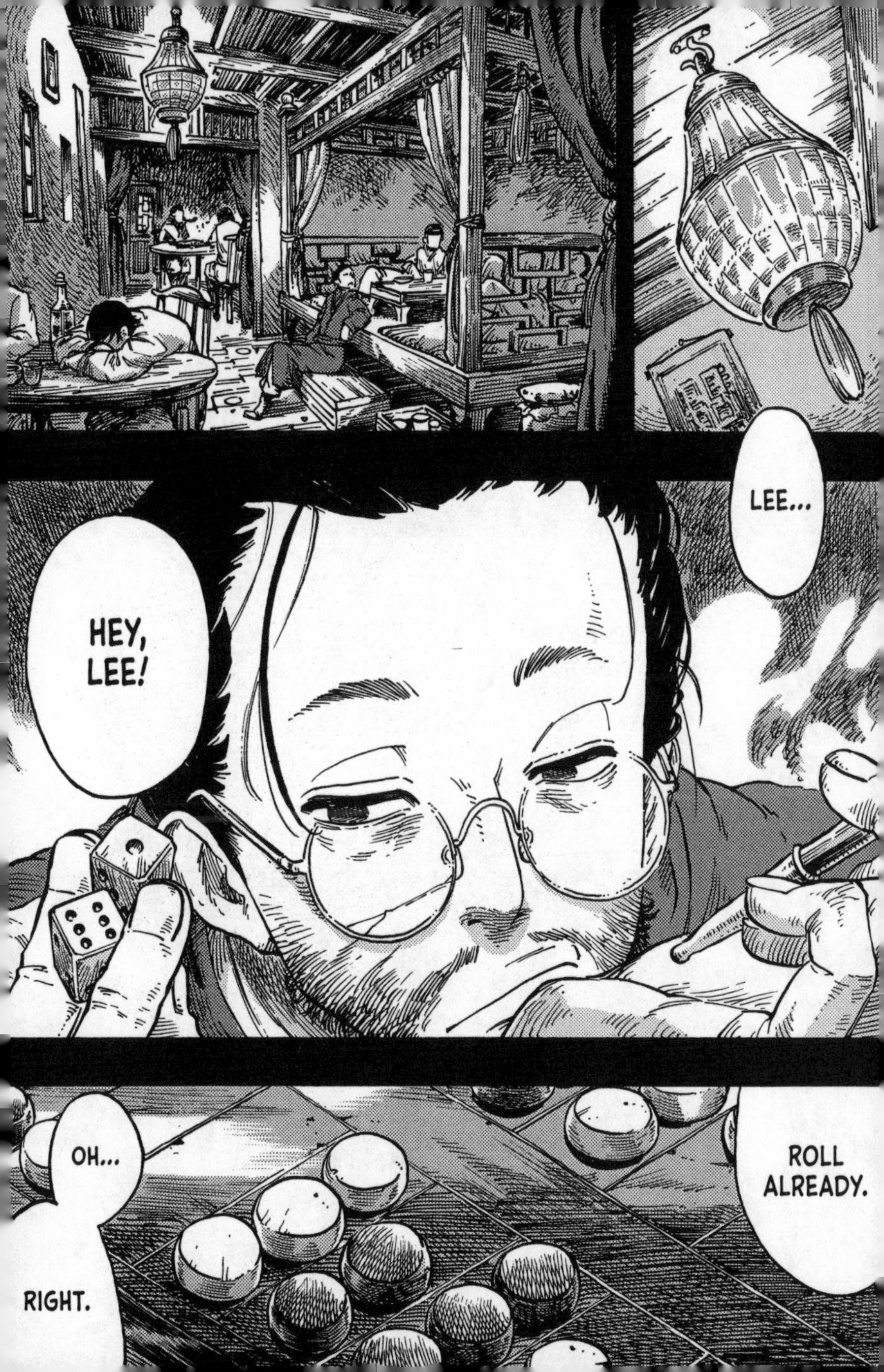
LEE...
HEY, LEE!
ROLL ALREADY.
OH...
RIGHT.

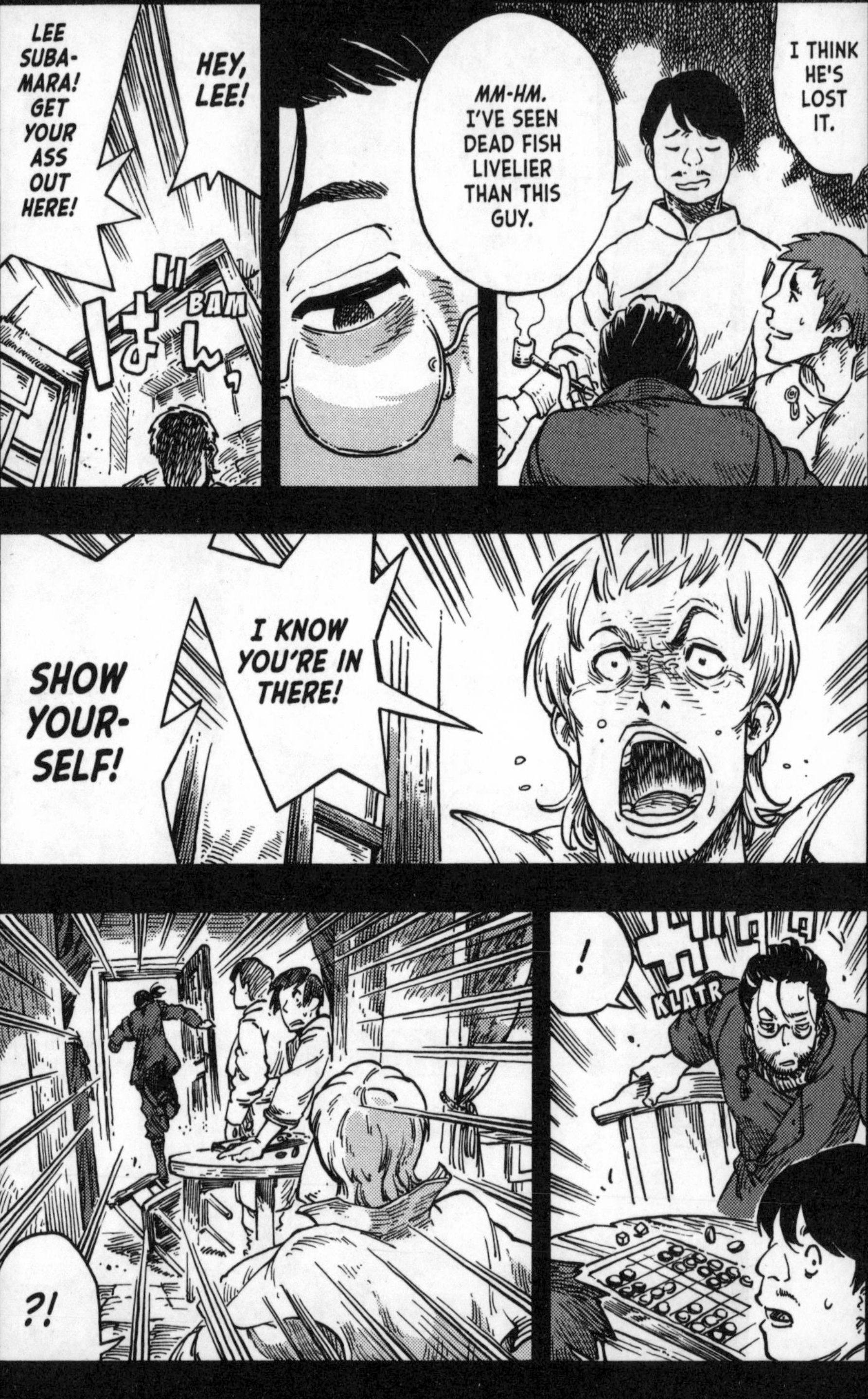
I THINK HE'S LOST IT.
MM-HM. I'VE SEEN DEAD FISH LIVELIER THAN THIS GUY.
HEY, LEE!
LEE SUBA-MARA! GET YOUR ASS OUT HERE!
BAM
I KNOW YOU'RE IN THERE!
SHOW YOUR-SELF!
!
KLATR
?!

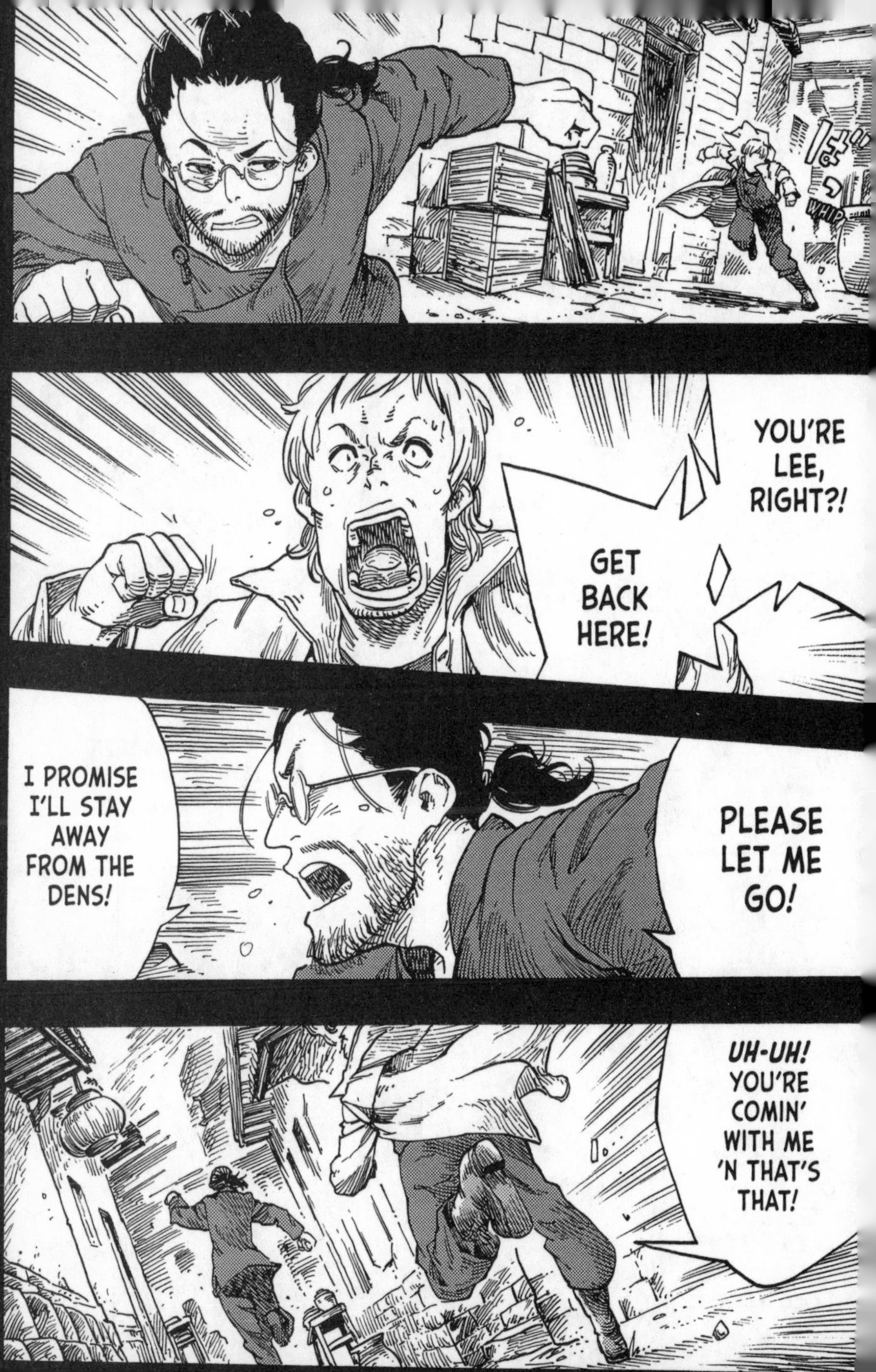
WHIP!
YOU'RE LEE, RIGHT?!
GET BACK HERE!
PLEASE LET ME GO!
I PROMISE I'LL STAY AWAY FROM THE DENS!
UH-UH! YOU'RE COMIN' WITH ME 'N THAT'S THAT!

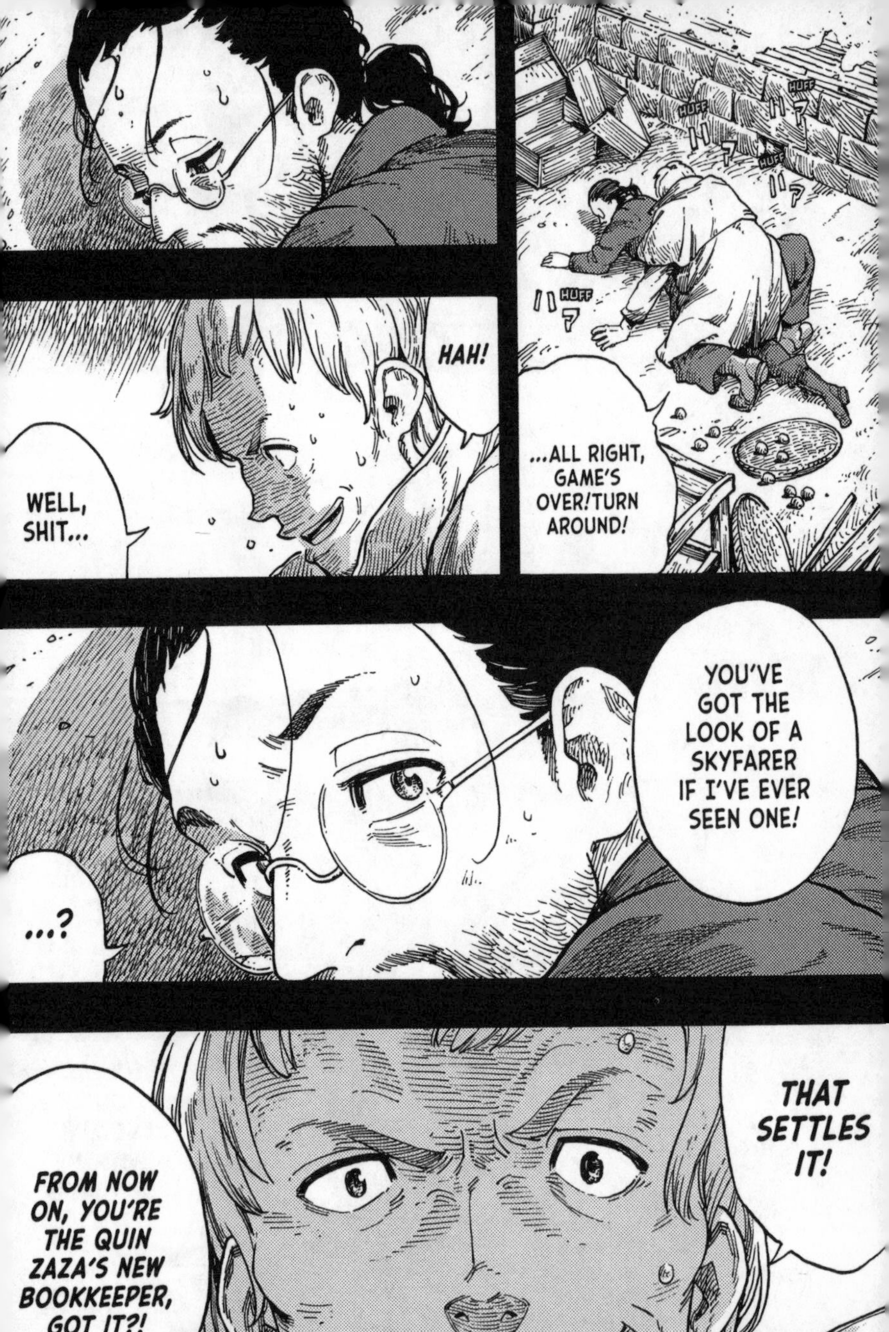
HUFF
HUFF
HUFF
...ALL RIGHT, GAME'S OVER! TURN AROUND!
HAH!
WELL, SHIT...
YOU'VE GOT THE LOOK OF A SKYFARER IF I'VE EVER SEEN ONE!
...?
THAT SETTLES IT!
FROM NOW ON, YOU'RE THE QUIN ZAZA'S NEW BOOKKEEPER, GOT IT?!

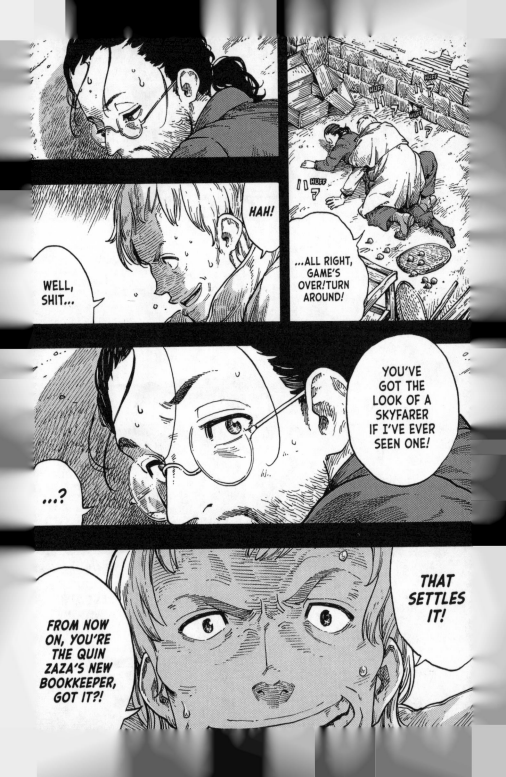

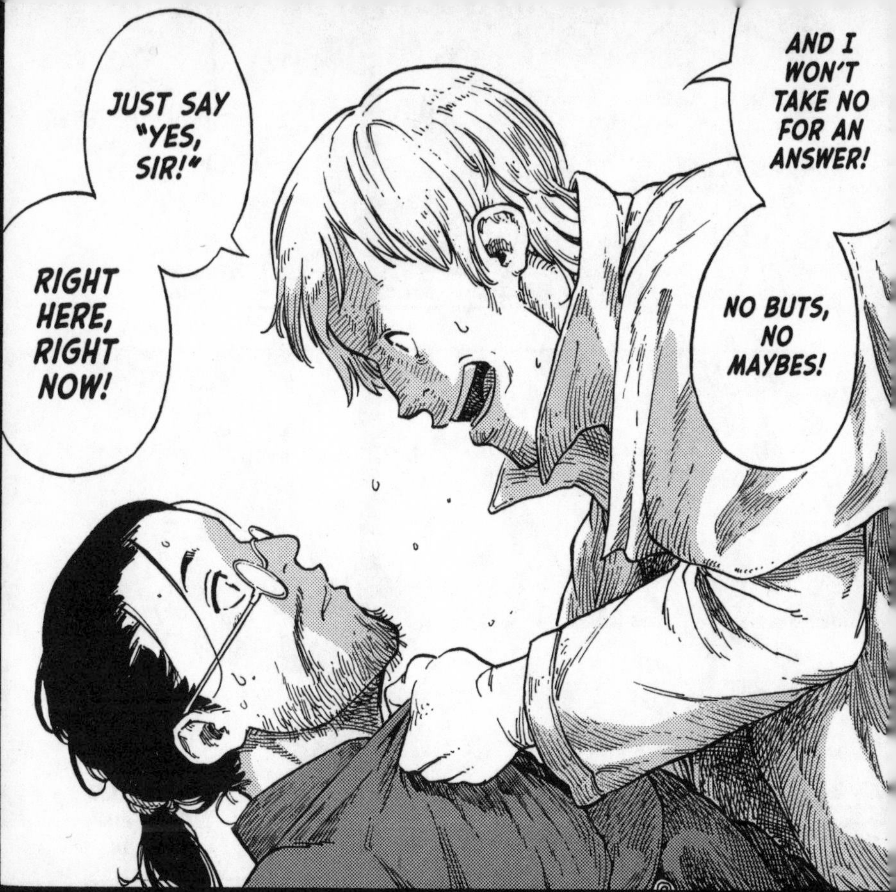
AND I WON'T TAKE NO FOR AN ANSWER!
JUST SAY "YES, SIR!"
NO BUTS, NO MAYBES!
RIGHT HERE, RIGHT NOW!

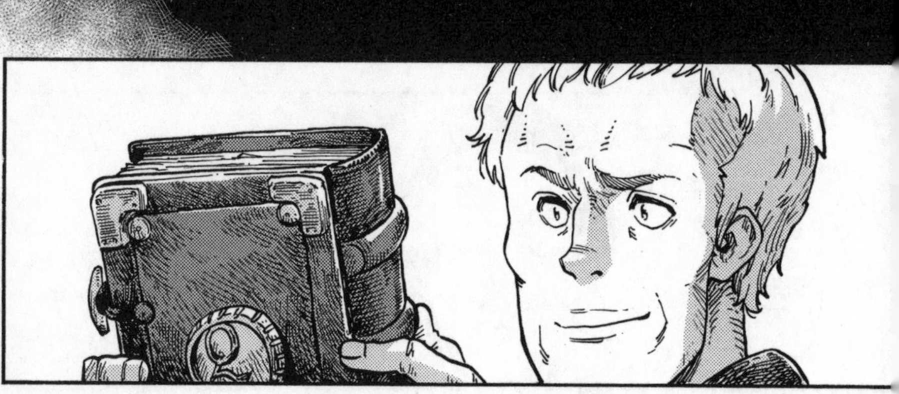

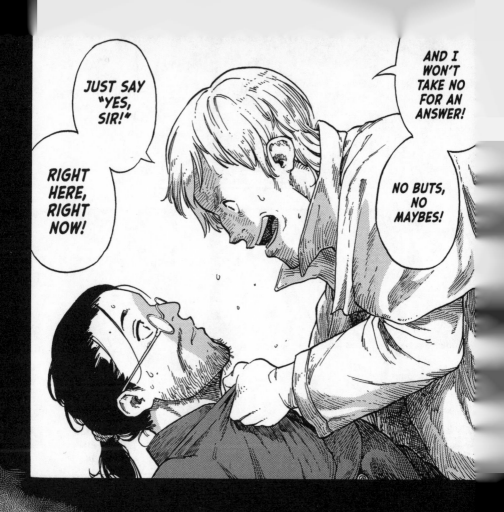

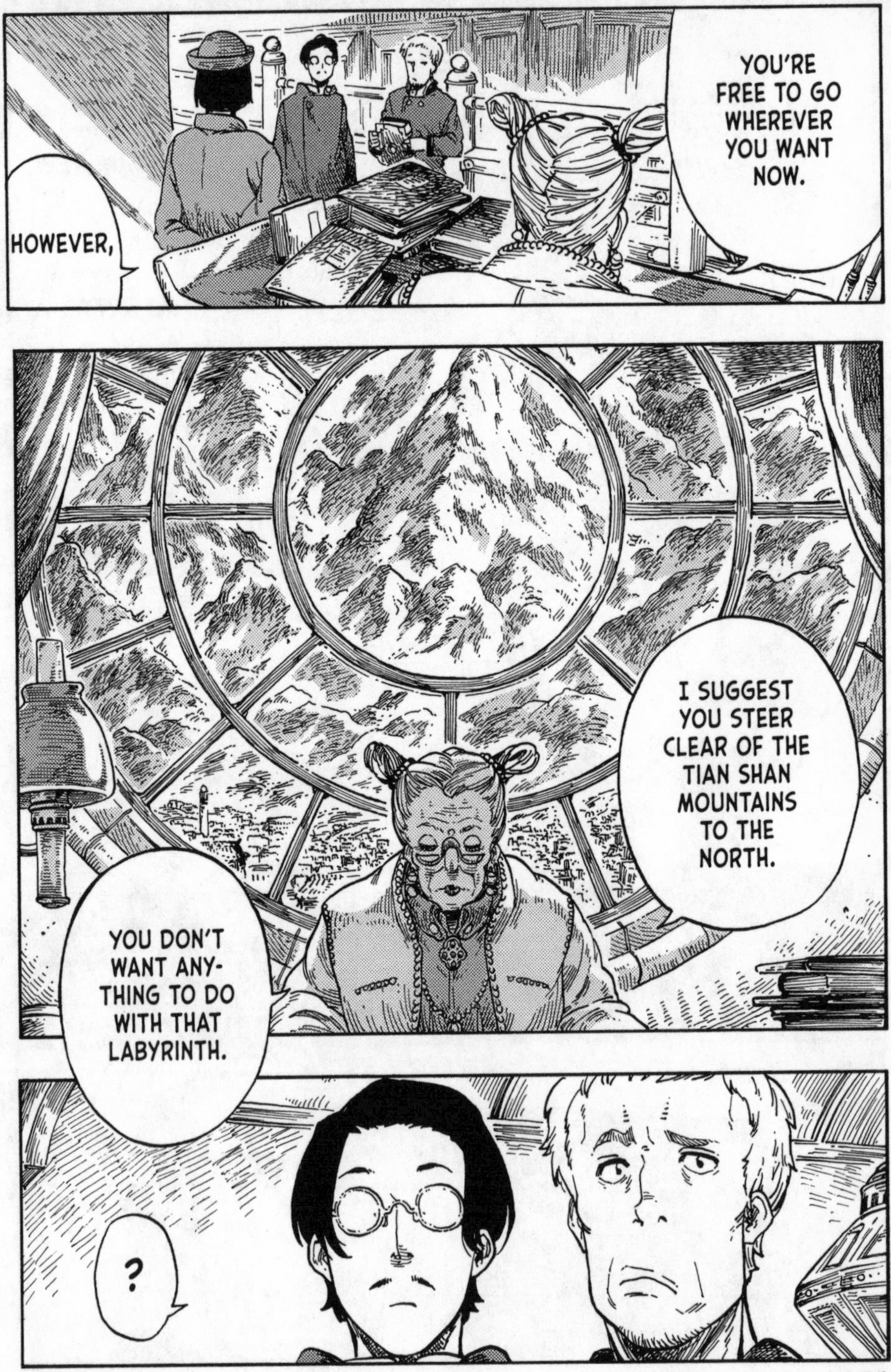
YOU'RE FREE TO GO WHEREVER YOU WANT NOW.
HOWEVER,
I SUGGEST YOU STEER CLEAR OF THE TIAN SHAN MOUNTAINS TO THE NORTH.
YOU DON'T WANT ANY-THING TO DO WITH THAT LABYRINTH.
?

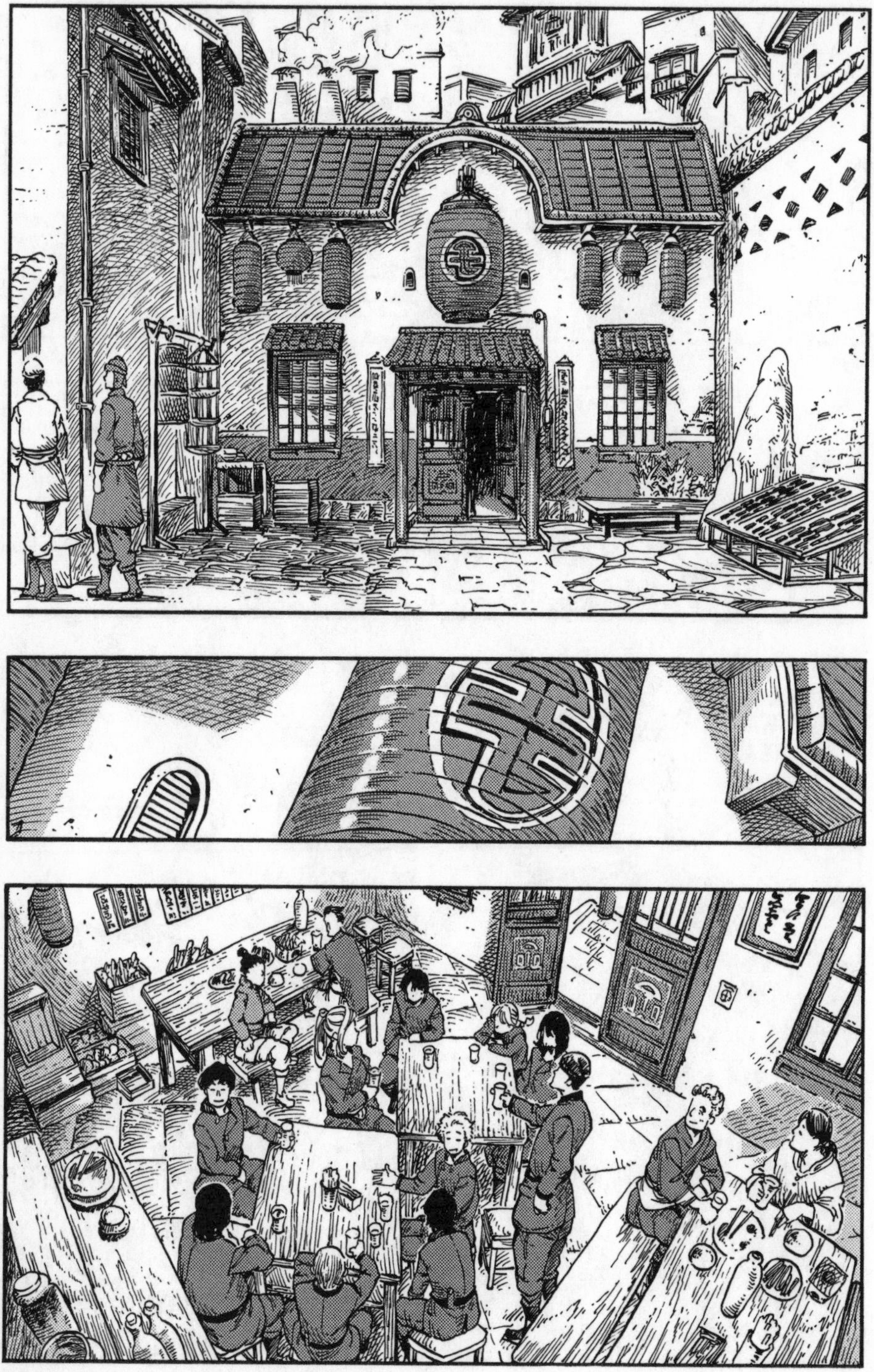

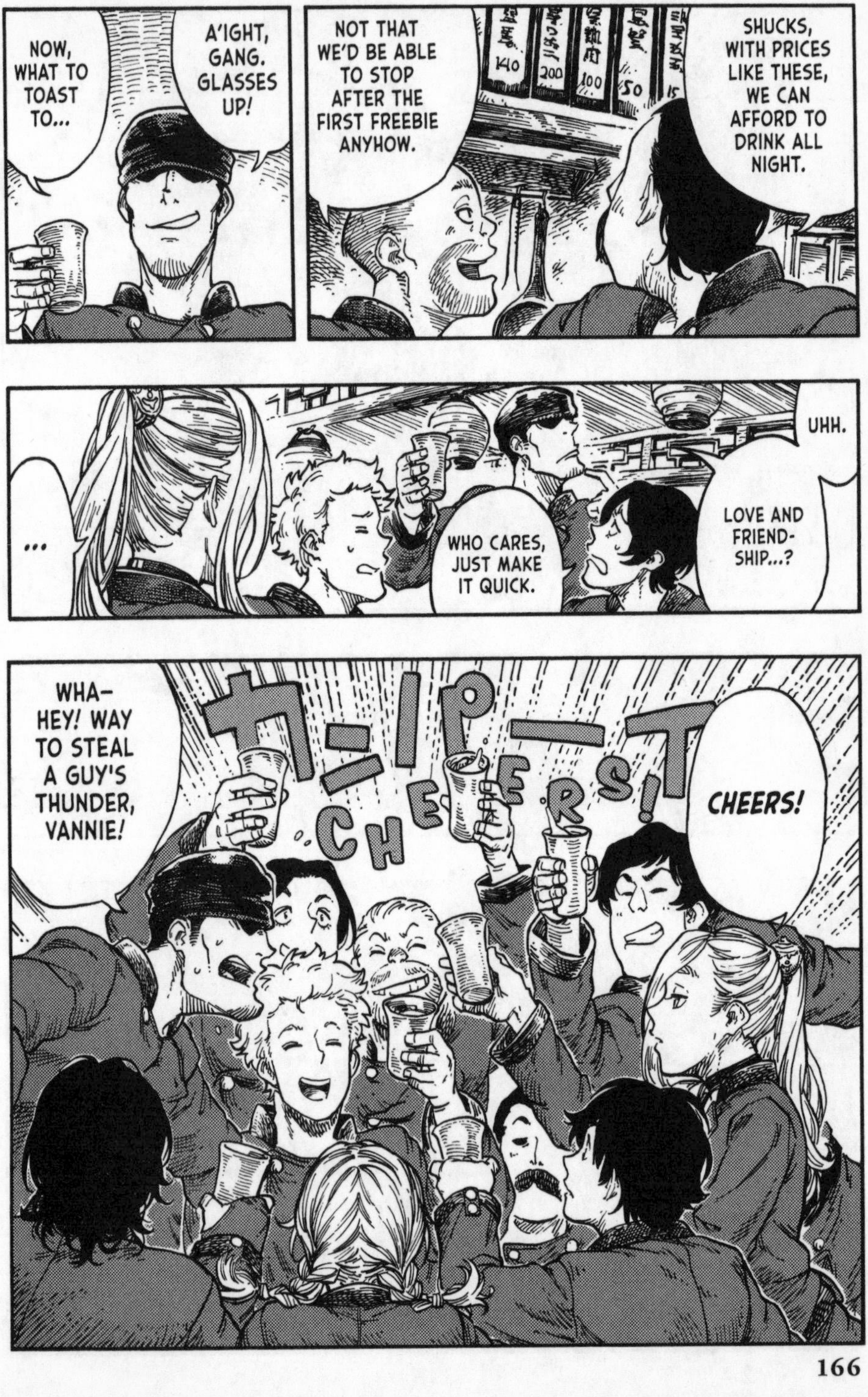
SHUCKS, WITH PRICES LIKE THESE, WE CAN AFFORD TO DRINK ALL NIGHT.
NOT THAT WE'D BE ABLE TO STOP AFTER THE FIRST FREEBIE ANYHOW.
A'IGHT, GANG. GLASSES UP!
NOW, WHAT TO TOAST TO...
UHH.
LOVE AND FRIEND-SHIP...?
WHO CARES, JUST MAKE IT QUICK.
...
CHEERS!
CHEERS!
WHA-HEY! WAY TO STEAL A GUY'S THUNDER, VANNIE!

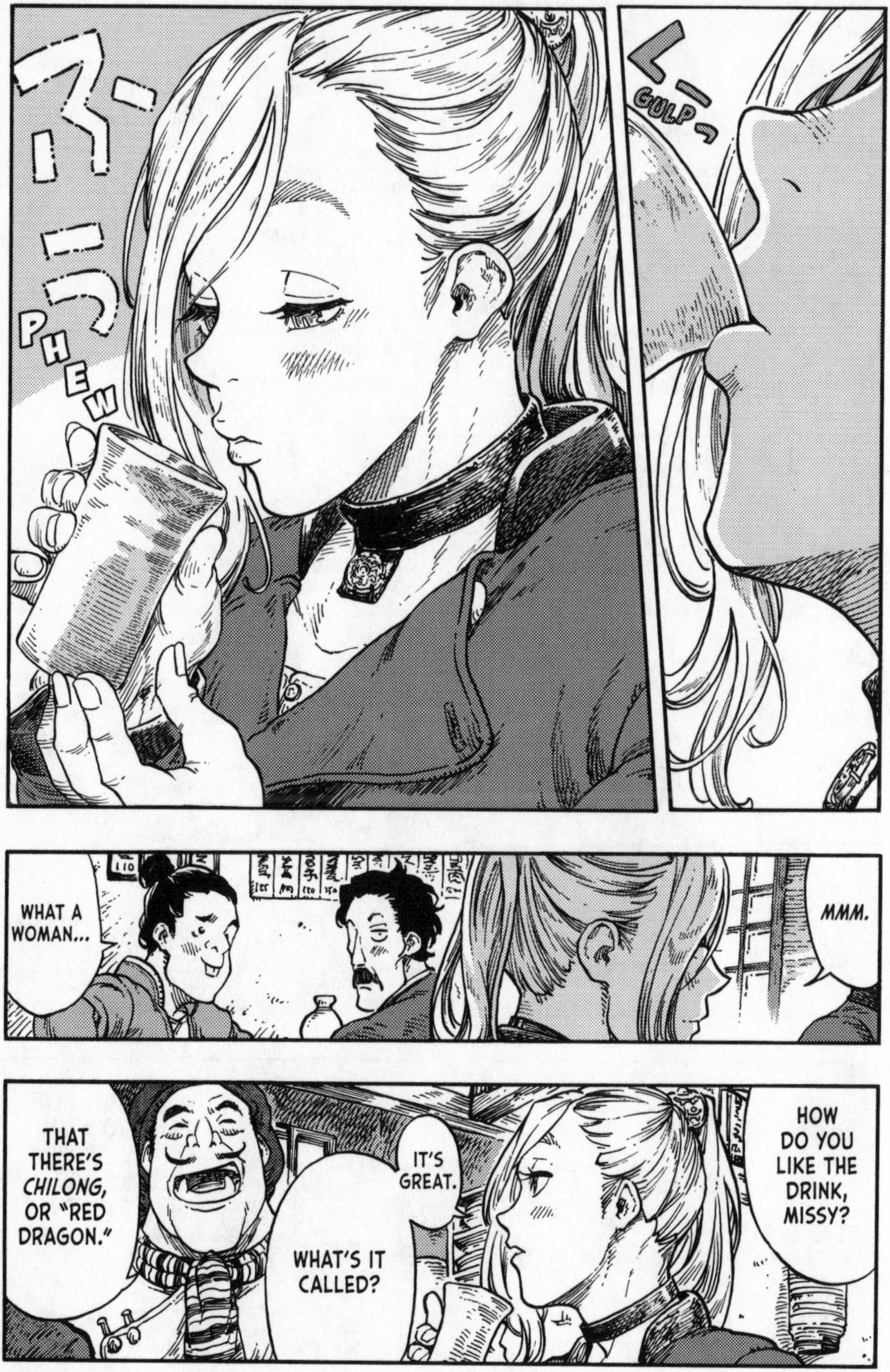
GULP
PHEW
MMM.
WHAT A WOMAN...
HOW DO YOU LIKE THE DRINK, MISSY?
IT'S GREAT.
WHAT'S IT CALLED?
THAT THERE'S *CHILONG*, OR "RED DRAGON."

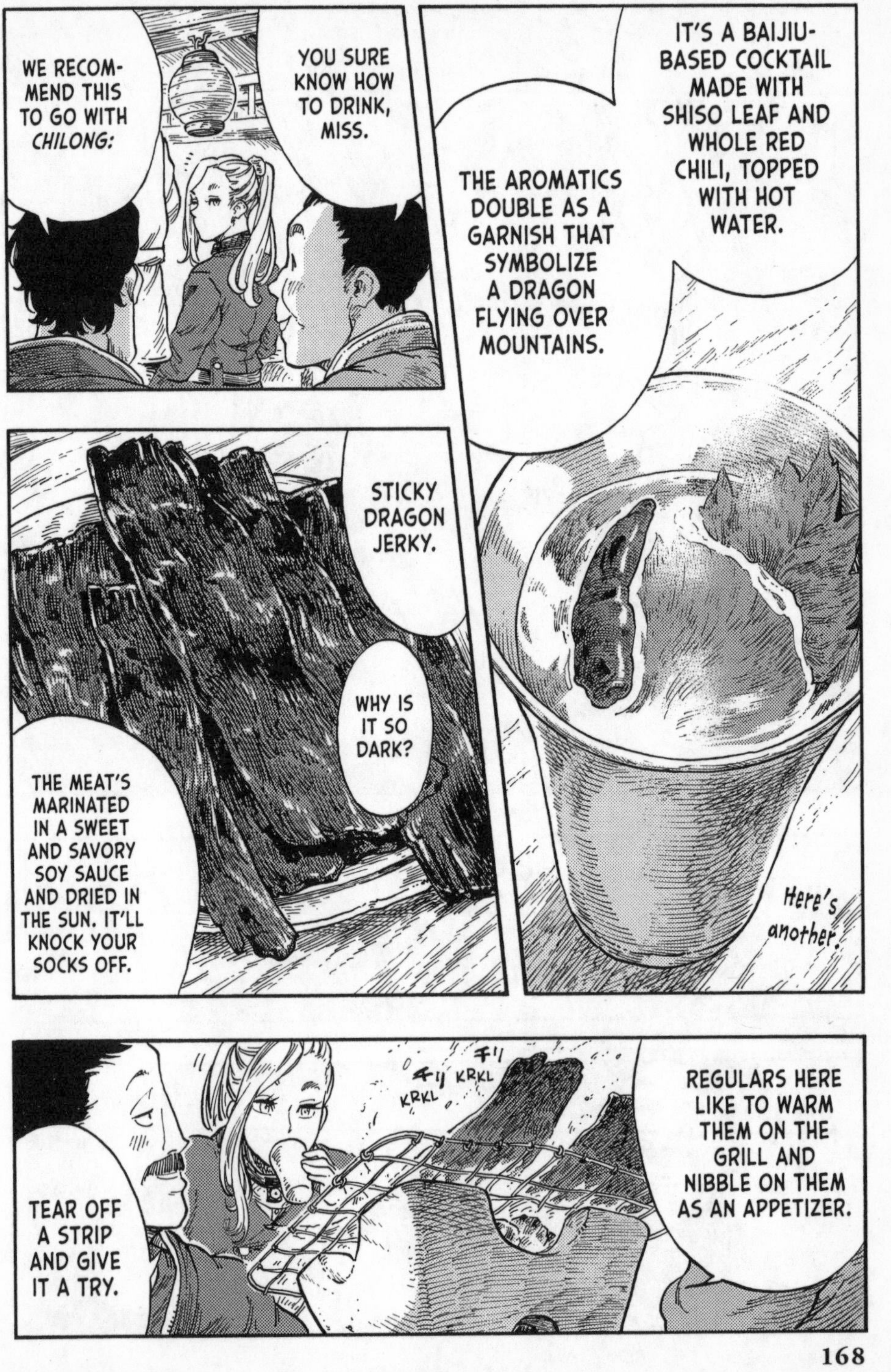
IT'S A BAIJIU-BASED COCKTAIL MADE WITH SHISO LEAF AND WHOLE RED CHILI, TOPPED WITH HOT WATER.
THE AROMATICS DOUBLE AS A GARNISH THAT SYMBOLIZE A DRAGON FLYING OVER MOUNTAINS.
Here's another.
YOU SURE KNOW HOW TO DRINK, MISS.
WE RECOMMEND THIS TO GO WITH *CHILONG:*
STICKY DRAGON JERKY.
WHY IS IT SO DARK?
THE MEAT'S MARINATED IN A SWEET AND SAVORY SOY SAUCE AND DRIED IN THE SUN. IT'LL KNOCK YOUR SOCKS OFF.
REGULARS HERE LIKE TO WARM THEM ON THE GRILL AND NIBBLE ON THEM AS AN APPETIZER.
チリ KRKL
チリ KRKL
TEAR OFF A STRIP AND GIVE IT A TRY.

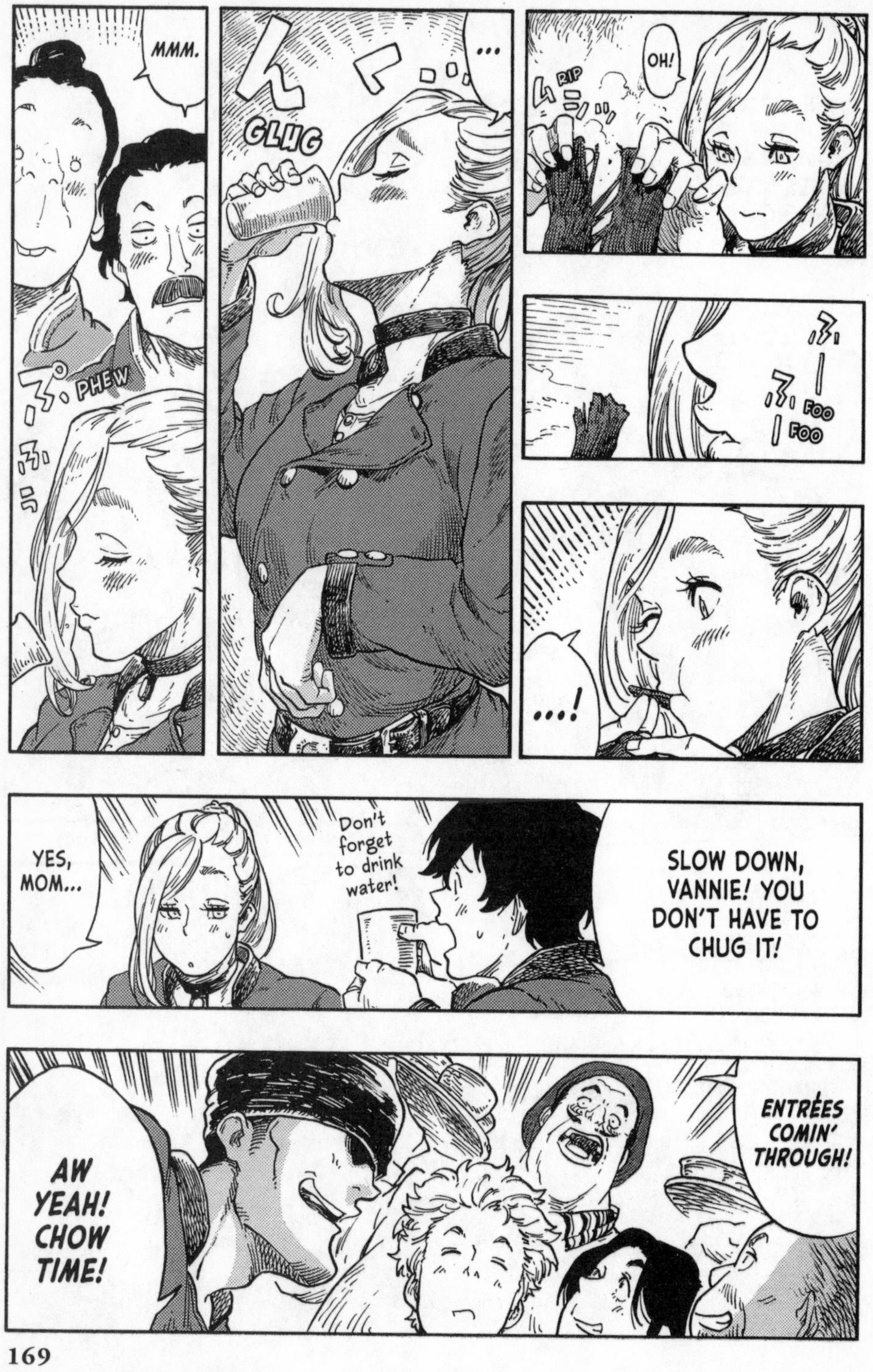
OH!
RIP
FOO
FOO
...!
...
GLUG
MMM.
PHEW
SLOW DOWN, VANNIE! YOU DON'T HAVE TO CHUG IT!
Don't forget to drink water!
YES, MOM...
ENTRÉES COMIN' THROUGH!
AW YEAH! CHOW TIME!

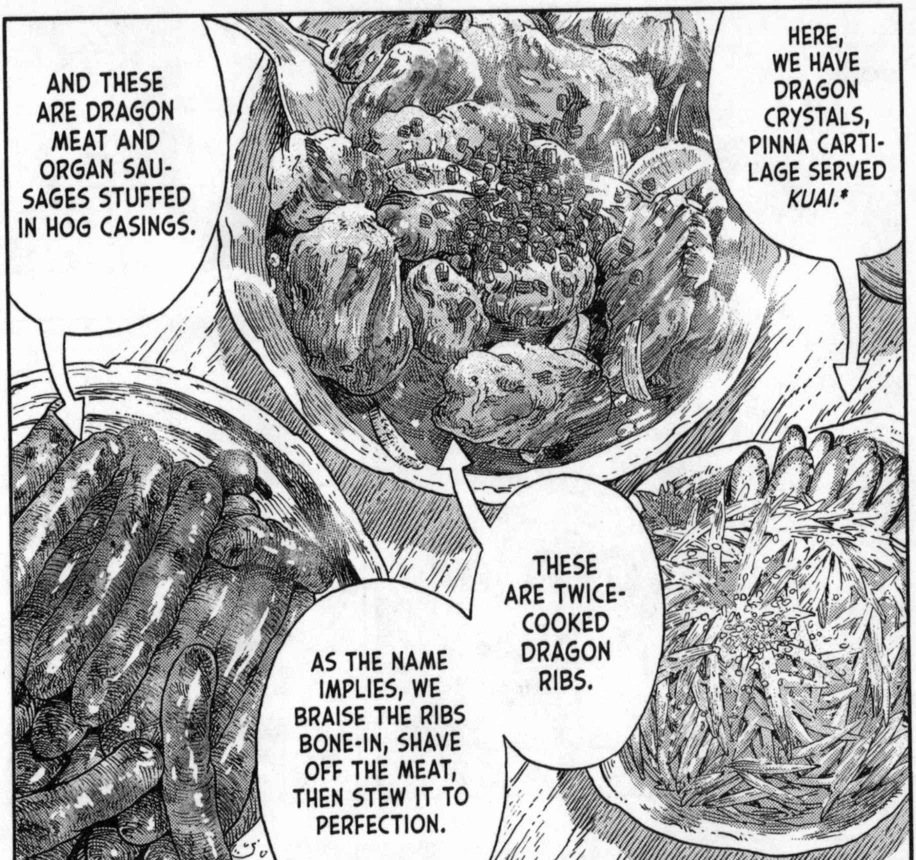
HERE, WE HAVE DRAGON CRYSTALS, PINNA CARTI-LAGE SERVED *KUAI.**
AND THESE ARE DRAGON MEAT AND ORGAN SAU-SAGES STUFFED IN HOG CASINGS.
THESE ARE TWICE-COOKED DRAGON RIBS.
AS THE NAME IMPLIES, WE BRAISE THE RIBS BONE-IN, SHAVE OFF THE MEAT, THEN STEW IT TO PERFECTION.

*Kuai: Thin strips of raw meat or seafood tossed in a vinegar sauce.

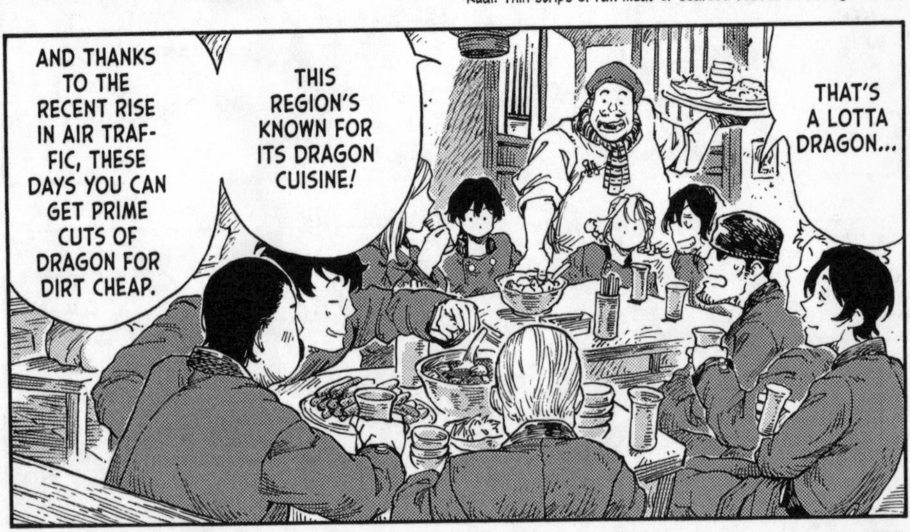
THAT'S A LOTTA DRAGON...
THIS REGION'S KNOWN FOR ITS DRAGON CUISINE!
AND THANKS TO THE RECENT RISE IN AIR TRAF-FIC, THESE DAYS YOU CAN GET PRIME CUTS OF DRAGON FOR DIRT CHEAP.

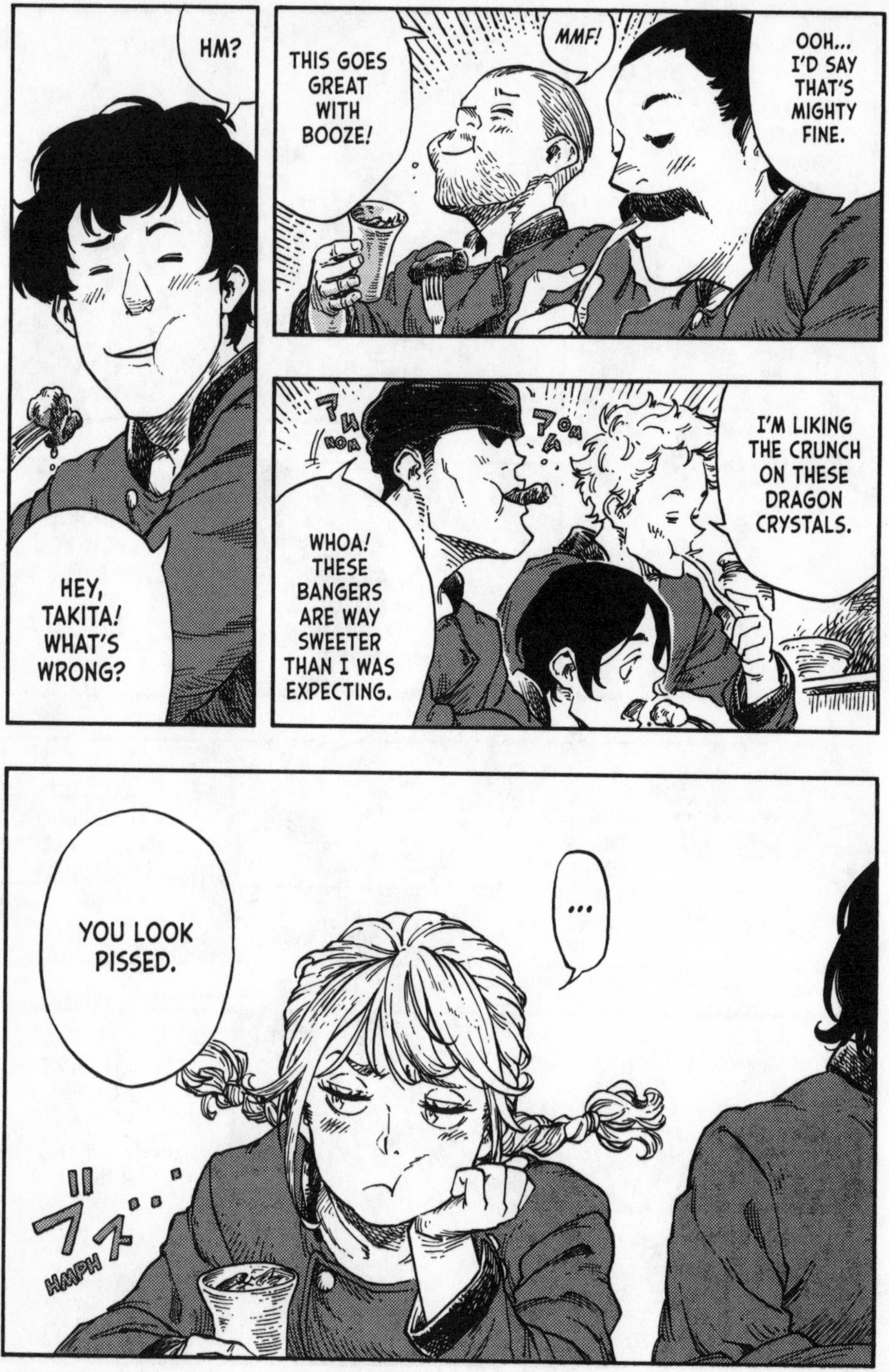
OOH... I'D SAY THAT'S MIGHTY FINE.
MMF!
THIS GOES GREAT WITH BOOZE!
I'M LIKING THE CRUNCH ON THESE DRAGON CRYSTALS.
NOM
NOM
WHOA! THESE BANGERS ARE WAY SWEETER THAN I WAS EXPECTING.
HM?
HEY, TAKITA! WHAT'S WRONG?
...
YOU LOOK PISSED.
HMPH

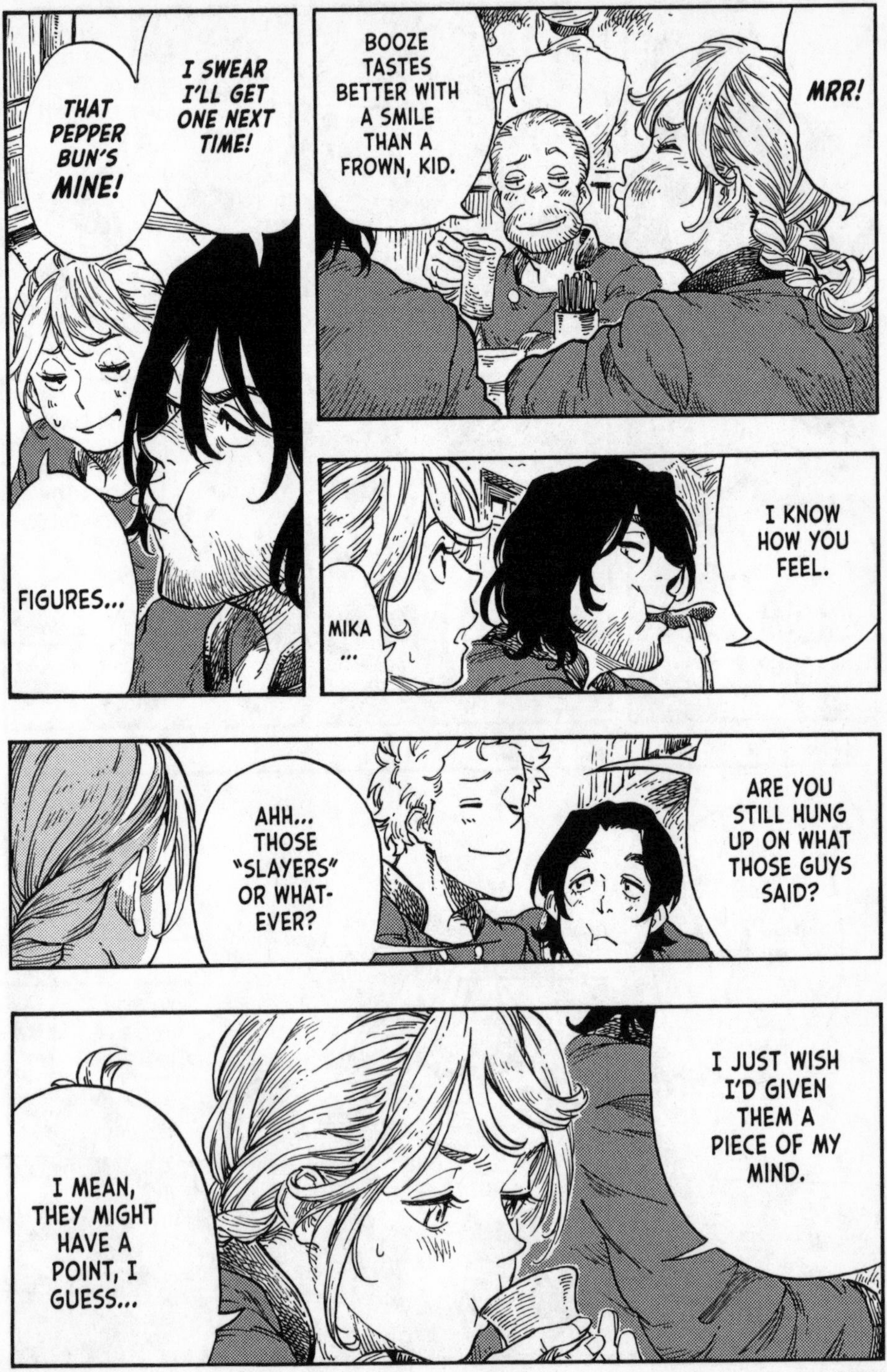
MRR!
BOOZE TASTES BETTER WITH A SMILE THAN A FROWN, KID.
I KNOW HOW YOU FEEL.
MIKA...
I SWEAR I'LL GET ONE NEXT TIME!
THAT PEPPER BUN'S MINE!
FIGURES...
ARE YOU STILL HUNG UP ON WHAT THOSE GUYS SAID?
AHH... THOSE "SLAYERS" OR WHAT-EVER?
I JUST WISH I'D GIVEN THEM A PIECE OF MY MIND.
I MEAN, THEY MIGHT HAVE A POINT, I GUESS...

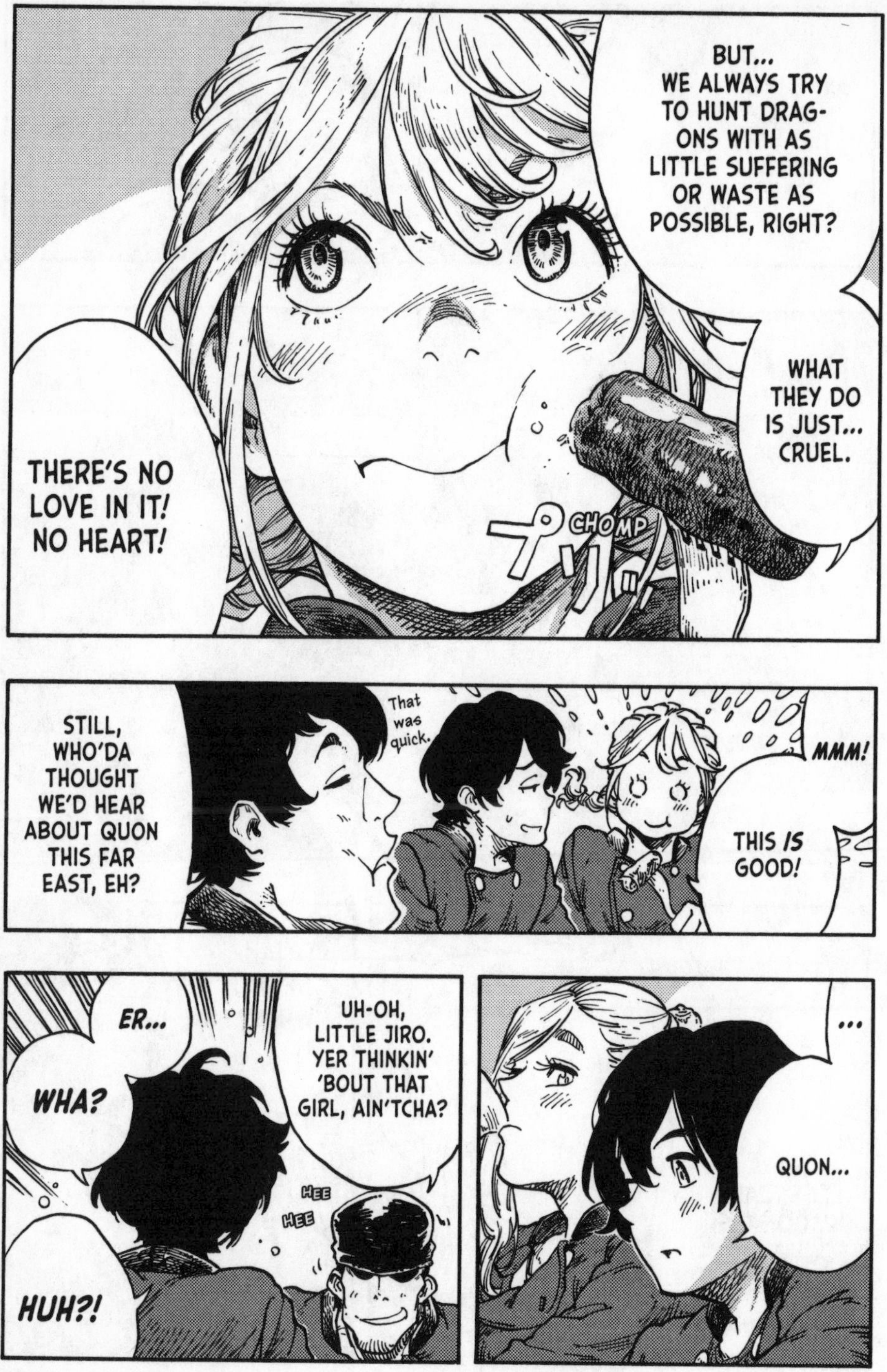
BUT... WE ALWAYS TRY TO HUNT DRAG- ONS WITH AS LITTLE SUFFERING OR WASTE AS POSSIBLE, RIGHT?
WHAT THEY DO IS JUST... CRUEL.
CHOMP
THERE'S NO LOVE IN IT! NO HEART!
MMM!
THIS *IS* GOOD!
That was quick.
STILL, WHO'DA THOUGHT WE'D HEAR ABOUT QUON THIS FAR EAST, EH?
...
QUON...
UH-OH, LITTLE JIRO. YER THINKIN' 'BOUT THAT GIRL, AIN'TCHA?
HEE HEE
ER...
WHA?
HUH?!

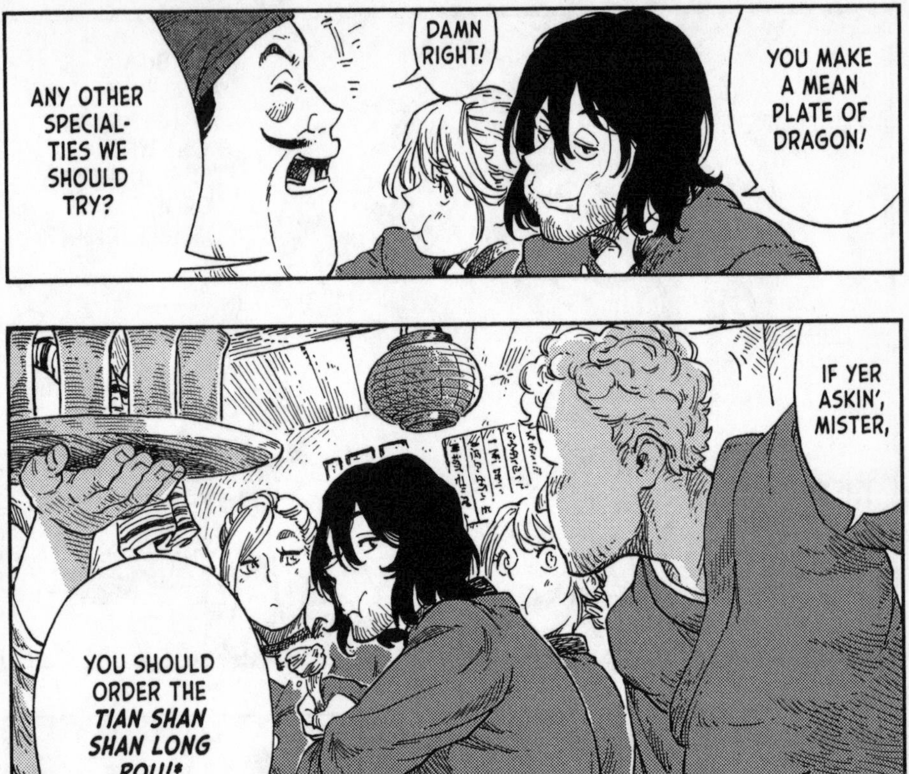
YOU MAKE A MEAN PLATE OF DRAGON!
DAMN RIGHT!
ANY OTHER SPECIAL-TIES WE SHOULD TRY?
IF YER ASKIN', MISTER,
YOU SHOULD ORDER THE *TIAN SHAN SHAN LONG ROU!**

*Tian Shan Shan Long Rou: Heavenly Mountain Dragon Roast

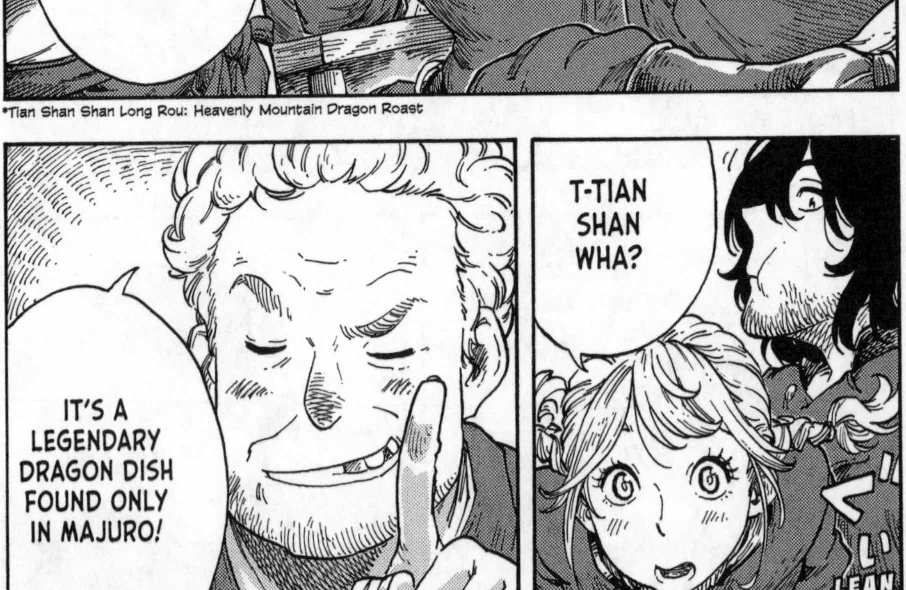
T-TIAN SHAN WHA?
LEAN
IT'S A LEGENDARY DRAGON DISH FOUND ONLY IN MAJURO!

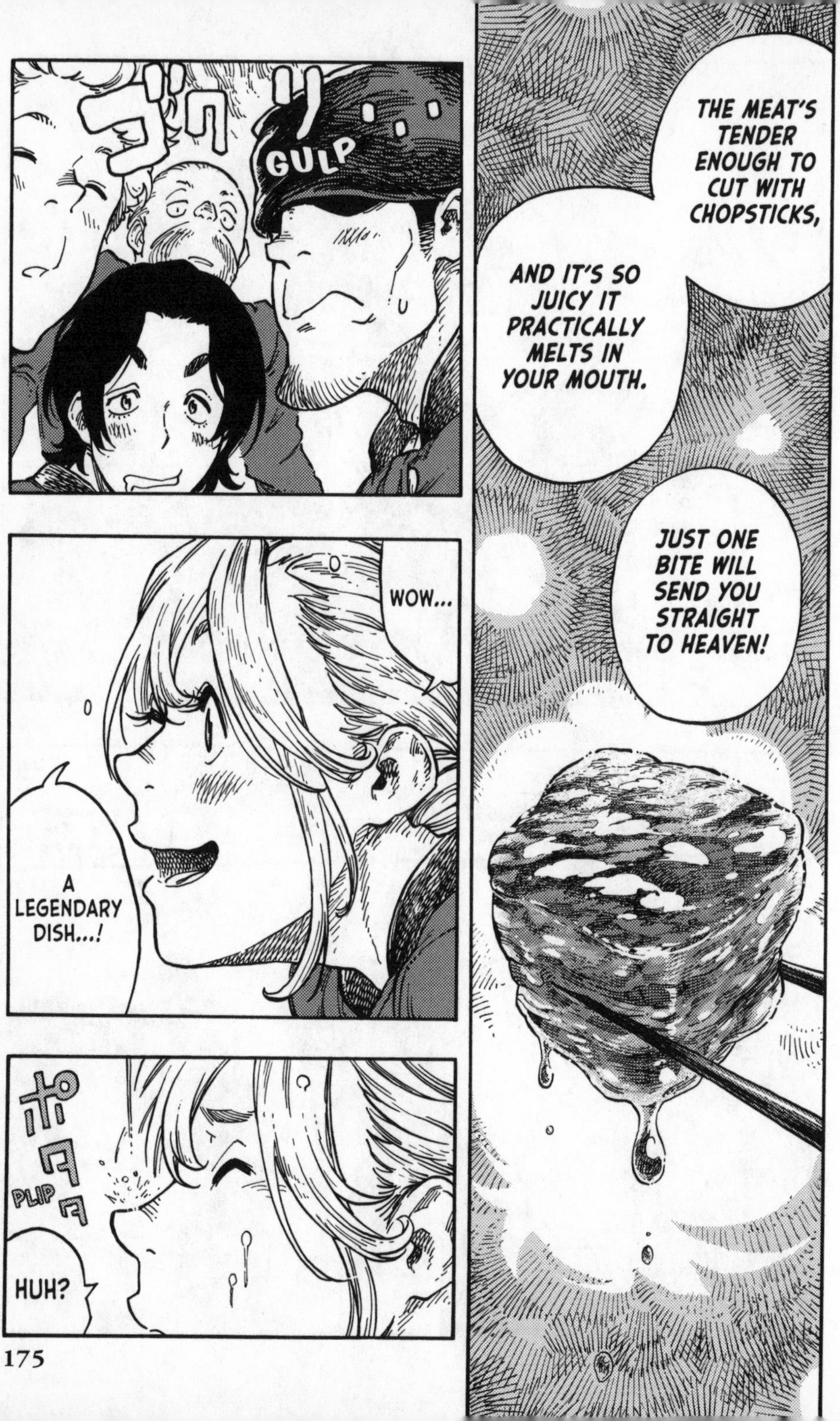
THE MEAT'S TENDER ENOUGH TO CUT WITH CHOPSTICKS,
AND IT'S SO JUICY IT PRACTICALLY MELTS IN YOUR MOUTH.
JUST ONE BITE WILL SEND YOU STRAIGHT TO HEAVEN!
GULP
WOW...
A LEGENDARY DISH...!
PLIP
HUH?

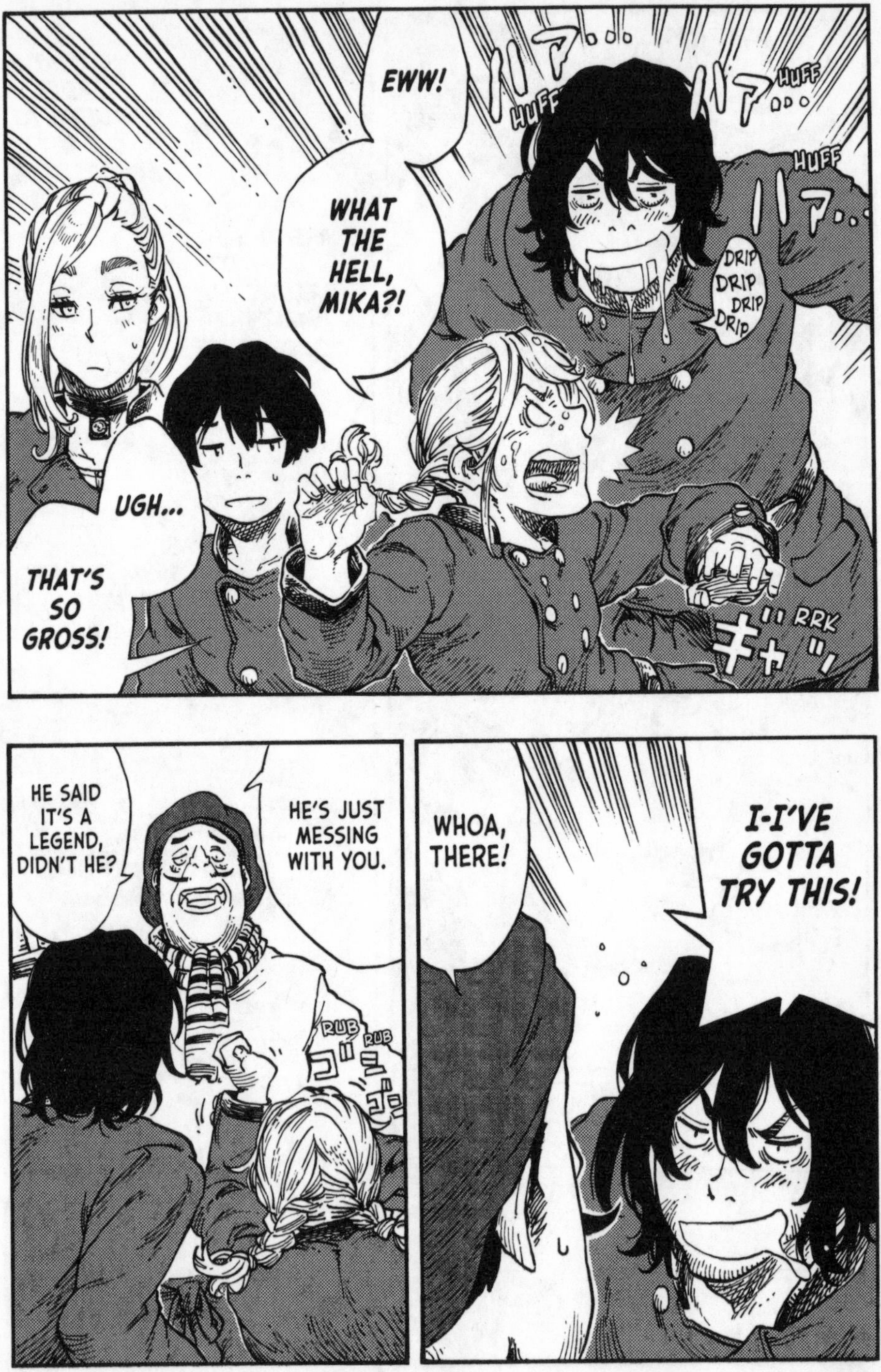
ハア… HUFF
ハア… HUFF
EWW!
WHAT THE HELL, MIKA?!
ハア… HUFF
DRIP DRIP DRIP DRIP
UGH...
THAT'S SO GROSS!
ギャッ RRK
I-I'VE GOTTA TRY THIS!
WHOA, THERE!
HE'S JUST MESSING WITH YOU.
HE SAID IT'S A LEGEND, DIDN'T HE?
RUB RUB

SUPPOSEDLY, THE DISH WAS ORIGINALLY MADE FOR ROYALS, BUT IT ISN'T ANYTHING TOO FANCY.

I EVEN HAVE A RECIPE.

THE PROBLEM IS THE *MEAT.*

WHAT DO YOU MEAN?

...?

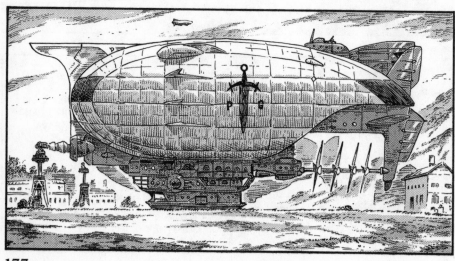

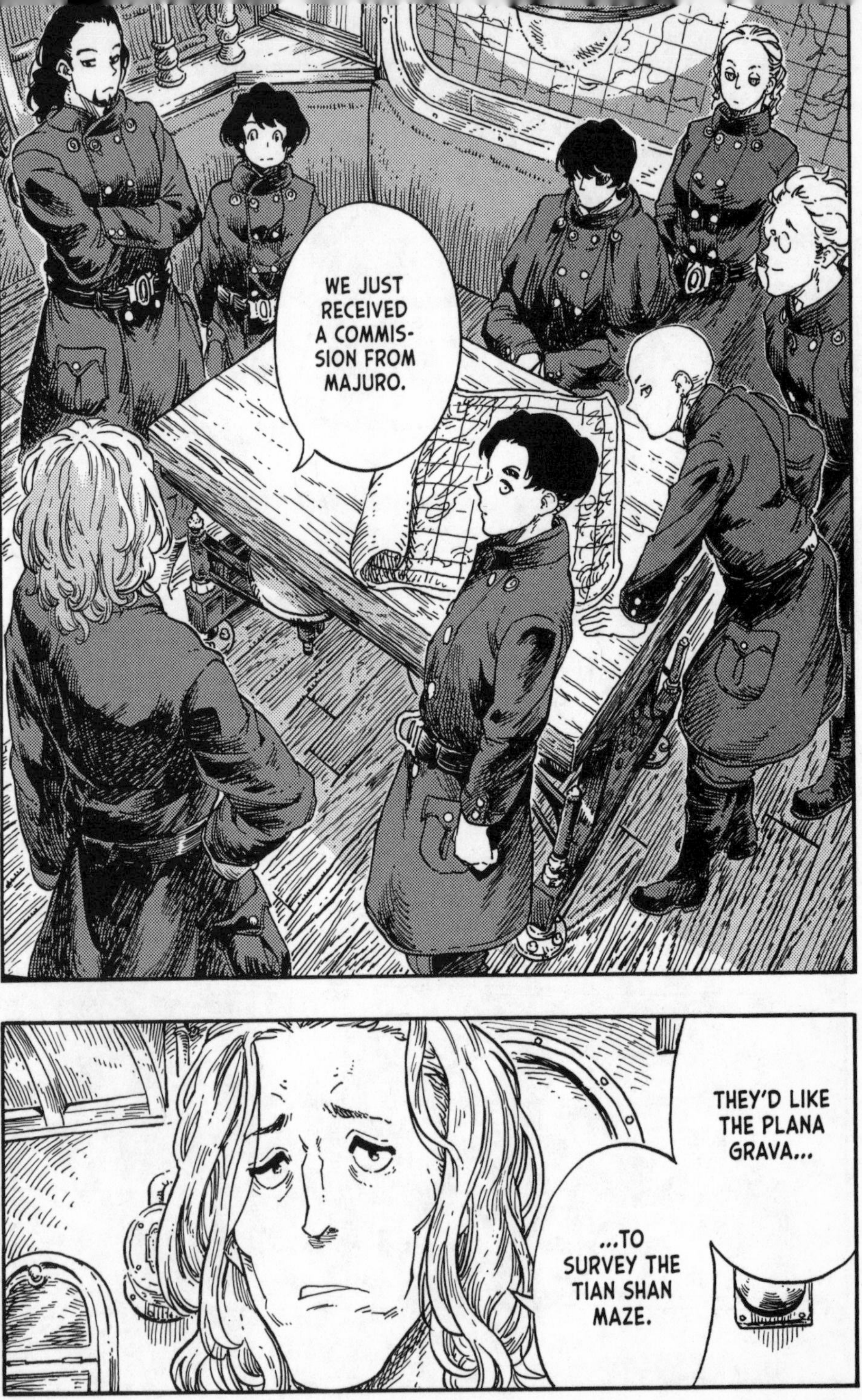
WE JUST RECEIVED A COMMISSION FROM MAJURO.
THEY'D LIKE THE PLANA GRAVA...
...TO SURVEY THE TIAN SHAN MAZE.

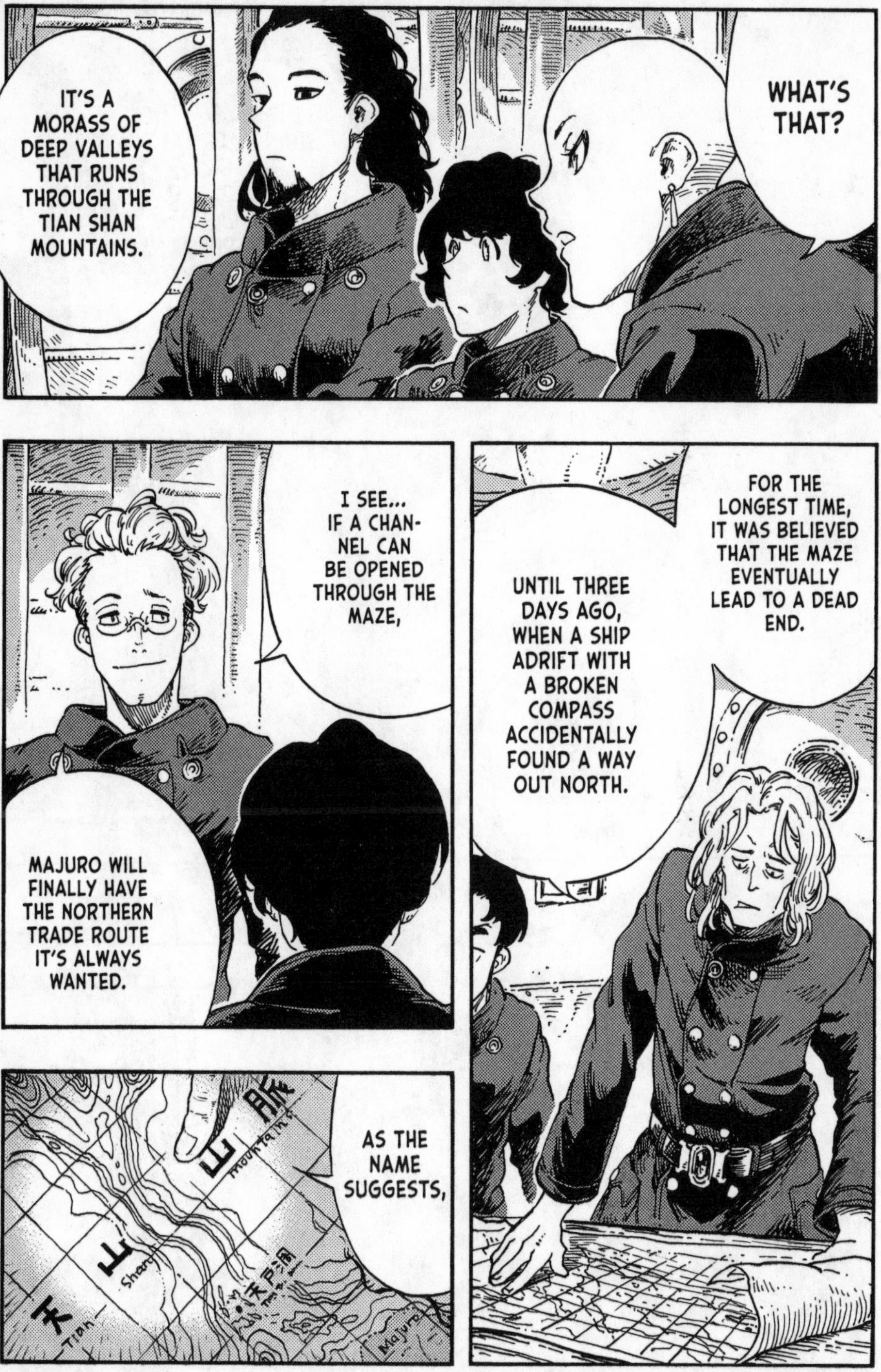
WHAT'S THAT?
IT'S A MORASS OF DEEP VALLEYS THAT RUNS THROUGH THE TIAN SHAN MOUNTAINS.
FOR THE LONGEST TIME, IT WAS BELIEVED THAT THE MAZE EVENTUALLY LEAD TO A DEAD END.
UNTIL THREE DAYS AGO, WHEN A SHIP ADRIFT WITH A BROKEN COMPASS ACCIDENTALLY FOUND A WAY OUT NORTH.
I SEE... IF A CHAN-NEL CAN BE OPENED THROUGH THE MAZE,
MAJURO WILL FINALLY HAVE THE NORTHERN TRADE ROUTE IT'S ALWAYS WANTED.
AS THE NAME SUGGESTS,
Tian
Shan
Mountains
Majuro

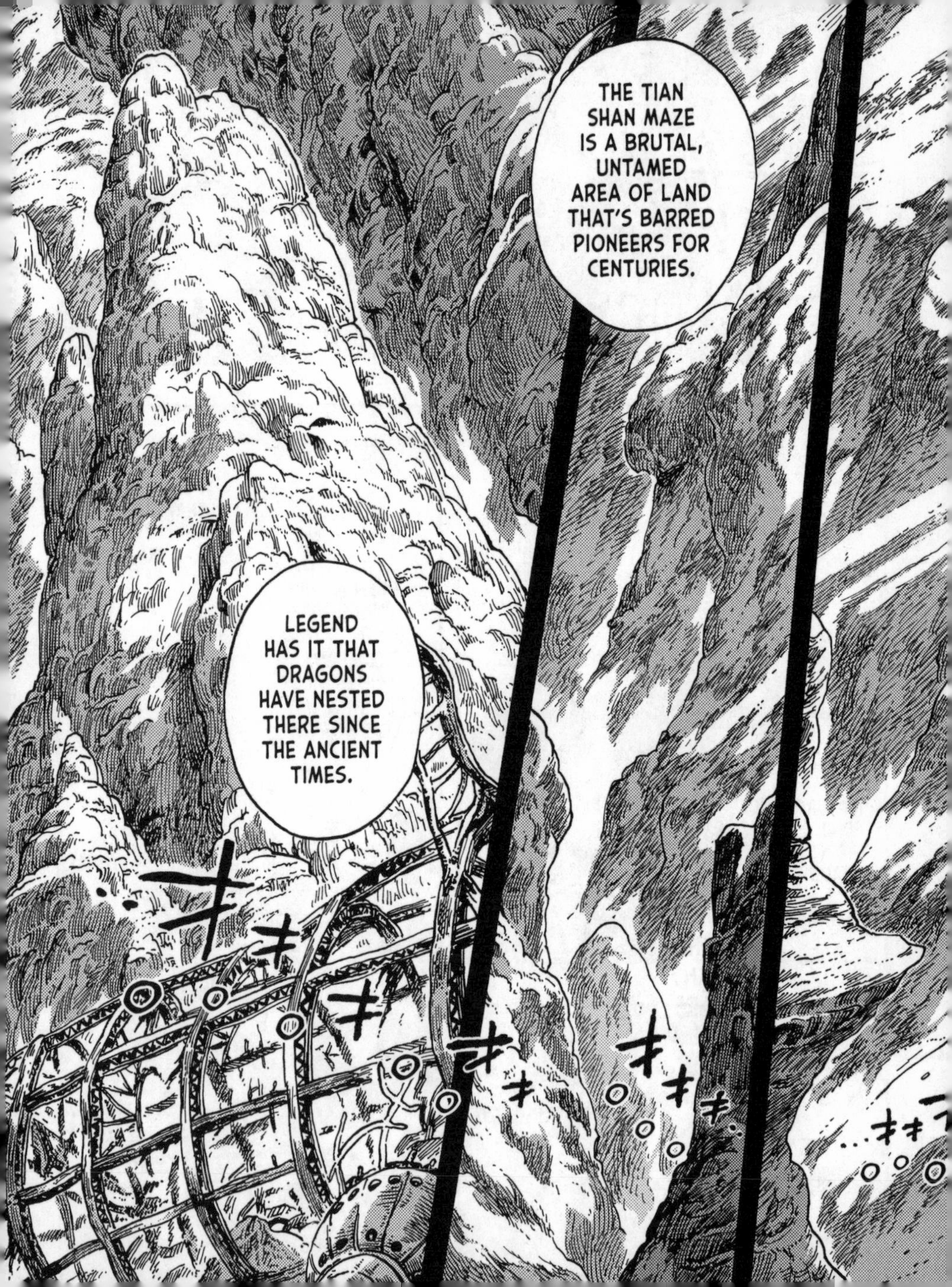
THE TIAN SHAN MAZE IS A BRUTAL, UNTAMED AREA OF LAND THAT'S BARRED PIONEERS FOR CENTURIES.
LEGEND HAS IT THAT DRAGONS HAVE NESTED THERE SINCE THE ANCIENT TIMES.

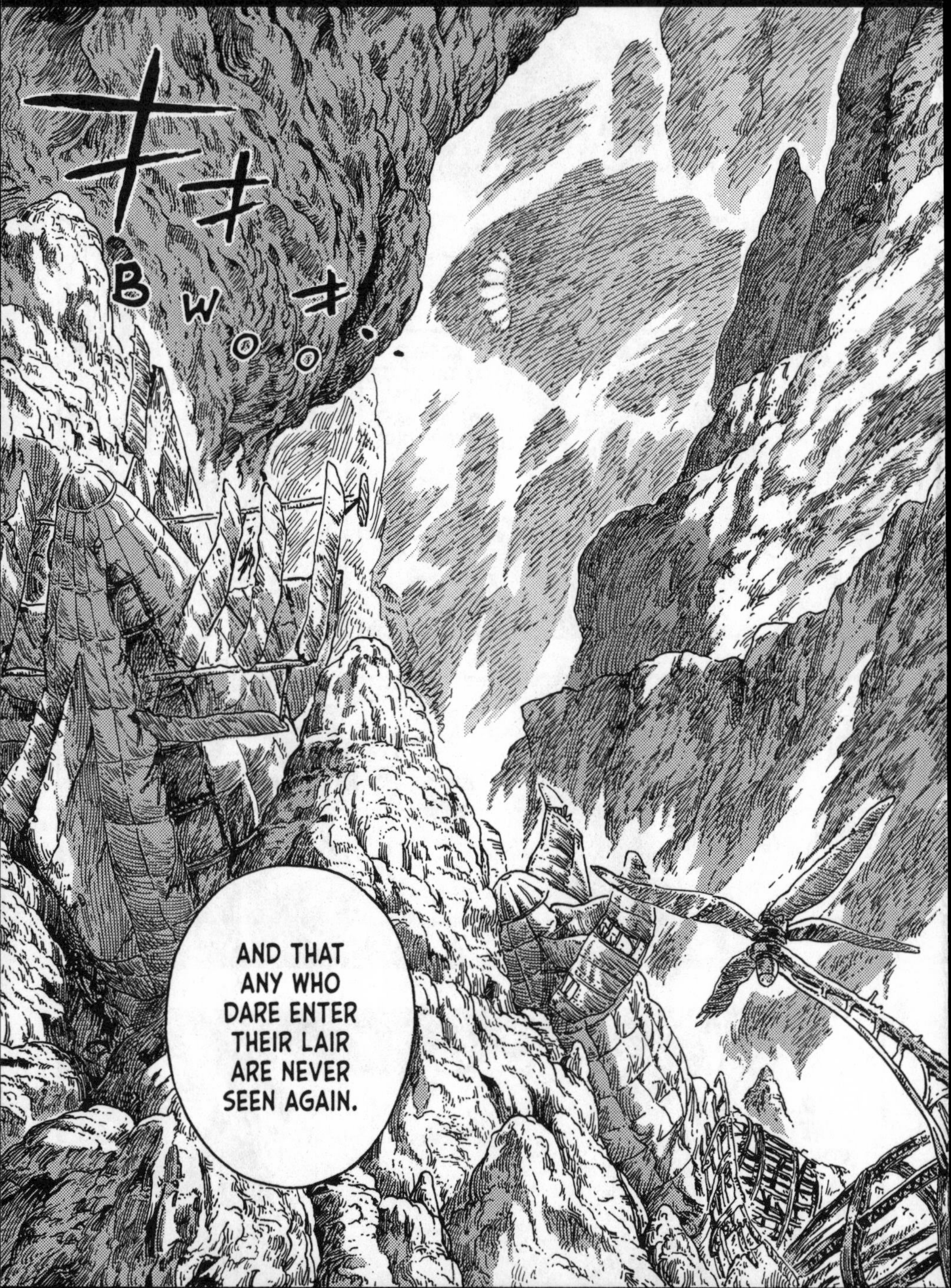
BWOO...
AND THAT ANY WHO DARE ENTER THEIR LAIR ARE NEVER SEEN AGAIN.

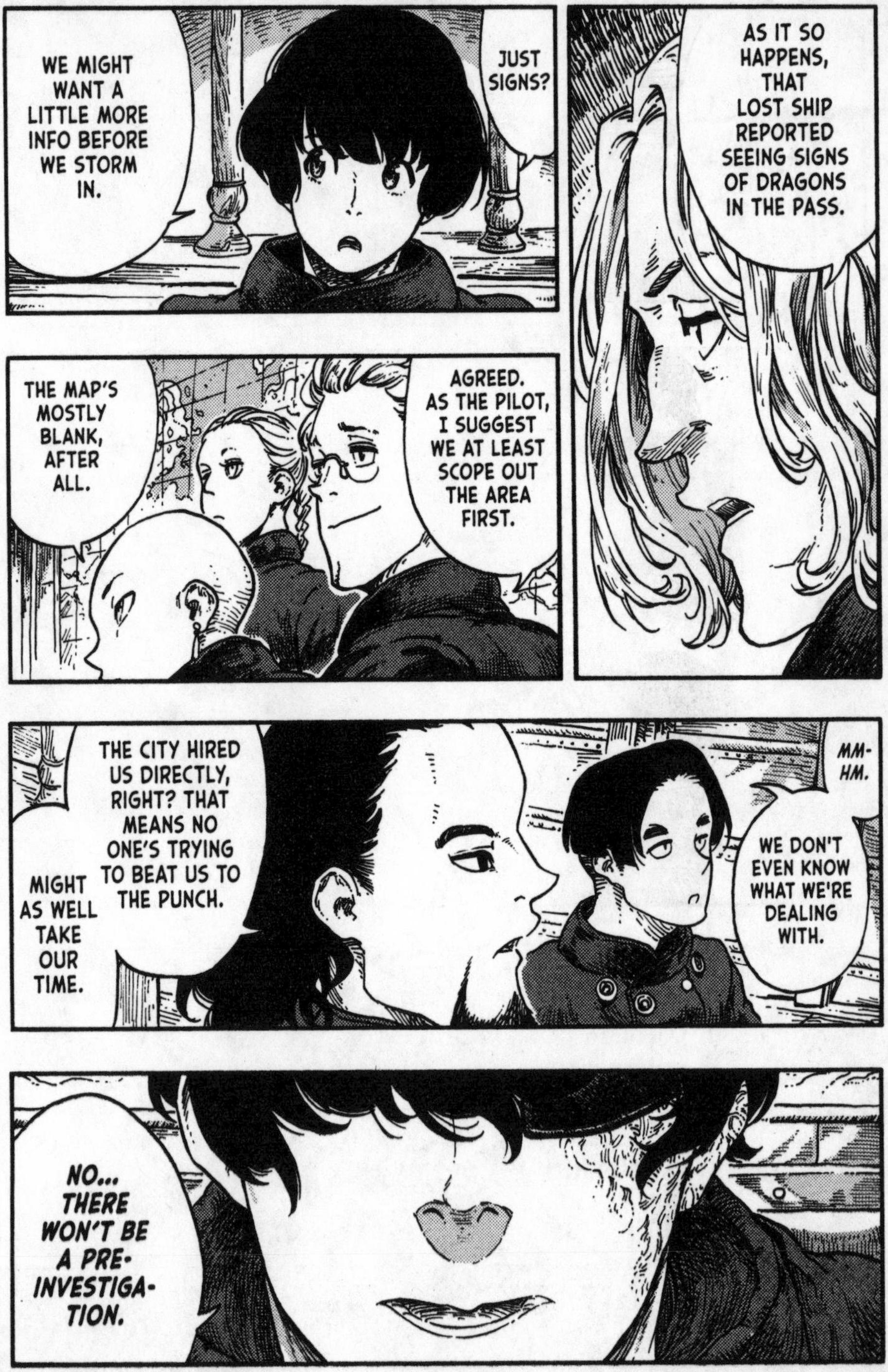
AS IT SO HAPPENS, THAT LOST SHIP REPORTED SEEING SIGNS OF DRAGONS IN THE PASS.
JUST SIGNS?
WE MIGHT WANT A LITTLE MORE INFO BEFORE WE STORM IN.
AGREED. AS THE PILOT, I SUGGEST WE AT LEAST SCOPE OUT THE AREA FIRST.
THE MAP'S MOSTLY BLANK, AFTER ALL.
MM-HM.
WE DON'T EVEN KNOW WHAT WE'RE DEALING WITH.
THE CITY HIRED US DIRECTLY, RIGHT? THAT MEANS NO ONE'S TRYING TO BEAT US TO THE PUNCH.
MIGHT AS WELL TAKE OUR TIME.
NO... THERE WON'T BE A PRE-INVESTIGATION.

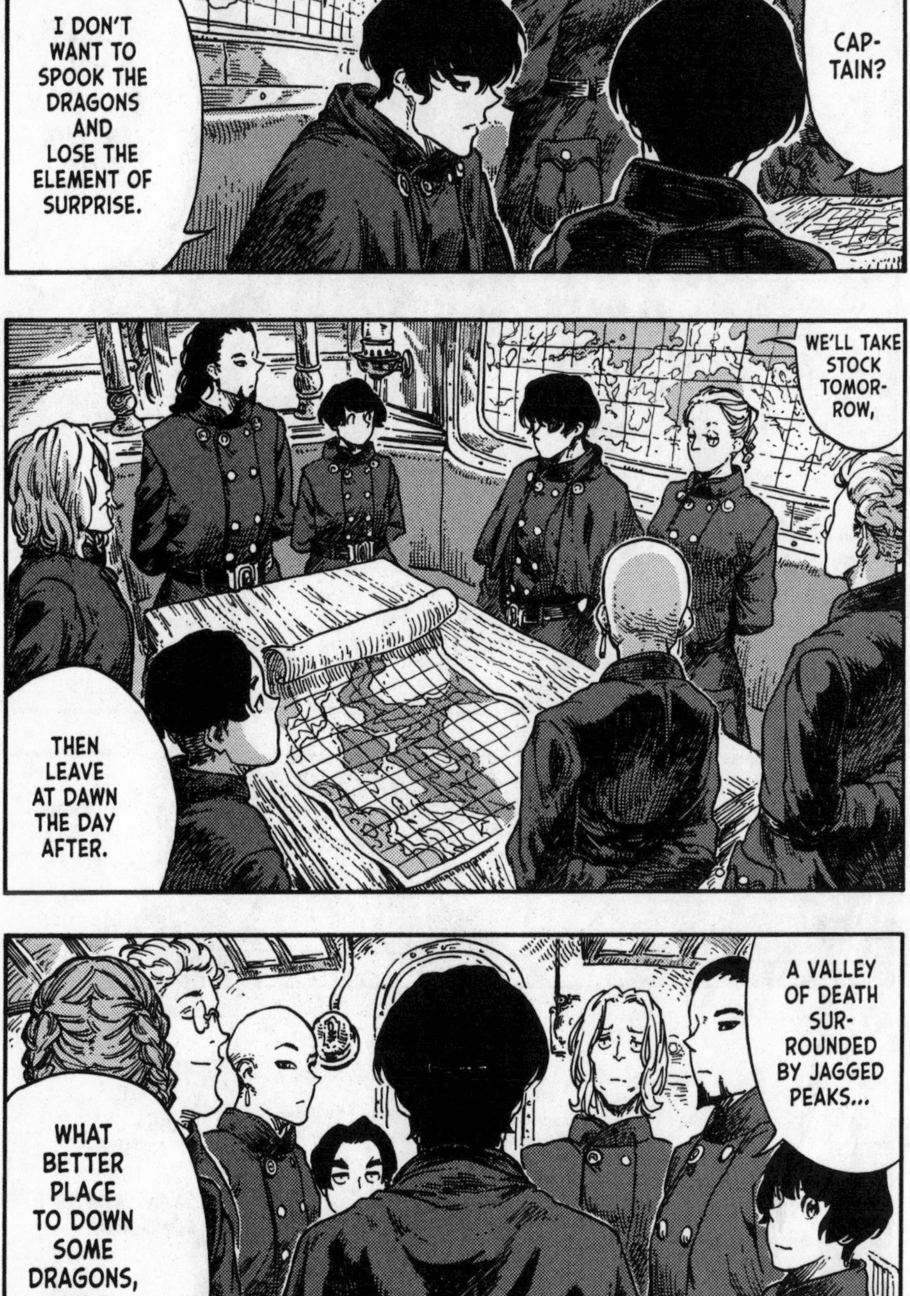
CAP-TAIN?
I DON'T WANT TO SPOOK THE DRAGONS AND LOSE THE ELEMENT OF SURPRISE.
WE'LL TAKE STOCK TOMOR-ROW,
THEN LEAVE AT DAWN THE DAY AFTER.
A VALLEY OF DEATH SUR-ROUNDED BY JAGGED PEAKS...
WHAT BETTER PLACE TO DOWN SOME DRAGONS, AM I RIGHT?

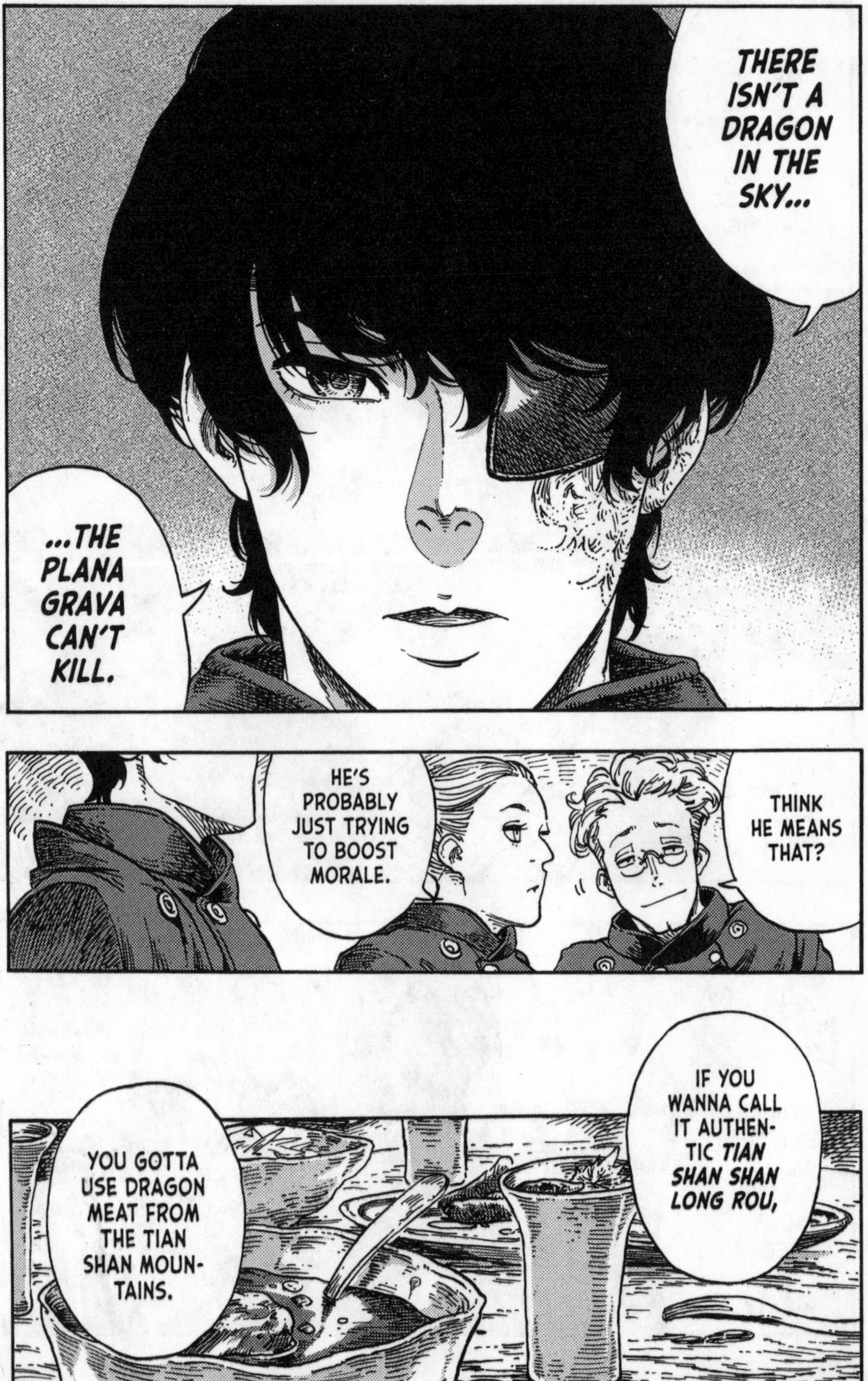
THERE ISN'T A DRAGON IN THE SKY...
...THE PLANA GRAVA CAN'T KILL.
THINK HE MEANS THAT?
HE'S PROBABLY JUST TRYING TO BOOST MORALE.
IF YOU WANNA CALL IT AUTHENTIC *TIAN SHAN SHAN LONG ROU,*
YOU GOTTA USE DRAGON MEAT FROM THE TIAN SHAN MOUNTAINS.

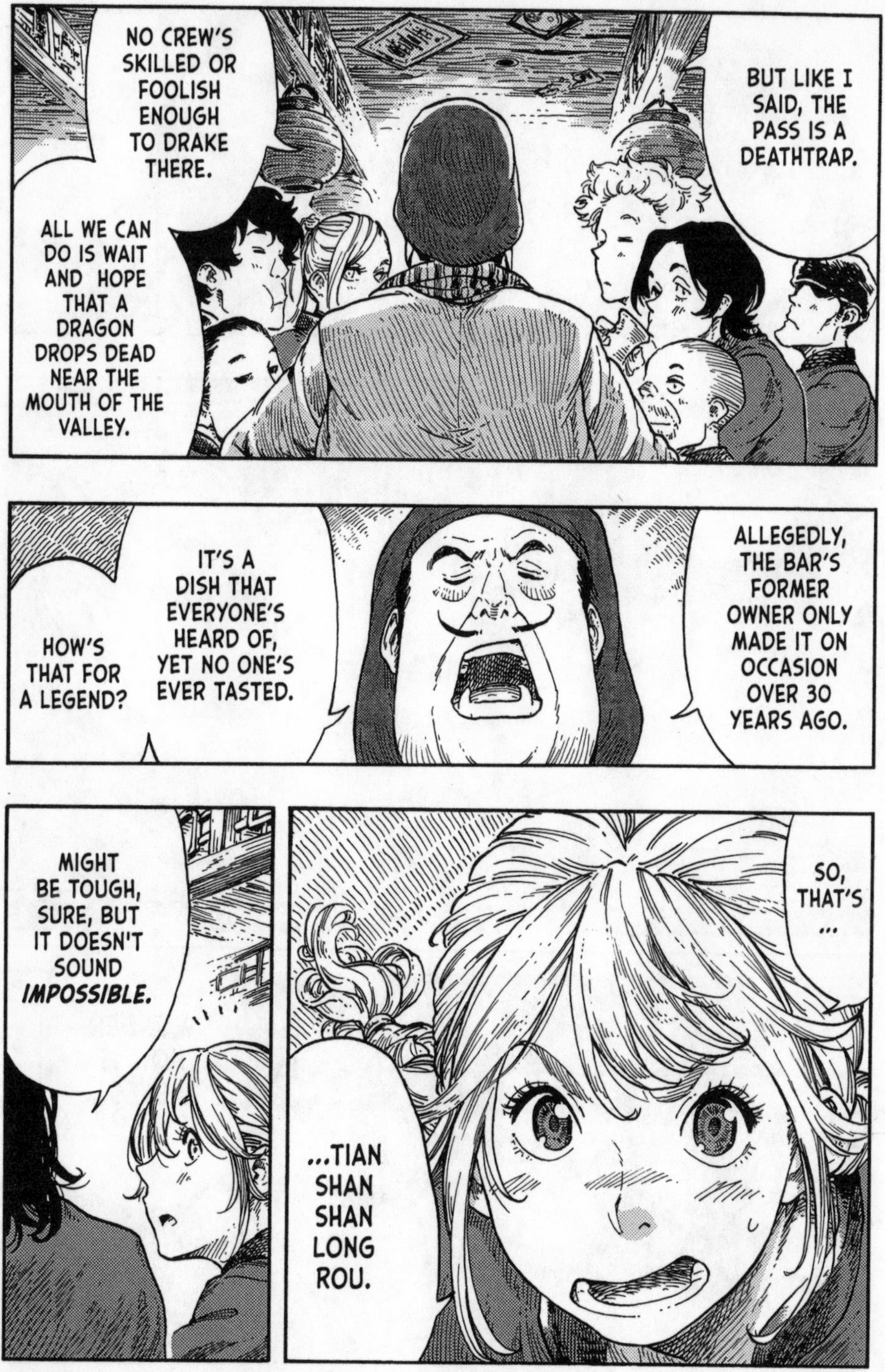
BUT LIKE I SAID, THE PASS IS A DEATHTRAP.
NO CREW'S SKILLED OR FOOLISH ENOUGH TO DRAKE THERE.
ALL WE CAN DO IS WAIT AND HOPE THAT A DRAGON DROPS DEAD NEAR THE MOUTH OF THE VALLEY.
ALLEGEDLY, THE BAR'S FORMER OWNER ONLY MADE IT ON OCCASION OVER 30 YEARS AGO.
IT'S A DISH THAT EVERYONE'S HEARD OF, YET NO ONE'S EVER TASTED.
HOW'S THAT FOR A LEGEND?
SO, THAT'S ...
...TIAN SHAN SHAN LONG ROU.
MIGHT BE TOUGH, SURE, BUT IT DOESN'T SOUND *IMPOSSIBLE.*

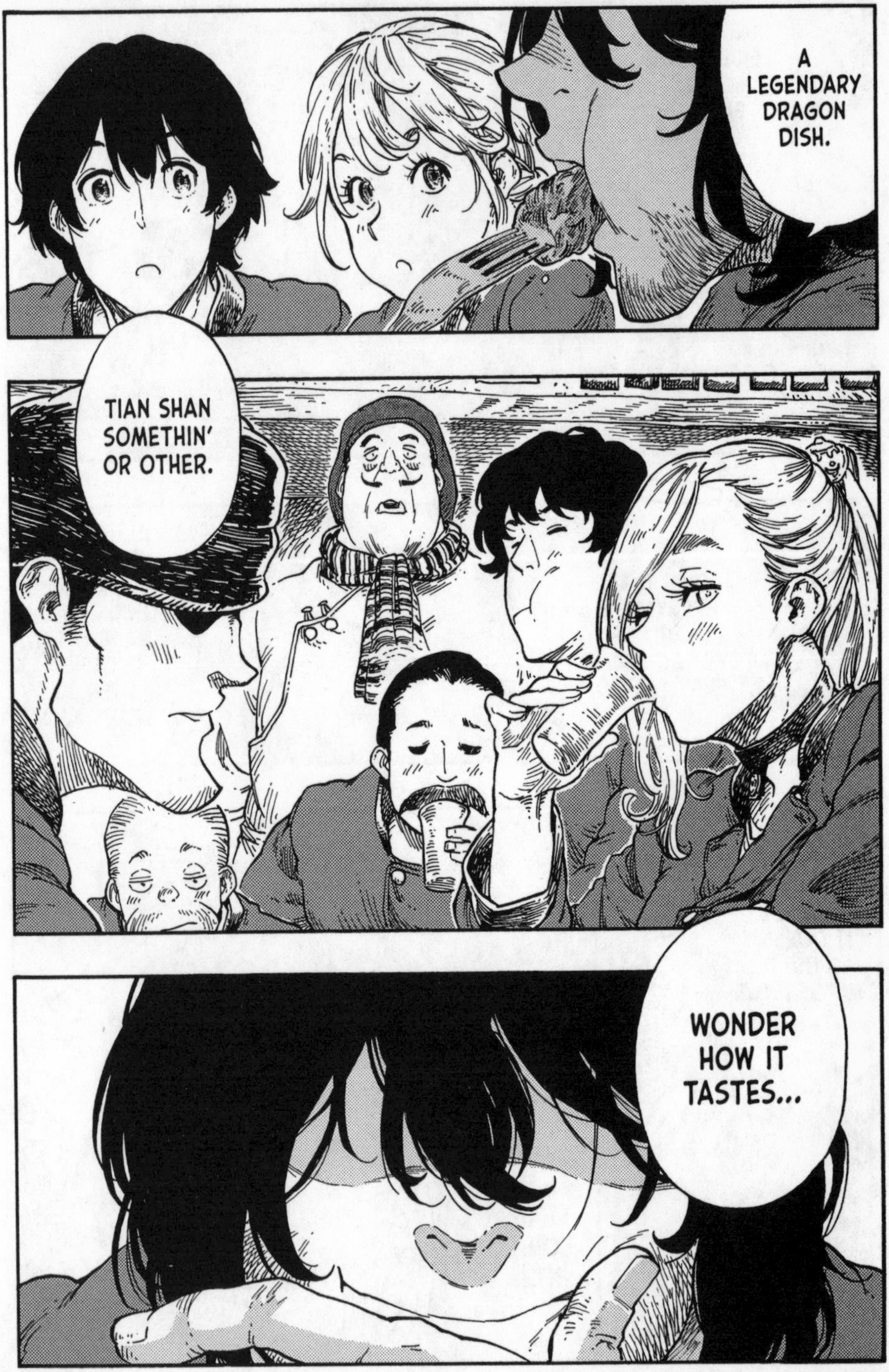
A LEGENDARY DRAGON DISH.
TIAN SHAN SOMETHIN' OR OTHER.
WONDER HOW IT TASTES...

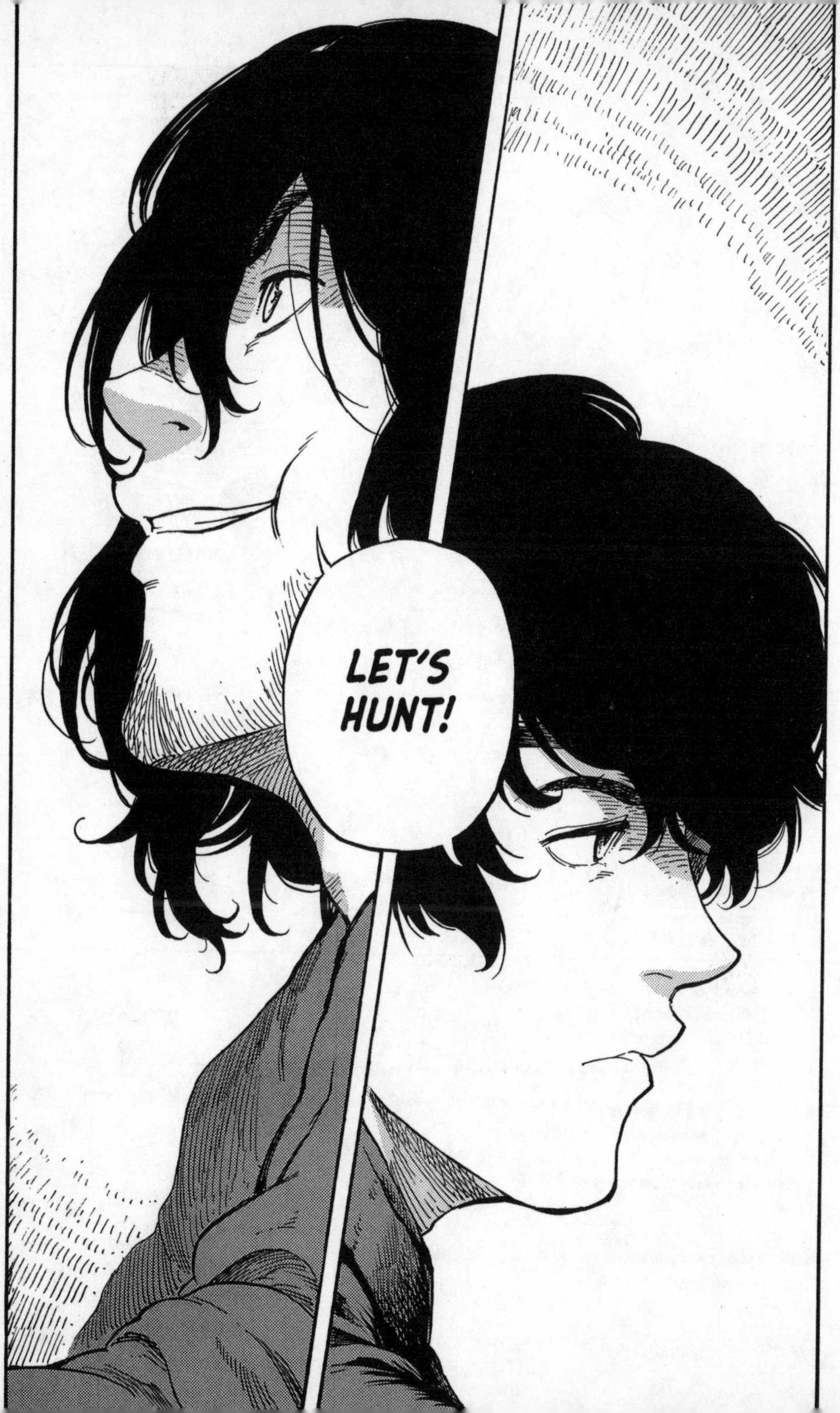
LET'S HUNT!

Dragon Crystals

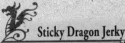

Ingredients (Serves 4)

- ✦ Dragon pinna cartilage: 300 g
- ✦ Salt: a pinch
- ✦ Vinegar: 120 cc (½ cup)
- ✦ Mirin: 1 tbsp
- ✦ Sugar: 1 tbsp
- ✦ ¼ of a lemon or other citrus of choice

01 Thinly slice the cartilage and rinse well under cold running water. Wipe off any excess moisture and rub salt into the surface. Leave to rest overnight.

02 The next day, wash the salted pinna well under cold running water and place in a bowl filled with water. Leave for three hours to desalinate. Meanwhile, over medium-high heat, combine mirin and sugar in a pot and mix well until the sugar is dissolved. Bring to a boil to burn off the alcohol and remove from the heat to cool.

03 In a jar or container, place cooked mirin, sugar, and vinegar and shake well to combine. Add sliced citrus and pinna to the container and let pickle overnight.

04 Slice pickled pinna into strips and serve on a platter garnished with citrus zest.

Sticky Dragon Jerky

Ingredients (Serves 4)

- ✦ Dragon sirloin (best to use fatty, tender cuts for this recipe): 600 g
- ✦ Salt: as needed
- ✦ Soy sauce: 100 cc (½ cup)
- ✦ Mirin: 100 cc (½ cup) ✦ Sugar: 45 g
- ✦ Sake: 60 cc (¼ cup)

01 Slice the sirloin into about 2-cm thick strips, salt liberally and let rest overnight.

02 The next day, wash the salt off the meat and drain well. Place the meat in a clean bowl and add soy sauce, mirin, sugar, and sake in a 2:2:1:1 ratio and mix well to coat. Let the meat marinate overnight.

03 Lay the strips out on a tray or rack and leave under the sun to dry for up to one day until hard and dry. Flame grill jerky strips before serving.

Chilong

Ingredients

- ✦ Baijiu
- ✦ One shiso leaf
- ✦ One chili pepper
- ✦ Hot water: as desired

01 Place shiso leaf and chili pepper in a glass and fill the glass up to ½ full with hot water.

02 Pour equal amount of baijiu (or to your liking) into the glass. Let the drink rest for a minute without stirring and serve.

HUFF...
HUFF
IT'S A MEAT PARTY!
DRIP DRIP DRIP DRIP
YOU HAVE TO SHARE, OKAY?!

Sausage

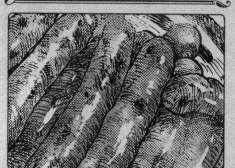

Ingredients (Serves 4) + Utensils

✦ Dragon (Best to use a variety of cuts. The more fat, the juicier the sausage): 1 kg

✦ Salted hog chitterlings: 2.4 m

✦ Salt: 20 g ✦ Pepper: 8 g

✦ Five spice powder: 2 g ✦ Sugar: 80 g

✦ Brandy: 30 ml (2 tbsp) ✦ A funnel

01 Dice the meat into 5 mm cubes.

02 Add the meat and seasonings in a bowl and mix well to combine.

03 Let the meat rest for 1-2 hours, mixing occasionally.

04 Soak the pork casings in water for 10 minutes to remove excess salt.

05 Slip one open end of the casing over the end of the funnel, pushing most of the casing up onto the nozzle. Tie off the other end of the casing.

06 Take small amounts of the meat mixture and push it through the funnel with your thumb or chopsticks. When you finish stuffing, tie off the other end and you'll be left with one very long sausage.

07 Twist the center of the sausage, dividing it in half. From the twist along one end, twist off two more 10 cm long links, forming a hoop. Pull the other end of the sausage through the hoop, tying the links in place. Repeat this process down the length of the sausage, tying the loose ends of the casings together with a square knot.

08 If there are air pockets in the sausage, perforate the casing with a needle to release the air.

09 Hang the links to dry for 1-2 days, then steam them for 20 minutes. Once cooked through, cool the links in cold water and drain thoroughly.

10 Grill the links in a pan or over charcoal until lightly charred and serve.

Twice-Cooked Dragon Shank

Ingredients (Serves 4)

✦ Bone-in dragon shank: 2 kg ✦ Oolong tea leaves: 100 g

✦ Daikon radish: 200 g ✦ Ginger root: 3 cm piece

✦ Garlic: 1 clove ✦ Yellow onion: ¼ large

✦ Welsh onion: 2 ✦ Sesame oil: 1 tbsp ✦ Soy sauce: 2 tbsp

✦ Oyster sauce: 1 tbsp ✦ Sake: 3 tbsp ✦ Sugar: 1 tbsp

✦ Five spice powder: 1 tbsp ✦ Water: 600 cc (2 ½ cups)

01 Bring a large pot of water to a boil. Add dragon shank and oolong tea and simmer on medium until the meat is tender.

02 Remove the shank from the pot and tear the meat off of the bone.

03 Slice the daikon into 1 cm thick half moons. Thinly slice yellow onion going with the grain. Thinly slice garlic and ginger as well.

04 Add sesame oil to a pot and cook garlic and ginger over medium heat until fragrant. Add the dragon shank, daikon, and onion and lightly stir fry.

05 Add water and bring the pot to a boil, then mix in seasonings and cover with a lid and simmer at medium-low heat for 50-60 minutes. Cook until the stock is reduced by half.

06 Serve stewed shank in a bowl and garnish with bite-sized welsh onion.

THE WORLD OF CLAMP!

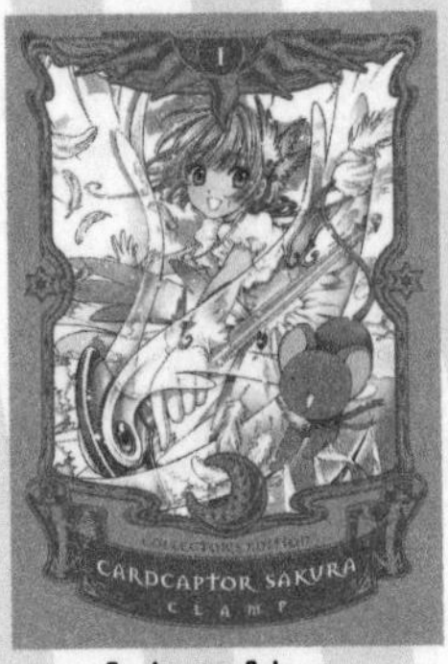
CARDCAPTOR SAKURA
CLAMP

Cardcaptor Sakura
Collector's Edition

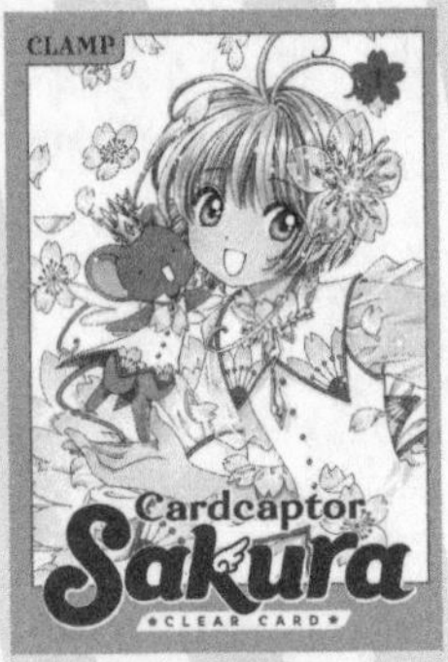
CLAMP
Cardcaptor
Sakura
CLEAR CARD

Cardcaptor Sakura:
Clear Card

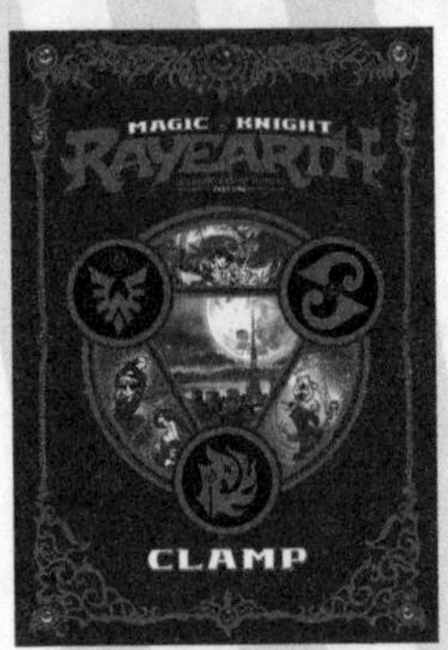
MAGIC KNIGHT
RAYEARTH
CLAMP

Magic Knight Rayearth
25th Anniversary Box Set

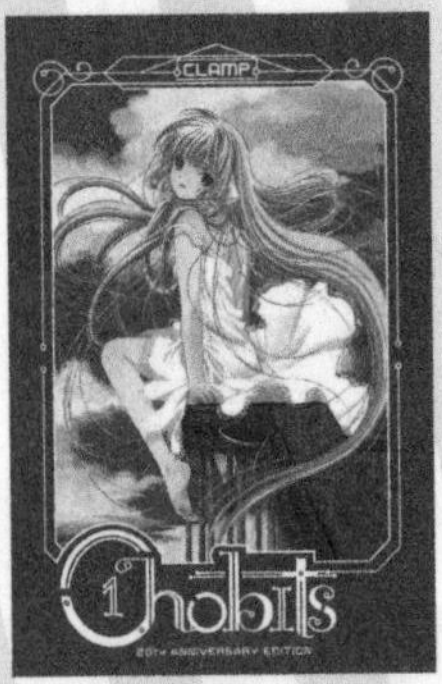
CLAMP
1 Chobits

Chobits

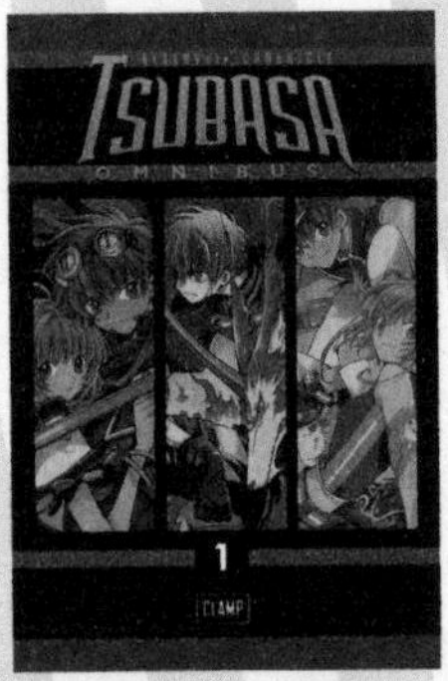
TSUBASA
OMNIBUS
1
CLAMP

TSUBASA Omnibus

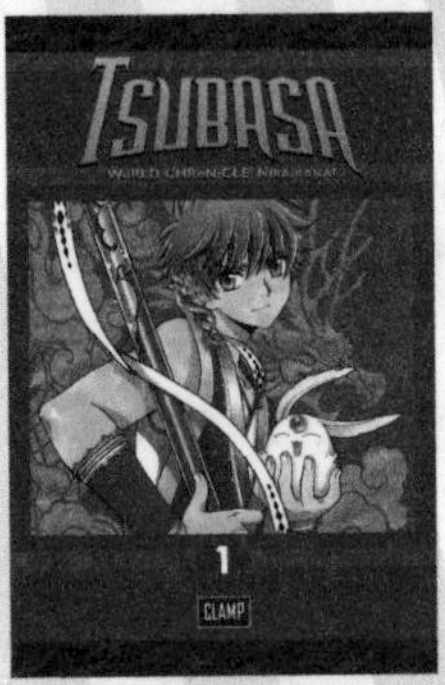
TSUBASA
1
CLAMP

TSUBASA WoRLD CHRoNiCLE

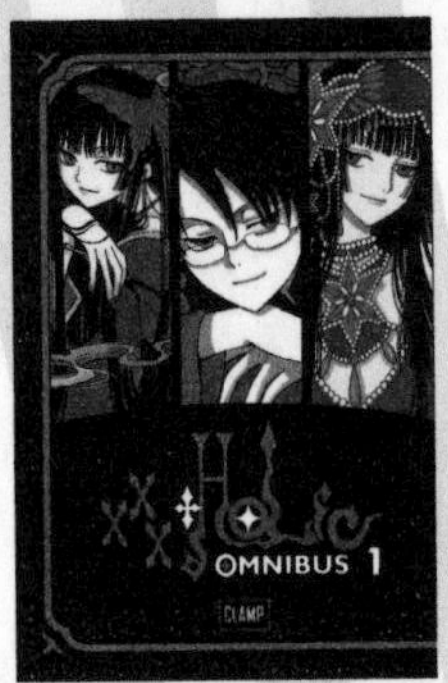
xxxHOLiC
OMNIBUS 1
CLAMP

xxxHOLiC Omnibus

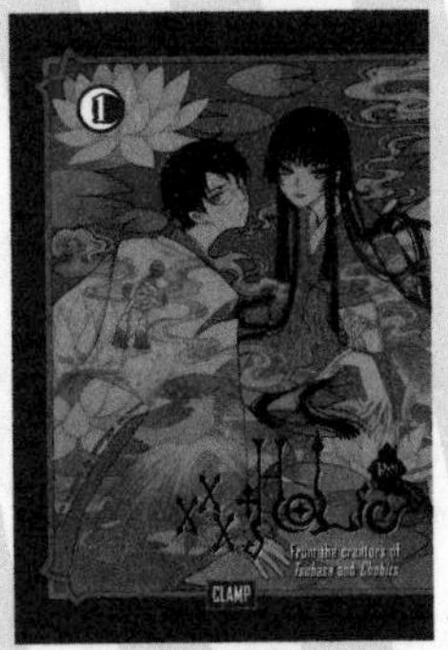
1
xxxHOLiC
From the creators of Tsubasa and Chobits
CLAMP

xxxHOLiC Rei

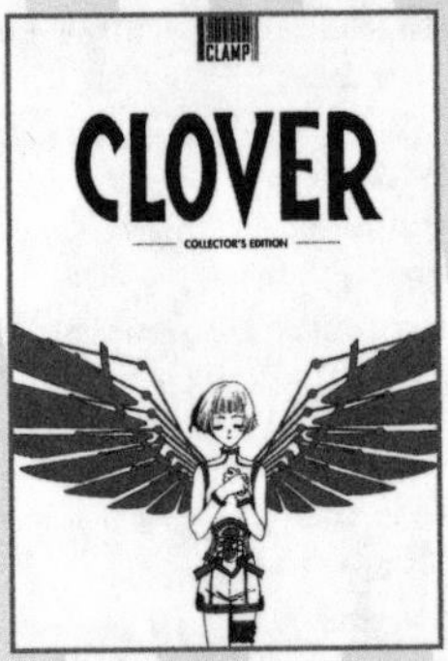
CLAMP
CLOVER
COLLECTOR'S EDITION

CLOVER Collector's Edition

KC KODANSHA COMICS

Kodansha Comics welcomes you to explore the expansive world of CLAMP, the all-female artist collective that has produced some of the most acclaimed manga of the century. Our growing catalog includes icons like *Cardcaptor Sakura* and *Magic Knight Rayearth*, each crafted with CLAMP's one-of-a-kind style and characters!

SAINT ☆ YOUNG MEN

A LONG AWAITED ARRIVAL IN PREMIUM 2-IN-1 HARDCOVER

After centuries of hard work, Jesus and Buddha take a break from their heavenly duties to relax among the people of Japan, and their adventures in this lighthearted buddy comedy are sure to bring mirth and merriment to all!

"Brilliant…the physical comedy and facial expressions will make you literally LOL."
—Sam Humphries
(host of *DC Daily*; writer, *Green Lanterns, Legendary Star-Lord*)

A Kodansha Comics Trade Paperback Original
Drifting Dragons 7 copyright © 2019 Taku Kuwabara
English translation copyright © 2020 Taku Kuwabara

All rights reserved.

Published in the United States by Kodansha Comics, an imprint of Kodansha USA Publishing, LLC, New York.

Publication rights for this English edition arranged through Kodansha Ltd., Tokyo.

First published in Japan in 2019 by Kodansha Ltd., Tokyo as *Kuutei doragonzu*, volume 7.

ISBN 978-1-64651-036-8

Printed in the United States of America.

www.kodanshacomics.com

9 8 7 6 5 4 3 2 1
Translation: Adam Hirsch
Lettering: Thea Willis
Editing: Jordan Blanco
Kodansha Comics edition cover design by Phil Balsman
YKS Services LLC/SKY Japan, INC.

Publisher: Kiichiro Sugawara

Director of publishing services: Ben Applegate
Associate director of operations: Stephen Pakula
Publishing services managing editor: Noelle Webster
Assistant production manager: Emi Lotto, Angela Zurlo